Rand Smith
1110 Madison St.
Evanston, IL 60202

Chirac's Challenge

Chirac's Challenge

Liberalization, Europeanization, and Malaise in France

Edited by
John T. S. Keeler and Martin A. Schain

ST. MARTIN'S PRESS
NEW YORK

CHIRAC'S CHALLENGE
Copyright © 1996 by John T.S. Keeler and Martin A. Schain
All rights reserved. Printed in the United States of America. No part of this book may be used or reproduced in any manner whatsoever without written permission except in the case of brief quotations embodied in critical articles or reviews. For information, address St. Martin's Press, Scholarly and Reference Division, 175 Fifth Avenue, New York, N.Y. 10010

ISBN 0-312-12270-5

Library of Congress Cataloging-in-Publication Data
Chirac's challenge : liberalization, Europeanization, and malaise in
  France / edited by John T.S. Keeler and Martin A. Schain.
    p. cm.
  Includes bibliographical references and index.
  ISBN 0-312-12270-5
    1. France--Politics and government--1981- 2. European Union-
  -France. 3. Chirac, Jacques, 1932- --Political and social views.
  4. France--Social conditions. 5. Political leadership--France.
  I. Keeler, John T. S. II. Schain, Martin, 1940- .
  DC424.C485 1996
  944.083'9--dc20
                                                          96-36044
                                                               CIP

First Edition: October 1996
10 9 8 7 6 5 4 3 2 1

Design by Milton Heiberg Studios

Printed in the United States of America by
Haddon Craftsmen
Scranton, PA

To M. Dominique Arnould and Mme. Dominique Arnould, who personify the very best features of *la France profonde*

and

To Marie-France Toinet, an excellent scholar and a wonderful friend, who left us too soon

Contents

Acknowledgments ix

Chapter 1—Mitterrand's Legacy, Chirac's Challenge
  John T. S. Keeler and Martin A. Schain 1

Part I. Institutions and the Policymaking Process

Chapter 2— Presidents, Premiers, and Models of Democracy in France
  John T. S. Keeler and Martin A. Schain 23
Chapter 3—Constitutional Politics and Malaise in France
  Alec Stone 53
Chapter 4—The Many Styles of Policymaking in France
  Frank R. Baumgartner 85

Part II. Business, Labor, and the Economy

Chapter 5—Business, the State, and the End of Dirigisme
  Vivien A. Schmidt 105
Chapter 6—Does the French Labor Movement Have a Future?
  Mark Kesselman 143

Part III. The Politics of Social Policy

Chapter 7—The Immigration Debate and the National Front
  Martin A. Schain 169
Chapter 8—Conflict and Consensus in French Education
  John S. Ambler 199
Chapter 9—Reforming French Health Care Policy
  David Wilsford 231

Chapter 10—Sexual Harassment, Gender Politics, and Symbolic Reform
   Amy G. Mazur 257
Chapter 11—The Limits of Malaise in France
   Marie-France Toinet 279

Part IV. The Challenges of Europe and the World

Chapter 12—The Maastricht Referendum and the Party System
   Andrew M. Appleton 301
Chapter 13—National Interest, the Dilemmas of European Integration, and Malaise
   David R. Cameron 325
Chapter 14—A Testing Time for the Pursuit of Grandeur
   Jolyon Howorth 383

About the Contributors 401

Index 404

ACKNOWLEDGMENTS

John Keeler: I would like to thank the Institut für Politikwissenschaft of the Eberhard-Karls-Universität Tübingen, where as a Visiting Professor in May 1995 I observed Jacques Chirac's victory in the second round of the presidential election and began the editorial work on this project. In Tübingen Roland Sturm, Rudolf Hrbek and Axel Markert were gracious hosts and Rudolf Steiert offered stimulating insights on the current status of French politics. Back in Seattle, Mark Schneider and Dan Valadez provided valuable research assistance and Katherine Kittel, Assistant Director of the Center for West European Studies at the University of Washington, did a superb job of organizing a conference on the theme of this book. Above all, I would like to thank M. Dominique Arnould and Mme. Dominique Arnould (yes, they are both named Dominique!), a remarkable French couple who befriended me as a graduate student twenty years ago and have made me feel at home in Pouilly-sur-Serre (Aisne) ever since. I could never adequately repay them for their many acts of kindness, but I hope the dedication will illustrate the depth of my appreciation for everything they have taught me about France and friendship.

Martin Schain: I would like to thank Pascal Perrineau, as well as friends and colleagues at CEVIPOF and CERI, who have provided a priceless intellectual community in Paris for many years. I would also like to thank Yvonne, Daniel and Jeanne, Sophie and Alain, Monica and Francis, Irène and Hugo, Pascal and Gisèle, Michel and Elisabeth, Patrick and Jean-Pierre, who guided me through the social crisis of December 1995, and who have helped make Paris my "second city." Finally, I would like to thank Henry Ehrmann, my friend and co-author who died in December 1994. Henry's thinking about French politics remains important in this volume.

Both of us would like to thank the editors of *French Politics and Society* for permission to reprint the article by Jolyon Howorth. We would also like to thank Mary Carter and Matthew McInnis of the Center for European Studies at New York University for their editorial contribution to this volume. Finally, we offer thanks and a joint dedication to our late friend Marie-France Toinet, whose contribution to this volume is, sad to say, her last published essay.

Chapter 1

Introduction:
Mitterrand's Legacy, Chirac's Challenge
John T. S. Keeler and Martin A. Schain

On May 7, 1995 Jacques Chirac, leader of the neo-Gaullist *Rassemblement Pour la République* (RPR), was elected the fifth president of France's Fifth Republic. During the electoral campaign Chirac had promised "profound change" and a "break with the past" personified by Socialist François Mitterrand, who at age 78 was leaving the Elysée Palace after a record 14 years as president.[1] As the press accounts stressed, Chirac seemed to possess the institutional power necessary for the introduction of substantial change. Aside from the presidency, Chirac and his conservative coalition controlled 80 percent of the seats in the National Assembly (as the result of a 1993 landslide victory), two-thirds of the Senate, 20 of the 22 regional councils and more than three-fourths of the department councils; moreover, Chirac's hand-picked successor replaced him as mayor of Paris while the conservative coalition also controlled most other large city governments. In short, Chirac as chief executive appeared able to claim a degree of power unprecedented in the history of the Fifth Republic and unparalleled in any other contemporary democratic system. With the Parisian daily *Le Figaro* proclaiming "Change: Chirac Wants to Go Fast," the new president rapidly named fellow neo-Gaullist Alain Juppé as his prime minister, assembled his cabinet and began attempting to deliver on his campaign promises.[2]

Now, after a year in power, what is most striking is how difficult it has been for Chirac to translate promises into a program, and a program into legislation. A year ago, even sympathetic observers had been quick to express skepticism. As Alain Peyrefitte cautioned, for example, Chirac's extraordinary "voluntarism"—what Americans might term his irrepressible "can-do" style throughout the campaign—aroused a variety of expectations that would prove difficult to fulfill.[3] In the eyes of Edouard Balladur, the prime minister from 1993 to 1995 and Chirac's principal rival on the Right in the recent election, the new president was to be faulted for "an accumulation of demagogic promises" that ignored the need for sacrifice and jeopardized the chances of enhancing economic growth.[4]

As a poll taken in April 1995 demonstrated, the major political asset of Chirac as a candidate was his ability to gain substantial support, unlike Balladur, from voters on the Left as well as the Right—was a reflection of his many promises and his mixed messages. Chirac managed to rank second to Lionel Jospin (22 percent to 41 percent) and far ahead of Balladur (8 percent) among "progressive" voters who viewed the state as obligated to maintain traditional welfare programs and alleviate inequality. At the same time, he ranked narrowly ahead of Balladur (30 percent to 25 percent) among conservative voters. Overall, he was the only candidate to obtain—in the fashion of de Gaulle—solid support across the ideological spectrum.[5]

It rapidly became clear that, as president, Chirac would have a difficult time retaining either the breadth or depth of support he was able to generate as a candidate. Detached analysts stressed that his economic program was contradictory in the extreme. The *Economist* noted that Chirac had promised "More jobs and spending, lower taxes and—*mirabile dictu*—a cut in France's public sector spending to meet the Maastricht convergence criterion [of a maximum budget deficit of 3 percent]. That was what Jacques Chirac promised. Something had to give, and it duly did." The first supplementary budget proposed by the Chirac-Juppé team in June–July 1995 included a "temporary" tax increase, a jobs-creation program that most critics believed fell woefully short of Chirac's goals, and spending cuts that would reduce the deficit from 5.7 percent to 5.1 percent but fall far short of the 3 percent Maastricht criterion.[6]

The early conflicts within the new government (and Chirac's own conflicts over policy choices) came to a head at the end of August, when the Minister of the Economy Alain Madelin, who had openly advocated stronger austerity measures, was forced to resign. Public support for the president and his prime minister fell to historic lows when Chirac finally opted for more painful cuts in state spending, and the government was challenged by the most intense strike movement since May–June 1968. (See chapters 2 and 6.)

Chirac's challenge appears even more formidable when set against the backdrop of the Mitterrand years. After all, while none of the governments of Mitterrand's presidency possessed quite the power that Chirac holds today, the institutions of the Fifth Republic gave them considerable governing capacity, yet they failed (to varying degrees) to solve the problems Chirac is now addressing. Moreover, one of those governments (1986-88) was headed by Chirac himself, and the most recent (headed by Balladur from 1993 to 1995) was controlled by his governing coalition.

To fully understand Chirac's challenge, therefore, one must first understand France's challenge of the past decade and the reasons why French governments have had such difficulties coping with it. The central purpose of this volume is to put Chirac's challenge in perspective by tracing the development of French public policy over the past decade. Our goal will be to show how the dilemmas faced by the new president have resulted from the failures—and, ironically, some of the achievements—of the Mitterrand era.

In the eyes of French voters, the principal failure of governments in recent years has been their inability to cope with economic problems, especially rising unemployment. Economic problems have, of course, been the rule rather than the exception in industrialized democracies since the oil shocks of the 1970s, but France has consistently had one of the highest unemployment rates of any of the large OECD states. Blaming the government for such economic problems has been a typical reaction of citizens everywhere, but the French case is distinctive in this regard as well.[7] The fact that governments in France have generally wielded relatively impressive executive powers has made it particularly difficult for them credibly to invoke—in the style of presidents in the United States or leaders of weak coalition governments elsewhere—institutional excuses for their shortcomings.[8] The net result of the inability of strong governments to deal effectively with economic problems and other related problems has been the emergence of a French malaise, the precise nature of which will be explored throughout this volume.

This malaise has deepened steadily with the successive socio-economic failures of French governments since the late 1970s. Mitterrand and the Socialists aroused considerable enthusiasm with their dramatic electoral victories in May–June 1981, in large part because most citizens believed that their economic program featuring extensive nationalizations and "redistributive Keynesianism" would alleviate what was then known as the "Giscard-Barre crisis."[9] Polls taken in the fall of 1981 showed that 61 percent of the French were confident in Mitterrand's ability to improve the economy and that a majority favored nationalizations largely because of their expected positive effects on unemployment.[10] The unemployment situation continued to worsen, however, and by 1983 a host of negative economic indicators had undermined support for the Socialist government and forced a major reorientation of policy.

In the wake of the abortive "Socialist experiment" of 1981-83, French governments of the Left as well as the Right sought to resolve the country's economic problems through multifaceted programs of liberalization. Indeed, as our subtitle suggests, liberalization became one of the most important trends and themes of the Mitterrand years. However, as figure 1.1 shows, neither the grudging liberalization of the Left nor the more assertive policies (including extensive privatization) pursued by governments of the Right have managed to cure France's economic problems. Inflation has been held in check since the mid-1980s, but other politically salient economic measures have been consistently disappointing. From 1983 through 1987 the unemployment rate continued to grow in France while it declined in most other major OECD countries. The French rate remained relatively high, even as it decreased slightly from 1988 to 1990, and during the 1990s the French rate has grown to become the highest among the major industrialized states.[11]

Throughout this period, the major politicians and parties of both the Right and Left have repeatedly paid an electoral price for their failures. After 23 years without *alternance* (a change of government between Right and Left), the Fifth Republic has experienced nothing but incumbent rejections (see figure 1.2) and the search for fresh policy solutions since 1981. Unemployment and economic crisis were the two major issues cited by voters when they ousted the Socialists in favor of a Chirac-led coalition in 1986, but the unimpressive record of Chirac's cohabitation government paved the way for the reelection of Mitterrand and the election of another Socialist government in 1988.[12]

Already by 1988, of course, the voters had learned not to expect miracles from a change of majority. The "generalized stymie of French public policy on the unemployment issue" was underscored vividly in the Mitterrand-Chirac debate during that year's presidential election. The candidates discussed the issue only briefly, despite the fact that it was again ranked as the

INTRODUCTION: MITTERRAND'S LEGACY, CHIRAC'S CHALLENGE

TABLE 1.1:
THE CYCLE OF ELECTORAL REJECTION IN FRANCE **1981-1995**

	Incumbent(s) and/or Majority Rejected	New Leader(s) and/or Majority Elected
1981	President Giscard d'Estaing	President Mitterrand
	Right Majority in National Assemby—Premier Barre	Left Majority in National Assembly—Premier Mauroy
1986	Left Majority in National Assembly—Premier Fabius	Right Majority in National Assembly—Premier Chirac
1988	Presidential candidate Chirac running while effective Head of Government in Cohabitation period	Mitterrand re-elected after serving for two years as effective Leader of Opposition during Cohabitation
	Right Majority in National Assembly—Premier Chirac	Left Majority in National Assembly—Premier Rocard
1993	Left Majority in National Assembly—Premier Bérégovoy	Right Majority in National Assembly—Premier Balladur
1995	Presidential candidate Balladur running while effective Head of Government in Cohabitation period—finished third on first ballot	President Chirac—portrayed himself in campaign as alternative to both the Socialists (Jospin tied to Mitterrand legacy) and Balladur

number one concern of voters. At one point President Mitterrand tersely stated that there had been "a continuity of failure" on this front, to which Chirac replied: "No, we haven't all failed in the same way." As Ronald Tiersky has quipped, this exchange represented "a remarkable moment of the new French consensus."[13]

By the next legislative elections of 1993 the Socialists' popularity had been eroded by a variety of issues, including corruption, but unemployment was again cited as the principal concern of voters as they delivered a landslide victory for the Right's RPR-UDF coalition. The new prime minister, Edouard Balladur, "quickly told the French that unemployment would get worse before it got better, which it did."[14] Political analysts marveled as Balladur's approval ratings remained high while the unemployment problem worsened in 1994, but the premier's teflon flaked sufficiently enough the next year for Jacques Chirac to edge him out as the leading candidate of the Right on the first ballot of the 1995 presidential election.[15] When Chirac defeated Socialist candidate Lionel Jospin in the second ballot of the election, 92 percent of the voters listed "the battle against unemployment" as

FIGURE 1.1:
UNEMPLOYMENT AND ECONOMIC GROWTH RATES IN FRANCE, 1979–1994

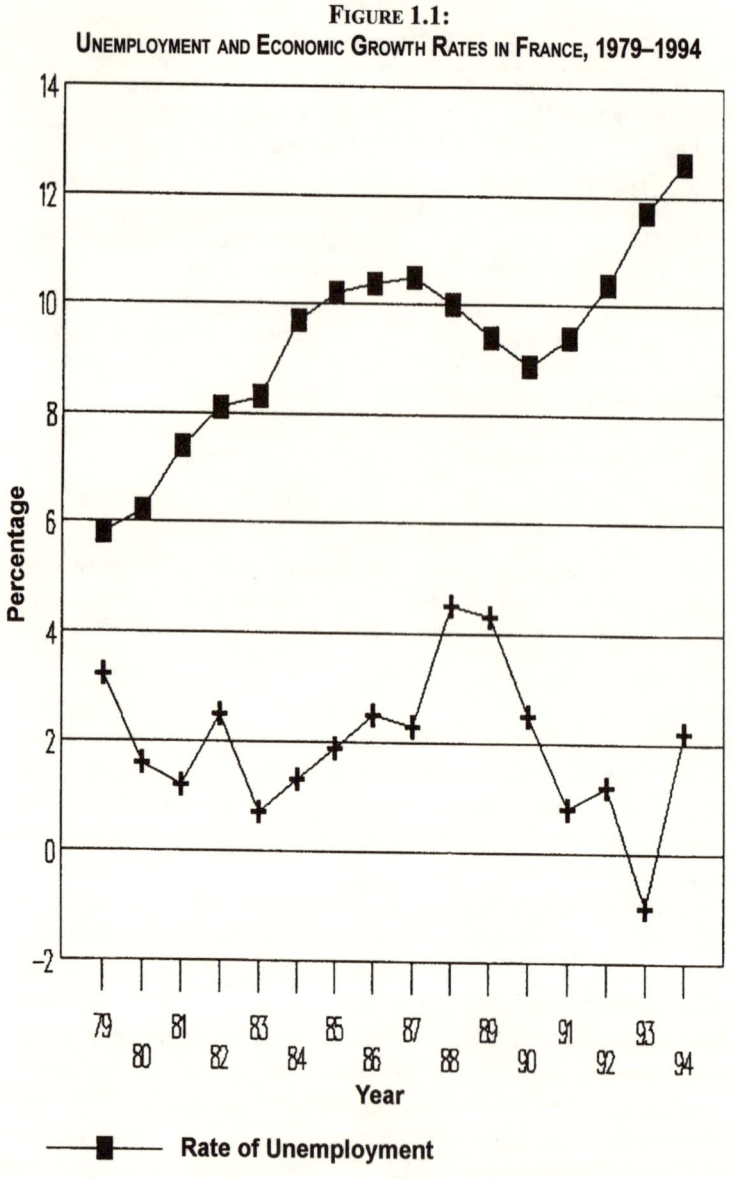

Source: *OECD Economic Outlook 57, June, 1995* (Paris: ORCD, 1995), and previous volumes

TABLE 1.2:
RESULTS OF THE 1995 FRENCH PRESIDENTIAL ELECTION

	First Ballot April 23	Second Ballot May 7
Lionel Jospin, PS	23.3%	47.4%
Jacques Chirac, RPR	20.8%	52.6%
Edouard Balladur, RPR	18.6%	
Jean-Marie Le Pen, FN	15.0%	
Robert Hue, PCF	8.6%	
Arlette Laguiller, LO	5.3%	
Philippe de Villiers, MPF	4.7%	
Dominique Voynet, Les Verts	3.3%	
Jacques Cheminade, FNS	0.3%	

Party Affiliations: PS (Parti Socialiste); RPR (Rassemblement pour la République); FN (Front National); PCF (Parti Communiste Française); LO (Lutte Ouvrière); MPF (Mouvement pour la France); FNS (Fédération pour une Nouvelle Solidarité).

Source: *L'Election présidentielle: Jacques Chirac, le défi du changement* (Paris: Dossiers et Documents du Monde, 1995), pp. 36 and 62.

their main concern, and 55 percent expressed confidence that the new president—who referred to unemployment as "this cancer of our society"—could improve the employment situation.[16]

The skepticism underlying that confidence (6 percent less than Mitterrand received on the same issue in 1981) was clearly revealed in other statistics from the 1995 election. On the first ballot, as table 1.2 and figure 1.2 show, Chirac not only finished second to Jospin but received the weakest support (20.8 percent) of any eventual winner since the two-ballot presidential election system was introduced in 1965.[17] A record 37 percent of the total vote on the first ballot went to fringe candidates of the extreme Right and Left (Jean-Marie Le Pen attracted a record 15 percent); moreover, a solid majority of the unemployed (58 percent) and working-class voters (55 percent) supported one of those candidates rather than Chirac or another moderate alternative.[18] In the second round, a record number (6 percent) of spoiled ballots made Chirac the first Fifth Republic president to be elected with less than half (49.5 percent) of the votes cast.[19]

As later chapters will discuss, this faltering confidence in the moderate politicians and parties of both the Left and Right (only 25 percent of the French as of 1994 said they felt "well represented by a political party") has resulted not merely from the inability of governments to cope with the central problem of unemployment, but also from their failure to prevent what is commonly viewed as a worsening *fracture sociale* (deep social division).[20]

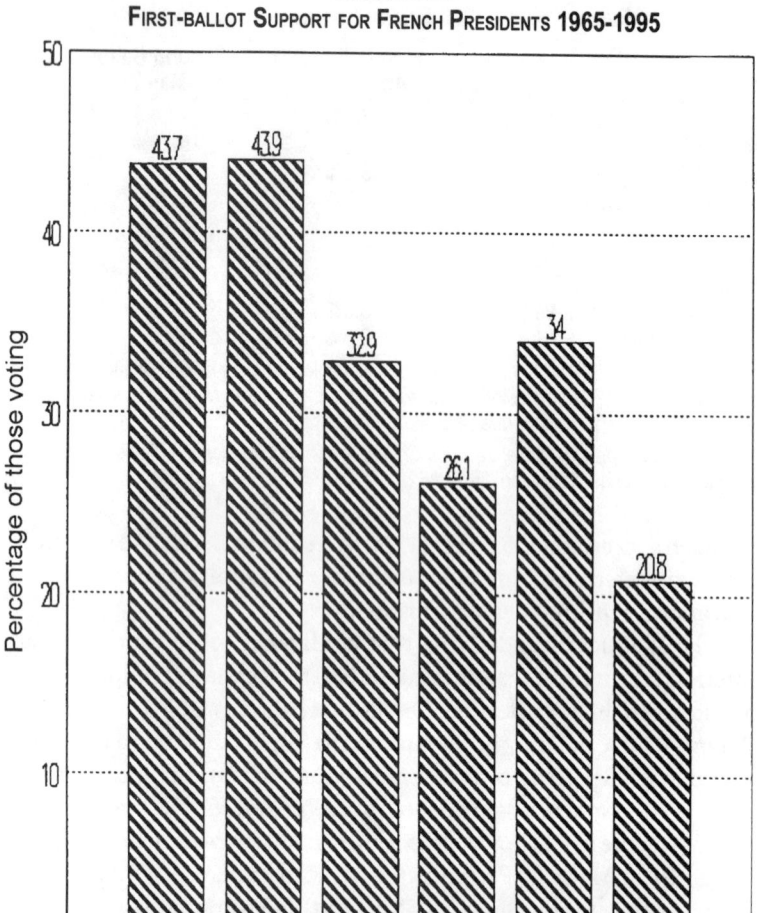

FIGURE 1.2:
FIRST-BALLOT SUPPORT FOR FRENCH PRESIDENTS 1965-1995

Source: Roy Pierce *Choosing the Chief: Presidential Elections in France and the United States* (Ann Arbor: Univ. of Michigan Press, 1995) and *Le Monde,* April 25, 1995.

On the eve of the 1995 elections, fully 89 percent of French voters declared that French society was divided, especially between the well-off and the "excluded" (66 percent), the employed and the unemployed (55 percent), and the French and the immigrants (52 percent).[21] Recent cuts in social programs made "social protection" (for example, health benefits and pensions) and "exclusion" (the homeless) the number two and number four most cited concerns of voters in 1995.

This demand for protection reflects a steady decline in confidence in the potential of liberalization as a cure for France's ills. Between 1990 and 1994 the number of French citizens who felt that "one must have confidence in business enterprises and give them more freedom" fell from 63 percent to 45 percent.[22] Whereas only 29 percent of the French felt that the state did not intervene enough in the economy in 1985, the figure had risen to 53 percent by late 1994 and to 67 percent by April 1995.[23] The poll of April 1995 also showed that a growing plurality (43 percent versus 40 percent) of the French now favored halting the privatization program and a majority (53 percent versus 41 percent) were hostile to proposals for increasing reliance on private health insurance.[24] Chirac's major challenge during his first year was to deliver on his campaign promise to maintain or even enhance, as previous governments have failed to do, social protection while simultaneously trying to stimulate job growth and reduce the public debt (which tripled in real terms during the Mitterrand years).[25] His decision in the autumn of 1995, to focus on debt and deficit reduction at the expense of social protection, led to the social upheaval of November-December, a clear warning of the limits of such policies in France.

At the same time, Chirac has been hard pressed to do better than past governments have at coping with the voters' number three concern of 1995, the explosive "immigration" issue. Anti-immigrant sentiments have been fueled for over a decade by the chronic unemployment problem. More fundamentally, however, they have derived from the perceived threat to French social identity posed by both the growth of the minority population and the development of the European Union. The record support (15 percent) received by Jean-Marie Le Pen on the first ballot of the 1995 presidential election, combined with the surprising success of his National Front in the municipal elections that followed shortly after, manifests the intensity of the challenge faced by Chirac on the immigration issue.[26] As polls of May 1995 showed, 33 percent of all French voters and 43 percent of those who voted for Chirac desire "that the ideas of the National Front (NF) be taken into account more by the new president."[27] During the first year the government did, in fact, take the ideas of the NF into account by considering new restrictions on immigration. Nevertheless, the influence of Le Pen continued to grow. By April 1996, 28 percent of voters (and 46 percent of government supporters) were sympathetic with Le Pen's ideas, as shown by an increase of 9 percent in two years (see chapter 7). Those citizens most concerned with immigration control favored not only sending illegal immigrants home, but also strengthening border controls even "for citizens of the other countries of the European Union."[28]

This latter fact underscores the extent to which Chirac's challenge involves another major trend of French policy over the last decade, Europeanization. In the eyes of many French, Mitterrand's greatest achievement was his commitment from 1984 onward to the building of the European Union (EU). For others, however, enhanced European integration has come to appear as not only a cause of France's economic problems—at a minimum, it seems, the "1992 program" and Maastricht were oversold as structural panaceas—but also a threat to France's autonomy and national identity. As later chapters will show, one of the ironies of the Mitterrand years was that, while a consensus emerged among the major parties of both the Left and Right over the necessity of Europeanization (and the related policy of domestic liberalization), many traditional supporters of those parties increasingly questioned whether this was the correct path to pursue.

A dramatic manifestation of this trend is the fact that on the first ballot of the 1995 election, fully 53 percent of the French who were opposed to the Maastricht Treaty voted either for Le Pen or for one of the other extremist candidates.[29] The EU issue in various ways is Chirac's greatest dilemma, given the tension between the extensive EU obligations to open borders and monetary union he has inherited and the strong divisions that the EU has generated among his constituents and coalition leaders. A decision of June 29, 1995 provided an early illustration of how Chirac has been tempted as president to continue straddling the Eurofence as he did during the Maastricht debate in 1992. Just before the deadline for implementing the Schengen Accords (which call for the elimination of French border controls vis-à-vis Germany, Spain, Portugal, and the Benelux countries), the French government invoked a safeguard clause allowing the controls to be maintained or reinstituted temporarily in special circumstances; concern over illegal immigration and drug traffic were the reasons cited to support this move. At the same time, the government was careful to explain to their European partners that "the Schengen Accords are not dead" and that "France is committed to Schengen, but a Schengen that works well enough to assure security." Then, at the end of March 1996, the government announced that it would open the frontiers with Germany,

Spain, and Portugal, but maintain controls on the Benelux border. Government spokesmen referred to the Benelux countries as a "narco-state".[30]

On the larger issue of European Union, as well, Chirac has continued to walk a careful tightrope. On one hand, his government, in its moves towards deficit reduction, in ministerial declarations, and in joint statements with the Germans, has more or less endorsed the general commitments of the Maastricht agreements, including monetary union.[31] On the other hand, at the time of the opening of the Intergovernmental Conference (to plan the future of the European Union) at the end of March 1996, there was still only tenuous agreement on the main lines of European construction within the government itself, and considerable conflict within the governing conservative coalition. Chirac himself continued to allude to his campaign promise of a referendum on "the construction of Europe," while the political bureau of the RPR was able to cobble together a statement on the European Union only in the absence of the two leaders, Séquin and Pasqua, who had led the anti-Maastricht forces in 1992.[32]

Nor were the December strikes very far from the thinking of the government: on the eve of the opening of the Intergovernmental Conference the president and prime minister announced that they would present a memorandum on "social Europe," a chance to place employment problems on the same level as monetary union. This "social model for Europe," Juppé argued would show that ". . . Europe attacks problems of daily life. Workers have rights, and the role of France in the construction of Europe is to recall that."[33] These efforts have yielded only the most limited political dividends for Chirac. By July 1995 his performance rating had fallen more precipitously during two months in office (from 59 to 44 percent "satisfied") than that of any previous president of the Fifth Republic. It continued to fall until the end of the December strikes (to a low of 27 percent—another record). By the end of February, Chirac's performance improved to 43 percent, and remained at that level through the end of his first year as president. A national survey indicated that large majorities found his style attractive, but equally large majorities were disappointed in his policies: 83 percent found him "dynamic," 76 percent "sympathetic," and 68 percent "close to the people;" on the other hand, 62 percent of those surveyed were disappointed in his economic and social policies, and 69 percent of the UDF supporters were disappointed in the first year of his presidency.[34] Thus, this has been an unexpectedly inauspicious honeymoon period for a president whose institutional power seemed so overwhelming only a year ago.

The 13 chapters that follow all address various institutional, economic, social, and political dimensions of Chirac's challenge. The chapters are divided into four thematic parts. Part I focuses on governmental institutions and the policymaking process in France, highlighting the extent and limits of executive power. In chapter 2, Keeler and Schain demonstrate how the dynamics of executive power have evolved since the "hyperpresidential" era of Charles de Gaulle. Governing in the style of a republican monarch, the general and his immediate successors led the French to believe that the "normal" mode of policymaking in the Fifth Republic would entail a degree of presidential dominance unparalleled in other democratic systems. However, as Keeler and Schain explain, political and institutional changes of recent years have tended to temper presidential power in important ways. Indeed, over the last decade the role of the prime minister in guiding the policymaking process has generally been either greater than that of the president (during the cohabitation era of 1986-1988 and 1993-1995) or nearly as significant (from 1988-1993). Although the 1995 presidential election seemingly set the stage for another era of hyperpresidentialism, Chirac—who as premier from 1974-1976 and 1986-1988 resented presidential encroachment on what he saw as the legitimate role of his office—announced his intention not to replicate the hyperpresidential practices of old and to leave considerable power in the hands of his prime minister.[35] After a year in office, one has good reason to be skeptical about his claim. Nevertheless, institutional changes at both the domestic level (see below) and the European level (see Part IV) assure that Chirac cannot wield the degree of power over policy that de Gaulle enjoyed.

The domestic institutional development alluded to above is what Alec Stone terms, in chapter 3, the "judicialization" of the policymaking process. Since the early 1980s, as Stone explains, an increasingly assertive Constitutional Council has employed its judicial review power in such a way as to constrain governments (of both the Right and Left) and alter the terms of legislative debate. Government officials are now forced to take constitutional jurisprudence seriously if they wish to avoid clashes with the Council, and leaders of the parliamentary opposition—bereft of means to obstruct the government in the Gaullist era—have been empowered by their ability to appeal juridically controversial bills to the Council. Although Robert Badinter, the influential president of the Council from 1986 until 1995, was rebuffed in some of his (and Mitterrand's) efforts to make the Council an even more formidable institution, his years in office have left a potent juris-

Introduction: Mitterrand's Legacy, Chirac's Challenge

prudential legacy. Given this fact, even a French president as powerfully situated as Chirac in 1995 is no longer able to exert his legislative will in the unobstructed fashion of de Gaulle.[36] On the issue of immigration, for example, Chirac should find it difficult to legislate more restrictive measures in light of the Council's landmark 1993 ruling on the *lois Pasqua*.

Whereas chapters 2 and 3 both portray the institutional context of policymaking in a general fashion, chapter 4 by Frank Baumgartner stresses that the style of policymaking in France actually varies substantially across issue areas and over time. At the heart of Baumgartner's analysis is the importance of variance in the "agenda status" of issues. When issues (even very important ones) are low on the agenda of partisan politics, they tend to be handled in a technocratic fashion by France's renowned high civil servants. In contrast, those issues that explode into the headlines through protest demonstrations, for which France is equally renowned—for example, education, social security, and immigration policy in recent years—generate partisan discord and the active involvement of the political elite. In certain cases, such mobilized social opposition can prove an insuperable obstacle to change. Jacques Chirac entered the Elysée having already learned the hard way how "the streets" can serve to limit the formidable powers of the French executive. During the winter of 1986-1987, Chirac as prime minister was forced by a burgeoning student movement to withdraw a major reform of the university system.[37] In December 1995, this time as president, he witnessed the power of protest once again.

Part II focuses on the evolution of economic policy and the status of business and labor in an era of increasing liberalization and Europeanization. As Vivien Schmidt explains in chapter 5, the past decade has featured a dramatic decline in traditional French *dirigisme*, or state intervention in the economy. The shift in this direction began with the Socialist government's economic U-turn of 1983, was accelerated in 1986 by the neoliberal government of Jacques Chirac that placed a premium on privatization and deregulation, and was reinforced during President Mitterrand's second term by both Socialist and conservative governments. While the trend toward domestic liberalization has altered the traditional pattern of business-state relations, so too has the Europeanization entailed in the Single European Act and the Maastricht Treaty. Business leaders have come to see Brussels as playing a role almost as important as that of Paris, and French governments have even encouraged the business community to enhance its lobbying activities at the Euro-level. The net results of liberalization and

Europeanization generated considerable enthusiasm in the late 1980s, Schmidt notes, but have become the source of some controversy since the economic slowdown began in the early 1990s. A crucial dimension of the current malaise, she argues, arises from the irony that the French state no longer possess the autonomy and interventionist capability of the past but is still expected by French citizens—not surprisingly, given the voluntarist rhetoric to which presidential candidates such as Jacques Chirac commonly resort—to resolve economic problems with forceful action.

The other side of this economic coin is the focus of chapter 6. Mark Kesselman explains how the liberalization and Europeanization of the last decade have generated an unprecedented crisis for the French labor movement, a crisis that has been slowed but not fundamentally changed by the massive strikes of December 1995. Labor movements in all of the industrialized countries have been experiencing severe challenges, he notes, but the problems in the French case have been exceptional. Since the Socialists' economic U-turn of 1983, governments of both the Left and Right have given priority to a strong franc, low inflation, and reduced wage costs. The French shift to conservative economic policy has been even more extreme than the global trend, and constraints posed by the EU have also reduced the French state's ability to provide the sort of legislative and regulatory concessions normally sought by labor. At the same time, accelerated European integration has enhanced the mobility of French capital while leaving labor behind. The most prominent results of these structural changes for the labor movement since the early 1980s have been a dramatic increase in unemployment and a decline of 50-70 percent in union membership.

Part III focuses on the politics of social policy in a number of key areas. In chapter 7, Martin Schain deals with immigration policy and the related rise of the National Front. It is often difficult to remember, he notes, that intense conflict over immigration emerged relatively recently in France. Since 1980, however, every new French government has proposed important new legislation related to immigration. A crucial factor in keeping this issue salient, Schain argues, has been the role of the National Front. The movement headed by Jean-Marie Le Pen has not only shaped the political agenda by compelling parties of both the Right and Left to treat immigration as a high priority issue, but it has also succeeded in expanding the terms of the debate from specific issues of immigrant integration to broader questions of French national identity. Ironically, Schain notes, the debates triggered by the National Front have masked the fact that there is broad agreement among the major parties on most issues related to immigration. Moreover, the intensity of the immigration debate has made it easy to overlook the fact that substantial progress has been made toward integrating immigrants into French society.

In chapter 8, John Ambler examines the evolution of education policy and highlights one of the achievements of the Mitterrand era: the vast expansion of secondary and higher education. Most striking, he notes, is the fact that the proportion of French youth completing a full secondary-school program increased from 34 percent in 1980 to 60 percent by 1990, with 75-80 percent now appearing as a realistic goal for the year 2000. The success of this drive to "democratize" education resulted from a surprising degree of Left-Right consensus, from the financial contributions of local governments (made possible by decentralization), to unprecedented cooperation between school authorities and business. However, as Ambler documents, the story of education policy has by no means been an unmitigated success. Some reforms have been aborted or diluted by factors ranging from protest demonstrations (especially by students) to the defense of *droits acquis* (established rights) by the teachers' unions, which have declined but remain relatively strong. Moreover, the bottom line has been disappointing, as the expansion and restructuring of education has failed to alleviate youth unemployment. Chirac thus inherited an educational system that, despite its achievements, is widely viewed as a source of the broader French malaise.

In chapter 9, David Wilsford deals with another important issue that has become a central political problem in France—and throughout the industrialized world—over the last decade: health care policy. Wilsford argues that France has done better than the United States at reaching the central goals of health policy (assuring high access and fairly comprehensive coverage while containing costs), but has done less well than Britain, Germany, or Japan. Some reforms of the health care system were achieved during the Mitterrand era, but the sort of major change deemed necessary by many analysts has proven unattainable in the face of broad support by both patients and doctors for the status quo. As a result, national health insurance ran a 26 billion franc deficit in 1993 and a 30 billion franc deficit in 1994, leaving major problems with which the Chirac presidency is now being forced to grapple. Readers will note that the Ambler and Wilsford chapters together provide excellent comparative case studies of the way the sectoral obstacles discussed by

Baumgartner can serve to frustrate reform efforts of the French executive, however powerful it is relative to those of other democratic systems.

Whereas chapters 7-9 deal with social issues that have long been high on the government's agenda, chapter 10 by Amy Mazur focuses on an issue that has acquired political salience in France only in the last decade: sexual harassment in the workplace. As Mazur notes, a variety of factors—the structure of policymaking, the legal culture, and societal attitudes—combined to keep the issue of sexual harassment off the French agenda for nearly a decade after it had been defined as a problem in many other countries. The issue finally made its way onto the legislative agenda in the early 1990s as a result of pressure not only from feminists within the Socialist Party but also officials at the European Commission. Indeed, one of the important lessons to be derived from this chapter is that the "Europeanization" of the last decade has involved not only economic constraints but also, in selected areas, considerable pressure for social policy harmonization. Although, as Mazur notes, a law on "abuse of authority in sexual matters in work relations" was finally passed in 1992, it was essentially a symbolic reform limited in content and devoid of effective enforcement mechanisms. Given the lack of concern manifested for this issue by the government of the Right elected in 1993, it is not surprising that policy in this area has not been high on the agenda for the Chirac presidency—and may thus prove again to be a point of discord with EU officials in Brussels.

Marie-France Toinet, in chapter 11, deals not with a specific policy area but rather with the broad question of social malaise in France. As Toinet explains, the current malaise reflects "identity turmoil" related to factors such as Europeanization and the growth of the immigrant population, economic anxieties stemming from high unemployment, and cynicism about politics resulting from recent policy failures of both right- and left-wing governments as well as corruption scandals. In terms of political behavior, the malaise has led to an increasing voter flight from the major parties (the RPR and UDF as well as the Socialists) and their presidential candidates while also producing a rise in abstention. However, as Toinet stresses, the malaise has fallen short of the sort of crises that have emerged at times in the French past and in other countries over the last decade. The major parties have not imploded as in Italy, no Berlusconi or Perot has captured broad public support, and voter turnout has remained relatively high. Moreover, the economy has performed quite well by some measures, the citizens have not (as in the United States) branded the government as the root of all problems. In fact, they have continued to support a considerable degree of state intervention, and social cohesion has been frayed less than in some other countries due, in part, to the retention of a substantial "social safety net." In short, argues Toinet, the legacy inherited by Chirac from Mitterrand is perhaps less problematic than some observers have contended.

Part IV is devoted to the challenges that the European Community or (as of 1993) European Union has posed for France since the onset of the Mitterrand era. In chapter 12, Andrew Appleton explains how the pivotal 1992 referendum on the Maastricht Treaty produced a "nervewracking period" for party leaders of both the Left and Right, especially Mitterrand and Chirac. The former called the referendum, as Appleton notes, to give his faltering Socialist government a much-needed and apparently certain victory—as the early polls showed wide support for Maastricht—and to expose divisions within the Right. As it turned out, Mitterrand's gamble almost produced a defeat that would have been a humiliation for the government and an enormous blow to the progress of the EU. Meanwhile, Chirac was forced to cope with profound divisions within the Right and was met with jeers from members of his own party when he announced that he would "vote yes without enthusiasm." The broader result of the referendum experience, as Appleton stresses, was to show that leaders of France's major parties seemed out of touch with the concerns of their constituents.

Chapter 13 by David Cameron deals more broadly with the Europeanization component of the Mitterrand legacy and the combination of achievements and malaise that it entails. As Cameron explains, while the Socialists' economic U-turn of 1983 seemed to represent a grudging acceptance of Euro-constraints, it was soon followed by a wholehearted commitment from Mitterrand and his government to the project of deepening European integration. From the French presidency of the EC Council of Ministers in 1984 to the elaboration of the "1992 Program" and the drafting of the Maastricht Treaty, Mitterrand consistently worked to build a new European Union that many observers view (despite the edifices that have mushroomed around Paris!) as his most impressive monument.[38] Polls taken from 1983 through 1987, show that the French public was increasingly supportive of this turn to Europe and was also more supportive of the integration venture than citizens, on average, elsewhere in the Community. However, this support has declined markedly since 1988 and by 1994 French citizens were less inclined to see the EU as a good thing than those in every other member country except Spain. As Cameron argues, this erosion of support for the EU has occurred for several reasons, most notably the failure of integration to deliver (at least in the short term) the sort of economic benefits that it had seemed to promise.

In the concluding chapter, Jolyon Howoth discusses the evolution of French nuclear policy in recent years and the most controversial decision to date of the Chirac presidency: the announcement in June 1995 that France intended to conduct a new series of nuclear tests in the South Pacific. As Howorth notes, Mitterrand authorized 86 nuclear tests during his tenure at the Elysée, but also declared a moratorium on such testing in April 1992. Chirac's departure from this policy "has raised a much bigger international hue and cry than any other event in France's nuclear history and has also proven unpopular with the French public." Howorth shows that the resumption of testing has not only led to unprecedented tensions with the countries of the Pacific but also compromised efforts to develop a Common Foreign and Security Policy (CFSP) within the European Union. In the short run, the political fallout from the nuclear test has generated a costly boycott of French products throughout the world.[39] In the long run, as Howorth argues, it may prove even more counterproductive by undermining France's efforts to establish a Euro-deterrent.

Notes to Chapter 1

1. See *The Economist*, May 13, 1995, p. 49.
2. See the headline of *Le Figaro*, May 9, 1995.
3. *Le Figaro*, May 9, 1995, p. 1.
4. *Le Monde*, April 19, 1995.
5. See *Le Monde*, April 11, 1995.
6. *The Economist*, July 15, 1995, pp. 34-35; see also *Le Monde*, June 23-24, 1995.
7. See Christopher Anderson, *Blaming the Government: Citizens and the Economy in Five European Democracies* (Armonk, N.Y.: M.E. Sharpe, 1995).
8. See John T. S. Keeler, "Executive Power and Policy-Making Patterns in France: Gauging the Impact of Fifth Republic Institutions," *West European Politics* 16, no. 4 (October 1993): 518-44.
9. Peter A. Hall, "The Evolution of Economic Policy Under Mitterrand," in George Ross, Stanley Hoffmann and Sylvia Malzacher, eds., *The Mitterrand Experiment* (New York: Oxford University Press, 1987), p. 55.

10. Elie Cohen, "Les socialistes et l'économie: de l'age des mythes au déminage," in Elisabeth Dupoirer and Gérard Grunberg, eds., *Mars 1986: La Drôle Défaite de la Gauche* (Paris: Presses Universitaires de la France, 1986): 78-80.

11. See Ronald Tiersky, *France in the New Europe* (Belmont, Calif.: Wadsworth, 1994): 175-77. The sources for the data in figure 1.1 are *OECD Economic Outlook 57, June 1995* (Paris: OECD, 1995) and earlier volumes in the same series.

12. See Lean-Louis Missika and Dorine Bregman, "La Campagne: la sélection des controverse politiques," in Dupoirer and Grunberg, eds., *Mars 1986...*, pp. 100-101.

13. Tiersky, 178.

14. Tiersky, 141.

15. On Balladur's popularity in 1993-94, see Elisabeth Dupoirer and Gérard Grunberg, "La Déchirure sociale," *Pouvoirs* 73 (April 1995): 149-51.

16. *Le Monde*, May 11, 1995, p. 9. Chirac's reference to unemployment as a French "cancer" was made in his May 19 speech to parliament; see *Le Monde*, May 21-22, 1995.

17. The sources for figure 1.4 are Roy Pierce, *Choosing the Chief: Presidential Elections in France and the United States* (Ann Arbor: University of Michigan Press, 1995), pp. 248-49 and *Le Monde*, April 25, 1995. For a discussion of Chirac's disappointment with the first ballot results, see *Le Monde*, April 25, 1995.

18. In light of this extraordinary vote for extremist candidates, Pascal Perrineau has argued that the 1995 contest should be seen as "a true crisis election" without precedent in the Fifth Republic. See *Le Monde*, April 26, 1995.

19. *The Economist*, May 13, 1995, p. 49.

20. See Dupoirer and Grunberg, "La Déchirure sociale," 154-56.

21. Ibid., 156.

22. Ibid., 153.

23. Ibid.; see also *Le Monde*, April 11, 1995.

24. *Le Monde*, April 11, 1995.

25. On the public debt, see *The Economist*, May 13, 1995, p. 26.

26. See Colette Ysmal, "La Droite modérée sous pression du Front National," *French Politics and Society* 13 (Spring 1995); *Le Monde*, June 13, and June 20, 1995.

27. *Libération*, May 9, 1995, p. 11, and *Le Monde*, April 13, 1996, p. 7.

28. *Le Monde*, May 11, 1995, p. 9.

29. See *Le Monde*, April 26, 1995.
30. See *Le Monde*, July 1, 1995. It should be noted that the safeguard clause has already been invoked a second time by the French government. After the terrorist bombing at the Saint Michel subway station in July, the government did so to reinstitute controls, which it had previously removed at airports for flights coming from so-called "Schengen space"; see *Le Monde*, July 28, 1995. These restrictions were partially lifted. The partial lifting of land controls was reported in *Le Monde*, March 26, 1996.
31. *Le Monde*, February 21, February 29, March 28, 1996.
32. *Le Monde*, January 19, 1996, where National Assembly President, Philippe Séguin, refers to Maastricht as "historic stupidity," at the same time that he speaks of the obligation to follow the decision made by the French people through universal suffrage in 1992; January 39, 1996, for Chirac's allusion to the referendum; February 9, March 25-25, March 26, 1996, for the struggle to develop a French position for the Inter-Governmental Conference.
33. *Le Monde*, March 26, 1996.
34. *Le Monde*, July 25, 1995; January 23, February 29, and May 3, 1996.
35. See *The Economist*, April 22, 1995.
36. One effect of the constitutional amendment passed on July 31, 1995 (see chapter 2) is that, on social and economic issues, presidents will be able to obviate Constitutional Council constraints by submitting matters to the voters in referenda. Some members of parliament proposed including in the amendment draft a requirement that all referenda be screened in advance by the Council, but the government rejected this idea; see *Libération*, July 6, 1995. For the opinions of two different constitutional experts regarding the advisability of requiring the advice of the Council on referenda, see Georges Vedel, "Une réforme constitutionelle sage et bienvenue," *Le Monde*, July 6, 1995 and Eric Dupin, "Court-circuiter le Conseil constitutionnel," *Libération*, July 13, 1995.
37. See John Ambler, "Why French Education Policy Is So Often Made on the Streets," *French Politics and Society* 12 (spring-summer 1994).
38. See *The Economist*, April 8, 1995, p. 43.
39. "Journal et revue de presse RFI," distributed by the Scientific and Technical Mission of the French Embassy in the United States, May 21, 1996.

Part I

Institutions and the Policymaking Process

Chapter 2

Presidents, Premiers, and Models of Democracy in France

John T. S. Keeler and Martin A. Schain

During the 1995 presidential election campaign, Jacques Chirac harshly criticized the "monarchical drift" of the presidency under François Mitterrand and promised, if elected, to take a more "modest" approach. Soon after he became president on May 17, Chirac moved on numerous fronts to make good on his pledge—at least in symbolic terms. He reduced the number of aides and guards at the Elysée Palace, disbanded the fleet of presidential jets, ordered presidential motorcades to halt the practice of sailing through red lights behind the sirens of a motorcycle escort, and reportedly told friends to continue addressing him by the familiar *tu* rather than adopting the formal *vous* normally employed with presidents.[1]

Despite such highly publicized "populist" changes in traditional presidential style, on more substantive matters Chirac's behavior during his first year in office has clearly been at odds with his declared intentions. Throughout the election campaign, Chirac insisted that he would be less interventionist than Mitterrand at the peak of his power in the early 1980s and that, while setting the broad outlines of policy, he would allow for a better balance between the role of the president and that of the prime minister and the government.[2] However, Chirac has proven to be a president intent on assuming a commanding position in the policymaking process. In the foreign policy sphere, the traditional "reserved domain" of the president, he has taken the lead on all important matters, ranging from the announcement of a controversial resumption of French nuclear tests in the Pacific to a historic reorientation of French defense policy.[3] At the same time, he has demonstrated that the key priorities in domestic policy are also to be determined at the Elysée Palace. Some French papers have referred to the dynamic new president as "Super-Chirac," while *The Economist* has noted that his message to the French seems to be: "The president is back!"[4] Contrary to the expectations aroused by his criticism of "the old regime," it thus appears that Chirac has attempted to restore the sort of republican monarchy or "hyperpresidential" system that last existed under Mitterrand before the 1986 elections.

To what extent is Chirac, a neo-Gaullist, likely to prove capable of governing in the hyperpresidential fashion that de Gaulle established as the "normal" mode of operation for the Fifth Republic? The central purpose of this chapter will be to answer that question by placing the Chirac presidency in a historical and comparative context. Our central argument is twofold: First, while current conditions are certainly permissive of a reversion to strong presidential dominance in the political system, the hyperpresidentialism of Chirac should be more constrained by both institutional and political factors than the original form developed by de Gaulle. Second, there is a reasonable possibility— given the "cycle of electoral rejection" discussed in chapter 1—that this latest experiment in hyperpresidentialism will not last beyond the next legislative elections due to be held by 1998. Within three years, then, it is quite possible that Chirac will be forced to govern in line with one of the other two models of democracy that have developed since 1974 (see table 2.1). A defeat for the RPR-UDF (the parties of the conservative majority) in that election would compel Chirac to play the minimal role pioneered by Mitterrand from 1986 to 1988 and 1993 to 1995. Alternatively, an increase in the power of the UDF relative to Chirac's RPR or a slim victory for the RPR-UDF coalition would force Chirac to govern in the "tempered presidential" styles of Giscard d'Estaing from 1974 to 1981 or Mitterrand from 1988 to 1993.

Section I will discuss the development of the "hyperpresidential" or "normal" model under de Gaulle and explain how, with some variance, this model reemerged under Mitterrand from 1981 to 1986. Section II will deal with the "tempered presidential" model that has been in evidence for 12

TABLE 2.1:
THE THREE MODELS OF DEMOCRACY IN THE FIFTH REPUBLIC

	Defining Elements	Cases	
The Hyper-presidential Model	The president is supported by a solid majority in the National Assembly. The president determines the essential goals of the government and manages the policymaking process on matters of highest priority. The premier is a "loyal lieutenant" of the president and possesses only as much autonomy as the president will allow.	1962-69 1969-74 1981-86 1995- *Note: The 1958-62 de Gaulle case is unique, with presidential dominance bordering on "liberal dictatorship" in times of crisis.	de Gaulle Pompidou Mitterrand Chirac

The Tempered Presidential Model	The president faces substantial opposition in the National Assembly. The premier derives considerable clout from his own parliamentary power base and/or the need for him/her to construct supportive coalitions for the passage of legislation.	1974-81 Giscard d'Estaing
		   Premiers: Chirac, Barre
		
		1988-93 Mitterrand
		   Premiers:
		   Rocard, Cresson,
		   Bérégovoy	

The Premier-Presidential Model
 	
(Cohabitation)
	The president faces a hostile majority in the National Assembly. The premier is the leader of the majority in the National Assembly and the effective head of government, with the president wielding very limited powers.	1986-88 Mitterrand
		   Premier: Chirac
		
		1993-95 Mitterrand
		   Premier: Balladur	

years (1974-81 and 1988-93) since the mid-1970s. Section III will analyze the "premier-presidential model" of 1986-88 and 1993-95. The concluding section will assess the Chirac presidency from a historical and comparative perspective.

I. The Hyperpresidential Model

The Fifth Republic's constitution did *not* institute a presidential regime in France. In fact, while the document did include some new powers for the president, it was clearly designed to produce a parliamentary regime. To understand how the regime moved rapidly toward a unique hyperpresidential model, one must appreciate the way in which de Gaulle and other pivotal political actors shaped institutional developments during the crisis years of 1958 to 1962.

The process of drafting the new constitution began in May 1958, when the Algerian crisis compelled the leaders of the Fourth Republic to negotiate the terms of a return to power by Charles de Gaulle, and ended with the formal presentation of the text on September 4 and its approval in a referendum on September 28. Michel Debré, appointed by de Gaulle to supervise the drafting process, categorized the purpose of the constitutional reform venture as being not to create a "presidential system" but rather to "renovate the parliamentary regime."[5]

This was to be a "rationalized parliamentary system" in the sense that the balance of power, which favored the parliament in the Fourth Republic, would be restructured to strengthen the government. For example: it was made more difficult for parliament to oust a government with a censure vote; the powers of parliamentary committees were curtailed; the government was granted more control over the parliamentary agenda and greater power to legislate through decrees. In addition, the government gained a variety of "constitutional weapons" that could be selectively employed to limit parliament's ability to shape legislation or delay the legislative process. Some of the most important "weapons" included the following: Article 44.3, the *vote bloqué* provision, enabled the government to require a house of parliament to vote on an entire bill and only on those amendments the government proposed or accepted; Article 49.3 allowed the government to declare a bill an issue of confidence and thus secure its passage if the National Assembly proved incapable of passing a motion of censure; Article 45.4 allowed the government to circumvent the Senate when that body proved uncooperative by sending the government's preferred version of a bill back to the National Assembly for a definitive vote.[6]

Under normal conditions, it appeared, most of the executive powers in the new regime would be exercised by the government (cabinet) under the direction of a prime minister, who would be appointed by the president but responsible only to parliament. According to Article 20, the government "shall determine and direct the policy of the nation," while Article 21 states that "the Prime Minister shall direct the operation of the government. He shall be responsible for national defense. He shall ensure the execution of the laws . . . he shall have regulatory powers and shall make appointments to civil and military posts."[7] Moreover, the text clearly stipulated that it would be the government (or prime minister), who would directly wield, without the necessity of presidential approval, the "constitutional weapons" designed to assure executive primacy over the "rationalized" parliament in the policymaking process.

The president was granted certain powers not provided to the chief of state under the Fourth Republic, for example, the right to dissolve the National Assembly ("after consultation with the Prime Minister"), the right to call a referendum (but only "on the proposal of the government"), and the right to invoke emergency powers under Article 16 ("after consultation with the Prime Minister" and others) under rare conditions.[8] In general, however, the role of the president was seemingly to be that of the guardian of the constitution, "who by his arbitration" in exceptional circumstances was to "ensure the regular functioning of the public authorities" (under Article 5).[9] An important implicit limit on presidential authority was the stipulation that the chief of state was to be elected by a large college of local notables (there were 81,764 electors in the indirect election of December 21, 1958).[10] As Debré noted, this mechanism would likely produce a political outcome very different from that related to direct election, for a "president who is elected by universal suffrage is a political leader bound by the daily work of government and command."[11]

Given the prospect that de Gaulle would serve as the regime's first president and the concern on the part of the many pro-parliamentary members of the Consultative Constitutional Commission (CCC) that the general might seek to interpret expansively the powers of the chief of state, the CCC compelled de Gaulle to address publicly what everyone saw as a crucial issue: relations between the president and prime minister. When asked directly whether he thought the president could *dismiss*—as well as appoint—the prime minister, de Gaulle responded: "No! For, if it were like that, he could not govern effectively. The prime minister is responsible to Parliament and not to the Chief of State in what concerns policy matters . . . The president of the Republic, I insist on this, is essentially an arbiter who has the mission of ensuring, no matter what happens, the functioning of the branches of government."[12] This statement and similar ones by other Gaullists largely "appeased the fears" of those who worried that "the spirit of the presidential regime" lurked in what looked like an essentially parliamentary text.[13] The final version of the crucial Article 8 on president-premier relations was worded as follows: "The President of the Republic shall appoint the Prime Minister. He shall terminate the functions of the Prime Minister when the latter presents the resignation of the Government."

Despite persistent concerns that de Gaulle as president might well extract resignations from prime ministers, most CCC members were convinced that the Fifth Republic was "parliamentary in text" and would certainly be so in practice after de Gaulle had passed from the scene.[14]

William Andrews summed up his review of the deliberations of the CCC as follows: "The original 1958 constitution established a parliamentary regime. This was the result of the drafting process, the intent of the framers, and the clear meaning of the key provisions of its text."[15] Right though Andrews is in most respects, a more precise wording would have been "the *publicly proclaimed* intent of the framers," for as he himself notes, de Gaulle would later acknowledge that he was not entirely honest in his exchanges with the CCC.[16] In his memoirs, de Gaulle mentioned that he had envisioned the president's role as "all-powerful," in contrast to the wishes of "the adherents of the outgoing regime." As de Gaulle stated in a 1966 interview, he had long thought "that the president of the Republic must govern, but in 1958 no one wanted that!" During the CCC deliberations, the former leader continued, "I could not say so. Then, gradually, we got there, with precautions, with detours, but, in the end, without much difficulty."[17]

Getting there, as de Gaulle put it, was greatly facilitated by two factors. First, the context of crisis over Algeria provided de Gaulle with many opportunities to wield extraordinary presidential power and thus, to the extent his actions proved successful, manifest the potential utility of institutionalizing a stronger presidency than envisioned in the constitution of 1958. Second, many of de Gaulle's institutional maneuvers were possible only because of his unique charismatic authority. His heroism and prescience as leader of the Resistance during World War II and his restoration of the Fourth Republic from 1944 to 1946, followed by 12 years in retirement, which allowed his legend to grow, had given him a "miracle-man" image in the eyes of most French citizens.[18] A poll showed that 80 percent of the public supported his return to power in June 1958 and most of them expected him to resolve not only the Algerian crisis but also the country's other pressing problems.[19] Almost 77 percent of the more than 80,000 electors voting for president in December 1958 supported him.[20] Looking back from the perspective of 1990, an opinion poll showed that most French considered him—mainly because of his role in the Resistance—the greatest Frenchman in history (ahead of Charlemagne and Napoleon I).[21]

The combination of extreme crisis and faith in (or resignation to the indispensability of) de Gaulle produced an era of "liberal dictatorship" that stretched from the end of the Fourth Republic through the first months of the Fifth Republic.[22] When de Gaulle was invested as the last premier of the old regime, an enabling act accorded him "full powers" for six months to take "the legislative measures necessary for the recovery of the nation." The powers thus conferred were essentially extended through February 4, 1959 by Article 92 of the new Fifth Republic constitution. While the rationale for granting such powers was the need for executive discretion in coping with Algeria, the powers were used so extensively that they touched virtually every area of public policy. Scores of important "bills" that would have been passed only in a slow and diluted fashion—if at all—under the old regime were now pushed through rapidly as ordinances.[23] It has been argued that "no legislative program has ever transformed French life so much so fast" as the 378 ordinances issued by de Gaulle's government between June 1958 and February 1959.[24]

While the formal period of liberal dictatorship ended in early 1959, for the next few years de Gaulle continued to define his presidential role in expansive terms and to wield great power in a fashion that generated constitutional controversy. In a speech at the Gaullist Party conference in November 1959, an associate of the president elevated into doctrine de Gaulle's apparent assumption that foreign policy, defense and Algerian affairs constituted a "reserved domain" of exclusive presidential power.[25] An outraged opposition spokesman, François Mitterrand, condemned this assertion as "the first legal coup d'Etat of the general" and also criticized the many political officials who seemed content to accept such audacity as long as de Gaulle was moving toward a resolution of the Algerian problem.[26] Two more "legal coups" followed in 1960. In March de Gaulle triggered a heated legal confrontation with Parliament when he refused to convene a special legislative session despite the fact that a majority in the National Assembly, in line with Article 29 of the constitution, had voted for one. Not only opposition leaders but many jurists questioned de Gaulle's claim that Article 30 (requiring a presidential decree to open special sessions) genuinely conferred discretionary power on the chief of state in the wake of an Assembly vote.[27] The next alleged "legal coup" took place in June when de Gaulle engineered a constitutional amendment allowing member states of the French Community to become independent while retaining their Community membership. While many opposition leaders supported the political thrust of the move, the amendment procedure employed was contested even by the Conseil d'Etat (Council of State) and deemed unconstitutional by most legal specialists.[28]

De Gaulle tested the limits of his constitutional prerogatives again in 1961 when, in response to an attempt by four generals to seize power in Algeria, he invoked the emergency powers of Article 16. While some commentators contested the need for reliance on Article 16 in this instance, many more questioned the legitimacy of de Gaulle's retention of full emergency powers for five months after the immediate threat to the regime had ceased.[29] It was only after the opposition had threatened a censure motion and stormed out of parliament in protest when their motion was ruled out of order, that de Gaulle "quickly decided to appease parliamentary frustrations by abandoning his emergency powers."[30]

For the future of the regime, the most significant moves of de Gaulle as a constitutional poker player were those of 1962. In April, just after the referendum confirming the Evian Accords on Algeria, de Gaulle ignored the letter of Article 8 and dismissed—or forced the resignation of—his prime minister, Michel Debré. There was no doubt about Debré's desire to retain the office, but he had manifested "abnegation without limits" throughout his twenty years of service to de Gaulle, so there was also no doubt that he would comply if asked to "resign."[31] This step, along with the nature of the new premier (Georges Pompidou, a close associate of de Gaulle who was not a member of parliament and had never held any elective office), signalled clearly that de Gaulle intended not to loosen, but rather to consolidate presidential dominance of the regime in the post-Algerian era. Although prominent opposition leaders condemned de Gaulle for forgetting the pledge he had made when Article 8 was being debated in 1958, they were unable to stop a power play that became an important precedent in later years.[32]

The single most important and controversial step taken by de Gaulle in reshaping the original 1958 constitution was announced in September 1962. In the wake of an assassination attempt that nearly succeeded, de Gaulle seized the moment to propose a constitutional amendment to institute the direct election of the president; such a reform, he argued, would give future presidents lacking his unique personal prestige the means to govern effectively. This change would have dashed the hopes of most party leaders for the reversion to a "proper" parliamentary regime in the post–de Gaulle era, and that was reason enough for them to oppose it. But de Gaulle made his proposal doubly objectionable by asserting that he intended to use what was almost universally viewed as an unconstitutional amendment procedure: a simple referendum under Article 11 (which seemed intended for more modest changes only) rather than a referendum following approval by both houses of parliament, as required by Article 89 entitled "amendment."

The greatest constitutional crisis of the Fifth Republic ensued. One member of de Gaulle's cabinet resigned in protest, others objected privately, both the Conseil d'Etat and the Constitutional Council advised against the move, and the National Assembly censured the government. Far from being swayed by such opposition, de Gaulle's perspective was that "to deny the people a right which belonged to them, seemed to me ... high-handed in that I myself was the principal inspirer of the new institutions, and it really was the height of effrontery to challenge me on what [these institutions] meant."[33] The referendum went ahead and, with de Gaulle pledging to resign if the outcome proved negative or merely weakly positive, 62 percent of the voters approved the amendment. Before the reform was promulgated, the president of the Senate used his power to send it back on appeal to the Constitutional Council. In one of the most hotly debated rulings it has ever delivered, the Council stated simply that on technical grounds it was not empowered to overturn the law. "The Constitutional Council has just committed suicide," charged Senate President Gaston Monnerville, while Mitterrand opined that the Council had proven itself "the derisory cap of a derisory democracy."[34]

In all of these steps from 1959 to 1962, the key to de Gaulle's success was his recognition that other relevant institutional actors in the regime would allow him, reluctantly or gladly, to overplay his hand. The opposition in the Assembly may have condemned him for abuse of power, but until the end of the Algerian War in 1962 they grudgingly tolerated his moves largely because they supported the general direction of his colonial policy. As Oliver Duhamel has noted, for example, whereas 295 opposition deputies voted for the special session in the March 1960 confrontation with the general, only 122 of them were willing to go so far as to censure his prime minister as well. Another factor that led opposition deputies to underplay their hands was their mistaken belief that de Gaulle's regime would represent "just a parenthesis in French history," as if the Fifth Republic would revert to its "proper" institutional balance (or even be formally changed) once the crisis had ended and de Gaulle was gone from the scene.[35]

De Gaulle's prime minister accepted the general's misreading of Article 8 out of political loyalty. It is intriguing to speculate what might have happened if de Gaulle's status had been a bit less exalted and Debré's proclivity to self-abnegation a bit less firm. Clearly the result could have been a crisis similar to that recently triggered in Russia by Yeltsin's difficult dealings with once-loyal backers in competing positions of power. De Gaulle's extraordinary authority seems all the more remarkable when one considers the experience of Poland's charismatic Lech Walesa, who "made" Tadeusz Mazowiecki prime minister and then could only "watch as a person he had treated as a tool started to outgrow him politically."[36]

The general public ignored de Gaulle's violation of the constitutional amendment procedure in 1962, despite the strong objections of most of their putative representatives in Parliament, because they supported the institution of direct election to the presidency and were reluctant to jettison the general.[37] The Constitutional Council, faced with what seemed to be a clear violation of the constitution, refused to overturn de Gaulle's amendment on procedural grounds seemingly out of deference to both de Gaulle (who had appointed three of its nine members and heavily influenced the appointment of three others formally chosen by the Assembly president) and the "sovereign" citizenry. Had any of these actors been more inclined to confront the Fifth Republic's first president, the institutions of the new regime would have been infused with a very different meaning.

Consolidating Hyperpresidentialism

Even though the Fifth Republic's institutional die had been largely cast by October 1962, its developmental process was far from complete. The key actors listed above still possessed considerable power, in one form or another, to shape the regime. Let us briefly examine how these actors contributed to the entrenchment of extraordinary presidential power in the Fifth Republic.

In November the general public facilitated the consolidation of presidential power by giving de Gaulle, for the first time, a solid majority in the National Assembly. The Gaullist Union for the New Republic (UNR) and its allies received nearly twice as many votes on the first ballot in 1962 as in 1958. Voters "massively turned away from deputies who had voted censure in favor of new Gaullist candidates," the UNR-led coalition gained almost sixty seats and now held more than 55 percent of the total.[38]

The behavior of the majority coalition in the National Assembly contributed to regime development as well, for an "ethos" pervaded the

Gaullist alliance according the executive an unusual degree of deference and autonomy.[39] The "timidity" of the majority in the Assembly was such that, during the entire decade of de Gaulle's presidency, parliament failed to set up even a single committee of inquiry to investigate the facts concerning some questionable executive actions.[40] Moreover, majority discipline was such that only a handful of Gaullist or allied Giscardian deputies ever supported a censure vote and few deputies of either group even diverged from the government's line on roll call votes.[41]

With assured support in the Assembly, the president was able to reappoint his loyal lieutenant Pompidou as prime minister. Over the next six years—with de Gaulle re-elected in 1965 and Pompidou retaining his office until 1968—the strictly hierarchical relationship between the two "heads" of the executive that conformed to Gaullist preferences was firmly entrenched as the "normal" mode of regime operation. Despite the 1962 amendment, the powers of the chief of state remained quite limited in purely formal terms. In fact, as comparative institutional studies by Maurice Duverger and by Matthew Schugart and John Carey have noted, the French president's *formal* powers in the Fifth Republic's "semi-presidential" system rank among the most meager accorded anywhere to a popularly elected president.[42]

What the French gradually began to view as the norm, however, was a far different reality that can best be described as hyperpresidentialism.[43] As Duverger has described the practice, presidents "exercised directly" the powers conferred on them by the constitution, and "exercised indirectly the prerogatives of their prime ministers and governments, by reducing the latter to obedience."[44]

Despite their protests against the direction the regime was taking under the Gaullists, the opposition parties also contributed significantly to the consolidation of (hyper)presidentialism. With great irony, given his status as the most formidable early critic of the Gaullist Republic, Mitterrand and his reformed Socialist Party played the most prominent role of this sort. From 1965, when he first ran for president, to the elections of 1974 and 1981, Mitterrand increasingly emulated de Gaulle's style as a presidential candidate and used the institution of direct presidential elections as a means for rebuilding and uniting the Left around himself and his party.[45] The Communists and centrists also gradually adjusted to, and grudgingly accepted various aspects of, the new regime.[46] Moreover, leaders of all major parties helped to consolidate the primacy of the presidency by seeking that office rather than aiming merely for the premier's role.[47]

The Pompidou Case

Georges Pompidou played an important role in regime development not only as the second premier, but also as the second president (1969-74). Those who had hoped hyperpresidentialism would disappear with de Gaulle were quickly disabused of this notion. Different though his style was in certain respects, "his view of the Presidency scarcely differed from de Gaulle's."[48] Backed by a large majority in the National Assembly, Pompidou had the power to perpetuate the general's vision of the president's role, including what was now viewed as the traditional relationship between the chief of state and the premier. Indeed, Pompidou emphatically affirmed de Gaulle's interpretation of Article 8 (and apparent disdain for parliament) by firing his first prime minister, Jacques Chaban-Delmas, just after the premier had received a massive vote of confidence from the National Assembly.[49]

The Mitterrand I Case

While the regime's "normal" hyperpresidential model gave way to another during the Giscard years (to be discussed below), it would be restored seven years later with the electoral success of Mitterrand and the Left. Mitterrand narrowly won the presidential election in May 1981, dissolved parliament, and then led the Socialist Party to a smashing landslide victory in the legislative elections. Far from using the vast power at his disposal to "reinvent" the regime in line with the parliamentary vision of his early critics, Mitterrand in essence chose to emulate (and legitimate) the hyperpresidential model developed under presidents de Gaulle and Pompidou. "France's institutions were not made for me," commented Mitterrand, "but they suit me well enough."[50] From the dawn of his tenure until 1986, when he lost majority support in the National Assembly, Mitterrand made it clear that he would provide the basic orientations of the government and that the premiers drawn from his own party (Pierre Mauroy until 1984, Laurent Fabius until 1986) would be expected to play the loyal lieutenant role perfected by Debré and Pompidou.

In general, Mitterrand also expected and received Gaullist-style deference from his party's National Assembly delegation. While he took fewer liberties with the constitution than de Gaulle had, Mitterrand made full use of his presidential powers and even seemed reluctant, despite an official plank of the Socialist Party platform, to call for a reduction of the president's term from seven to five years.[51]

The only major way in which hyperpresidentialism under Mitterrand differed from the earlier post–1962 versions was that, due to developments of the Giscard era (see below), the government was now somewhat constrained in its policymaking capacity by the "counter-power" of an activist Constitutional Council.[52] The Council, to which the opposition appealed with alacrity, struck down as unconstitutional at least several key articles of important Socialist reform bills and deterred other policy steps by its mere presence. Despite this constraint, the experience of the first phase of the Mitterrand presidency (1981-86) was far closer to the Gaullist regime model than the more "tempered" presidential periods to be discussed below.[53]

II. The Tempered Presidential Model

In a number of respects, 1974 marked a turning point in the development of the Fifth Republic. First, a non-Gaullist was elected president. Valéry Giscard d'Estaing, the leader of the "minority" of the traditional majority coalition who had served as a minister under both de Gaulle and Pompidou, narrowly won the special election to replace the deceased Pompidou. Second, Giscard became the first president who was not the leader of the largest party in the National Assembly; Giscard's authority was limited by the fact that his own loosely organized party held only 55 seats versus 183 for the neo-Gaullist UDR (renamed the RPR in 1976) from 1974 to 1977, and 119 versus 155 from 1978 to 1981.[54] Third, given the neo-Gaullist "majority within the majority," Giscard became the first president who felt compelled to appoint, at least initially, someone other than a loyal lieutenant as premier; for his first two years in office he was forced to work with the leader of the neo-Gaullists, Jacques Chirac, as prime minister. Finally, Giscard became the first president to establish an institutional reform that would at least modestly empower the opposition and thus check governmental power; he sponsored an amendment that, in effect, granted the parliamentary opposition the Right to appeal bills to the Constitutional Council for judicial review. All together, the three political changes would temper the traditional hyperpresidentialism of the Fifth Republic in the short run while the institutional amendment would do so, to some extent, in the long run.

What the new political landscape of the Giscard era underscored was the extent to which effective presidential power in the Fifth Republic, which de Gaulle had envisioned as a regime allowing the chief of state to govern "above" the parties, very much depended on the balance of party power in the National Assembly; this had been true before 1974, of course, but the reality was now more visible. From 1974 to 1976, Giscard attempted to govern essentially in the traditional hyperpresidential fashion, counting on Chirac to replicate the traditional Gaullist role of obedient premier and to deliver the support of the Gaullists in the Assembly. Even during the new president's honeymoon period, however, his lack of control over the "majority of the majority" forced him to abandon or water down a host of policy initiatives in the face of Gaullist opposition. Moreover, Chirac soon made it clear that he felt his status as leader of the Assembly's largest party entitled him to more autonomy vis-à-vis the president than that previously allowed any premier of the Fifth Republic.[55] When it became clear in 1976 that he would be granted neither "the means nor the liberty" that he expected, Chirac resigned, thus becoming the first premier in the regime's history to resign of his own volition.[56]

With Chirac back in the Assembly working to establish his status as the genuine leader of the majority (in part to position himself to defeat Giscard at the next presidential election), and with the Gaullists increasingly asserting "their autonomy, their identity, their independence and their disobedience," Giscard "reigned more than he ruled" for the remainder of his term.[57] The president's limited authority meant that his second premier, Raymond Barre, would come to appear as much a rival (with an eye toward the presidency) as an assistant to the extent that he was successful. The institutions of the regime still allowed for governmental stability (for example, Barre would continue as prime minister until the 1981 elections). Moreover, the constitutional weapons available to the executive (now used with unprecedented frequency), reinforced by majority solidarity in the face of increasing competition from the Left, still allowed for a good measure of governmental effectiveness. This mode of governing, however, was no longer the "normal" model of hyperpresidential government; it was at best a tempered or "rationalized" presidentialism.[58]

In the context of a different balance of party power, therefore, the key traditional players (from the president and premier to the electorate and the Assembly delegations) in the governmental game gave new meaning to the regime's institutions. In addition, during this period a *formal* change in institutions combined with unprecedented assertiveness to make the Constitutional Council a player of importance—a player that would henceforth serve to temper governmental power in a fashion de Gaulle had never envisioned. Not until 1971 (two years after de Gaulle's departure from the scene) did the Council overturn a government-sponsored bill on constitutional grounds.

Before Giscard's 1974 amendment empowering sixty senators or sixty deputies (that is, the opposition) to appeal a bill to the Council, however, the judicial body had received few cases to review.[59] In the wake of the 1974 amendment, appeals increased and more significant government bills were overturned—on the basis of norms of reference which the Council expanded with every ruling—than ever before. The Council would play a far more important role during the later reform governments of the Socialists (1981-86) and the Right (1986-88), when vast policy agendas led to proliferating appeals and waves of negative rulings.[60]

The Mitterrand II Case

The second instance of tempered presidentialism emerged following the 1988 elections, when François Mitterrand won reelection to the presidency but was supported by a mere "relative" majority in the National Assembly. The logic of the Giscard model applied once again from 1988 to 1993 in a number of major respects: the policymaking capacity of the president, and the executive generally, was constrained by the absence of a stable and disciplined majority; the prime ministers of the era (Michel Rocard, Edith Cresson and Pierre Bérégovoy) were able to obtain their central policy goals only by frequently resorting to the executive's "constitutional weapons," with Rocard breaking the record for use of Article 49.3 and Cresson for 44.3 (see figure 2.1); the need for premiers to use such weapons and arrange evanescent majorities in Parliament accorded them a degree of power and autonomy unknown in hyperpresidential eras; and the president felt compelled to work with at least one premier (Rocard), who was a major political rival with an eye on a future presidency.[61]

Despite these similarities, Mitterrand enjoyed more power in this period than Giscard had earlier, due to both his personal stature in the Socialist Party and his greater partisan assets in the National Assembly.[62] The Gulf War also provided the president with numerous opportunities to demonstrate his "absolute preeminence" in the "reserved domain" of defense.[63]

III. The Premier-Presidential Model

Even more than 1974, 1986 marked a leap into uncharted political territory for the Fifth Republic. The legislative elections of that year produced, for the first time, a National Assembly majority hostile to the president; the two major parties of the Right held only a fragile edge, with the neo-Gaullists again the leading component, but their position was strong enough to

FIGURE 2.1:
USE OF ARTICLES 44.3 & 49.3 IN NATIONAL ASSEMBLY

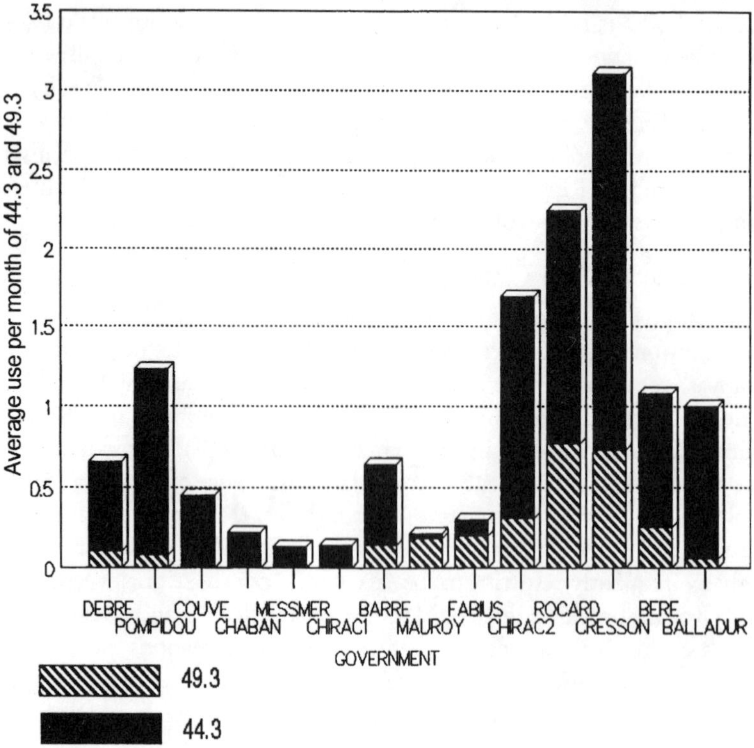

Source: *Bulletin de l'Assemblée Nationale: Statistiques* (Annual).

require Mitterrand to appoint one of their leaders as premier.[64] Mitterrand's choice of neo-Gaullist chief Jacques Chirac launched the first experiment with what the French termed "cohabitation," that is, the awkward sharing of the Fifth Republic's dual executive by the Left and Right.

Without a supportive majority in the Assembly and thus unable to wield "indirectly" powers granted to the premier, the limits to the formal powers of the president were more starkly manifested than ever before. For the most part, prime minister Chirac was able to function as the acknowledged head of government and to manage Parliament through manipulation of the executive's constitutional weapons. It should be noted, however, that in the French case what Arend Lijphart has termed "parliamentary-phase semi-presidentialism" was hardly reducible to an analogue of British parliamentarism. "Premier-presidentialism" is a useful description for the model that emerged, for though the premier was predominant in most respects, both the president and the premier's aspirations to the presidency continued to play major roles in the political game.[65]

As for the president, Mitterrand continued to exercise considerable if selective power. At the outset, Mitterrand announced that he would be guided by "the constitution, nothing but the constitution. But all of the constitution."[66] In line with both the constitution and tradition, he was especially insistent on retaining a major say in the "reserved domain" of foreign policy and defense. His rival, Chirac, was poorly positioned (as leader of a movement that traced its origins to de Gaulle) to contest an expansive reading of presidential power in this area. Mitterrand was thus able to use his appointment power (Article 8) to veto Chirac's original nominees for foreign minister and defense minister and obtain acceptable (that is, politically neutral) replacements. He also managed to maintain a high profile in diplomacy (though Chirac insisted on accompanying him to international summits) and to assert his authority on a variety of important matters related to defense.

On domestic matters, Mitterrand deferred for the most part to Chirac and his government. However, Mitterrand did intervene in this sphere when he thought he could find and justify suitable institutional levers to push. For example, just as de Gaulle had read presidential discretion into Article 30 in the March 1960 controversy, Mitterrand invoked Article 13 (requiring the president's signature on ordinances and decrees) to veto ordinances on matters such as privatization and the redrawing of electoral districts; such moves could not stop the Chirac government from achieving its goals, but they did cause delay and allow for parliamentary debate. Mitterrand also used his media access to speak out against government policy on certain issues, particularly social policy.[67]

Throughout the first cohabitation era, the games played by Chirac and Mitterrand were affected by their calculations regarding the looming presidential election of 1988. Both the premier and president seemed constrained in their assertions of power by the fact that the public was watching, and would soon be judging them at the polls. Voters generally responded negatively to actions that provoked constitutional crises. Chirac was doubtlessly prevented from attempting to "radically undermine the office of the presidency" by the fact that his sights were set on that prize.[68] In the end,

Mitterrand's restrained and statesmanlike behavior, combined with the public's tendency to blame the more powerful premier for economic and other problems, enabled the president to achieve reelection in 1988.

Cohabitation II

The 1993 parliamentary elections triggered what became known as "cohabitation II," as Mitterrand's Socialists were routed in an unprecedented landslide that gave the two major parties of the Right (the RPR and UDF) more than 80 percent of the seats in the National Assembly. Now that this second political-institutional experiment has ended, with the 1995 presidential election, it is clear that two of its features merit special mention here. On the one hand, the mode of governance manifested in cohabitation II was probably as close as the Fifth Republic system will come to the pure parliamentary model. Even though the premier of this era, neo-Gaullist Edouard Balladur, was less confrontational in style than Chirac had been (leading observers to speak of a more "gentle" cohabitation), his relative authority was far greater. Whereas Balladur was backed by the largest majority in Fifth Republic history, Mitterrand was tied to a Socialist Party routed at the polls in the wake of scandals, internal divisions and numerous unpopular policy moves. Moreover, for most of this period Balladur's approval ratings held at a remarkably high level—in light of the country's continuing economic problems—while Mitterrand's never rose much above 40 percent. Finally, Mitterrand's attempts to assert influence waned as his lame-duck status became more pronounced, as the cancer, which he made public and drained his strength, and as his image was tarnished further by revelations surrounding his record under the Vichy regime. Even in the foreign policy realm, therefore, Balladur's primacy seemed evident.[69]

On the other hand, the Elysée Palace continued to shape political developments to some extent during this era. Before his interest and health gave out, Mitterrand showed that even a president with minimal assets could remain a factor in a cohabitation setting. Having learned in 1986 that a hostile premier could delay his receipt of diplomatic dispatches routed through the Ministry of Foreign Affairs, Mitterrand had prepared for cohabitation II by ordering in 1990 the installation of electronic decoding equipment in the Elysée so that all dispatches would be at his immediate disposal. The president's extensive network of governmental contacts, combined with his appointment of a host of loyal personnel to sensitive diplomatic posts just before the 1993 election, guaranteed early on that he could not be easily excluded from the traditional reserved domain of foreign affairs and defense. While Prime Minister Balladur quickly asserted his right to play a role in diplomatic efforts on several fronts, he also showed a willingness to cooperate with the president. A pattern of institutionalized consultation between the president, the prime minister, the foreign minister (Alain Juppé) and other relevant cabinet ministers was developed through the mechanism of a *conseil restreint*—a restricted meeting of ministers involved in foreign affairs, chaired by the president—after each formal meeting of the Council of Ministers.[70]

At the outset of cohabitation II, the primacy of the presidency as a political prize was also underscored in a remarkable manner: Jacques Chirac, frustrated by his two prior attempts to govern as premier, declined to accept the Matignon role in 1993 (despite his party's supremacy within an 80 percent majority) the better to prepare himself for another run at the presidency in 1995. Chirac's gamble almost proved fatal to his political career. Balladur's continued popularity, which stunned everyone, led the premier to renounce his pledge not to run against Chirac in the 1995 election, and until just months before the vote Balladur looked like the certain winner.[71] Ultimately, of course, Chirac's assumption—based on bitter personal experience—that the incumbent premier's popularity would erode substantially proved prescient (with the aid of corruption scandals and Balladur's poor campaign style) and paved the way to his presidential election.

IV. The Chirac Presidency in Perspective

When Chirac won the election of May 1995, it was commonly thought that the French governmental system would automatically shift back into its "normal" mode of presidential dominance. Indeed, since he inherited an unprecedented RPR-UDF majority in the National Assembly, Chirac seemed more than capable of governing in a hyperpresidential fashion reminiscent of Mitterrand I or Pompidou if not de Gaulle in the mid-1960s. On the surface, at least, the first months of Chirac's term have certainly met these expectations. The president has named a classic "loyal lieutenant" (Alain Juppé) as his premier, selected a cabinet dominated by members of his own party, and assumed a commanding position in the policymaking process.

When measured against the standard of earlier cases of hyperpresidentialism, however, the potential of the Chirac presidency looks less impressive in several respects. First, Chirac's authority within his governing coalition pales next to that of de Gaulle and compares poorly with that of Pompidou and Mitterrand. As noted in chapter 1, Chirac obtained the dubious distinction of receiving the lowest vote total (20.8 percent) on the first ballot of any president elected since 1965; moreover, he was the first president ever to receive less than 50 percent of the votes cast on the second ballot (6 percent of the ballots cast were "spoiled," generally a way of expressing protest through the ballot-box). As early as July 1995, a leader of the Parti Républicain (the largest branch of the UDF) was openly ridiculing Chirac by noting sardonically that his RPR-dominated government "represented only 20.8 percent of the French."[72]

The political position of the president and the prime minister rapidly deteriorated at the end of August and then grew alarmingly worse during the next three months as the government drifted into the worst political crisis since the "events" of May–June, 1968. The crisis emerged from a combination of ineptitude, bad luck, and real conflicts within the governing majority. When the Minister of the Economy, Alain Madelin, questioned the civil service retirement scheme he was dismissed the next day by M. Juppé.[73] Just over a month later the government, under pressure from increasing unemployment and a more general economic decline, announced reforms of the social security system (as well as the nationalized railway system) that incorporated many of the proposals for which Madelin was fired.

The citizen's reaction to the civil service and railway unions was not unexpected, but the breadth of support for these reactions was not anticipated. The unions called for strikes against the reforms (the "Juppé Plan," see Chapter 6 by Mark Kesselman.) By the end of November the strikes had grown into a vast social movement of civil servants and transport workers— but the movement also included university students, who were striking for other reasons—that virtually shut down the country for the first three weeks in December 1995. Public opinion was generally sympathetic to the strikers, and confidence in the president and prime minister fell to historic lows by early November, a decline that continued through early 1996.[74] By early January, a compromise of sorts was reached with the major unions, but the political damage endured long after that.

The crisis of the winter of 1995 has exacerbated a situation in which Chirac has enjoyed less parliamentary deference than that which enabled de Gaulle to establish the hyperpresidential tradition. On the one hand, many of the 260 members of Chirac's own RPR compare him unfavorably to such rivals as Balladur and Philippe Séguin, the president of the National

Assembly (and a leading critic of Chirac's support for the Maastricht Treaty). On the other, Chirac must deal with a "minority of the majority"—the UDF—that holds 214 seats (37 percent of the total) in the National Assembly, and that includes many legislative leaders loyal to Balladur and harshly critical of departures from his policy orientations. What this means, for example, is that the budget must be steered through an Assembly finance committee chaired by a former minister of justice under Balladur, Pierre Méhaignerie, who is said to relish playing the role of *contre-pouvoir positif* (a positive counter-weight).[75]

Only two months into Chirac's presidency, relations between the government and the parliamentary majority were said to be characterized by "impatience, irritation, annoyance and frustration."[76] All of Chirac's first major initiatives—the budget, the proposal to amend the constitution (see below), and the resumption of nuclear weapons tests—generated considerable dissent.[77] Moreover, such grumbling was encouraged by the fact that Chirac's approval rating fell more sharply—from 59 percent to 44 percent—during his first two months in power than that of any previous president of the Fifth Republic.[78]

Not surprisingly, in the aftermath of the crisis criticism and disarray grew within the majority and touched every major reform proposed by the government. Agreement was difficult to reach, not only between the RPR and the UDF but within each of the two components of the majority.[79]

Criticism was also encouraged by a second problem with which the president has been forced to deal. The National Assembly is no longer as structurally enfeebled as it was in the days of de Gaulle or even Mitterrand I. In September 1993 Séguin sponsored the institution of a package of procedural reforms designed to enhance the status and efficiency of the Assembly.[80] Moreover, since Chirac's election Séguin has worked to bolster Parliament's ability to monitor and control the government. He pushed for a constitutional amendment—adopted with Chirac's blessing on July 31, 1995—that substantially increases the number of days per year Parliament meets in regular session; Parliament now meets not in two sessions of three months each, but rather, in a single nine-month session. While celebrating the achievement of this "coup," Séguin prepared legislation (again with Chirac's support) to create two new parliamentary offices that would reinforce the ability of the Assembly and the Senate to prepare and scrutinize legislation: an *office parlementaire d'amélioration de la legislation* (Parliamentary

Office for the Improvement of Legislation), that would act to simplify legislation and check the tendency towards "legislative inflation;" and an *office d'évaluation des politiques publiques* (a Parliamentary Budget Office), to give parliament independent budgetary expertise similar to the Congressional Budget Office in the United States. These new institutions, in conjunction with the extended single session, clearly give the parliamentary majority more potential as a counterweight to the executive than it has possessed in the past.[81]

While Chirac has publicly supported these moves, he is well aware that Séguin's role as a "vigilant censor" of the government is in part motivated by his rivalry with both the president and prime minister, Alain Juppé. Séguin, disappointed not to be appointed premier himself, refused to accept any lesser post within the government and thus returned to his position at the head of the National Assembly with a mission as a critical parliamentary leader that must be cause for some concern at the Elysée. The enhanced position of Séguin was also cause for some concern among leaders of the Senate and the opposition. Passage of the legislation to create the two new parliamentary offices was delayed for more than a year because the Senate (and the opposition) leaders argued that the new offices would strengthen, above all, the power of the president of the National Assembly and the majority.[82]

It has yet to be determined, of course, to what extent the actions led by Séguin will actually serve to "modify the institutional equilibrium" in favor of Parliament in the long run.[83] As long as party discipline remains strong and the executive retains the constitutional weapons discussed above, especially those of Articles 49.3 and 44.3, the French Parliament will remain far less of an impediment to government action than the American Congress. Nevertheless, the support of the majority must now be negotiated with care and compromise.[84]

It can be expected that the other major component of the 1995 constitutional amendment—an extension of the range of issues that may be submitted to a referendum so as to include "reforms related to the economic and social policy of the nation"—will enhance to some degree the position of the president and his government vis-à-vis Parliament.[85] Given the political risks involved with calling referenda, few observers expect that Chirac or future presidents will use this new power with great frequency. However, as Georges Vedel and others have noted, the simple possession of such power should be useful as a "weapon of deterrence" against parliamentary obstruction regarding issues on which the president enjoys broad public support.[86]

Third, the electorate that has to be faced by 1998 must be more of a concern for Chirac than it was for the previous Gaullist presidents, de Gaulle and Pompidou. In their era the Right benefited from the fact that voting for the Left entailed the twin fears of a leap into the unknown and a possibility of participation in the government by a strong Communist Party.[87] The situation now, of course, is totally different. The Socialist Party has held power for two-thirds of the past 15 years and is now viewed as a pragmatic party of government; despite its massive legislative losses in 1993, the Jospin phenomenon of 1995 showed that the Socialist Party is capable of a rapid comeback. In fact, since September the Socialists have benefited from a string of by-election victories, both for departmental assemblies and for the National Assembly as well as significant gains in the (indirect) Senate elections.[88] Meanwhile, the Communist Party is now not only much weaker than in the past, but also far less of a cause for concern than in the post–Cold War era.

Two additional factors make the prospects for a continuation of hyperpresidentialism doubtful after the next legislative elections. First, French voters have manifested a remarkable propensity to oust incumbent leaders and legislative majorities since 1981. If Chirac is to retain a majority in 1998, he must become the first leader in two decades to break the cycle of electoral rejection. However, a year after Chirac's election, the prospect of cohabitation in 1998 was uncomfortably realistic to his RPR nemesis, Charles Pasqua: "What would be the value [to the Gaullists] to have reconquered the leadership of the state, only to return it so soon to those who led the state to where we found it three years ago?"[89] No doubt he had been glancing at the recent polls, which revealed that Socialist support was increasing, while support for Right was declining quickly.[90]

Second, the French electorate no longer suffers from the same fear of cohabitation that it possessed years ago. While cohabitation was once viewed as likely to plunge the nation into a severe constitutional crisis, it has now been tried twice with minimal turmoil. Moreover, much to the consternation of some political leaders, polls show that many French citizens have actually viewed the two cohabitation periods as positive experiments in political consensus building.[91] After the first 21 months of cohabitation II, for example, 70 percent of those polled expressed satisfaction with the way the governing process had worked and most (47 percent versus 38 percent) thought it was more positive than negative for France.[92]

In short, therefore, the renaissance of hyperpresidentialism under Chirac may well prove to be brief. By 1998 at the latest, President Chirac could find himself functioning within either the premier-presidential model or the tempered presidential model as outlined above. Even if he avoids that fate, Chirac's rendition of hyperpresidentialism is destined to entail a lesser degree of presidential control over the policymaking process than has been known in the past. Aside from the constraining factors discussed above, two institutional developments to be examined later in this volume will limit his freedom to maneuver.

As David Cameron makes clear in chapter 13, the enhancement of European integration will restrict Chirac's policy options on certain issues in a fashion that de Gaulle would have found unthinkable (and unacceptable!). In addition, as Alec Stone explains in the next chapter, the evolution of the Constitutional Council since the early 1980s has made it a counterpower far more formidable than it was early in the Fifth Republic. Although the expansion of the referendum power has provided the president with a means for attempting to circumvent the Council in extraordinary cases (since bills approved by referendum may not, unlike those approved by parliament, be appealed to the judicial body), *les sages* retain the capacity to obstruct a wide variety of governmental initiatives.[93]

Notes to Chapter 2

1. *The Economist*, July 1, 1995; see also *Libération*, July 15-16, 1995.

2. See *L'Election présidentielle: Jacques Chirac, le défit du changement* (Paris: Dossiers et Documents du Monde, 1995): 32; *The Economist*, April 22, 1995.

3. For example, see *Le Monde*, June 15, 1995, January 31, February 3, and February 24, 1996.

4. See *The Economist*, July 1, 1995.

5. William G. Andrews, *Presidential Government in Gaullist France* (Albany: SUNY Press, 1982): 3, 32, 22.

6. For a detailed discussion of the Fifth Republic's constitutional weapons, see John T.S. Keeler, "Executive Power and Policymaking Patterns in France: Gauging the Impact of Fifth Republic Institutions," *West European Politics* 16 (October 1993).

7. Henry Ehrmann and Martin A. Schain, *Politics in France*, 5th ed. (New York: HarperCollins, 1992): 425.

8. See Vincent Wright, *The Government and Politics of France*, 3d ed. (New York: Holmes and Meier, 1989): 15-16.
9. On Article 5, see André Hauriou as cited in Marie-Anne Cohendet, *La Cohabitation: Leçons d'une expérience* (Paris: Presses Universitaires de France, 1993): 54.
10. Didier Maus, *Les grands textes de la pratique institutionnelle de la Ve République* (Paris: La Documentation Française, 1992): 28.
11. Cited in Ehrmann and Schain, 290.
12. Andrews, 18.
13. Ibid.
14. Ibid, p. 21.
15. Ibid., 38; see also Olivier Duhamel, *La Gauche et la Ve République* (Paris: Presses Universitaires de France, 1980): 154.
16. Andrews, 25.
17. Ibid., 26.
18. Philip M. Williams and Martin Harrison, *Politics and Society in de Gaulle's Republic* (New York: Anchor Books, 1980): 30.
19. Roland Sadoun, "De Gaulle et les sondages," in *De Gaulle en son siècle, vol. 1: Dans la mémoire des hommes et des peuples* (Paris: La Documentation française/Plon, 1991): 321.
20. Maus, 28.
21. Jérôme Jaffré, "L'enquête d'opinion de la SOFRES," in *De Gaulle en son siècle, vol. 1: Dans la mémoire des hommes et des peuples* (Paris: La Documentation française/Plon, 1991): 327.
22. Maurice Duverger, *La Ve République* (Paris: Presses Universitaires de France, 1963): 18.
23. For excellent examples drawn from the case of health care, see Ellen M. Immergut, *Health Politics: Interests and Institutions in Western Europe* (New York: Cambridge University Press, 1992), chapter 3.
24. Andrews, 128-30.
25. See Jean-Louis Quermonne, *Le gouvernement de la France sous la Ve République*, 2nd ed., (Paris: Dalloz, 1983), p. 182. The notion of this "reserved domain" seemed implicit in many of de Gaulle's statements and actions, and it is indisputable that the concept has continued to shape perceptions of presidential power. However, de Gaulle himself clearly felt that the primacy of the presidency legitimately extended to domestic affairs as well. See Ezra Suleiman,

"Presidential Government in France," in Richard Rose and Ezra Suleiman, eds., *Presidents and Prime Ministers* (Washington: AEI, 1980): 113.

26. François Mitterrand, *Le Coup d'Etat permanent* (Paris: Juillard, 1984): 98.
27. Duhamel, *La Gauche*, 172-74.
28. Williams and Harrison, 37; Duverger, *La Ve République*, 16.
29. See Duverger, *La Ve République*, 57-58; Andrews, 135-38.
30. Williams and Harrison, 42.
31. Lacouture, 569.
32. Duhamel, *La Gauche*, 178.
33. Charles de Gaulle, *Memoirs of Hope* (New York: Simon and Schuster, 1971): 314-15. De Gaulle's conception of his special relationship with the regime's institutions is developed in detail in his memoirs. One chapter begins with the assertion: "The new institutions were in place. From the summit of the State, how was I to shape them? To a large extent it was incumbent upon me to do so. For the reasons which had led me to this position, and the conditions in which I exercised it, did not derive from written texts . . . If I had now assumed the country's highest office, it was because . . . I had come to be accepted as its final refuge. This was a fact which, alongside the literal provisions of the Constitution, had inevitably to be taken into account. Whatever interpretation might be given to such and such an Article, it was in any case to de Gaulle that Frenchmen turned. It was from him that they expected the solution of their problems" (pp. 270-71).
34. See Alec Stone, *The Birth of Judicial Politics in France: The Constitutional Council in Comparative Perspective* (New York: Oxford University Press, 1992): 60-66. See also Louis Favoreu and Loic Philip, eds., *Les Grandes décisions du conseil constitutionnel*, 4th ed. (Paris: Sirey, 1986): 172-83.
35. See Stanley Hoffmann, "Paradoxes of the French Political Community," in Hoffmann et al., *In Search of France* (New York: Harper, 1963): 96-97; Duhamel, *La Gauche*, part II.
36. See Jaroslaw Kurski, *Lech Walesa: Democrat or Dictator* (Boulder: Westview, 1993): 100.
37. De Gaulle was fully aware that opinion polls had long shown direct election of the president to be popular with the public, however much it was opposed by members of Parliament. It should be also noted that support for the institution has increased dramatically since it was first put into effect. As of 1990, 88 percent of the public approved it, including even 64 percent of Communist voters. See Jaffré, 329.

38. Williams and Harrison, 48; Frank L. Wilson, *French Political Parties under the Fifth Republic* (New York: Praeger, 1982): 171.

39. Wilson, 170-71.

40. Françoise Dreyfus, "The Control of Governments," in Peter A. Hall, Jack Hayward and Howard Machin, eds., *Developments in French Politics* (New York: St. Martin's, 1990): 138.

41. See Wilson, 174.

42. Maurice Duverger, "A New Political System Model: Semi-Presidential Government," in Arend Lijphart, ed., *Parliamentary Versus Presidential Government* (Oxford: Oxford University Press, 1992): 145-47; Matthew S. Shugart and John M. Carey, *Presidents and Assemblies* (New York: Cambridge University Press, 1992): 155; the Schugart and Carey ratings, based on an analysis of strictly formal powers, give the French president a total power score of only 4, compared to 11 for the American president and 8 for the Finish president.

43. See Olivier Duhamel, *Le Pouvoir politique en France* (Paris: Presses Universitaires de France, 1991): 71.

44. Duverger, "A New Political System Model," 145.

45. See Duhamel, *La Gauche*, part II; see also R.W. Johnson, *The Long March of the French Left* (New York: St. Martin's Press, 1981).

46. See the chapters by Jean Baudouin (on the Communists) and Serge Sur (on the centrists) in Olivier Duhamel and Jean-Luc Parodi, eds., *La Constitution de la Cinquième République* (Paris: Presses de la Fondation Nationale des Sciences Politiques, 1985).

47. On the Austrian case, see Shugart and Carey, 72.

48. Suleiman, 117.

49. Suleiman, 110.

50. For Mitterrand's ideas on the presidency, see *Le Monde*, Dec. 11, 1981.

51. See Olivier Duhamel, "The Fifth Republic under François Mitterrand," in George Ross, Stanley Hoffmann and Sylvia Malzacher, eds., *The Mitterrand Experiment* (New York: Oxford University Press, 1987). Mitterrand's government did replace the original Gaullist electoral system for the National Assembly with a variant of proportional representation in 1985, but that system was used only once (in 1986) before the old system was reinstituted by Chirac's cohabitation government.

52. See John T. S. Keeler and Alec Stone, "Judicial-Political Confrontation in Mitterrand's France," in Ross et al., *The Mitterrand Experiment* (New York: Oxford University Press, 1987).

53. In a recent paper, Olivier Duhamel rates (based on a scheme that breaks presidential "resources" into seven categories) the power of Mitterrand in this period as 17 compared to de Gaulle's 20 and Giscard's 9. See "Président, Premier ministre, Gouvernement, les différent cas de figure" (paper presented to the conference on "Presidential France 1962-1992," NYU Institute of French Studies, New York, December 4-5, 1992): 12.
54. Ehrmann and Schain, 242-43; Duhamel, *Le Pouvoir,* 41.
55. Maurice Duverger, *Bréviaire de la cohabitation* (Paris: Presses Universitaires de France, 1986): 36-38.
56. Françoise Giroud, *La Comédie du pouvoir* (Paris: Fayard, 1977): 234-35.
57. Duhamel, *Le Pouvoir,* 41.
58. See the citation of Claude Emeri in Duhamel, *Le Pouvoir,* 42.
59. According to the constitution's original provisions, only the president of the republic, the prime minister, or the president of either assembly could send bills on appeal to the Council.
60. See Stone, *The Birth of Judicial Politics*; Louis Favoreu, *La Politique saisie par le droit: alternances, cohabitation et conseil constitutionnel* (Paris: Economica, 1988); Léo Hamon, *Les Juges de la loi, Naissance et rôle d'un contre-pouvoir: le Conseil Constitutionnel* (Paris: Fayard, 1987).
61. See Keeler, "Executive Power."
62. Using the rating system alluded to in endnote 52, Duhamel scores the power of "Mitterrand III" as 11 versus 9 for Giscard.
63. See Duhamel, *Le Pouvoir,* 166-67.
64. Ehrmann and Schain, 243.
65. The term premier-presidentialism is taken from Shugart and Carey, 23.
66. Cited in Wright, 71.
67. See Wright, 70-74.
68. Wright, 70.
69. See Jean Charlot, *La Politique en France* (Paris: Editions de Fallois, 1994): 191-97; Jean-Louis Bourlanges, "Le Maitre du pouvoir et le roi de la jungle," in Olivier Duhamel and Jérôme Jaffré, eds., *L'Etat de l'opinion 1995* (Paris: Seuil, 1995); Elisabeth Dupoirier and Gérard Grunberg, "La Déchirure sociale," *Pouvoirs* 73 (April 1995): 143-57.
70. See Jean-Claude Zarka, "Le Domaine réservé à l'épreuve de la seconde cohabitation," *Revue Politique et Parlementaire* (March-April 1994); for an analysis of the institution of the *conseil restreint,* see Ehrmann and Schain, 307.

71. By the fall of 1994, as Balladur's popularity ratings remained high and he began to appear an almost certain bet to win the presidency in 1995, Chirac's frustrated ambitions had become the target of jokes and satirical publications. For the most sardonic example of this genre, see Les Guignols de L'Info, *L'Agenda secret de Jacques Chirac* (Paris: Canal + Editions, 1994). In this book, presented as Chirac's pocket calendar for 1993, a desperate Chirac scribbles next to defaced pictures of Balladur: "Il m'a piqué mon boulot de dans 2 ans . . ." (He stole my work of two years from now . . .).

72. *L'Express,* August 3, 1995, p. 23.

73. *Le Monde,* August 27-28, 1995.

74. *Le Monde,* November 8, 1995.

75. See *Le Monde,* July 13, 1995.

76. Ibid.

77. See *Le Monde,* July 7, 13, 14, and 19, 1995; *Libération,* July 12 and 19, 1995.

78. *Le Monde,* July 25, 1995; see also *L'Express,* August 3, 1995, p. 23.

79. See *Le Monde,* January 23, 1996,

80. See Charlot, 189-190.

81. *Le Monde,* May 21-22, 1995; see also *Le Figaro,* May 11, 1995 and *Le Monde,* May 14-15, 1995.

82. See *Le Figaro,* May 11, 1995; *Le Monde,* June 22, 1995.

83. See *Le Monde,* May 21-22 and June 22, 1995.

84. *Le Monde,* April 16, 1996.

85. Some members of the opposition denounced the extension of referendum power as a dangerous "presidentialization of the regime." Socialist Bernard Derosier, for example, branded it "Napoleon III plus television"; see *Le Monde,* July 12, 1995.

86. See *Le Monde,* July 6, 1995.

87. See J. R. Frears and Jean-Luc Parodi, *War Will Not Take Place* (New York: Holmes and Meier, 1979).

88. See *Le Monde* September 26, 1995 and April 10, 1996 for a summary of the Senate and the by-election results.

89. *Le Monde,* April 6, 1996.

90. Summarized in *Le Monde,* April 10, 1996.

91. See Charlot, 196-197.

92. Dupoirier and Grunberg, 146.
93. As Eric Dupin reported in *Libération* on July, 13 1995, the goal of avoiding constitutional control of legislation was "very consciously pursued by certain leaders of the present majority" in approving the July amendment. In fact, he noted, such leaders have openly acknowledged that the proposal to hold a referendum on education—which Chirac has promised—is "motivated precisely by the desire to be liberated from constitutional constraints." It should be noted, however, that some members of the majority, especially within the UDF, have already expressed their opposition to the plan for such a referendum; see *Le Monde,* August 2, 1995.

Chapter 3

Constitutional Politics and Malaise in France

Alec Stone

The establishment of the Fifth Republic initiated a constitutional revolution: a virtually immediate, remarkably durable transformation of the core relationships among policymaking structures. Assessments of French policymaking since 1958 have rightly focused on the executive-legislative dyad, and the enormous extent to which the constitution redistributed capacity from Parliament to the president and prime minister. Analysis of lawmaking patterns, over a span of more than three decades, reveals an extraordinary continuity.[1] The Gaullist model, of a dominant, two-headed executive and a relatively docile (or at least controllable) Parliament, is not only intact in 1995, it is without visible rival.

One Gaullist institution, however, is virtually unrecognizable from the standpoint of the first decade of the Fifth Republic. The Constitutional Council was established to guarantee executive predominance, just one of the many useful weapons deployable by the government in conflicts with Parliament. By the 1980s the Council had emerged as a powerful policymaking actor in its own right, operating primarily to constrain rather than to facilitate the government's work.[2] The Council is the only clearly "post-Gaullist" institution on the constitutional landscape, successfully reinventing itself, and also the greater political environment of which it is part.

The purpose of this chapter is to describe and evaluate this development from a policymaking perspective.[3] Part I reviews the structural determinants of *constitutional politics*, by which I mean the complex and multidimensional interaction between the government, Parliament, and the Council in the making of public policy and the building of constitutional law. Part II provides a conceptual framework for observing and evaluating the impact of constitutional review on both legislating and judging. Part III employs this framework, focusing on the 1981-93 period. Part IV assesses arguments about an alleged political malaise from the perspective of constitutional politics.

I. The Institutional Setting of Constitutional Politics

Majority rule (the ideology of the "general will") and its twin corollaries, statutory sovereignty and the prohibition of judicial review, have been precepts of the French legal order for more than two centuries. This order was not formally overthrown by the 1958 constitution; rather the constitution transferred effective power over the production of statutes to the executive, and added an extra stage, that of constitutional review by the Council, to the legislative process. Today, as in 1790, a statute once promulgated remains supreme, immune to judicial challenge.[4] If the ideology of statutory sovereignty remains *formally* intact, it has been all but obliterated as a matter of day-to-day legislative politics. A rival ideology has emerged, that of constitutionalism. For the purposes of this chapter, constitutionalism is the notion that (1) constitutional norms occupy the highest position within a hierarchy of enforceable norms, and that (2) constitutional norms must take precedence in any conflict with lower order norms, including legislative ones. In France, the higher law status of constitutional norms is defended or enforced by the Constitutional Council.

Viewed comparatively, the Constitutional Council can be assimilated into a family of institutions that are today called *constitutional courts*. Like all European constitutional courts, the Council is a specialized state organ whose central purpose is to render authoritative interpretations of the constitution. The Council, however, is unlike other European constitutional courts in a number of respects. Most important, the Council's *constitutional review authority*—its power to declare legislation unconstitutional and therefore void—is exclusively *a priori* and abstract. *A priori* constitutional review is the constitutional control of legislation that has been adopted by the legislature but has not yet been promulgated. It is *abstract* in that the Council is asked to take a position on the constitutionality of a pending statute in the absence of a case or controversy. It does this by comparing the legislative text with the constitution. French constitutional review, therefore, is a purely exegetical exercise: if a legislative text is read by the Council to be in conflict with the constitution, it is annulled. Abstract review contrasts sharply with the more familiar and widely spread *concrete* review, which is triggered by litigation (in American parlance, a judicial "case or controversy"). French review proceedings are initiated exclusively by politicians, who refer legislation adopted by parliament but not yet promulgated directly to the constitutional court for a ruling. American courts, including the United States Supreme Court, may only engage in concrete review (in accord with the prohibition against "advisory opinions"). The constitutional courts of Austria, Germany, Portugal, and Spain exercise both concrete and abstract (but not *a priori*) review, but abstract review activities constitute only a tiny fraction of each court's caseload.[5]

The magnitude of the role that politicians play in the French system of review is also exceptional. Politicians appoint the nine-member Council to nine-year terms. The president of the Republic, the president of the National Assembly, and the president of the Senate each names one member every three years. They do so freely—ratification procedures or other means of blocking appointments do not exist. There are no formal prerequisites for membership, other than minimum age (18 years) and French citizenship. Prior legal training, mandatory for membership on every other European constitutional court, is not a requirement for Council membership. In practice, the single most important criterion for selection has been partisan affiliation. Since the Council's creation in 1958, former government ministers and parliamentarians have *always* constituted a majority of its members. Although only four professional judges have ever been appointed, certain eminent law professors have had enormous influence on the Council's jurisprudential development (François Luchaire in the 1970s, Georges Vedel in the 1980s, and, in this decade, Jacques Robert).

This mode of recruitment all but guarantees that the Council's composition will eventually reflect the political majority in place at any given time. The Council's Gaullist character was virtually an axiom until the mid-1980s. The Left appointed its first member in 1983, increased its share of seats to four in 1986, and, having won the elections in 1988, was able to achieve its first majority of appointments in 1989. Although the recruitment process is a highly partisan one, the impact of the Council's composition on it's internal decisionmaking dynamics is virtually impossible to study. Official secrecy shrouds the body's work: the Council deliberates and votes in privacy, and dissenting and concurring opinions are not allowed.

The power to initiate the constitutional review of legislation is also monopolized by national politicians. Until 1974, only four officials—the president of the Republic, the prime minister, the president of the Assembly, and the president of the Senate—could petition the Council for a ruling. In 1974, a constitutional amendment extended this power to any sixty deputies or sixty senators. The act of referral automatically suspends a law's promulgation pending a ruling by the Council as to its constitutionality. No authority may block such referrals, and the Council is obliged to render a judgment, within a maximum of thirty days. The Council must decide (there is no French "political question" doctrine); and its decisions are final (no appeal is possible).

Constitutional Rights and Jurisprudential Activism

As is well known, the Council's original function was to guarantee executive control over Parliament, a control that was to be virtually absolute. In its first decade, the Council performed this function impeccably, exhibiting few signs of independence. Concerns about "judicial independence" would have been misplaced anyway. In the 1960s, no one—not politicians, not law professors, not judges—thought of the Council as a court (or even a specialized "court-like" body). The institution was a "council," an obedient servant of General de Gaulle, his prime ministers, and the new constitutional order. Indeed, the framers were wary of conferring any judicial status to the institution. They summarily rejected proposals to establish the Council as a kind of constitutional court of appeal, like those found in Austria, Germany, or Italy. Equally important, the framers refused to grant the Council jurisdiction over a charter of rights (which was the fundamental reason constitutional courts elsewhere in Europe were established). In fact, the new constitution did not contain a general catalog of rights binding on legislators. Although the preamble to the 1958 Constitution declares the "solemn attachment" of the French people to the preamble of the 1946 Constitution, the framers (in 1958 and 1946) insisted that neither preamble possessed *constitutional status* (i.e., capable of being enforced as a supralegislative body of norms). These limitations were necessary, Gaullists argued, in order to maintain statutory sovereignty and to avoid a "government of judges" situation.[6]

In a famous 1971 decision, the Council "incorporated" the preamble into the Constitution by asserting jurisdiction over it.[7] In doing so, the Council elevated certain texts proclaimed or alluded to in the 1946 Preamble to constitutional (supralegislative) status. As developed in the 1970s, the following texts now constitute the French bill of rights, and, when combined with the constitutional text that follows the Preamble, make up the Council's norms of reference:

- the 1789 Declaration of the Rights of Man (simply mentioned in the 1946 preamble), which enumerates rights of due process, equal treatment under the law, free speech, conscience, and property ownership;
- the "Fundamental Principles Recognized by the Laws of the Republic" (FPRLR), mentioned but not enumerated in the 1946 preamble; and,
- "the political, economic and social principles particularly necessary to our times" (the 1946 principles), which constitute the vast bulk of the Preamble, proclaiming (among many others) the following: equality of the sexes; the rights to work, to join a union, to strike, and to obtain social security; and the responsibility of the state to guarantee a secular school system, and to nationalize all industries that have taken on the character of a monopoly or public service.

The 1946 Preamble thus encompasses radically opposed notions of individual and collective rights. The 1789 Declaration, particularly its pronouncement that property rights were "sacred," was dear to the political Right and an anathema to the Left. The 1946 principles constituted the then majority's (the Left) version of a bill of rights; and the vague phrase, the FPRLR, was actually a bid by center and center-right Catholics to protect the private school system. What is certain is that, had the framers foreseen the Preamble's incorporation by the Council, only the 1946 principles would have stood a chance of inclusion. In fact, denounced as expressing an "outmoded conception" of property rights, the direct incorporation of the 1789 text into the 1946 Constitution was rejected overwhelmingly by the Constituent Assembly.[8]

The Council's 1971 decision and its subsequent jurisprudence of the Preamble radically expanded the Council's own capacity for discretionary lawmaking. From a legislator's perspective, this jurisprudence introduced an extraordinarily high degree of uncertainty into the policymaking process. This was so because the exact content and nature of the obligations contained in the Preamble were either unknown or in dispute. Nevertheless, nearly all of the Council's most important decisions since 1971 have been based on the Preamble, and the Council's authority to develop the text has been at the heart of controversies about the Council's expanding influence over legislation since the mid-1980s.

II. The Judicialization Phenomenon

The development of constitutional review is essentially a story of *judicialization*, the process by which the norms of legal discourse gradually penetrate and are absorbed by policymakers and the Council itself. Judicialization is an ongoing, dynamic, transformative process, the outcome of which is now more or less certain.

The Judicialization of Policymaking

Policy processes can be described as *judicialized* to the extent that constitutional jurisprudence, the threat of future constitutional censure, and the pedagogical authority of past jurisprudence alter legislative outcomes.[9] The definition is sensitive both to direct impact (a ruling of unconstitutionality is a veto) and to indirect impact (policy outcomes may be altered by anticipatory reactions, the government and its majority anticipating the future attitude of the Council on a given bill). In part III the judicialization phenomenon will be illustrated with a wide range of examples. Here I wish only to make the following four general points.

First, judicialization can be empirically verified and evaluated. While a court's direct impact is obvious, indirect influence can be measured by tracing legislation through the policy process to determine how and why it is altered as a result of constitutional arguments. In France, this effect is called *autolimitation:* the exercise of self-restraint on the part of the majority in anticipation of an eventual negative decision of the constitutional court.

Second, judicialization is neither permanent nor uniform. Disaggregating constitutional court impact by the policy sector reveals that each area manifests its own dynamic of constitutional possibility and constraint, conforming to the development of constitutional control. Legislative processes are more or less judicialized as a function of this variation. In France, nationalizations and privatizations, media policy, penal law, electoral law, and immigration are examples of highly constrained policy areas.

Third, constitutional courts and political oppositions are connected to one another by a kind of jurisprudential transmission belt. Oppositions judicialize legislative processes in order to win what they would otherwise lose in "normal" (majority rules) political processes. Their referrals provide the Council with opportunities to construct constitutional law, to extend jurisprudential techniques of control, and (the same thing) to make policy. As constitutional jurisprudence grows more dense and technical, so do grounds for judicial debate and the potential for higher levels of judicialization.

Fourth, the Council has developed creative techniques of control, in part to cushion the impact of negative decisions. These techniques often function to strengthen Council dominance over policy outcomes. Following the practice of the German and Italian courts, the Council has asserted the power to attach *strict guidelines of interpretation* (SGIs, which are called *réserves d'interprétation* in France) to otherwise constitutional legislation. This occurs when the Council rules that a bill is constitutional—and therefore capable of being promulgated—only if it is interpreted as the Council has in its decision. The pronouncement of SGIs often results in unambiguous lawmaking, or as written amendments that attach to a law. The Council may also decide not only to declare a law unconstitutional, but also to tell legislators how they ought to have written the law in the first place. In such cases, a *corrective revision process*—the reelaboration of a censured text in conformity with constitutional jurisprudence in order to secure promulgation—is often generated.

The Council as a Third Legislative Chamber

In most cases, legislative bills are introduced by the government into the National Assembly; after amendment and adoption the bill moves on to the senate. If it is an important bill, it goes to a third place, the Constitutional Council. Constitutional jurisprudence is the lasting, written record of a final "reading" by a third body, the Council, which is required to pass on legislation before promulgation. Put in this way, students of French policymaking have good reason to conceptualize the Council as a specialized third (legislative) chamber, specialized because the Council's work is meaningfully restricted to decisions about constitutionality.

The third chamber thesis has been criticized on two main grounds: that the Council (1) is not self-activating and (2) does not possess the same discretionary powers as the National Assembly and the Senate.[10] These criticisms merit response. First, if all third chambers must be self-activating, then the Council is not a third chamber. However, if such a definition were to be accepted, we might not be able to include the British House of Commons or the French National Assembly in a list of legislative chambers. Neither is self-activating. Both are examples of what Polsby calls "arena legislatures," to be contrasted with "transformative legislatures": the former does not legislate, but instead ratifies policy choices made by the executive, while the latter (the US Congress) legislates free from formal outside control.[11] In France, the executive dictates the legislative agenda; the Assembly cannot pass laws or adopt amendments over the government's objection; and the Senate's veto can be overturned by a majority vote of the Assembly. In fact, the Council's policy preferences are the only preferences the government cannot ignore, reverse or quash.

Second, the Council is clearly not the National Assembly. It is a constitutional court that exercises *a priori* review authority over legislation. It does, however, exercise discretionary powers that are legislative in nature—that is, the legal norms generated by the Council's jurisprudence are general and prospective in precisely the same way that legislation is. When ruling for the first time on a given legislative issue area or where accumulated precedence is thin, the Council enjoys enormous discretion. Further, the notion that Parliament has greater "liberty of choice" than does the Council does not stand up to scrutiny. It is an empirical fact, for example, that the Council's impact on many laws far outweighs that of the Assembly or Senate; that is, the Council's amendments have been more extensive and significant than were Parliament's.

French politicians, too, think of the Council as a third chamber and employ variations on the metaphor constantly. In 1986 one parliamentary supporter of constitutional review described the Council's evolution as a gradual transformation "into a kind of second parliament adding, on its own, to the content of legislation and dictating the conduct of the first parliament."[12] The same year, neo-Gaullist Jacques Toubon called the Council "a new kind of legislator" and a "parliament of judges."[13]

The Judicialization of the Council

The Council is clearly not a judicial body in the way that the term *judicial* has traditionally been understood in legal theory. Judicial bodies are those that meet certain minimum criteria: they must (1) be composed of professional judges who are (2) primarily engaged in settling disputes brought by (3) real-life litigants who (4) argue a case before them according to (5) fixed, contradictory procedures. They resolve these disputes by applying existing law to the case at hand.[14] For most of this century, French legal science was extraordinarily hostile to any form of review that was not performed by the courts, that is, institutions that conformed to the above criteria. But by the end of the 1970s, consensus had been reached among French constitutional law specialists that the Council ought to be considered a "court-like" body because it possesses the power to determine the content and applicability of constitutional law.[15] It makes little difference, these specialists argue, what process yields the opportunity to make such determinations; the result is the same.

The Council certainly performs a powerful judicial role within the legislative process once this process has been extended to include a constitutional review stage. Like all constitutional or supreme courts, the Council makes final decisions with respect to the constitutionality of legislation, and these decisions are expressed in the form of and constitute a jurisprudence. Further, the Council's output has been *judicialized*, if what we mean by this is that the Council's jurisprudence has gradually become more dense, technical, and attendant to the norms of legal discourse. Further, the Council decision-making processes have come to resemble, over time, those of other constitutional courts. In a typical case, the Council receives petitions from the opposition, often written by constitutional law professors employed on an ad hoc basis by the political parties. Since the late 1970s, petitions have gradually come to resemble full fledged legal briefs, containing lengthy analyses of the Council's past jurisprudence and its relevance to the law referred. The Council then invites submissions from the government and from the parliamentary majority (a practice unknown two decades ago), and these "briefs" are combined with the reports of the parliamentary commissions and the transcripts of parliamentary debates. Thus, the Council has itself encouraged and formalized practices that look something like adversarial proceedings. The dossier is completed by doctrinal commentaries published in law journals, and- if other European courts have decided similar constitutional issues—foreign jurisprudence is also included.[16]

Viewed comparatively, the Council lacks judicial, or court-like, status in at least one crucial way. Unlike all other constitutional courts, it is formally detached from the judiciary, that is, the Council does not hear cases on appeal from either the ordinary or administrative courts. Nevertheless, two recent developments deserve to be followed closely. First, the Council has begun to call upon the judicial system to implement its jurisprudence, stating in its decisions, for example, that judges are expected to treat SGI's as formal law. Although no systematic research on the judicial implementation of the Council's jurisprudence exists, substantial resistance to Council tutelage certainly remains. In August 1993, for example, the Professional Association of Judges issued a press release calling on judges and prosecutors to ignore all SGI's, which they characterized as nothing but "trivial gloss."[17] Second, the Council, the Council of State (France's highest administrative court), and the Court of Cassation (France highest appellate court in the non-administrative court system) are making efforts to harmonize their respective jurisprudence—in the interest of coherence, but not out of obligation.

Finally, while he was president of the Council (1986–1995), Robert Badinter (former socialist minister of justice in the Mauroy and Fabius governments, 1981-85) pressed to transform the Council into a full-fledged constitutional court. In 1988, Badinter proposed a constitutional revision to allow litigants in the ordinary or administrative courts to challenge the constitutionality of trial-relevant legislation on the grounds that the legislation had violated their constitutional rights. Once requested, the high appellate courts—the Council of State and the Court of Cassation—would decide if the challenge was a serious one and, if so, refer the matter to the Council. Had the revision been successful, the ideology of legislative sovereignty definitively would have been put to rest, since promulgated legislation could be attacked as unconstitutional in judicial proceedings. It would also have placed the Council in direct contact with litigation and with the citizenry, consolidating its position as *the* defender of constitutional rights in France. With the wholehearted support of President Mitterrand, the Rocard government formally submitted the constitutional amendment to Parliament in 1990, but it was killed by the rightist Senate (the Senate possesses an absolute veto only with respect to constitutional changes). A similar proposal was debated again in 1993, with the same result. The Right generally opposes the revision on the grounds that the Council already possesses too much power; it argues further that an expansion of the Council's jurisdiction over constitutional rights would only be acceptable after the imprecise 1946 Preamble was replaced by a new bill of rights. The revision has no chance of being adopted in the near future. After 1988, Badinter pleaded—also unsuccessfully—for changes in the Council's procedures to include public hearings, open debate between the petitioners and representatives of the government, as well as testimony from parliamentary commissions and other bodies. Failing such fundamental changes, the judicialization of the Council has probably reached its outer limits.

Legislators as Constitutional Judges

If in judicialized environments, the Council behaves as a legislator, this is also true: the degree to which any legislative process is judicialized is equivalent to the degree to which parliament behaves as a constitutional judge. As mentioned above, French doctrinal specialists today conceptualize the Council as a judicial body, a court whose principal function is to produce constitutional jurisprudence. This conclusion was reached by defining those institutions that have the power to determine "what the applicable law is" as "court-like" bodies. Because the Council determines what the constitutional law is, it should be treated the same as any other court, as least with respect to doctrinal activity. One scholar writes: "although the [Council's] intervention is one stage of legislature procedure, it constitutes a judicial stage."[18] From the vantage point of constitutional politics, this effort cannot separate what the Council does from what Parliament does. In a sentence, if the Council is to be considered a judicial body by virtue of the fact that it is at times charged with definitively determining the constitutionality of legislation, then so must Parliament. This is the logical result of applying the new definition of "things judicial" to an institution other than the Council.

In judicialized settings, legislators behave as constitutional judges. In fact, such behavior is formalized in parliamentary procedure as *motions d'irrecevabilité* (motions of unconstitutionality). Parliamentary motions of unconstitutionality require Parliament to debate and rule on a bill's constitutionality. Such a motion, written and presented in the form of a judicial decision, interrupts the chamber's work for a debate on the bill's constitutionality. During this debate, parliamentarians attack or defend a bill while citing constitutional texts, legal scholarship, and past Council jurisprudence. If the motion passes, the bill is declared unconstitutional, and it is killed. These motions are today a regular part of legislative life. Table 3.1 shows the extraordinary increase in their use. In the 1981-87 period, the National Assembly alone debated and voted on 94 such motions, a figure to be compared with 93 Council decisions. Logic, if little else, might well compel the conclusion that the National Assembly behaves more often as a constitutional court than does the Council.[19]

To sum up, in judicialized environments the Constitutional Council often behaves legislatively, as a specialized, third chamber of Parliament. For its part, the legislature behaves "judicially" when it debates and rules on motions of unconstitutionality and when it makes law with reference to the dictates of constitutional jurisprudence. In France, lawmaking and the building of constitutional law are often one and the same process.

TABLE 3.1
MOTIONS OF UNCONSTITUTIONALITY IN THE FRENCH NATIONAL ASSEMBLY *

	1967-73	1974-80	1981-87	1988-90
Motions Raised	2	35	20	35
Average per Year	.29	5	2.9	11.7
Motions Voted	1	35	93	23
Average per Year	.14	5	13.2	7.7

* Motions of Unconstitutionality are requests for debate and then a vote on the allegation that a bill is unconstitutional. If a majority supports such a motion, the bill in question is rejected. Motions are virtually always raised by the opposition, and the vote is virtually always along party lines.

Source: *Statistiques, Bulletin de l'Assemblee nationale, numero speciale* for each of the years cited. The statistical bulletin does not present figures for the pre–1967 period, probably because no such motions were raised.

III. Constitutional Politics

The Council's impact on legislative processes and outcomes is both direct and indirect. As a matter of direct impact, every decision constitutes the final stage of one legislative process and sometimes the opening stage of another. But the Council also exercises an indirect impact, essentially the "feedback" or pedagogical effects of its jurisprudential corpus. The Council's jurisprudence functions as a set of rules that (1) instruct legislators as to the correct routes to be taken or avoided, and (2) arm the opposition with constitutional arguments that can be used to cajole or force the government and majority to compromise initially-held policy choices. Many of the most important reforms of the past decade have been substantially altered as a result of such compromises.

Direct Effects: Annulments

Since at least 1981, the Council's intervention in the policymaking process can be described as systematic. Table 3.2 summarizes the Council's constitutional review activities. Immediately obvious is the explosion in activity after 1974: the 1971 decision incorporating a bill of rights and the 1974 amendment extending the power to petition the Council combined to expand the system's procedural and substantive capacity to generate review. After 1974, every budget and nearly every important or controversial piece of legislation has been the subject of referral, nearly all of which have been made by parliamentary minorities. French constitutional politics are, therefore, oppositional politics. The number of referrals grew dramatically after 1981, and has since stabilized. In the 1974-80 period, the Giscard d'Estaing

TABLE 3.2
THE CONSTITUTIONAL REVIEW ACTIVITY OF THE FRENCH COUNCIL: 1958-1993

	1959-73	1974-80	1981-87	1988-93
Referrals	9	66	136	97
- President	0	0	0	0
- Prime Minister	6	2	0	3
- President of the National Assembly	0	2	0	1
- President of the Senate	3	0	2	4
- 60 Deputies, or 60 Senators	-	62	134	89
Decisions*	9	46	92	69
- Censuring Text	7	14	49	38
- Favorable to Text	2	32	43	31

* Due to multiple referrals, the number of referrals since 1974 is larger than the number of decisions.

Source: Table compiled by author from the *Recueil des décisions du Conseil constitutionnel*, 1959-93.

presidency, 46 laws were referred to the Council, 6.6 laws per year; in the 1981-87 period, the first Mitterrand presidency, 92 laws were referred, or 13.1 laws per year. Since 1981, about one-third of all legislation has been referred,[20] an extraordinary ratio given the fact that most legislation passed is politically uncontroversial. The figures also indicate why referrals are so popular with the opposition, and why the government and its parliamentary majority must take seriously the opposition's threats to go to the Council. Referrals have a high rate of success: since 1981, far more than half (57 percent) of all referrals ended in some form of annulment by the Council.

Total annulments, decisions that invalidate an entire law, are rare but potentially explosive political events. The most spectacular ever rendered was the Council's 1982 annulment of the Socialists' nationalization law. The law, which sought to nationalize 5 industrial conglomerates, 36 banks and 2 financial investment companies, was the centerpiece of the Socialists' legislative program. The fate of the legislation proved to be tied to the resolution of the central controversy of French constitutional law, the nature of the relationship between three seemingly contradictory texts: Article 34 of the 1958 Constitution, the 1789 declaration, and the 1946 principles. Article 34 grants to Parliament the power to legislate in certain specified subject matters, a grant that includes the exclusive authority to nationalize and to privatize. In French legislative discourse, appeals to the sanctity of Article 34 are appeals to majority rule and parliamentary sovereignty. The 1789 declaration, however, lists constraints on lawmaking, of which Article 17 declares that "property being inviolable and sacred, no one can be deprived of it in the absence of public necessity, legally declared, obviously warranted, and without just and prior compensation." Finally, line 9 of the 1946 principles, intended to supersede the 1789 text, proclaims an obligation to nationalize in certain circumstances: "Every asset, every enterprise, whose exploitation is or has acquired the character of a national public service or of *de facto* monopoly, must become the property of the collective." In the absence of an enforceable Preamble, these contradictions, like so many others in French constitutional history, would be harmless. Article 34 would have simply triumphed without a fight.

The bill was adopted after nearly three months of tortuous constitutional debate in parliament. Although the right-controlled Senate rejected the bill as unconstitutional, the Assembly overrode the veto, and the bill was referred to the Council by both senators and deputies. The Council ruled that nationalizations were constitutional in principle, under Article 34, but that the authority to nationalize could only be exercised in accordance with "principles and rules possessed of constitutional status," that is, those rules dwelling in the Preamble.[21] However, it vetoed the bill on the grounds, among others, that the compensation formula did not meet the constitutional requirements laid down by Article 17 (1789). The Council then went on to state in precise detail how the Socialists should have handled payment in the first place, in effect elaborating a new compensation formula that would be ratified in a corrective revision process.

In terms of constitutional law, the decision established a general hierarchy of legal norms to be protected by constitutional jurisprudence. First, the Council declared that the "sacred and inviolable" nature of the right of property contained in Article 17 (1789) had not eroded and, in fact, was even supplemented by an unwritten principle that the Council now elevated to constitutional status: the *liberté d'entreprendre* (the right to engage in free enterprise). The Council then ruled that the 1946 principles (as well as the FPRLR) could only "complement" the 1789 declaration and could never contradict or limit the enjoyment of the rights that the latter text contains. Line nine (1946) was judged to have no legal effect on the question at hand. The Council thus imposed an interpretation of the preamble that was wholly antithetical to the founders' intent in 1946. The discordant terms of the preamble were fully harmonized: as a legal text, the 1789 declaration must, in all instances, take precedence over the

1946 text, which henceforth may serve only a complementary and never a contradictory jurisprudential function.

In the first months of the new Balladur government (spring-summer 1993), the Council rendered two total annulments. In the first, the government produced a bill to establish, as a matter of formal law, the independence of the Bank of France. The prime minister, a committed advocate of central bank independence in the service of law inflation rates, had sought to get a jump on the anti-Maastricht forces in Parliament (the most important of which belong to his own party) by introducing the bill during his "honeymoon" period. The Maastricht Treaty's provisions on European Monetary Union (EMU) require all member states of the European Union to guarantee central bank independence as one step toward the establishment of an independent European central bank (which would possess the power to manage a common European currency). In its 1992 decision on the constitutionality of the Treaty, the Council had ruled that only a constitutional amendment would permit France to participate in the EMU, since the constitution prohibited "transfers of competence" to a supranational body in those domains "essential to the exercise of sovereignty." A constitutional amendment providing for participation in EMU was then adopted, and the Treaty was ratified by France.[22] On August 15, 1993, the Council annulled Balladur's law on the grounds that since the Treaty had not yet entered into force, French constitutional provisions giving it effect were also not yet in force. The ruling left the law (which prohibits the Bank from "soliciting or accepting instructions from the Government") in contradiction with the 1958 Constitution, which states (Articles 20, 21) that the government alone defines and "conducts national policy." The Maastricht Treaty entered into force November 1, 1993, removing the constitutional (if not the political) obstacles to central bank independence. The bill was adopted during the fall term of 1994.

The Council also annulled a central plank of the Right's 1993 electoral platform, the decentralization of university governance. Although governments on both the Left and the Right have worked to restructure the education system since the mid-1980s, neither has been very successful. Reform efforts have been blocked by entrenched interests, union activity, and mass protests. In 1986, the Chirac government had sought to resolve some of the structural problems of French universities, such as overcrowding, underfunding, and overregulation, by devolving meaningful decision-making authority from the national ministry of education to the universities themselves. Within certain limits, universities would have had the authority to weaken the role of governing councils (made up of teachers, students, and administrators), limit enrollment, charge tuition, issue their own diplomas, and establish special programs adapted to regional conditions and constituencies. When parts of this plan were floated in the fall of 1986, huge demonstrations were organized and turned violent (one student was killed by police forces and parts of Saint Michel were set aflame and barricaded), and students and teachers went on strike. The law was opposed as representing a first step toward the "Americanization" of higher education, and a retreat from the a social entitlement according to which every citizen that passes the high school examination, the *baccalauréat*, is entitled to a free education, and university diplomas are both national and formally equal in status. Within days, the bill was simply suppressed by the government. In 1993, the new Balladur government hoped to avoid this fate by waiting until the school year had ended and by keeping its intentions purposefully vague. The bill that was finally introduced in the legislature simply authorized universities and the ministry to set certain rules of university governance, without being precise about the ultimate scope or nature of the reforms. After a detailed judicialized debate in Parliament, the Council agreed with the opposition: if the government and its parliamentary majority want to experiment with new governing structures, a law must "define precisely the nature and scope of these experiments."[23] Not wishing to focus national attention on the issue, the government immediately declared that university reform would have to wait at least two years—until after the presidential elections of 1995.[24]

The vast majority of annulments are "partial annulments." In such cases, the Council deletes from the bill—"amputates" in French parlance—those provisions judged to be unconstitutional, but then allows what remains to be promulgated. Partial annulments are more flexible techniques of constitutional control, since they allow the government and its majority to claim some measure of absolution. Nevertheless, some partial annulments constitute what are in effect vetoes, to the extent that the bill once amputated is no longer equipped to achieve its purposes. The period of the first Socialist government (1981-85) provides a number of such examples. In a November 1982 decision on the Socialists' municipal elections law, the Council struck down a provision that sought to require that all ballots contain at least 25 percent women candidates (expanding women's representation in parliament had been a campaign promise).[25] Although the Socialists had argued that they were seeking to give concrete meaning to the 1946 principle of "equality of the sexes," the Council, ruled that Article 6 (1789)—which guarantees French citizens (actually the language is "men") equality under the law—rendered such quotas unconstitutional. In January 1984 the Council annulled a bill that would have given all faculty equal rank for the purposes of university elections thereby establishing meaningful rights of participation for the majority of teachers who were not full professors.[26] The Council blocked the reform. It relied on Article 11 (1789), which consecrates the freedom of expression, and a newly minted FPRLR, which the Council labelled "professorial independence."

The Council's reworking of the 1984 press law is perhaps the most spectacular example of a partial annulment that thwarted the legislature's central intent.[27] The general purpose of the 1984 law was to establish an enforceable anti-trust policy to counter the rapid concentration of the newspaper industry that had begun in the early 1970s. The anti-trust rules then in place required a strict one person/one paper standard, but they had never been enforced. Indeed, the rules had been openly flouted by the right wing (RPR) deputy and press baron, Robert Hersant. In a series of shady deals made during the 1970s, Hersant was able to amass a press empire that included 19 dailies, 7 weekly newspapers, and 11 magazines. After the 1981 elections, Hersant mobilized his papers, especially his flagship daily, *Le Figaro*, to oppose the Socialist government and to promote Jacques Chirac's emerging neoliberal agenda. Thus, while the government could justly claim that its bill was designed to protect diversity in the industry and to restore respect for the rule of law, its partisan aspects were crudely evident.

The legislative battle was waged primarily in the language of constitutional law, but arguments were no less recognizable as pro- or anti-Hersant. For Socialists, the collective had a responsibility to restrict the rights to property when the exercise of such rights has the effect of infringing the enjoyment of non-economic rights. Freedom of the press was conceived as the right of readers to choose from a variety of papers representing the diversity of opinion within society. This right could no longer be guaranteed, claimed one minister, because "certain men" had engaged in "fraud," "cheating," and "embezzlement." The opposition argued that talk of rights only obscured the government's true motive, which was to take revenge on Hersant. For the Right, freedom of the press was conceived in terms of ownership, in terms of what Jacques Chirac called the "inseparable principles of the freedom of expression, the right of private enterprise and the rights to property."

In its final rendition, after judicialized debate in parliament had radically revised the bill, the law relied on a "fixed market ceiling" anti-trust mechanism—maximum percentages of total circulation for daily newspapers that any press group could fill. The law forbade any one group from controlling more than (1) a 15 percent share of the national (Parisian) market or 15 percent of the total regional circulation or (2) 15 percent of the national market and 10 percent of the regional market. A special regulatory body, the Commission on Financial Accountability and Press Pluralism (CFAPP), was created to police the rules and to force sell-offs if necessary. In practice, the law would have forced Hersant to choose to divest either his regional papers or *Le Figaro*.

In one of its most complex decisions ever,[28] the Council annulled parts of ten different Articles of the law. As a matter of constitutional interpretation, the Council agreed with the government that the protection of the rights of readers to choose was the issue. Relying on Article 11 of the 1789 declaration (consecrating freedom of expression), the Council deduced that "pluralism," though not mentioned in any constitutional text, was "an objective possessed of constitutional status." In terms of its concrete legislative impact, the decision destroyed the bill and saved the Hersant empire. Though the Council affirmed legislative competence to set fixed ceilings, it ruled that the CFAPP could not apply the ceilings to "existing situations" (i.e., press groups could not be forcibly dismantled) unless: (1) these situations had been illegally acquired or (2) pluralism was actually threatened. The Council then judged that neither condition had been met. In so ruling, it willfully ignored the lengthy parliamentary discussions of the illegality of Hersant's situation. It also unambiguously substituted its judgment for that of the government and of the majority, declaring that pluralism was "not currently weakened in a manner so serious that it would be necessary to apply [anti-trust provisions] to existing situations." The Council's decision is impossible to reconcile with the oft-repeated claim that the Council does not exercise discretionary powers comparable to those of Parliament.[29]

What was left of the bill was promulgated. But bereft of an effective enforcement mechanism, it could not fulfill its intended purpose. Not only did the law make it legally impossible for any other group to increase its market share to the level enjoyed by Hersant, but also the press baron was emboldened to acquire more regional dailies. By March 1986, when the Right returned to power, the Hersant press group controlled more than 38 percent of the national market and more than 26 percent of the regional one, including an absolute monopoly in the nation's largest multi-paper regional market, the Rhone Valley. In comparative terms, the percentage of the total French market controlled by Hersant is today greater than that controlled by any press group in any western democracy.

Partial annulments are rarely as dramatic as the Council's decision on press pluralism. Such annulments may accumulate within a given sector, adding up to what is in effect the virtual "constitutionalization" of rules governing legislating. The best example of this phenomenon is to be found in French penal law, a body of law composed of the penal codes and the codes governing judicial procedures. While technical, penal code reform is largely the story of ongoing legislative tug of war between the Left and Right that has been played out since 1980. While in power, the Socialists have generally worked to liberalize the codes—to reduce sentences, restrict police powers, and enhance the rights of the accused.[30] Right-wing governments have worked to reverse these changes, and, in some areas, to radically recast the codes in the opposite direction. The Council has been called upon to referee this struggle, rendering dozens of partial annulments of penal code reforms, while laying down precise rules—and SGIs—meant to govern how these codes must or must not be revised in the future. The thrust of this line of jurisprudence is liberal, and since 1986, aggressively so.[31] In consequence, reformers today must be prepared to maintain Council-mandated standards of due process, non-retroactivity, equality before the law, and so on.

The first year of the Balladur government was dominated by a controversial reform package known as the Pasqua laws (after Charles Pasqua, the minister responsible for drafting the legislation). The package included four laws whose purposes were, among other things: to extend the powers of police and prosecutors to verify citizenship, to demand identity cards, and to hold suspected criminals for lengthier periods for questioning without benefit of counsel; to provide the state with new means of fighting illegal immigration and rejecting political asylum requests; and to tighten the requirements for obtaining citizenship. The Pasqua laws are far too complex to analyze in their entirety here, as are the intense and fully judicialized parliamentary debates that preceded their adoption. To summarize, the Left challenged the constitutionality of all four laws, and in response the Council rendered four partial annulments and attached a number of SGI's to each. Most important:

- The Council proclaimed that the right to a counsel during the initial "detainment period" *(garde à vue)* is an "inalienable right," guaranteed by a FPRLR.[32] Further, detainment may not exceed prescribed limits (that is, four days for those suspected of the most heinous crimes). The government had sought to reverse a Socialist reform (the last law passed before the 1993 elections) providing for counsel to all detainees, by suppressing or delaying the right to counsel for those suspected of drug trafficking, terrorism, pimping, or extortion.
- The Council ruled that the principle of "individual liberty" (invented by the Council in the 1970s) precluded "general and arbitrary" identity checks, or personal searches by police.[33] Pasqua's law had sought to legalize sweeping, blanket checks and searches by police, whereas the law in place, a Socialist text of 1983 drafted by Badinter's ministry, permitted checks only when the authorities had concrete basis for suspecting that an individual had committed a crime or was preparing to commit one. The Council rewrote the law, in essence, reconstituting the 1983 status quo.
- In response to a comprehensive immigration reform law, the Council established a regime protecting the rights of foreigners residing in France. The Council's decision on the immigration bill was the longest (and one of the most complex) ever rendered. In it, the Council ruled that foreigners possess: the right to be treated equally before the law; certain rights of due process, defense, and appeal; and rights to marry, divorce, and reunite their families while remaining in France. In all, the Council annulled eight different provisions, most of which were designed to make it easier for the state to control immigration or to punish and expel illegal immigrants.
- The Council decided that foreigners requesting asylum in France possess the constitutional right to remain on French territory pending the processing of their claims, replete with the right to counsel and appeal.[34] The Council relied on line four of the 1946 Preamble, which provides for a right to asylum for those persecuted on the basis of race, religion, nationality, or political activity. Before this decision, line four had been assumed by constitutional scholars to be a dead letter (in legal terms, the provision was "non self-executing," or without "direct effect"). The decision, as discussed below,

would lead the government to quash the Council's ruling by revising the constitution.

Indirect Effects: Autolimitation and Corrective Revision

When the Council vetoes legislative provisions its impact on policy is direct and negative. But the Council also exercises *indirect and creative* impact, to the extent that governments and their parliamentary majorities decide to draft, amend, or suppress legislative initiatives in order to satisfy the requirements, real or divined, of constitutional jurisprudence. Restated, this impact constitutes the reception—or implementation—of constitutional jurisprudence by legislators.

Two factors are crucial. The first of these is the existence of a leading decision (or line of decisions) relevant to the legislation currently being debated by the government or Parliament. By "leading decision," I mean a constitutional ruling that either specifies, for the first time, those rules governing policymaking in a given legislative sector, or radically reinterprets existing rules. Nearly all leading decisions are annulments, precisely because the best moment for laying down general principles meant to constrain legislators is when legislators are actually being constrained. At the same time, the judges may construct quite detailed prescriptions meant to guide future policymaking in that sector, in order to avoid such "misunderstandings" in the future. It is nearly impossible, however, for lawmakers, within a given legislative process and *in advance* of a leading decision, to know the exact nature of the constitutional constraints which face them. A leading decision has the effect of at least partly codifying these constraints. A succession of decisions on legislative initiatives within the same policy sector can, as with the example of penal law, lead to the virtual constitutionalization of that sector. In this way, constitutional uncertainty is gradually replaced by constitutional obligation.

The second factor is the extent to which parliamentary oppositions exploit review processes for their own political ends, facilitating or reinforcing the control of constitutional courts over policy outcomes. Because governments can not avoid having their legislation referred to constitutional courts, and because decisions bind legislators without the possibility of appeal, abstract review referrals are powerful weapons of opposition. Put crudely, oppositions exploit abstract review procedures—which are virtually costless—in order to win from constitutional courts what they can never win in Parliament.

Put in a power-centric language of social science, indirect effects are anticipatory reactions structured by constitutional politics. Dahl's formula[35]—A has power over B to the extent that A can make B do what B would otherwise not do—can be altered to explicitly account for anticipatory reactions. Thus: A (the constitutional court) has power over B (the government and its parliamentary majority) to the extent that B anticipates A's interest and constrains its behavior accordingly. As constitutional review has developed, A's interest has been more and more precisely articulated, in a growing corpus of policy-relevant, constitutional rules binding legislators; and B's interest in conforming to A's interest has been, in turn, made more compelling. Oppositions facilitate anticipatory reactions by threatening referral to the court *during* parliamentary debate and, at times, even before that debate begins.

Anticipatory reactions can occur at each stage of the legislative process, beginning with the drafting of a bill by government ministers. Cabinet deliberations are formally secret in France, but we do know that the process by which bills are produced has been transformed as a result of the evolution of constitutional review. As the government's legal advisor, the Council of State reviews every bill for possible inconsistencies between the legislative text and constitutional jurisprudence.[36] While difficult to verify (given cabinet secrecy), constitutional considerations can lead governments to alter and even suppress entire bills. The Socialists radically altered the compensation formula contained in the 1982 nationalization bill, on the advice of the Council of State. The Council of State had suggested that the government could enhance its constitutional security by taking into account certain profits and assets, raising the cost of nationalizing by some 20 percent. As we have seen, the Constitutional Council would later invalidate the formula as insufficient. In 1986, the right-wing, Chirac government (1986-87) undertook a revision of the laws governing French nationality and citizenship and proposed to privatize the prison system. Both reforms were dropped, the government citing, among other things, worries about constitutionality. After the Socialists won the 1988 parliamentary elections, the first act of the new prime minister, Michel Rocard, was an order that all bills be harmonized with relevant constitutional jurisprudence.[37]

Once a bill is submitted to parliament, open constitutional debate begins. Some political parties employ full-time constitutional specialists, usually law professors, who advise them on how to attack or defend the constitutionality of a bill, and to draft referrals to the court. On the chamber floor any National Assembly deputy or Senator can raise a procedural "motion of unconstitutionality" (discussed above), which forces debate about the precise relevance or meaning of specific decisions of the Constitutional Council. Subject to strict party discipline, motions of unconstitutionality are virtually never adopted. Their importance, however, is to warn the government, explicitly, that its bill will be referred to the Council if it does not agree to compromise and amend the bill in the amending process to come.

Constitutional debate leading to government compromise is today a banal part of the parliamentary process. Oppositions have learned to state their partisan objections to a bill in terms of constitutional law; the majority has little choice but to respond in kind. Hundreds of amendments, rewriting dozens of important bills, have been adopted as a result of such debate. The 1982 decentralization bill is the classic example, adopted after having been rewritten by a record 500-plus amendments, after turgid debates about constitutionality.[38] The 1984 Press Law was also radically deformed. The bill submitted to Parliament bore slight resemblance to the one finally adopted nearly a year later. Of the law's original 42 Articles, 26 were substantially rewritten, and most of these changes were made under the threat of referral.[39] (As discussed above, the Council would nevertheless defang the bill, at least with respect to its application to Hersant.) In 1986, the Council rendered five decisions on a series of bills (an earlier set of Pasqua laws) to tighten the penal codes. The fact that a leading decision[40] had already laid down a set of basic rules contributed to the nearly total judicialization of the parliamentary processes by which these bills became law.[41]

Some decisions constitute not only the final stage of one legislative process, but the opening stage of a corrective revision process. Corrective revision processes occur after full or partial invalidations. They are highly structured, because the Council has already made its legislative choices explicit, and because oppositions (who can always refer the corrected law to the Council again) work to guarantee the government's compliance with the terms of the decision. Corrective revision processes lead to Council-written legislation. A few examples, drawn from dozens available, will suffice to illustrate the point. As noted above, in 1982 the French Constitutional Council annulled the 1982 nationalization bill, on the grounds that stockholders of companies to be nationalized would not be compensated fairly for their shares. It then went on to tell the government—in precise detail—how a *constitutional* compensation formula should have been elaborated in the first place. This new formula, which raised the costs of nationalization by another 30 percent, was simply copied—virtually word for word—into a new, revised bill. In 1986, the Chirac government proposed to deregulate the communications sector as a whole by, among other things, privatizing the radio and television industries, and abrogating the market-ceiling, antitrust provisions of the 1984 Press Law. After a long summer of heated constitutional debate, the government agreed to establish anti-trust mechanisms. The Council nonetheless censured important parts of the reform on the grounds that these mechanisms were not enough to protect media pluralism. In response, the government rewrote the bill, replacing the amputated provisions with the Council's own language. An elaborate anti-trust regime—relying on market-ceilings and governing the whole of multimedia communications—emerged, despite the Chirac government's commitment to rid French law of such ceilings.

The logic of corrective revision is simple. Once the Council has annulled a bill and stated in detail what a constitutional version of the bill would look like, the government is faced with a choice. It can ratify the Council's policy choices by rewriting and resubmitting the bill to Parliament, or it can forego the reform entirely. The latter choice is often no choice at all (imagine the Socialists renouncing nationalizations simply because the Council had ordered more compensation). Another option exists—the government can elect to revise the constitution in order to make constitutional what the Council has censured. In 1993, for the first time ever, the Balladur government decided to do just that.

In its decision on Pasqua's immigration law, the Council had ruled that French authorities must process all demands for asylum, and that as long as this process was underway, asylum seekers could remain on French territory. The decision required what earlier law had made discretionary. The 1985 Schengen Accords, signed by the member states of the European Community, had agreed that, within EC territory, only one state is responsible for processing asylum claims. The purpose of the treaty was to block claimants from moving from one state in the EC to another, in effect shopping for asylum. Although in 1991 the Council had ruled that the Schengen Accords did not violate the constitution, its 1993 decision prohibited France from taking advantage of Schengen's provisions. Rather than accept the Council's decision, the government decided to revise Article 53 of the constitution, in essence, incorporating the Schengen rules directly into the constitution. The revision was adopted on November 19, 1993, and entered into force on November 25, 1993. The next day, the government introduced legislation reinserting the original provisions on asylum censured by the Council, as well as a number of corrections required by the Council's other annulments of the immigration bill.[42]

IV Conclusion: The Council and Malaise

John T. S. Keeler has argued that France today suffers from a "distinctive" form of political "malaise."[43] Ironically, this malaise is partly due to the very success of the constitutional revolution that is the Fifth Republic. Since 1981, governments of first the Left and then the Right have fueled unreasonably high public expectations about the capacity of government to transform French society. Building on the demonstrated capacity of executives to have their legislation ratified by Parliament since 1959, successive governments, employing a strident rhetoric of "radical reform," promised impressive reform packages. In fact, although governments delivered on the most important of these promises, the public largely focused on the gap between the rhetoric of fundamental transformation and the perceived sameness of political life despite this rhetoric. Reform mania quickly became normal politics, and the public wearied of reformism just as quickly.

This malaise is partly determined by structural factors, partly by ideological factors. The post-1981 period has been an era of intense ideological polarization, and governments, whether Socialist or neoliberal, have felt compelled to counter one vision of *gouverner autrement* (transform government) with another. As Keeler's data demonstrates, the very permissiveness of the French policymaking process has further encouraged governments to be more rather than less audacious. Even the alleged exception—the Rocard government (1988-91)—"appear[s] modest only against the megastandards of 1981-86."[44] Focus on a seemingly omnipotent, but ultimately ineffective, executive is only one side of the coin. The perceived impotence of Parliament, which is the cost of permissiveness, is the other.

In evaluating the impact of constitutional politics on malaise, I will offer two quite different perspectives. The first focuses on the enhanced role of the Council in policymaking as a contributor to the problem. The second argues that the Council's impact on malaise has not been entirely negative, but may provide part of the antidote.

The Council as an Obstacle to Reformism

Viewed comparatively, the frequency of sustained, public judicial-political confrontations in France is extraordinary, testimony to the resilience of the ideology of legislative sovereignty in the face of an ever rigorous constitutionalism. In no other European country have conflicts between lawmakers and the constitutional court approached the high levels achieved in France in 1981-82, 1986, and 1993. In each of these periods, government ministers and parliamentarians complained of a "government of judges," and made more or less veiled threats to abolish the Council, to alter its institutional mandate, and to overturn its decisions by constitutional amendment or referenda.[45]

There is a pattern to these outbreaks. They occur after an *alternance,* elections yielding a new governmental majority and a transfer of power from the Left to the Right or vice versa. The era of *alternance* is the post–1981 era, but also the eras of (1) reform mania, and (2) the judicialization of policymaking. The logic of confrontation is thus the following: new governments come to power, overload the legislative system with extensive reform legislation, and then have to suffer the Council's interventions. In the first session of Parliament presided over by new governments in 1981, 1986, and 1993, for example, about half of all legislation was referred to the Council by the opposition, including virtually every important bill. In this context, the Council is easily assimilated into the opposition by the new majority, and easily characterized as an illegitimate obstacle to the government's reform efforts. This reaction is even more understandable when one adds another element—the composition of the Council. In the 1981-83 period, the new Left majority faced a Council composed entirely of appointees made by the Right; in 1986, the Chirac-led Right majority had lost the Council presidency and four of nine seats; in 1993, the Balladur-led Right majority faced a Socialist Council (6-3). If the Right wins all national elections in the 1995-98 period, it will regain a majority of the Council's seats only in 1998. Thus, we may very well expect renewed confrontations in 1995-96. Finally, judicialized policy processes are capable of eviscerating not only the legislation, but also the rhetorical-ideological momentum of a new government. Judicialization can transform what ought to have been an energizing, triumphant crusade to *changer la vie* (change the world) into a tedious, numbingly technical discussion and application of the Council's jurisprudence.

Comparatively, has the Council been a greater obstacle to reform than have other European constitutional courts? The answer is partly no and partly yes. In exercising constitutional review, all European constitutional courts participate in legislative processes and regularly generate legislative outcomes that conflict with the policy preferences of governments and parliamentary majorities. Further, the possibility for elected officials to overturn a decision of unconstitutionality is far greater in France than in other European countries. Juridically, a constitutional court decision declaring a piece of legislation to be in violation of the constitution can only be reversed by amending the constitution, as the Balladur government chose to do in 1993 in order to promulgate its immigration reforms. In Germany and Spain, polities in which abstract review coexists with concrete review, it is virtually impossible to overturn most important constitutional decisions. In Germany, the constitution itself categorically forbids any amendment of the constitution that would impact fundamental rights. In Spain, a constitutional amendment impacting fundamental rights can only be adopted by the same procedure as an entirely new constitution, that is, by a super-majoritian vote of the legislative chambers followed by a popular referendum. In France, by contrast, a disgruntled government needs only (1) a three-fifths majority in the Assembly and the Senate,[46] or (2) a majority vote of the people in referendum to overturn a constitutional decision.

As if this permissiveness were not enough, the constitution of the Fifth Republic also allows the president of the Republic to submit legislation for adoption by the people in referendum. The original terms of Article 11 restricted this power on the basis of subject matter, namely, to reforms of "the organization of public authority" or to ratify certain treaties. After the 1995 presidential elections, President Jacques Chirac and Prime Minister Alain Juppé asked parliament to extend the president's Article 11 powers to include the authority to propose legislation by referendum to "economic and social policies" and to "the organization of public services." The revision easily sailed through the parliamentary process and was approved on July 31, 1995. From the perspective of constitutional politics, the amendment is important to the extent that it will permit the president to bypass constitutional review mechanisms, since legislative bills so proposed cannot be referred to the Council by any authority.[47]

At the same time, we have to remember that French constitutional review evolved in a relatively hostile environment. In Germany, Italy, and Spain, constitution-makers, imbued with the ideology of constitutionalism, explicitly authorized constitutional courts to defend constitutional rights against legislative encroachment. In France, the ideology of constitutionalism was not meaningfully present in 1958, but developed gradually as an adjustment to the Council's jurisprudence. Attacks on the Council are but one manifestation of this process of adjustment.

Constitutional Politics as a Partial Antidote to Malaise

Following others, Keeler has noted that "the malaise of the 1980s [may have] had a bright side," to the extent that public disillusionment with reformism left the masses more pragmatic and modest in their expectations. What remains is for politicians "to respond to these clues" by, among other things, becoming less ideologically driven, and more consensual both in legislating and in their dealings with each other.[48]

It could be argued that the Council can and has played a structural role in emitting and reinforcing these clues. Constitutional politics function to produce, by the sustained interaction between the Council and parliamentarians, rules that narrow reform options. As these rules multiply, reform impulses may be moderated. Louis Favoreu argued in 1989 that a primary "function" of constitutional review in France was to "pacify" ideological conflict, by constraining excesses, and thus create the conditions for centrist politics.[49] I have criticized this view at some length,[50] but Favoreu and I would surely agree on the following related points. First, constitutionalism—the notion that all acts of government must conform to constitutional law in order to be considered legitimate—is today an ascendant counter-ideology to that of parliamentary supremacy. Lawmakers may grumble and even scream about the Council's capacity to make policy, but they have not yet gone further to curb its authority. Second, once out of power, the same politicians who complained of an intolerable "government of judges" situation, have unashamedly used referrals to the Council as a means of obstructing the legislative agenda of the *new* majority. These referrals serve to legitimate constitutional review, and thus reinforce constitutionalism. Third, viewed from the perspective of the executive-legislative dyad, the growth of constitutional politics constitutes a (slight) reinvigoration of parliamentary life, to the extent that parliamentary oppositions are able to use referrals and threats of referral to more effectively participate in the policy process.[51]

Notes to Chapter 3

1. John T. S. Keeler, "Executive Power and Policy-Making Patterns in France: Gauging the Impact of Fifth Republic Institutions," *West European Politics* 16 (1993): 518-44.

2. John T. S. Keeler and Alec Stone, "Judicial-Political Confrontation in Mitterrand's France: The Emergence of the Constitutional Council as a Major Actor in the Policy-Making Process," in Stanley Hoffmann, Sylvia Malzacher

and George Ross, eds., *The Mitterrand Experiment* (New York: Oxford University Press, 1987): 161-81.

3. The chapter updates and extends arguments presented in: Alec Stone, *The Birth of Judicial Politics in France* (Oxford University Press: New York, 1992); and Alec Stone, "Where Judicial Politics are Legislative Politics: The French Constitutional Council," *West European Politics* 15 (1992): 29-49.

4. The law of August 16, 1790, which remains in force, reads: "Courts can not interfere with the exercising of legislative powers or the application of the laws."

5. Alec Stone, "The Birth and Development of Abstract Review: Constitutional Courts and Policymaking in Western Europe," *Policy Studies Journal* 19 (1990): 81-95.

6. See Stone, *The Birth of Judicial Politics in France*, chapters 1, 2.

7. Decision 71-44, *Recueil des décisions du Conseil constitutionnel* (1971): 29.

8. The vote was 429-119, see Stone, *The Birth of Judicial Politics in France*, pp. 145-47.

9. This section is based on Alec Stone, "Judging Socialist Reform: The Politics of Coordinate Construction in France and Germany," *Comparative Political Studies* 26 (1994): 443-69.

10. A full discussion is at Stone, *The Birth of Judicial Politics in France*, chapter 8.

11. Nelson Polsby, "Legislatures," in Fred I. Greenstein and Nelson Polsby, eds., *Handbook of Political Science* (Reading, Mass.: Addison, Wesley, 1975) vol. 5, p. 277.

12. Pierre Pascallon, "Le Conseil constitutionnel: un deuxième parlement," *Revue politique et parlementaire* 925 (January 1986): 3.

13. *Le Monde*, September 5, 1986.

14. See Martin Shapiro, *Courts: A Comparative and Political Analysis* (Chicago: University of Chicago Press, 1980): 1-2.

15. Stone, *The Birth of Judicial Politics in France*, 33-40, 95-98.

16. Since 1987, the Council has participated in the Conference of Constitutional Courts, a pan-European assembly of constitutional judges established in 1972.

17. *Le Monde*, August 9, 1993.

18. Michel de Villiers, "Note 16," *Revue administrative* (November-December 1984): 587.

19. In 1928, the eminent law professor and future Council member Marcel Waline argued that Parliament behaved as a "constitutional jurisdiction" whenever it debated such motions (which at that time came under the rubric of the *ques-*

tion préalable); the argument was then attractive because no constitutional court at that time existed. Marcel Waline, "Eléments d'une théorie de la juridiction constitutionnelle,' *Revue du Droit Public* 45 (1928): 441-62.

20. Excluding the ratification of international agreements.

21. Decision 81-132, *Recueil des décisions du Conseil constitutionnel* (1982), p. 18.

22. The Council's three decisions on the Maastricht Treaty are analyzed in Alec Stone, "Ratifying Maastricht: France Debates European Union," *French Politics and Society* 11 (1993): 70-88.

23. Article 34 says that legislation "fixes rules concerning the creation of public establishments," universities being among such establishments. Decision 93-322, *Journal officiel (Lois...)* (1993), p. 10750.

24. *Le Monde*, July 20, 1993.

25. Decision 82-146, *Recueil des décisions du Conseil constitutionnel* (1982), p. 66.

26. Decision 83-165, *Recueil des décisions du Conseil constitutionnel* (1984), p. 30.

27. The following is based on Stone, "Where Judicial Politics are Legislative Politics," 38-40.

28. Decision 84-181, *Recueil des décisions du Conseil constitutionnel* (1984), p. 73.

29. A claim made by the Council itself in its jurisprudence, and constantly repeated by legal scholarship.

30. The best review of the Socialist's achievements in this area is William Safran, "Rights and Liberties Under the Mitterrand Presidency: Socialist Innovations and Post-Socialist Revisions," *Contemporary French Civilization* 12 (1988): 1-35.

31. In 1986, Robert Badinter became president of the Council. Badinter had long advocated a liberalization of the penal codes.

32. Decision 93-326, *Journal officiel (Lois...)* (1993), p. 11599.

33. Decision 93-323, *Journal officiel (Lois...)* (1993), p. 11193.

34. Decision 93-325, *Journal officiel (Lois...)* (1993), p. 11722.

35. Robert Dahl, "The Concept of Power," *Behavioral Sciences* 2 (1957): 201-15.

36. See Alec Stone, "Legal Constraints to Policymaking: The Constitutional Council and the Council of State," in P. Godt, ed., *Policymaking in France* (New York: Columbia Univ. Press, 1989): 32-33.

37. The text of Rocard's *circulaire* was published in Le Monde, May 27, 1988.

38. Decision 82-137, *Recueil des décisions du Conseil constitutionnel* (1982), p. 38.

39. Documented in Stone, *The Birth of Judicial Politics in France*, 181-86.

40. Decision 80-127, *Recueil des décisions du Conseil constitutionnel* (1981), p. 15.

41. See Alec Stone, "In the Shadow of the Constitutional Council: The Juridicisation' of the Policymaking Process in France," *West European Politics* 12 (1989): 22.
42. *Libération*, November 27-28, 1993.
43. Keeler, "Policy-making Patterns in the Fifth Republic," 534-38.
44. Keeler, "Policy-making Patterns in the Fifth Republic," 537.
45. For accounts and assessments of the pre-1993 confrontations, see Keeler and Stone, "Judicial-Political Confrontation in Mitterrand's France"; Stone, "In the Shadow of the Council"; and Stone, *The Birth of Judicial Politics in France*, 78-92. In 1993, ministers (Balladur and Pasqua) and numerous parliamentarians engaged in public Council bashing; see especially *Le Monde*, August 17, August 25, August 27, October 22, 1993, November 20, 1993. The intensity of government-sponsored Council bashing in 1986 and 1993 even led the President of the Council, Badinter, to publish rebuttals on the front page of *Le Monde* (e.g., November 11, 1993).
46. I am simplifying a slightly more complex procedure.
47. This was not the only motivation. The amendment was also tailored to bypass the kind of social protests that have characterized efforts at reforming the educational system. A referendum designed to authorize the government to undertake educational reform is now in the works.
48. Keeler, "Policy-making Patterns in the Fifth Republic," 535.
49. Louis Favoreu, *La politique saisie par le droit* (Paris: Economica, 1989).
50. Stone, *The Birth of Judicial Politics in France*, chapters 4, 7.
51. This reinvigoration has also enhanced the role of parliamentary commissions and those that control them, i.e., the majority.

Chapter 4

The Many Styles of Policymaking in France

Frank R. Baumgartner

Who governs France? In response to this simple question, scores of French and foreign scholars have provided varied and sometimes confusing answers. Many excellent and detailed descriptions of the roles of elite civil servants, elected officials, interest-group leaders, and popular protesters have been offered, but the results of these disparate studies do not always fit together easily. Scholars often emphasize the role of the high civil service, but in many cases popular protest renders these insiders virtually powerless. Elected officials often seem secondary in importance to career officials, but changes in the presidency, the prime ministership, and other political positions nonetheless appear to affect policy outcomes. Government officials often work in relative obscurity, but important press coverage and public debate often accompany the preparation of new policies. Interest-group leaders are often seen as outsiders, but in many areas they play an important role in providing information, advice, and warnings. International partners are generally seen only as minor actors, but increasingly the rulings and policies of the European Union play an important part in shaping domestic French public policies. In sum, our collective response to the deceptively simple question of who governs France seems inconclusive, partial, and contradictory.

I propose a simple factor, not typically given explicit attention in many studies of the policy process, that may help explain some of these seeming contradictions: the question of agenda-setting. In this chapter, I review a number of studies of the French policy process and point out how explicit consideration of the agenda status of the issues being discussed might help clarify why descriptions of the process often seem to differ. In France, as in any country, decisions high on the national political agenda are those discussed in public, in the media, and by the nation's top political leaders. These high-agenda items are often controversial. Issues discussed on the nightly news programs, on the front page of national newspapers, and in the speeches of politicians differ systematically from issues lower on the political agenda. Issues low on the political agenda are treated in relative obscurity, often by career government officials operating according to standard operating procedures, with little political oversight or interference, and in close consultation with affected interests.

In studies of American policymaking, attention to the agenda status of public issues has long been the norm.[1] Study after study in American politics has documented the entrenched interests dominating political "subsystems" that flourish when important issues or industrial organizations are kept out of the political limelight and remain, therefore, "off the agenda."[2] This literature has some echo in studies of British politics, where scholars have also paid explicit attention to the question of agenda-setting and to the idea that there are contending arenas of policymaking, each with different characteristics.[3] In comparative politics more generally, and in French politics in particular, these questions have rarely received the careful attention they deserve.

Students of comparative politics have more traditionally discussed questions of pluralism, corporatism, statism, and other systems of policymaking. These studies, based either on descriptions of entire national systems or on studies of individual sectors of the economy, have rarely considered the agenda status of the issues with which they deal.[4] Considering that pluralism seems to describe a system in which political conflicts often generate loud and public debates whereas corporatism denotes a more secretive and controlled process, it would seem paramount for scholars in comparative politics to consider more carefully the question of agenda setting. A potential reason for the conclusion that a particular country is characterized by highly public and conflictual policy processes might be that a study has systematically chosen only high-status agenda items for consideration. Similarly, a study based mostly on the observation of issues treated away from public attention would be more likely to reach a conclusion closer to corporatism. Of course, every country is simultaneously home to some issues that are high on the political agenda and others that are low. This may help explain why scholars have found it so difficult to place countries on a putative "corporatism-pluralism continuum." In any case, students of comparative politics have rarely made explicit whether their studies were based on issues with a high or low on a nation's political agenda.

Studies of policymaking in France have rarely paid attention to the question of agenda setting. In a study of thirty different issues in the area of education policy in 1983 and 1984, however, I found that the process of decision-making differed dramatically depending on the agenda status of the issue.[5] Political leaders became involved systematically depending on a series of considerations: Was there conflict among affected interest groups or government agencies? Was there media coverage? Was the issue an expensive one? Could it be linked to the nation's partisan cleavages? Did the Opposition in Parliament seize on the issue? Were there street demonstrations? In that study, I pointed out that policymakers in France were strategic in their efforts to push issues either higher or lower on the political agenda. Depending on their estimates of who would make the decisions (and on what basis), policymakers attempted to portray the issue in a manner that would cause it to rise or fall on the political agenda. Clearly, civil servants and other elite government actors stood more to gain if they could convince others that certain issues were "merely" technical matters of no great import. Others wanted to treat the issue as a "political" question demanding partisan intervention and public debate. Depending on the outcome of these struggles, the policy process differed dramatically: either few policymakers became involved and the process centered on the elite civil servants often described by others as dominating large areas of French policymaking, or many policymakers became involved and the process was highly political, controversial, and subject to public debate. I found it impossible to conclude that any single style of policymaking dominated, even within the relatively narrow range of education policies that I studied during one twelve-month period.

Studies of the policy process in France differ systematically in their use of high- and low-agenda issues as an empirical base. In the pages to follow, I review a number of prominent studies of the policymaking process in France in order to show that the varied conclusions that authors have reached may often be explained by this simple consideration. In examining the importance of whether an issue is decided amid the public, partisan, and media attention that accompanies a high position on the national political agenda or whether the issue is decided in the relative obscurity of the bureaucracy, I will not argue that either environment is accurate or more important. Rather, a great number of policymaking styles naturally coexist in France as in any other country.

No single policy style is "typical" of France. Certainly, a range of constitutional, institutional, political, and cultural factors create a common context for policymaking in France and cause France to differ systematically from other countries. However, these national differences often pale in comparison to differences in policy styles within a country, based on agenda-status. Even within France, it is possible to observe tremendous differences in how policies are made from one economic domain to another, from issue to issue, and over time. Rather than attempting the impossible task of identifying a single French style of policymaking, we should set our sights on describing the variety of styles that occur in France and on explaining this diversity. In this chapter, I focus on a single aspect, the agenda status of an issue, in an effort to help explain some of the discrepancies that are apparent in published studies of the policy process in France.

The Diversity of Policymaking Styles in France

The grandest and most influential studies of policymaking in France are those that focus on the powerful role of elite civil servants. Among American authors, Ezra Suleiman has been particularly accurate in his descriptions of the power of the *grands corps*.[6] Others such as Harvey Feigenbaum have reinforced the general theme of powerful career officials playing key roles in a range of economic domains.[7] There is no question that the *grands corps* and other elite groups of civil servants play a paramount role in French policymaking. International comparisons have also reached this same conclusion.[8]

Anne Stevens gives an apt summary of the view that the French state, through its civil servants, took responsibility for running the post-war economy. She describes how a feeling of self-confidence animated these graduates of the *grandes écoles* and how they felt that "the renewal and growth of the country depended on us."[9] Clearly, leaders of the Parisian ministries were the most important element in the post-war economic boom that defined France even during a period of remarkable political instability. The

Fifth Republic, like the Fourth, has also been characterized by the importance of this cohesive civil service.

Peter Hall compared British and French economic policymaking and noted the close ties linking government and banking elites in France.[10] Generally, partisan issues were unimportant in France during the time that he studied these questions: the making of economic policy was successfully portrayed as a "technical" question best left to the experts. John Zysman also emphasizes the power of the civil service in forging monetary and investment policy.[11] A recent study of the actions of the French Treasury *(le Trésor)* by Philippe Jurgensen and Daniel Lebègue makes a point of emphasizing the technically arcane nature of the discussions, the small number of people who can understand the issues involved in manipulating the national market for credit, and the secrecy in which most of these actions are shrouded.[12] It seems clear that large areas of the French economy, and macroeconomic policymaking in particular, feature a cohesive set of government and private actors sharing a vision of what they should accomplish. With this shared vision comes a tradition of relative independence from (and distrust of) partisan politics. Many important areas of policy seem to be removed from public discussion because of the cohesiveness of the actors involved.

Two issues in particular serve to demonstrate the policy importance of agenda-setting and the value to elites of steering clear of partisan politics. The civilian nuclear power program, implemented by Parliament in response to the 1973 oil embargo, is one of the most remarkable engineering and public works projects in the western world. France, by implementing the Messmer Plan, moved from generating less than 8 percent of its electricity from nuclear power in 1974 to getting over 70 percent from that source just 12 years later. Equally remarkable to the engineering and financing of this effort have been the successes in avoiding political controversy over, and, to some extent, public discussion of nuclear issues. Nuclear power in France simply does not correspond to a partisan cleavage. With the Communist Party a firm supporter of the nuclear power program from its inception (and with the affiliated Confédération Générale du Travail (CGT) the dominant union among energy workers), and with the Socialist Party out of power, Conservative officials were able to build a consensus in favor of a high-tech solution to the nation's "dangerous dependence on foreign sources of energy." By the time the Socialists came to power the program was so far under way that the abandonment of a single power plant, at Plogoff in western Brittany, marked a way for the Socialist Party not only to indicate a change from previous policy, but also to adopt the remainder of that policy as its own. At this point, nuclear power is a non-issue among the leaders of the major political parties in France. The relative acceptance by the French of the nation's nuclear program is because of the lack of elite-level partisan differences, not because of mass-level opinion in favor of the program. Public opinion surveys in 1983 showed that the French do not differ much from their European neighbors, but are more hostile towards nuclear power than Americans.[13] With an elite consensus that neither side would exploit the issue for political advantage, with a single electrical utility company enjoying a good reputation for technical competence, with spending carefully spread out to hundreds of local governments of all political persuasions, and with a weak set of environmental groups, France rarely debates nuclear power in spite of its great importance to the nation. In the United States, the issue is much more likely to inspire public debates in spite of the virtual abandonment of the technology by American utilities and its relatively minor historical importance.[14]

Edward A. Kolodziej describes almost an identical situation in the case of arms procurement and manufacturing in France. With an all-party consensus that France's military must be strong, with spending spread through the country to ensure a wide distribution of economic benefits, and with a public image as a high-tech industry suited only to guaranteeing the national independence, the French arms industry has been able to avoid the "heat of partisan debate and the glare of public disclosure."[15] Clearly, staying off the agenda is sometimes a powerful strategy in policymaking, so long as one has the support of the relevant state agencies and industrial leaders. Both the nuclear power and the arms industry examples point to this conclusion.

It is clear that traditional French policymaking studies explore ways in which the high civil service is able to exert its tremendous power. Whether these powers are described using the terms "corporatism," "statism," "elitism," or any other phrase, they are distinctive in that they imply a tight control by a small number of specialists, usually a group of elite civil servants, who make policy and generally work in relative obscurity.[16] Further, it is equally clear that the bulk of studies focusing on these bureaucratic powers have been based on the analysis of issues devoid of partisan and public debates. Another large research tradition in French policymaking studies is to focus on those cases where bureaucratic power is low.

Virtually every author who has written about the French political system as a whole has insisted on the "crisis-prone" nature of the system. Michel Crozier has given the most complete explanation of this process in his description of the "blocked society."[17] The state remains distant from the people, most of the time resisting reform, but occasionally pressures build to such an extent that they can no longer be contained. Protest, crisis, and heroic change are seen as an integral, if troublesome, part of the system. In a political system generally marked by tight control by civil servants, one cannot ignore the occasional revolt. Considering the importance of such revolts in overturning various French regimes since the monarchy, political leaders in particular are certainly aware of their potential importance.[18]

The myriad studies of French political life that mention the importance of protest stand in contrast to those focusing on the importance of the civil service, for the job of the civil service is precisely to avoid social unrest. It is important to build an explanation of the policy process that can accommodate the involvement of powerful civil servants, but it is also important to recognize that protest, street demonstrations, and disorderly conduct are equally common features of the French policy process.

One of the reasons for protest is the lack of effective representation—in the form of interest groups—of many societal segments. Though the French support a seemingly endless array of interest groups, many of them are small, and relatively few segments of society are represented through a single, powerful organization that can speak for its members and represent them in the halls of government when decisions are being made. As decisions in many areas are made in the absence of effective interest groups, protest ensues. A variety of authors have described a state of interest-group politics in France in which the labor unions and other associations are typically weak and unable to speak for the vast majority of their members.[19] Of course there are areas of strong groups (nothing is that simple in French politics), but in many cases the desires of civil servants to engage in negotiations with affected interests are thwarted due to a lack of *interlocutors valables*. The result? Protest, crisis, and a loss of control by those government actors usually best able to manage such policymaking negotiations.

Martin Schain points out that French industrial unions are typically so weak that they cannot control the mobilization of their members and yet, paradoxically, this lack of control sometimes reinforces their power in negotiating with government officials.[20] In the 15 years since that chapter was published, its point has only become more accurate. Even if government officials were willing to bargain with the leaders of well organized interest groups, most of the groups in the area of labor are too weak to bargain with authority. Does this make them powerless? Surprisingly, no. Once their members (or potential members) go on strike, government officials are desperate for bargaining and negotiating partners who can speak in the name of the protesters, and union officials are typically the only ones available. In the complex arena of protest politics in France, the very weakness of some interest groups can lead paradoxically to a strength.[21] The crises generated by a street protest or a prolonged and seemingly uncontrolled strike often create a new dynamic. As the issue hits the national political agenda, pressure for resolution is much greater. Given the importance of public salience even in simple bargaining situations, it is clear that policymakers have an interest in promoting or in inhibiting the rise of certain issues onto the political agenda. Crisis is an effective way to achieve this.

Besides a series of studies that focuses on the roles of elite civil servants and another series that considers the importance of protest, heroism, and unconventional politics, we can identify a range of sectoral studies that describe relatively diverse patterns of policymaking within different industrial sectors. Studies of agriculture,[22] health care,[23] science,[24] nuclear power,[25] industrial relations,[26] local administration,[27] and a variety of other issues[28] have shown variation in policy styles due to the different organization of state structures, economic slack, and organization of interests in each of these areas. We can see, therefore, many different national styles of policymaking in just a short review of such studies.

Still, another type of difference is change over time. James Hollifield[29] and Martin Schain[30] describe how important changes have been made over the decades to immigration policy as that issue has become more politically sensitive. Whereas immigration was once considered only from the point of view of labor-flow management and industrial policy, today it is much more likely to be the subject of political controversy (if not partisan exploitation and electoral grandstanding). As public understanding of the issue has changed, so too has the list of political actors who feel the need to become involved. A small group of obscure civil servants working in close contact with leaders of industrial corporations have been replaced by a large and heterogeneous group of policymakers with no clear consensus on what they should do.

Studies of other issues also make clear important differences in how a single issue is treated at two different points in time. Alcohol issues, once at the center of what was considered the weakness of the French state because of the power of the local pressure groups (especially in the case of the infamous *bouilleurs de cru* of the Fourth Republic)[31] are now much more tame. The shopkeepers of the Poujade Movement have not been able to keep up the level of political mobilization that led them to momentary prominence decades ago. In sum, it is not difficult to find examples over the years of single issues where the relative mobilization of interests on each side, and the degree of public prominence given to the question, have waxed and waned considerably. In short, levels of public attention strongly affect the nature of the policy process. Each can change over time.

In sum, we can note from this quick review of several recent French and American descriptions of the policy process in France that a great number of different styles of decision-making operate within France. Bureaucratic control is often extreme, but street protest and open political debate are also common. Certain areas of the economy sustain cohesive and powerful interest groups, but other areas feature only divided or weak organizations. Some issues are treated as high-agenda items for a period of time only to recede from the political limelight in later years. With few exceptions, most issues most of the time are treated in relative obscurity by government officials and affected interests. Certain issues, such as macroeconomic policy, are routinely covered in the press and are of interest to large segments of the business community, but even these issues rarely mobilize the public. Most issues, in fact, rarely emerge as high-agenda items. Scholars recognize that periodic and temporary exposure to the glare of public debate is just as much a part of the normal policy process as the more common periods of obscurity. However, most explanations of the two styles of policymaking are not integrated. Michel Crozier comes the closest with his idea of a "blocked society" lurching through a crisis only after pressure builds up during long periods of bureaucratic rigidity.[32]

Policymaking in every area can be affected by long periods of relative obscurity and incrementalism followed by short bursts of public attention and dramatic change. Bryan Jones and I found such patterns in a variety of American public policies over several decades of study.[33] In proposing a punctuated-equilibrium model of the policy process in a democracy, we found that the dynamics of agenda-setting are an integral, even a fundamental, part of the normal policy process. As issues move away from public attention or as they become the object of increased public and media interest, the nature of the policy processes surrounding them (and the subsequent actions of government) change dramatically.

Certain areas of the economy seem particularly insulated from public discussion, and those are the ones most commonly described by scholars as being dominated by powerful civil servants and technocratic decision-making styles. Other areas seem particularly prone to controversy and to partisan discussion. These differences are worth systematic consideration and explanation, for they are part of a single system of policymaking: each democracy is home both to controversial issues and to consensual ones, and a complete description of the policy process in any country must account for these differences. With greater attention to the dynamics of agenda-setting in our studies of policymaking, we may better propose an integrated set of explanations for what otherwise appear to be disparate processes.

John Keeler and Martin Schain demonstrate in their introductory essay that the French Fifth Republic has gone through many important stages since its inception in 1958. Longitudinal changes are clearly important to consider. Throughout the chapters of this volume, various authors point in particular to a long-term decline in ideological divisions among the major political parties. These longitudinal changes have important consequences for the policy process as certain issues, once closely associated with the partisan cleavages, lose their partisan relevance and other issues become more prominent. Issues that have long been central to the French partisan cleavages have to do with the clerical divide associated with the Revolution, with the social class divisions associated with industrial production, and, to a lesser extent, with the events of the Occupation and the Resistance. Many professional and social organizations, including labor unions, teachers' associations, parents' groups, and recreational organizations were created partially in reference to these grand divisions. When these groups have been involved in policy disputes in the past, they have often used their common ideological affinities as a direct line to politicize certain debates if it served their interests. Even without an active effort to politicize—when groups are organized into such large, ideological families—appealing to one's allies is a natural tendency and one that cannot be avoided. There is no question, for example, why an issue like reform of the private schools can put millions of French people into the streets: almost every major political party and social organization in France has some tie to the clerical/anticlerical divisions that once dominated French political life.

New social issues such as feminism, immigration, the environment, European integration, homelessness, and global-economic restructuring have not prompted the creation of organizations with close ties to new political parties and party leaders. However, as each political party struggles to retain its relevance to the public, ties will grow between the parties and the organizations even though each represents a different position on these new issues. Indeed, one can observe the beginnings of these trends today.

A second important secular trend is apparent in the essays gathered in this volume. Along with a decline in ideology there is increased public skepticism towards politics, and increased distrust of politicians. This has to do in part with a series of public corruption scandals over the past decade. France, like the United States, Italy, and many other western countries, faces a confidence crisis in its political elite partly due to a perception of conflict of interest.[34] However, more is involved here than only the ethical standards of the individual politicians. Changes in the nature of the policy problems facing the French have caused both a decline in ideological confrontation, as mentioned above, and an increase in skepticism.

Political parties must be related to choices of public policy in order to retain their relevance to public life in a democracy. If the parties are attached to positions that the voters do not recognize as important, voters wonder about the purpose of the politicians' posturing and public statements. Skepticism, if not outright hostility, is a likely outcome of a system where parties fail to offer meaningful choices on important issues. One of the reasons for public skepticism about the nation's political parties is that these parties and their leaders are tied to the past through their long-standing organizational alliances. The Communist Party will not lose its connections with the labor unions, just as the Gaullists and Conservatives will not become disassociated from religious organizations. However, as these old ties lose their relevance to the voters, such organizational links must change or the parties risk extinction. As massive changes take place in the nature of the economy that seem to make old political cleavages less important, new positions must be staked out. This process, however, is likely to take decades.

Parties will remain relevant to the voters, and voters will lose their skepticism towards them, only to the extent that the parties can adopt to the new issues. This will occur only when new interest groups organize and forge links with these new politicians, a process that can already be observed as the Socialist Party moves haltingly to develop ties with groups such as the environmentalists or those dedicated to protecting immigrants and second-generation French. In the meantime, the traditional political parties act as an anchor, tying modern France to the core issues of its history.

French politics includes a great range of policy styles, as this chapter has recounted. An important distinction among the various styles of policymaking discussed is how policy decisions become linked to the partisan cleavages and therefore to the voters. One intriguing element of this review is that many of the most important issues of French national life seem to be the subjects of an all-party consensus that effectively grants control to elite government actors. If civil servants are as important as so many scholars point out, then of what use are the parties (and therefore the voters)? In order for a democracy to have meaning, voters choosing among political parties must feel that they are at the same time making some policy choices of consequence. The challenge for the French political system in the years to come will be for the political parties to offer policy positions on the new issues that matter to the French. This is surely going to lead to important changes in the policy process as European integration, womens' rights, the environment, minority rights, immigration, and industrial restructuring begin to replace old issues of wages, national independence, and the role of the Church as the defining elements of partisan debate. In this renewal, if it occurs, the parties will find their relevance to the French voters. If it does not occur, there will be increased reinforcement of the powers of civil servants to run society in the absence of any serious public and democratic debate about the direction they choose to lead the country. Such a trend in a country already seen by many to be a technocracy would probably only fuel further public skepticism towards the parties and the institutions of democracy.

Understanding and Explaining Diversity in Styles

This chapter has reviewed a range of findings about policymaking in France, discussing how many studies emphasize the powerful roles of civil servants and how others equally and accurately describe much more politicized, controversial, and public styles of policymaking. I have argued that only by making the links between partisan choices and policy choices clear can a democracy continue to ensure the input of the public, and therefore, expect to retain its support. As the public-policy problems facing a country change over the decades, however, partisan cleavages are often slower to change. Maintaining a link between political parties and the policy choices that a government makes is, however, in the long run a central element to the success of a democracy. The parties will have to offer more relevant choices or the system as a whole will lose the support of the public.

Besides these concerns regarding the future relevance of the French party system, this chapter has focused on some more methodological concerns about the study of policymaking in a modern democracy. There is not and never has been a single "French" style of policymaking. Many different styles of policymaking coexist simultaneously in France, as they do in any complex country. Some may bemoan this fact because it makes the comparative study of policymaking more complex. Others may revel in this fact because it produces such a variety of French idiosyncracies to be explained, analyzed, and discussed. As the comparative study of public policy becomes a subject of more interest, our theories and understandings of how policies are made will be advanced further if we are careful to address common conceptual issues. One such conceptual issue that deserves attention is the agenda-setting process. Issues debated in public differ systematically from those that are treated "off the agenda" in ways that are central to our ideas of how policies should be made in a democracy. For our descriptions of the policy process to be comparable, we need to be clear about which types of issues we are describing and why.

At least four levels of analysis in comparative studies of policy processes seem clear. These might be described as: 1) the macro-level, in which the unit of analysis is the entire country; 2) the meso-level, in which issue domains or economic sectors within countries are compared; 3) the micro-level, where particular issues are compared to each other; and 4) the longitudinal, in which changes over time are explained. In the study of French politics as in that of any single country, of course, the first level is ruled out. However, our studies of French politics are clearly bound by a set of "constants," that together form the national context of policymaking such as the constitutional structure of the country, the political culture, and the organization of interest groups and political parties. In a macro-level comparison, these national-level constants would indeed be variables with explanatory power, but within a given country we cannot rely on these to explain our findings. The studies mentioned in this chapter have all necessarily been at one of the three lower levels of analysis, but the chapter has clearly demonstrated that even at these lower levels of analytic view, abundant differences remain to be explained.

Each analytical approach is associated with a set of theories that can be addressed and, more importantly, a set of questions that cannot be addressed. The studies in this book help to develop a clearer understanding of several of these theories: the particular institutional and political contexts of French policymaking that may be compared to those of other states, and the internal variation over issue domains—from issue to issue and across time—that can lead us to understand the impact of different political environments within even the same country. In this chapter I have attempted to show the importance of considering the agenda status of the issues under consideration, though other variables are clearly important as well. By studying a range of issues within a single national context, we can contribute to a broader understanding of the policy process in general. French politics and policymaking are striking in their diversity. Happily, however, this diversity is subject to some of the same explanations that appear to apply in other countries as well. By remaining sensitive to the range of issues to be addressed in the comparative study of policymaking, students of French politics can contribute to a much broader understanding of how policies are made in modern democracies, and why.

Notes to Chapter 4

1. See E. E. Schattschneider, *The Semi-Sovereign People* (New York: Holt, Rinehart and Winston, 1960); Roger W. Cobb and Charles D. Elder, *Participation in American Politics: The Dynamics of Agenda-Building* (Baltimore: Johns Hopkins University Press, 1983); John W. Kingdon, *Agendas and Alternatives in American Politics* (Boston: Little, Brown, 1984); Frank R. Baumgartner and Bryan D. Jones, *Agendas and Instability in American Politics* (Chicago: University of Chicago Press, 1993).

2. See Arthur F. Bentley, *The Process of Government* (Chicago: University of Chicago Press, 1908); Douglass Cater, *Power in Washington* (New York: Random House, 1964); A. Lee Fritschler, *Smoking and Politics,*. 4th ed. (Englewood Cliffs, N.J.: Prentice-Hall, 1989); Ernest S. Griffith, *The Impasse of Democracy* (New York: Harrison-Hilton Books, 1939); Arthur Maass, *Muddy Waters: The Army Engineers and the Nation's Rivers* (Cambridge: Harvard University Press, 1951); Emmette S. Redford, *Democracy in the Administrative State* (New York: Oxford University Press, 1969); David Vogel, *Fluctuating Fortunes: The Political Power of Business in America* (New York: Basic Books, 1989).

3. See Brian W. Hogwood, *From Crisis to Complacency? Shaping Public Policy in Britain* (New York: Oxford University Press, 1987); A. G. Jordan and J. J. Richardson, *British Politics and the Policy Process* (London: Allen and Unwin, 1987); Martin J. Smith, *Pressure Power and Policy: State Autonomy and Policy Networks in Britain and the United States* (London: Harvester Wheatsheaf, 1993).

4. See Gabriel Almond, "Corporatism, Pluralism, and Professional Memory," *World Politics* 35 (1983): 245-60; Alan Cawson, ed., *Organized Interests and the State: Studies in Meso-Corporatism* (London: Sage, 1985); Gerhard Lehmbruch and Philippe C. Schmitter, eds., *Patterns of Corporatist Policy Making* (London: Sage, 1982); Philippe C. Schmitter, "Still the Century of Corporatism?" *Review of Politics* 36 (1974): 85-131; and Philippe C. Schmitter and Gerhard Lehmbruch, eds., *Trends Towards Corporatist Intermediation* (London: Sage, 1979).

5. Frank R. Baumgartner, *Conflict and Rhetoric in French Policymaking* (Pittsburgh: University of Pittsburgh Press, 1989).

6. Ezra N. Suleiman, *Politics, Power, and the Bureaucracy in France* (Princeton, N.J.: Princeton University Press, 1974); *Elites in French Society* (Princeton, N.J.: Princeton University Press, 1978); and *Private Power and Centralization in France: The Notaries and the State* (Princeton, N.J.: Princeton University Press, 1987).

7. Harvey B. Feigenbaum, *The Politics of Public Enterprise* (Princeton, N.J.: Princeton University Press, 1985); see also Pierre Birnbaum, *Les Sommets de l'état* (Paris: Seuil, 1977) and *La Classe dirigeante française* (Paris: Presses Universitaires de France, 1978); Jean-Luc Bodiguel, *Les Anciens élèves de l'ENA* (Paris: Presses de la Fondation Nationale des Sciences Politiques, 1978); Jean-Luc Bodiguel and Luc Rouban, *Le Fonctionnaire détroné?* (Paris: Presses de la Fondation Nationale des Sciences Politiques, 1991); Pierre Bourdieu, *La Noblesse d'état* (Paris: Editions de minuit, 1989); Elie Cohen, *Le Colbertisme "high tech"* (Paris: Hachette, 1992); Monique Dagnaud and Dominique Mehl, *L'Elite rose* (Paris: Editions Ramsay, 1982); Jean G. Padioleau, *L'Etat au concret* (Paris: Presses Universitaires de France, 1982); Jean-Louis Quermonne, *L'Appareil administratif de l'Etat* (Paris: Seuil, 1991); Pierre Rosanvallon, *L'Etat en France* (Paris: Seuil, 1990); René Rémond, Aline Coutrot, and Isabelle Boussard, *Quarante ans de cabinets ministériels* (Paris: Presses de la Fondation Nationale des Sciences Politiques, 1982); F. Ridley and Jean Blondel, *Public Administration in France* (London: Routledge and Kegan Paul, 1964); Luc Rouban, *Le Pouvoir anonyme* (Paris: Presses de la Fondation Nationale des Sciences Politiques, 1994); and Jean-Claude Thoenig, *L'Ere des technocrates: Le cas des Ponts et Chaussées* (Paris: Editions d'Organisation, 1974).

8. See Joel D. Aberbach, Robert D. Putnam, and Bert A. Rockman, *Bureaucrats and Politicians in Western Europe* (Cambridge: Harvard University Press, 1981), p. 251; Mattei Dogan, ed., *The Mandarins of Western Europe* (New York: Wiley, 1975).

9. Anne Stevens, "The Higher Civil Service and Economic Policy-Making," in Philip C. Cerny and Martin A. Schain, eds. *French Politics and Public Policy* (London: Frances Pinter, 1980), p. 83.

10. Peter Hall, *Governing the Economy* (New York: Oxford University Press, 1986).

11. John Zysman, *Governments, Markets, and Growth* (Ithaca: Cornell University Press, 1983).

12. Philippe Jurgensen and Daniel Lebègue, *Le Trésor et la politique financière* (Paris: Montchrestien, 1988), pp. 1-2 and passim.

13. See Ronald Inglehart, "The Fear of Living Dangerously: Public Attitudes Toward Nuclear Power," *Public Opinion* 7 (1984): 41-4.

14. See Baumgartner and Jones, *Agendas and Instability,* chapter 4; Frank R. Baumgartner and David Wilsford, "France: Science Within the State," in Etel Solingen, ed., *Scientists and the State,* (Ann Arbor, Mich.: University of Michigan Press, 1993), p. 81.

15. Edward A. Kolodziej, *Making and Marketing Arms* (Princeton, N.J.: Princeton University Press, 1987), p. 402. France's recent displacement of the United States as the world's number one supplier of arms to third world countries shows the power of these relationships.

16. See Dominique Colas, ed., *L'Etat et les corporatismes* (Paris: Presses Universitaires de France, 1988); Bruno Jobert and Pierre Muller, *L'Etat en action* (Paris: Presses Universitaires de France, 1987).

17. Michel Crozier, *La Société bloquée* (Paris: Seuil, 1970).

18. See Charles Tilly, *The Contentious French* (Cambridge: Harvard University Press, 1986); Frank L. Wilson, "Political Demonstrations in France: Protest Politics or Politics of Ritual," *French Politics and Society* 12 (1994): 23-40.

19. See, for examples, Jean Meynaud, *Les Groupes de pression en France* (Paris: Armand Colin, 1958); and *Nouvelles études sur les groupes de pression en France* (Paris: Armand Colin, 1962); René Mouriaux, *Les Syndicats dans la société française* (Paris: Presses de la Fondation Nationale des Sciences Politiques, 1983); and Frank L. Wilson, *Interest-Group Politics in France* (New York: Cambridge University Press, 1987).

20. Martin A. Schain, "Corporatism and Industrial Relations in France," in Philip C. Cerny and Martin Schain, eds., *French Politics and Public Policy,* (London: Frances Pinter, 1980).

21. See also John S. Ambler, "Why French Education Policy Is So Often Made on the Streets," *French Politics and Society* 12 (1994): 41-64; Frank R. Baumgartner, "The Politics of Protest and Mass Mobilization in France," *French Politics and Society* 12 (1994): 84-96; Martin A. Schain, "Ordinary Politics: Immigrants, Direct Action, and the Political Process in France," *French Politics and Society* 12 (1994): 65-83; and Wilson.

22. John T. S. Keeler, *The Politics of Neocorporatism in France* (New York: Oxford University Press, 1987).
23. David Wilsford, *Doctors and the State* (Durham, N.C.: Duke University Press, 1991).
24. Baumgartner and Wilsford; Robert Gilpin, *France in the Age of the Scientific State* (Princeton, N.J.: Princeton University Press, 1968); Pierre Papon, *Le Pouvoir et la science en France* (Paris: Editions du Centurion, 1978); Don K. Price, *The Scientific Estate* (Cambridge: Harvard University Press, 1965).
25. Lawrence Scheinman, *Atomic Energy Policy in France under the Fourth Republic* (Princeton, N.J.:Princeton University Press, 1965).
26. William J. Adams and Christian Stoffaës, eds., *French Industrial Policy* (Washington: Brookings, 1986); Andrew Cox and Jack Hayward, "The Inapplicability of the Corporatist Model in Britain and France: The Case of Labor," *International Political Science Review* 4 (1983): 217-40; Schain.
27. Catherine Grémion, *Profession: décideurs* (Paris: Gauthier-Villars, 1979).
28. Denis Segrestin, *Le Phénomène corporatiste: Essai sur l'avenir des systèmes professionnels fermés en France* (Paris: Fayard, 1985).
29. James F. Hollifield, *Immigrants, Markets, and States* (Cambridge: Harvard University Press, 1992).
30. Martin A. Schain, "Immigrants and Politics in France," in John S. Ambler, ed., *The French Socialist Experiment* (Philadelphia: Institute for the Study of Human Issues, 1985) and "Patterns of Policy-making in France: The Case of Immigration" (paper presented at the annual meeting of the American Political Science Association, Chicago, Il., 1992).
31. See Philip M. Williams, *Crisis and Compromise: Politics in the Fourth Republic* (Garden City, N.Y.: Anchor Books, 1966).
32. Crozier.
33. Baumgartner and Jones.
34. See Yves Mény, *La Corruption de la République* (Paris: Fayard, 1993).

Part II

Business, Labor, and the Economy

Chapter 5

Business, the State, and the End of Dirigisme

Vivien A. Schmidt

Traditional French dirigisme (state intervention in the economy) is not dead, but it is very much diminished. The policies of successive governments of the Left and the Right through the Mitterrand years have effectively undermined an approach to economic policymaking that goes back to Louis XIV and his minister Colbert, although it had its heyday in the post-war period. The state no longer has the macroeconomic tools and microeconomic policy instruments that in the past had ensured that the state would lead and business would follow. Moreover, business today needs the state less for guidance and support. This is a result not only of the new deregulated environment and the opening up of non-governmental sources of financing but also of the changes in the structure of business. Business is now both more international in consequence of the rash of cross-border mergers, acquisitions, and joint ventures beginning in the middle to late 1980s and more interdependent as a result of the cross-shareholdings among public and private enterprises.

Dirigisme in France has always indicated both a set of interventionist policies and directive policymaking processes. In the post-war period, the policies were epitomized by the indicative plans and industrial policies that focused on *grands projets* (big state-led initiatives) and encouraged the creation of "national champions" in both public and private sectors. These policies put tremendous resources in the hands of planners and industrial policymakers in the form of subsidies, grants, and loans as well as nationalized enterprise, thereby enabling them to exercise extensive control over business. During the Mitterrand years, the nationalization and restructuring of major industries represented the culmination of this dirigiste policy tradition, with the Socialists' 1983 U-turn in monetary policy and their concurrent deregulatory reforms having begun the move from a state-directed to a more market-oriented economy. The neoliberal Right, with privatization and continuing deregulation, only took this farther. And yet, even privatization, while engineering the retreat of the state, was dirigiste in the way in which it determined control of the newly privatized firms. In fact, even as dirigiste policies were superseded by liberal policies as early as 1983, dirigiste policymaking processes continued. Only as of 1988 did dirigisme as a set of directive policymaking processes abate, as government began to follow business more than lead it, despite occasional rhetorical flourishes or grand initiatives. Even so, significant changes in state ownership and control occurred along with further deregulation.

Dirigisme as a set of policymaking processes has traditionally been characterized by close relationships between ministry and industry and a "statist" pattern of policymaking in which governments formulate "heroic" policies minus business input. Although often using other terms, most French scholars have taken account of the dirigiste or heroic aspects of the statist pattern. They generally portray France as the ideal-typical, strong state, insulated from the political community but centralized enough to ensure at least partial autonomy.[1] They find institutions that provide the state with "tactical advantages" that enable it to take independent action[2] and to manifest a policy style notable for its capacity not merely to initiate far-sighted planning efforts but also to impose them where it deems necessary.[3] Moreover, they outline a political system in which the state remains central, dominating the political agenda and monopolizing the construction of the populace's worldview, organizing and controlling societal interests, and taking charge of the implementation of public policies.[4] Finally, scholars see policy not only identified by a small group of the administrative elite, the central decision-making milieu,[5] but also implemented by it with minimal public debate.

Often left out of this equation, however, is the part of the statist pattern that has always attenuated the dirigisme. However strong the state may appear, it suffers from many weaknesses. First of all, the image of the strong state hides great fragmentation caused by rivalries both between and within ministries.[6] Secondly, in numbers of instances where policies are more "everyday" than heroic, the boundaries between "state" and "society" become blurred, and societal interests may even take over government's policy formulation role (this was the case with the notaries.)[7] Finally, however much the government may seek to impose its policies without consultation, societal interests can and do effectively resist them.[8] The state is not really able to govern by decree because "the system will not function unless private organizations give their willing collaboration to the pursuit of public purposes."[9]

France's statist pattern of policymaking, then, is one in which government's ability to be dirigiste—that is, to take unilateral action at the policy-formulation stage without prior consultation with those most interested in the policy—is tempered by its need to respond to societal interests at the implementation stage, where policymaking is characterized by the politics of accommodation, cooptation, or confrontation.[10] Much depends upon the centrality of the policy to the government, the policy's potential impact on the most affected interests, and these interests' level of access, upset, and organization. Business in particular, despite often having been portrayed as the victim of state dirigisme, has in fact managed to get its way much of the time, given top managers' special access to decision-makers as a result of personal relationships, old school ties, and the system of *corporatisme* (membership in prestigious civil service corps). What changed, beginning in 1988, is that dirigiste or heroic policies formulated absent business input gave way to more everyday policies that resulted from a consensus between business and government on what was to be done.

The problem for France today is that, although this shift away from dirigisme in both policies and policymaking processes had initially been greeted with great enthusiasm, as France slid into recession in the early 1990s some, including business heads, began questioning the diminished role of the state in directing the economy. The difficulty for the state, however, is that the liberal policies of the recent past have ensured that it no longer has its traditional interventionist capability and, therefore, the state cannot effectively return to a more directive role. The European Union, moreover, now carefully scrutinizes any government attempts to intervene—particularly regarding subsidies to nationalized enterprise—at the same time that it has, for the most part, dashed French hopes for European level industrial policy to take the place of that given up at the national level. Finally, by the end of Mitterrand's second *septennat* (second seven-year term), even as the economy appeared to be pulling out of recession, other problems had added to the malaise. Not only had business heads come under increasing scrutiny on questions of misappropriation of company funds as well as involvement in illegal campaign financing, but also (and more importantly) their reputation as being "the best and the brightest" had come under increasing attack as the unemployment rate remained high and some enterprises suffered severe losses, despite large and repeated government investment.

President Jacques Chirac and the government led by Alain Juppé will therefore face a number of problems in their first years in office without the dirigiste policy instruments, financial resources, or policymaking freedom that enabled their predecessors to wield tremendous influence over business. But perhaps they will not need them.

The Changes in Policies Toward Business

Historically, the French state, supported by strong, cohesive bureaucratic institutions and a culture receptive to government leadership in the economy, has always played a key role in managing the economy and in owning and/or controlling business. Indeed, the *étatisme* (statism) involved here has generated its own vocabulary: *colbertisme*, indicating the first major state intervention by Colbert, and *neo-colbertisme*, its modern equivalent; dirigisme, first used positively to denote directive industrial policy in the Fourth and early Fifth Republics, now more negatively used to indicate excessive state intervention; and *volontarisme*, (voluntarism) the latest term in vogue among those who advocate a continued role for the state in industrial policy.

For all this interventionist history, however, there has also been a countercurrent of "liberalism,"[11] and periodic reactions against state interference in the market. Even in liberal times, however, the state continued to play a role. During the Third Republic in particular that role was as protector of industry, limiting competition with protective tariffs and controlling the market by business arrangement and political action.[12] By contrast, the role of promoter came to the fore after World War II, with modernization and an opening to international markets replacing the focus on protecting the domestic market.

From the post-war period up until the Mitterrand years, the state benefitted from ever expanding powers over industry, gaining policy instruments and public enterprises (either through acquisition or creation) that enabled it to control business more and more. And yet, simultaneously, ever since the signing of the Treaty of Rome in 1957, membership in the European Community, with its "liberal" bias, has acted as a major spur for French governments to move away from a state-directed economy to one with a greater emphasis on the market. This has been a gradual but ineluctable process, one in which each action in conformity with EC policy has, taken together with other exogenous factors, so undermined the effectiveness of the traditional set of policies that it literally forced governments to adopt new EC-inspired policies, which brought even greater market openness and a larger commitment to European integration. The conflict between the two competing strands of economic management policy, that is, of dirigisme and liberalism, came to a head in 1983, when the Socialist government, faced with a choice between abandoning major elements of its dirigiste policies or the European Community, decided in favor of the latter and, therefore, of liberalism. From that point on, the dirigisme that had its symbolic culmination in the Socialists' nationalization and restructuring program was in retreat, with deregulation and privatization the order of the day.

But while the disengagement of the state was carried out in heroic fashion by the Socialists in power from 1983 to 1986 and then by the neoliberal Right in power from 1986 to 1988, this disengagement subsequently became a more everyday affair.

From Dirigisme to Disengagement: Government Policies toward Business, 1981 to 1986

The beginning of the end of traditional state dirigisme in the post-war period began with the move away from France's traditional protectionism, as mandated by the European Community in the 1960s, along with the abandonment of a number of specific policy instruments such as preferential taxation and public procurement policies, non-tariff barriers and certain kinds of industrial subsidies.[13] These measures, which opened the domestic market to greater competition, taken together with a whole panoply of problems related to external economic constraints in the 1970s—such as the end of the fixed exchange-rate system that had enabled French governments to correct payment deficits through devaluation, the impact of the two oil crises, and increasing international competition—decreased the French government's ability to manage the economy.[14] These constraints undermined not only the French governments' traditional macroeconomic tools for controlling the economy (for example, the *encadrement du credit,* or the system for rationing credit), but also its microeconomic tools, such as the national plans that no longer accurately forecast economic trends and the industrial policies that no longer adequately sorted out the most appropriate industrial investments.[15] By Giscard's presidency, the *trente glorieuses* (thirty glorious years of economy prosperity) had ended, and with it faith in the state's economic leadership.

By the 1970s, moreover, the national champions that had been the focus of de Gaulle's industrial policies had become lame ducks, more interested in catering to protected home markets than competing in the international economy. And government policymakers were no help. The special relationship between planners and big business that had contributed to the strength of France's industrialization efforts in the Fourth and early Fifth Republics had become a weakness because it excluded not only the business associations that would have impeded modernization but also organized labor.[16]

Confronted in 1981 with the decreased competitiveness of French industry, the general slowdown in economic growth, and the relatively high unemployment rate, as well as the after-effects of the two oil crises and the worldwide economic climate, the Socialist government of Prime Minister Mauroy felt that the economy was in need of heroic measures and a revival of the traditional state dirigisme that had proven so successful in the past. Therefore, in direct opposition to Barre's neoliberalism, and instead of instituting austerity measures as most foreign governments were in the face of recessionary pressures, the government engaged in a high degree of market interventionism along with economically expansionist policies focused on investing in industry.[17] Specifically, the government instituted reflationary economic policies such as raising the minimum wage by 10 percent; increasing allowances to the elderly and the handicapped by 20 percent and those for family lodging by 50 percent; reducing the work week to 39 hours, with the extra hour remaining in workers' paychecks; adding a fifth week of paid vacation; allowing retirement at sixty; providing for the hiring of another 100,000 public employees; and establishing manpower training programs and various employment protection statutes. In addition, the government launched a costly, wide-scale nationalization program that left the state in possession of all but a few family-owned banks, 13 of the 20 largest firms in France, and a controlling share in many other French companies, that together provided the government with at least a foothold if not a full share in most sectors of the economy and control over 96 percent of deposits.[18] This was combined with a highly interventionist industrial policy containing a mandate to refinance and restructure the nationalized industries, including the chemicals industry, electronics, computers, and steel, as well as certain industries in the private sector such as machine tools, textiles, furniture, leather goods, and toys.[19] At the same time, however, the government also remained committed to European integration and intent on staying within the European Monetary System (EMS) that the Barre government had joined in 1979. Within a very short time, that commitment led to a crisis for the Mauroy government, whose expansive macroeconomic and expensive microeconomic policies were totally out of step with those of fellow European Community members.

French exceptionalism could not last long in an increasingly interdependent global economy and in an integrating Europe. By 1983, instead of the break with capitalism that the Socialists had promised in their economic projects from the 1940s until their victory in 1981 (although by the 1981 election campaign this break was primarily a campaign slogan, side by side with slogans promising to modernize capitalism and strengthen traditional values), the break was with Socialism.[20] Epitomizing this break was the shift in macroeconomic policy. The main question over which the Socialists agonized between June 1982 and March 1983 was whether to stay in the EMS, and thereby begin to reduce the budget deficit and deflate the economy, or whether to exit, and thereby sustain reflation by devaluing the franc and putting up protectionist barriers to imports in order to stabilize the trade deficit.[21] For some, only the discipline of the European Monetary System would permit France to retain its place in the global competition; for others, the only quick escape from the crisis was to get out from under the Community environment with its impossibly high interest rates.[22] With Mitterrand's decision to stay in, France had to reduce public spending, scale back aid to industry, in particular to the nationalized industries, and allow more bankruptcies. It also had to cut back on its social policies, since bringing down inflation necessarily took the place of bringing down unemployment rates.

Moreover, minus the resources that its inflationary policies had generated, the Socialist government was no longer able to stimulate industry through demand using its traditional industrial policy instruments. It therefore had to improve the competitiveness of French firms through more supply-side measures. This had actually started even before the great U-turn of 1983, in 1982 with the deindexation of salaries on prices, and the 1983 law on savings, which allowed the introduction of new debenture shares and investment certificates. With the decision to stay in the EMS and therefore to embrace European integration wholeheartedly, liberalization now anticipated European Community directives as much as followed them.

The liberalization accelerated under Prime Minister Fabius, who put an emphasis on profit and faith in the market. In 1984, the Socialists began putting through measures encouraging competition in the banking system, relaxing regulations in the financial markets, authorizing many new financial instruments, loosening controls over exchange rates, partially eliminating price controls, and reducing a variety of business taxes, including the *prélèvements obligatoires* (payroll taxes), and the tax on revenues. In the capital markets in particular, the Socialists established a second market in unlisted securities and a third in financial futures. Finally, in 1985 they even went so far as to consider a law on competition that, though never passed, would have reinforced anti-trust measures and loosened restrictions on competition. Moreover, public sector wages were held down and regulations affecting firms' ability to lay off workers loosened.

Business benefitted greatly from this liberalization of the economy. The opening of the markets under the Mauroy and Fabius governments enabled business to gain new non-governmental sources of financing—including stocks, money market funds, mutual funds, negotiable certificates of deposit emitted by banks, and treasury bills and negotiable treasury bonds emitted by companies—thus diminishing business' dependence upon government for subsidies and its vulnerability to government pressure. Equally importantly, however, liberalization also enabled business to reduce its dependence upon the banks. Whereas in 1978, business financing from non-banking sources came to only 30.7 percent of that from financial institutions, by 1985, it had jumped to 60.6 percent and by 1986 to 153.6 percent.[23] For the first time, as a result, the banks had some real competition, which forced them to become more competitive in their lending rates. Moreover, businesses themselves, able to finance investment out of retained earnings as a result of their improved performance and profitability, had to borrow less.

Thus, by the time they lost the elections to the neoliberal Right, the Socialists had reversed their macroeconomic policies completely, going from Keynesian expansionism to liberal austerity, and from dirigiste policies focused on expanding the purchasing power and social benefits of workers to liberal ones concentrating on promoting the productive power and investment of business. A similar reversal also occurred for the nationalized enterprises, although it was not quite as dramatic. The need of the nationalized industries for more capital at a time when the government could not spare any led the Socialists in 1984 to allow privatization informally through the illegal sale of subsidiaries and even earlier than this, in 1983, through the floating of non-voting shares and investment certificates. Simultaneously, the new realities of market competition led the government to again respect the traditional autonomy of public enterprise as early as spring 1983. By the time the neoliberal government came to power, many of the nationalized firms were profitable again and in need of new capital that only privatization could provide.

Dirigiste Disengagement: Government Policies toward Business, 1986 to 1988

The neoliberal Right's policies generally continued in the direction first charted by the Socialists. Like Fabius, Chirac's government focused first and foremost on bringing down inflation and the budget deficit, although it was even more supply-side in its approach to industry, cutting taxes rather than increasing financial aid to corporations. Moreover, the government decontrolled prices and created the Council on Competition. It also went further in the deregulation of securities, futures, and foreign exchange markets; in the reduction of payroll taxes, corporate taxes (by 37 billion francs over two years), and the business tax; in the ending of most price controls; and in the passage of the law on competition that replaced the two ordinances on competition of June 30, 1945 (along with approximately 30,000 rules that had grown up around them).[24]

On top of policies that simply extended those of their Socialist predecessors, the neoliberals introduced a number of entirely new policies. Most notably, they overhauled monetary policy as of January 1, 1987, by replacing the system of rationing bank credit, the *encadrement du crédit* (which they themselves had instituted in 1974 when they were known as conservatives) with a system in which the Banque de France would control the money supply by manipulating interest rates. They also liberalized controls on corporations' stock issues and passed the law on savings which facilitated leveraged management buyouts (LMBO) and employee stock ownership plans (ESOP) as well as encouraged employees to buy shares in the firms for which they worked (especially in the newly privatized ones). Moreover, they created what Balladur dubbed the *petit bang* (the little bang), which broke the 180 year monopoly of the sixty official French stockbrokers, replacing the old system with one in which the administrative tasks related to the running of the stockmarket are separated from the regulatory and oversight functions carried out by an elected council. This anticipated the scheduled end to the stockbrokers' monopoly way in advance of 1993, when the 12 member countries of the EC would be able to trade on the Paris Bourse and the six regional stock exchanges.

The neoliberals' privatization program—which involved selling off such symbols of state authority as the national television station, TF1, the industrial firm Saint-Gobain, and the bank Société Générale, and which was halted only as a result of the stock market crash in October 1987 with 40 percent of the 65 companies on the original list privatized—was the center-piece of their liberalization efforts.[25] It was designed to end the state interventionism that limited firms' flexibility of operation and politicized the appointment process for CEOs; to reduce the state's budgetary burdens while allowing the privatized enterprises new sources of funding; and to ensure greater recourse to the national and international financial markets by the privatized companies after their return to profitability. In addition, privatization was designed to enable France to meet the challenge of European integration by permitting firms to be as free as their European competitors for strategic purposes as well as by giving a boost to the newly opened French *bourse* (stock market).

For all this, however, neoliberal privatization was no paean to Thatcherian laissez faire, since the state tightly managed the process, choosing to whom to grant control of the companies to be privatized in order to ensure stability of French ownership and to protect against foreign takeover. In fact, while claiming to end state dirigisme and set up a "people's capitalism," the neoliberals were highly interventionist as they picked the *noyau dur* (hard core) of investors (including state-owned banks) to hold anywhere from 15 percent to 30 percent of the stock in the newly privatized firms; and they were not very populist since, although they ensured a vast increase in small, individual shareholders, they did not provide for their representation on the boards of directors. The result was in some sense a return to the "protected capitalism" of the cross-shareholdings of the past, but with one very important difference: the banks and insurance companies were involved for the first time, thus bringing French financial and industrial firms closer to the German model of industry-banking partnership and to a more dynamic capitalism.[26]

Thus, the heroic policies of the Left had been followed by heroic policies of the Right, in both cases with strong government initiatives that altered the landscape of French business and industrial policy. Subsequent governments were to continue this process, but with much less heroism. As of 1988, everyday policymaking substituted itself for the heroics that had come before, and the pace of liberalizing reforms only intensified even as the heroic rhetoric subsided.

Europe, moreover, was to become an increasingly important element in the economic equation. Although the impact of European integration had already been felt as of 1983 with regard to the macroeconomic sphere, the effects of the Single European Act of 1987 on the microeconomic sphere were yet to be felt. The public as a whole was generally unaware of the changes that were about to take place, and would remain so until the ratification of the Maastricht Treaty in 1991 incited a major public debate. French business, however, was already very much aware of the potential changes, and very much in support of them.

Everyday Disengagement: Government Policies toward Business, 1988 to 1995

For governments from 1988 onward, the direction of economic policy was set. Deregulation and privatization, either officially or unofficially, remained the order of the day, pushed by the imperatives of European integration as well as by the capital needs of firms. These had become everyday matters, however, as the heroic policies formulated without significant consultation gave way to ones that seemed to follow business much more than to lead it, and as the *coup par coup* (blow by blow) took the place of any coordinated industrial policy. In this period, there were to be no heroic economic projects, whether on the Left or the Right, and certainly no heroic industrial policies to make them a reality. Moreover, a new consensus on the appropriate role of the state in the economy was emerging, one in which liberal macroeconomic and microeconomic policies were to be accompanied by a certain amount of state interventionism, and in which business was to work together with government to formulate strategies for the future.[27]

In fact, heroic policymaking seemed a thing of the past, the heroism of those initial seven years during Mitterrand's first presidential mandate having exhausted the public and the politicians, as well as the font of ideas. The lesson, gleaned from seven years of *va-et-vient* (back and forth) on economic policies and ideology, is that through nationalization and privatization, through state control of business and proclaimed state non-intervention, as well as through government-sponsored industrial cooperation and government promotion of seemingly unbridled competition, business operates as business.[28] Moreover, the lesson from the neoliberals in particular, with their

Thatcherite and Reaganite policies of laissez-faire capitalism, was that the free market, with all that entailed in terms of unbridled competition and uncontrolled business, was not the panacea anticipated. When the public voted for the Socialists in 1988, they were voting for stability and an end to both left- and right-wing economic ideologies.

Between 1988 and 1995, all governments emphasized what Pierre Bérégovoy, minister of finance under Prime Ministers Rocard and Cresson and then prime minister himself, called "competitive disinflation," by giving priority to budget reduction and focusing on supply-side microeconomic policies. The Rocard government reduced corporate taxes by 10 billion francs in its 1989 budget, cut taxes on individuals by 5 billion francs and increased public spending in line with inflation, that is, by 4.5 percent. Moreover, it reduced taxes on revenue from savings and on consumption (by reducing the TVA [value-added tax], as mandated by the EC, despite Rocard's criticism of its "pauperizing" effect on the State). At the same time, however, Rocard spent a lot on a variety of measures for poor workers, on public employees' salaries, on the national education system, and on modernizing the public sector. Similarly, while Prime Minister Cresson continued with tight monetary policies, she sustained spending to modernize the public sector, although she reduced spending for the health sector and for the military. Her successor, Pierre Bérégovoy, in addition to keeping inflation down in order to maintain stable prices and keep a strong franc, reduced fiscal pressures on business yet again, in particular by reducing the rate of taxation on profits (it went from 50 percent in the early 1980s to 33 percent for 1993). Finally, the major preoccupation of right-wing Prime Minister Edouard Balladur, elected in March 1993, as of left- and right-wing governments before him, continued to be keeping the franc strong and inflation down, even if this meant keeping interest rates high and thereby slowing growth in an already recessionary economy.

For all this economic austerity, however, French industry, small- and medium-sized as well as large, still received major subsidies from the government. This was as true for Balladur's right-wing government, which pledged a record amount of subsidies to business, as it was for its left-wing predecessors. Moreover, the heroic industrial policy initiatives of the past were not entirely dead, they were simply unsuccessful, as with Cresson's attempt to create an electronics-to-nuclear energy superfirm combining Thomson and CEA (Commissariat à l'Energie Atomique). By contrast, most successful were those everyday industrial policies that produced changes in state ownership and control of French industry every bit as extensive as, although much less dramatic than, the heroic policies of nationalization and privatization.

Between 1988-91, the period during which official policy put a stop to privatization without reinstituting nationalization (the policy of the *ni-ni*, or neither privatization nor nationalization), the Rocard government responded in two ways to the demands of capital-starved public enterprises for much needed funds. First, it allowed them to trade shares in one another and thereby also circumvent the EC Commission's dim view of direct governmental subsidies by making them indirect. In so doing, Rocard's government actually succeeded in creating a new set of oversight arrangements for nationalized enterprises where, instead of direct governmental control, nationalized enterprises began to control one another through participation in their capital as shareholders, much like the privatized firms. Secondly, Rocard progressively weakened the policy of ni-ni unofficially through the sale of shares of nationalized enterprises in order to promote strategic alliances with or acquisitions of foreign companies (this began with Péchiney, which sold 25 percent of its shares on the market to finance its acquisition of American Can, and continued with Volvo's acquisition of a 25 percent stake in Renault) until there was nothing left to do but officially allow nationalized firms to be privatized up to 49 percent. This inaugurated the "post-ni-ni period" of 1991-93 under Cresson and Bérégovoy, which saw the Japanese computer maker NEC's acquisition of a 5 percent stake in Bull, the reduction of the state's direct stake in the oil company Total from 31.7 percent to 5 percent, the partial sales of Elf and of Crédit Local de France, as well as the further trading of shares among nationalized banks and industries.

With these two kinds of actions, Rocard began a process continued by Cresson and Bérégovoy that ensured that the bulk of large French industry, public as well as private, would become controlled by a *noyau dur* (hard core) of large corporate investors made up of banks and insurance companies as well as other industries.[29] In addition, because Socialist governments also changed the status of public enterprises in the service sector such as France Télécom and EDF (Electricité de France) in order to increase their autonomy of action, all nationalized enterprises found themselves increasingly in the position of private French enterprises—able to make their own strategic decisions with minimal government interference and able to turn to non-governmental sources for financing.

Finally, although Bérégovoy did not get his wish to substitute the *et-et* (and-and) for the ni-ni, that is, continued nationalization for public enterprises in monopolistic service sectors and total privatization for those in competitive sectors, the Balladur government of 1993-95 did it for him. Its ambitious privatization program, although very much an everyday affair by comparison with the heroic policy of 1986-88, nevertheless had by spring 1994 already succeeded in selling off such companies as BNP (Banque Nationale de Paris), Elf, Rhône-Poulenc, Hervet Bank, and UAP (Union Assurances de Paris), with AGF (Assurance générales de France) and Bull scheduled before the end of the year.

Thus, as much if not more was done to alter the structure of French capitalism during the era of everyday policymaking than in the previous, more heroic period. By progressively diminishing state ownership and weakening state control over the course of Mitterrand's second *septennat*, governments of the Left and Right succeeded in creating a truly mixed economy in which public and private financial and industrial concerns own and control one another following the German model of banking-industry partnership. Except, instead of resulting from sweeping, heroic governmental policies formulated without societal input, it came from a growing consensus between government and business about what should be done, and from government decisions that were for the most part the everyday responses to the needs of the moment rather than publicly proclaimed heroic policies.

By the early 1990s, in short, France's statist pattern of policymaking, distinctive for its heroism and at its apogee throughout the *trente glorieuses*, had lost not only the means to make heroic industrial policies but also the will, thus having become—at least in comparison to the past—an empty shell devoid of its traditional content. But much of this, at least in the early to mid-1980s, had been accomplished in heroic statist fashion.

Since the middle to late 1980s, moreover, heroic policymaking, if anything, was transferred to the supranational level, with governments focusing on the making of Europe, with the Maastricht Treaty, and on the making of European industrial policy. The results, however, were not always as anticipated. The French had expected that, by giving up control over national monetary policy, they could manage to control European and French macroeconomic policy from the EC, and thereby better handle the external constraints that had made the economic environment so unpredictable in the 1970s. Moreover, at the microeconomic level they had assumed that, by liberalizing and thereby giving up many of their industrial policy instruments at the national level, they could regain these and more at the European level by creating an interventionist European industrial policy.

At first, at least, the French were not wrong. As long as the world economy was booming, everyone profited (except the unemployed) from an integrated economic system and the tight monetary policies. However, as the world slid into recession, led by the United States, French economic growth began to slow and some opinion leaders began to question the politics of the strong franc to which governments remained faithful, since this meant slowing economic growth and doing little to reduce unemployment. Similarly, the hopes for European level industrial policy, fueled by the early to mid-1980s EC history of programs such as Esprit, Brite, Euram, Race, Eureka, and Jessi,[30] were disappointed, particularly in terms of initiatives in the high technology area such as HDTV (high definition television). Finally, the French saw themselves disadvantaged with regard to bureaucratic politics at the level of the European Commission, by what they felt was an "Anglo-Saxon" bias when it came to decisions on mergers and on state grants to nationalized enterprises by the Competition Directorate-General. (In fact, the French suffered from only one major setback with regard to proposed mergers—the de Havilland Decision of 1991—and from minimal interference in the case of state subsidies to nationalized enterprises such as Bull, Renault, and Air France).[31]

For all this, however, the French state remains, continuing to influence business indirectly, not only through its more supply-side macroeconomic policies and microeconomic incentives, but also through personalities. The state's colonization of business by way of state-trained, former civil servants at the head of major French banks and industries, whether public or private, means that there remains a single interpenetrating elite setting the course of the French economy.[32] As a result, the retreat of the state in response to deregulation, privatization, and European integration has not brought the end of state influence over business, only a different and perhaps more modern kind of influence—to match the internationalization of French business itself. And all of this has spelled great changes in the traditional statist process of policymaking as reflected in the relations between ministry and industry.

The Changes in Industrial Policymaking Processes

In the industrial policymaking process, although the state often appears to dominate, business usually manages to have its way. Generally, this has meant that heroic policies formulated without business input have been altered in the implementation, with government accommodating or even being coopted by business, and with only the occasional confrontation. While in the 1960s Andrew Shonfield saw the national planning relationship as constituting almost a "conspiracy to plan" between ministry and industry,[33] in the 1970s Charles Lindblom explained that same relationship as "in some part even an explicit exchange of favors,"[34] and by the 1980s Jack Hayward could argue that industrial policy, which had replaced planning as the preferred governmental tool, "frequently amounts to an industrialists' policy."[35] In fact, even at the height of state interventionism, with the restructuring of the newly nationalized industries, there was much less confrontation than might have been expected, mainly because government capitulated to industry demands or, when it did not, sweetened the deal with promises of capital grants or loans.[36]

There are a variety of reasons for this particular business-government relationship. Most important for the process itself is France's administrative model of policy implementation, which allows civil servants tremendous discretion in applying the rules—so much so that exceptions are granted as often as not. In de Tocqueville's oft-repeated phrase, the rules are rigid but the application flexible. This is clearly in contrast to regulatory models of implementation such as those of the United States and the European Union, where exceptions are not tolerated.[37] But even when civil servants are unwilling to grant exceptions, business often triumphs anyway, generally because it is able to take advantage of interministerial rivalries by pitting one ministry against another or by going up the ministerial hierarchy, appealing to higher officials within a ministry and even the prime minister or the president for an arbitration.

This has been as true for the nationalized enterprises as it has been for private firms. Despite the formal powers ministry officials have over nationalized enterprise through their *tutelle* (oversight function), through their ability to nominate and revoke the CEO, and through the state-industry planning contracts, public sector heads have nevertheless managed to maintain their independence and to benefit from a tradition of autonomy that has enabled them to run their firms and set overall strategies with a minimum of interference from the state.[38] This results from a large variety of factors, including the CEOs' own personal political power; their individual relationships with ministry officials based on shared elite state education, membership in the *grands corps* (prestigious civil service corps) and ministerial cabinet experience;[39] their collective influence as members of the grands corps; their role as protectors of the national interest;[40] and the inability of the ministries to exercise control through the planning contracts. In fact, the planning contracts that were intended to balance out public enterprises' autonomy by ensuring their accountability were, for the most part, little more than gentlemen's agreements, generally consecrating public enterprises' own decisions.[41]

Finally, adding to the advantages of business in recent years has been European integration. The primacy of the EU in policy formulation has decreased the independence of French government, which no longer has the authority to make policy unilaterally, and increased the independence of business, which now looks as much to Europe as to the nation-state for policymaking.

Planning and Industrial Policymaking Processes Prior to 1981

During the post-war period, for all the talk of dirigisme and extreme state interventionism, the relationship between business and government was essentially cooperative, although over time mutual accommodation began to look more like cooptation, as governments led less and the initiative often shifted to business. When national planning was in its heyday from the mid-1940s to the early 1960s, with policies formulated in formal consultation with business, implementation was more bound up with the formulation process, as business agreed in planning sessions to the goals, plans, and policies initiated and implemented by civil servants. This process, as Shonfield saw it, involved "an act of voluntary collusion by senior civil servants and senior managers of big business," bypassing politicians and organized labor. Business benefitted greatly from the resulting public investments while the planners controlled the content of the plan and ensured business' "voluntary" compliance[42] through the institutional mechanisms at their disposal, including positive measures such as subsidies, credit, and so forth, and negative ones, such as price controls, regulation, and taxation.[43]

As planning became less effective, more ambitious, and more politicized from the mid-1960s on, however, government led less, and accommodation began to look more and more like cooptation. This was especially the case with the Sixth Plan, when the CNPF (Conseil National du Patronat Français), the national confederation of France's major businesses, took the initiative, so much so that the government which followed its recommendations was left with the appearance of having been captured by industry, such that *l'impératif industriel* (the industrial imperative) seemed to have become *l'impératif des industriels* (the imperative of industrialists).[44] It was also true in the case of sectoral planning for the steel industry, where the relationship between the industry's trade association and government was akin to a "corporatist-style collusion" to the benefit of the industry, given that government poured in increasing amounts of money without imposing sufficient constraints or exercising adequate oversight over the declining industry.[45]

In the case of the oil industry, cooptation also became the rule, but here the results were not at all disastrous. The oil industry prospered even though state elites became the "ideological captives of the private sector,"[46] because the oil companies, in some sense, dictated state policies as a result of their greater expertise.[47] There were, however, also instances of accommodation, when top officials allowed Elf to invest in a United States petrochemical firm only if that company opened a branch in France;[48] and there was confrontation, such as the repeated clashes from 1978 to 1981 between the CEO of Elf and the minister of industry, although the government generally capitulated in the end.

Cooptation to this degree, however, was not necessary for other sectors of industry, whether public or private, to have their way. For private firms such as Thomson and CGE (Compagnie Générale d'Electricité), the planning contracts ensured that, while the State took the technical and industrial risks, the enterprises carried out the industrial projects and disposed liberally of the resulting profits.[49] For the automobile industry, too, sectoral policies essentially followed the desires of the companies. As long as companies did not need state funds, they could basically do what they wanted, and CEOs fought hard to maintain this.[50] Such freedom from interference was harder for monopolistic public firms in the transportation sector, such as Air France, which managed to resist many government demands on technical grounds but could not avoid the move to the Charles de Gaulle airport; and the SNCF, the national railway, which, although it mostly had its way, suffered lengthy delays on approval of its plans for the TGV (trains à grande vitesse).

The politics of accommodation and cooptation were not the rule for all industries, however, especially for firms in less concentrated sectors of industry during times of economic downturn. The case of the textile industry is one in which the kind of relationship characteristic of heavy manufacturing developed late and was not very successful.[51] This was equally true for the machine-tool industry as well as for the computer industry. The Plan Calcul, which involved the expenditure of vast amounts of money in an effort to create a national champion in computers to match the national champions in other sectors, proved a disaster. Industrial success went hand in hand with relative industry independence from government interference only with the national champions that were already well-established. But with the national champions, government policymakers had difficulty exerting control, having to subsidize generously in order to ensure their participation in the *grands projets,* unable to exert pressure over them by going to a rival, and without any leverage by virtue of their size and therefore the numbers of jobs they controlled.[52]

The state's sectoral plans and policies, in short, increasingly followed, rather than led, big business. Elie Cohen and Michael Bauer, in summarizing the relationship between state and industry, differentiate between three kinds of relationships, none of which suggests that government is very strong. In the face of powerful industrial firms such as Thomson, the firm even if nationalized, imposes its own strategy on the government. However, even where the firm is in a weakened position through bankruptcy, the government does not manage to take a successful leadership role: its attempts to create powerful industries through mergers among weak firms, as in the machine-tools industry, invariably fail. Finally, although the government may have great successes in sectors where no powerful industrial firms existed, such as its initiatives in oil, nuclear, aerospace, and armaments, these successes only lead to a reversion to the first instance, where the newly powerful firm can exert its influence over the government.[53] If an industry is viable, in other words, it controls itself; if it is not, nothing government does will alter that. This was as true after the 1981 nationalization of many major industries as it was before.

Industrial Policymaking through Nationalization and Restructuring

With the extensive nationalization of industry under the Socialists, heroic policymaking returned full force. The policy was formulated by an extremely restricted group of Socialist members of the government and close advisors and implemented without significant outside input. The political parties as such had no direct role in the formulation process; and Parliament, although an integral part of the process, also had little real impact on the policy, which it passed with great speed despite a good deal of debate.

The restructuring policies as carried out by the ministries, by contrast, although often equally heroic in formulation (some CEOs learned of the plans for the restructuring of their companies from the newspapers), in implementation responded to the politics of accommodation and cooptation. There was only the occasional confrontation (for example, the resignation of the CEO of Rhône-Poulenc in protest of Minister of Industry Jean-Pierre Chevènement's proposed restructuring of the chemicals industry). Moreover, almost immediately after that incident, with the replacement of Chevènement by Laurent Fabius, the Ministry of Industry restored its traditional respect for the autonomy of public enterprises, leaving most internal management decisions up to the firms themselves and relying on negotiated contracts between the state and the public enterprises regarding the firm's goals and objectives and the state's commitments.

During the restructuring process, the state exercised varying degrees of control while it left internal decisions up to the firm. Thus, despite a high degree of interventionism with a declining industry such as steel, where the government had mandated extensive restructuring, mutual accommodation was at play. By contrast, a similar degree of interventionism in the case of Saint-Gobain, where the government's industrial policy promoting the vertical integration of firms was at issue, led to confrontation over the sale of Olivetti shares. Even here, however, although the Ministry of Industry interfered with Saint-Gobain's strategic autonomy, it did not interfere with the company's managerial independence. As Jean-Louis Beffa, CEO of Saint-Gobain after Fauroux noted, "It was management, as with any other shareholder, that proposed the strategy.... To be perfectly frank, the state let us do what we wanted at the point at which we did not ask for money." In fact, nationalization as a whole, he insisted, did not change much of anything: "It was a parenthesis. It allowed Saint-Gobain to continue with its *politique* (policy) that has gone on for over 300 years."[54]

The chemicals industry experienced a similar set of interactions. Although even more dramatic confrontations occurred with the restructuring policy, with the resignation of the CEO of Rhône-Poulenc and the non-reappointment of the CEO of Elf, in general accommodation characterized the ministry-industry relationship. The negotiations among the various industrial groups involved dragged on, until Chevènement preempted everything when he announced his "devolution policy." This, however, led to a renewed round of discussions, which then again dragged on until Fabius became minister of industry—with the final resolution occurring in June 1983 to the satisfaction of most of the industrialists involved, with all firms other than CDF-Chimie in a position to turn themselves around, and with all expected to except CDF-Chimie.[55]

Thus, even in one of the most apparently interventionist of restructurings, the desires of most firms were accommodated. In all other ways, moreover, cooptation was the rule. Thus, in the case of Rhône-Poulenc, because the company was in relatively good financial shape, making its money in the international market, the government had an essentially hands-off policy, leaving it with basic control over its own planning, restructuring, and social policies both before and after nationalization.[56]

In the case of other, healthier sectors that were less out of line with government industrial policy, ministries were less interventionist, and tended to respond to the desires of the industry. In the case of CGE, the telecommunications manufacturing giant (later Alcatel-Alshtom), in fact, CEO Georges Pébereau noted that during the period of nationalization, "the state fulfilled all of its obligations as a shareholder and I never was subjected to the least constraint, in any domain, which was not the normal one of any shareholder."[57] Moreover, he was totally free to decide to whom to sell companies or which to buy and at what price, insisting that he would "not have stayed one lone minute if it had been otherwise." The state in its role as major shareholder could have put him in a minority on the board of directors but, "If at any given moment I was in disagreement with my shareholder, I asked to be received by the Minister himself and, on leaving, either we were in agreement or I was revoked."[58]

The electronics industry was similarly subject to relatively little unwelcome interventionism, with the government creating incentives for development primarily to encourage private as well as public enterprises to invest in certain areas, for example, integrated circuits.[59] Thomson itself benefitted the most from restructurings that left some firms in other industries unhappy. For example, when Saint Gobain was forced to give up one of its operational areas to Thomson, the former saw the state as highly dirigiste, while the latter saw it, rather, as an arbiter in the restructuring process.[60] Similarly, Bull was less than pleased when it was forced to take over one of Thomson's troubled subsidiaries. Bull, in fact, got the raw end of most deals, as the company also had to acquire some of CGE's losing operations, all of which explains former CEO Francis Lorentz's insistence that the first two years of the Socialists' tenure in office were "madness."[61]

Most firms, in short, but certainly not all, got their way in the implementation of industrial policies even at times of great interventionism. This should help explain why CEOs of major nationalized firms, although eager for denationalization as a way of increasing their flexibility and their access to capital investment, did not attack state control unduly. Moreover, in the Socialist government's granting of permission to sell non-voting shares and in its turning a blind eye to the illegal sale of subsidiaries, the government not only let firms have their way, it effectively undermined its own policy of nationalization, thus paving the way for the privatizations of the neoliberal government.

Only firms in the non-competitive sector did not, for the most part, find accommodation, either under the Socialists or the neoliberals who followed them. The pharmaceutical companies, for example, suffered from the fragmentation of state action: prices were kept artificially low because the Ministry of Social Affairs, which was more interested in the physical health of citizens, had tended to prevail over the Ministry of Industry, which was interested in the economic health of companies, primarily because the Ministry of Finance, most interested in the macroeconomic health of the country, had tended to support the former over the latter.[62] For similar reasons, moreover, the Ministry of Finance subjected the electric utility, EDF, to a *contrôle tatillon*, ("nit-picking" control), which kept its price rises well below the amount agreed upon in the planning contract, which was necessary for it to engage in adequate industrial investment.

Industrial Policymaking Processes through Privatization and Deregulation

Privatization under the neoliberal government of 1986 to 1988 was as heroic an affair as nationalization and restructuring. Its major outlines were sketched out even before the Right took office: Parliament played less of a role than in the case of the Socialists, and there was no consultation on the choice of companies to privatize, although often the general inclinations of industry were followed. The decisions on privatization were entirely those of Minister of Finance Edouard Balladur, with no outsiders involved, including the CEOs of the soon-to-be privatized firms—even if management's views on privatization sometimes played a role (for example, Crédit Agricole was privatized, despite opposition; Dassault was not, despite great interest).

Moreover, only in a few instances did top management play a major role in the choice of the hard-core of investors (for example, CGE and Paribas). Most CEOs did, however, suggest names in response to the Ministry's query as to their special preferences for certain companies as related to their international, industrial, or financial plans.[63] When they had serious objections to any one potential hard core member, however, this was taken into account.

For the most part, then, privatization was a heroic affair which, although it involved minimal consultation on the choice of firms to be privatized and somewhat more consideration on the hard-core memberships, generally satisfied the participants with a few exceptions, and was therefore not seen as highly dirigiste. Policies with regard to mergers and acquisitions, by contrast, were occasionally much more interventionist.

Although the government was generally liberal regarding competition policy, it did not hesitate to intervene where it deemed necessary. Although Chirac did nothing with certain big mergers and acquisitions in 1987—for example, the *épousaille* (marriage) of BSN and Fiat, the merger of Moët-Hennessy and Louis Vuitton, the failed takeover attempt by Chargeurs on Textiles Prouvost, and the development through various takeovers of the consulting giant Cap Gemini Sogeti—he actively encouraged the takeover of Générale Occidentale by the privatized CGE. Similarly, although Minister of Industry Madelin agreed to Thomson's acquisition of the American firm RCA and the merger of its electronics operations with the Italian public enterprise SGS, he actively tried to exclude John Kila, placed by Fabius as shareholder and CEO of the paper company Chapelle Darblay, and replace him with the French group Pinault. Finally, at the same time that, in the interest of competition, Minister of Transportation Douffiagues allowed the charter airline UTA to compete with Air France on certain routes, he forbade UTA to land in New York under pressure from the CEO of Air France, Jacques Friedmann (a good friend of Chirac).[64]

Ministry-Industry Relations through the Periods of Neither Nationalization Nor Privatization, Partial Privatization, and Renewed Privatization

As of 1988, with the shift from heroic to everyday policymaking, ministry-industry interactions became almost entirely relations of accommodation and cooptation. Succeeding governments for the most part either lacked the will or the means to impose decisions on business that looked less to the government for guidance—as firms became increasingly subject to the imperatives of world competition, the constraints of the market, and the demands of technological advancement—or for support, as alternative sources of financing have grown. Most government actions came from the proposals of business, whether they involved the growing intermixing of the economy through the trading of shares in nationalized enterprises as under Rocard, through the trading of shares between nationalized and private firms under Cresson and Bérégovoy, or through the outright privatization of nationalized enterprises under Balladur. There were, nevertheless, a certain number of instances where governments intervened, often over objections from business.

With the return of the Socialists to power, the industries' only problems with the ministries involved their seeking to sell subsidiaries in strategic areas. Otherwise, the state was exceedingly accommodating, in particular by allowing for the trading of shares in nationalized companies. This is where formulation and implementation blur, as the politics of accommodation became the everyday policies of governments without many heroic initiatives. But although business for the most part initiated, it did not always entirely get its way. Accommodation, rather than cooptation, was often the operative concept. The Volvo-Renault alliance is a case in point. As the CEO Louis Schweitzer explained, the initiative came from the company, which negotiated a preliminary deal with Volvo to turn Renault into a holding company, with the operational units as subsidiaries jointly controlled by Volvo. This, however, was vetoed by President Mitterrand, who nevertheless accepted Volvo's acquisition of a 25 percent stake in Renault.[65]

Under Rocard, in fact, the relationship between ministry and industry was highly cooperative, leading to much accommodation and few confrontations. Even in the case of the restructuring of the chemical and nuclear industries, although the initiative came from the government's concern that there was too much competition, the process was characterized by lengthy consultation—which only partially succeeded.[66] By contrast, the restructuring failed entirely in the nuclear industry in the case of Framatome, where responsibility for the case was ultimately shifted from the minister of industry to the minister of finance.

Under Cresson, the government was, in certain instances, more interventionist, but again industry seemed to win out. In two major cases where company-proposed alliances had received the go ahead from the Rocard government (Bull's alliance with the Japanese NEC and its alliance with the American IBM), Cresson threatened to veto them, but ultimately capitulated in exchange for industry concessions.

Which companies were subject to more government pressure depended, as in the past, upon the strategic importance of the industry as well as on questions of personality and history. Thus, numbers of industries had no problem making alliances with foreign companies, such as Elf with Sterling drug (the pharmaceutical subsidiary of Kodak), or Roussel-Uclaf with the Japanese Ajinomoto; and others such as Pechiney, Rhône-Poulenc, and

Atochem were given relative liberty in management and alliance as long as public funds were not requested. Other firms, however, in nuclear energy, computers, and electronics, were subject to a significant amount of interventionism, for example, on the agreement between Framatome and KWU (the nuclear subsidiary of Siemens) to export and construct a 1000 megawatt reactor.[67]

The Cresson government, in short, precipitated many more confrontations than the previous government, although ultimately its impact was not very different. Moreover, such confrontations occurred not only in the case of alliances with foreign firms, but also in the trading of shares among nationalized enterprises. What under Rocard had been a sometimes reluctant response to company initiatives was now actively encouraged by the government, and occasionally imposed. For example, although the BNP and Crédit Lyonnais insisted publicly that their acquisition of 10 percent stakes in Air France and Usinor-Sacilor respectively were done under their own initiative, privately BNP acknowledged that it had only agreed to the Air France deal in return for government help with raising the bank's capital the previous year—and BNP did refuse to exercise its option to acquire shares in Usinor-Sacilor.[68] Moreover, although the head of France Télécom insisted that its acquisition of shares in the Banque Hervet represented an opportunity for the company rather than an instance of state dirigisme, he made certain subsequently to institute state-industry planning contracts that protected France Télécom from such "opportunities" in the future.[69] In fact, the planning contract signed in November 1991, in which France Télécom agreed to cut its debt, modernize its network, and expand abroad, proved timely, since the contract helped protect Télécom from the Cresson government's pressure soon thereafter to increase its share in Bull from the 17 percent stake it had already acquired.

Perhaps the most newsworthy of such cases was the proposed merger of Thomson and CEA into a superfirm. Here, CEA tended to resist, since while Thomson stood to gain a lot in terms of financial help, CEA stood to lose financial reserves that it had set aside to cover the costs of dismantling nuclear installations. Once the Bérégovoy government came to power, the deal fell through. CEA-Industrie took only a minority interest in the company, which meant that Thomson had to go elsewhere to find more capital.

This was not the end however of the "Meccano Industriel," as the French call this kind of operation. Although the Bérégovoy government essentially encouraged continued trading of shares without such dramatic flights of "voluntarism," the Balladur government came up with a new suggestion involving firm mergers for reinvigorating Thomson. In other ways, too, the Balladur government took a more interventionist role, especially with regard to the nationalized industries in trouble. The CEOs of both Bull and Air France were let go very quickly; in the case of the CEO of Air France, this was only after the minister of transportation, who had requested a radical restructuring program, forced the withdrawal of the plan in response to employee strikes.

Other than in these two cases, however, the Balladur government seemed to be following the same pattern as its immediate predecessors with regard to respecting the traditional autonomy of public enterprise. Once a new CEO was appointed who had the confidence of the government, the hands-off policy returned. Privatization, moreover, would only serve to consecrate that autonomy.

The actual process of privatization in the Balladur government reflected the change in policymaking processes. It was more of an everyday affair than privatization in the Chirac government, and the work of more individuals. There was a consensus, in the first place, about the appropriateness of privatization and about how it was carried out. Secondly, there was a great deal more consultation with the CEOs about which firms were ready, and about which shareholders should be part of the noyau dur. Pragmatism essentially determined the choice of companies to be privatized. All companies that represented potential problems were delayed or eliminated from the list: Thomson because of Ministry of Defense opposition; the three insurance companies because of profitability and alliance issues. Moreover, the government was not about to privatize Renault since "to privatize Renault in the current state of affairs would result in giving the control to the Swedish manufacturer."[70] This, no doubt, contributed to the Swedes' ultimate decision to pull out of the planned merger.

Thus, Balladur's government was no more dirigiste than previous governments since 1988. And for good reason, since it did not have the capability to be dirigiste any more than those governments, given governmental policies favoring privatization, deregulation, and Europeanization that progressively diminished the state's ability to intervene. First, privatization has diminished the number of companies subject to close ministry scrutiny. Second, deregulation has stripped governments of the policy instruments that they had used in the past to gain business compliance with their policies, in particular price and exchange controls, competition policy, and sectoral rules governing business. Third, financial deregulation has opened up new, non-governmental sources of financing and decreased governmental control over the allocation of credit at the same time that austerity budgets have deprived governments of the money that they traditionally used to influence business. Finally, the new structure of capital ownership and control, within which public and private industrial and financial concerns own and control one another, has left ministries with much less direct influence over industry. In fact, even with regard to the ministries' *tutelle* (oversight) over the nationalized enterprises, opportunities for confrontation have diminished significantly, and cooptation tends to be the order of the day. Only when a firm is losing money, and therefore must go to the government for capital grants, does accommodation or even confrontation occur, as in the cases with Bull and Air France. But even here, government intervention tends to limit itself to the appointment of a new CEO.

In short, government policies through the Mitterrand years have reduced current and future governments' ability to influence business, not only because government no longer has the regulatory or financial tools to "persuade" business to do as it wishes, but also because business needs government guidance or support less because of the new competitive environment and the opening up of non-governmental sources of financing. The outcome is a loosening of the ties that bind business to government, and this has only increased as a result of European integration.

The Impact of European Integration

The primacy of the European Union in policy formulation, which has become more and more significant as the Single European Act was followed by the Maastricht Treaty, means that French governments have lost their traditional independence of decision-making. Decisions that were formulated unilaterally in the past are now made at the EU level in consultation with member states. Moreover, societal interests that were always excluded from the policy formulation process at the national level find that they have access at the EU level. Big businesses in particular now find themselves the privileged interlocutors of the European Union Commission, and partners rather than supplicants of French ministries in the lobbying efforts of the nation. As a result, businesses have gone from a system in which they had their say primarily at the implementation stage to one in which they also have input at the formulation stage when it comes to European regulations and directives.[71]

Business heads themselves recognize these changes, and have come to see Brussels as almost as important as Paris for policymaking, especially since Paris no longer has veto power over decisions made in Brussels (with the qualified majority rule).[72] Moreover, business is expected by Brussels to make its views heard directly, as well as through the intermediary of the French mission. In consequence, lobbying activities that are still regarded as illegitimate by French authorities at the national level are actually encouraged by them when it involves the EU.[73] One need only make note of the countless exhortations in the late 1980s and early 1990s by French officials to French business to, as Edith Cresson put it when she was minister of european affairs: *Agir pour ne pas subir,* (act so as not to be acted upon.)[74] And business has responded, organizing itself to lobby in Brussels not only as charter members of European business associations such as UNICE, the European Employers' Federation, and various European groupings of national umbrella organizations, but also as members of national associations, or even as individual firms.[75] On their own, moreover, French CEOs also have direct, albeit informal, impact through face-to-face meetings with European commissioners. In short, whether as part of European business associations, national associations, or as individual firms, French business plays a role not only in influencing policy, but also, in some instances, initiating it, since European business often participates with the European Commission in seeking to impose a policy on reluctant governments.

French business' access to the policy formulation process has further increased its independence from the national government, since business is now as much a partner with national ministries in efforts to influence the EU as it is a supplicant of national ministries to influence the EU for it. Moreover, as a partner in the EU lobbying effort, government tends to see business more as the defender of the interests of the French nation than as a lobby that might have its own interests at heart, and not those of France in particular or Europe at large. It is as if the old notion attached to public enterprise—in which public enterprise was seen to act as a catalyst for social reforms and industrial innovation, leading the nation forward—has been generalized to all big French businesses, despite the fact that increasing numbers are private or on the road toward privatization, and that their goals, whether public or private, are profitability above all.

This sense that however independent business is, it still serves the national interest, pervades not only interaction related to European policy formulation, but also continues to characterize the entire French business-government relationship. The only problem, however, is that it has become increasingly one-sided, as government gives and business takes. As Elie Cohen explains it, the "attributes of sovereignty" that French business gained in the past from its relationship with government remain, leaving unchallenged the idea that French business operates in the national interest through the creation of French jobs and factories and through the trade balance, and that in exchange the state owes it attention, assistance, and protection.[76]

Business independence, in short, has been ensured not only by changes in the policymaking processes but also by the conviction that business acts in the public interest. And this can only have been enhanced by the fact that at the head of the major business firms, as often as not, are individuals whose education and career paths have been state-centered. This means that in many cases the very civil servants who helped shape the policies formulated by French governments are the same CEOs who are now helping shape the policies formulated by French governments in conjunction with their European partners (for example, the current head of Renault was in Delors' cabinet, the former number two at the BNP was formerly director of the Treasury, and the current head of Aerospatiale was director-general of industry).

Conclusion

Over the course of the Mitterrand years, the heroic policies of the past have for the most part given way to more everyday ones as governments, absent their traditional interventionist policy instruments, could no longer command, and therefore consulted a great deal more. Although relations between business and government are still close, the ties that bound them inextricably to one another throughout the post–war period, first through planning and then industrial policies, have been loosened. Ministries have become partners rather than leaders of industry, while industries that used to look almost exclusively to the state for guidance and resources now turn more to one another for strategic advice and equity investment, and to the enlarged stockmarket for funds. Even the nationalized enterprises have become mostly autonomous, as the state-industry planning contracts have become more vague and less binding, and as the trading of shares among nationalized enterprises has substituted an indirect system of state oversight for the more direct state *tutelle*. Finally, the European Union has only served to increase business independence by increasing business' access to policymaking.

This is not to suggest, however, that France is no longer statist in its pattern of policymaking. Governments have not stopped seeking to guide business, albeit in indirect ways, more in keeping with the new international economic environment and the dictates of the European Union. They as always play a primary role in deciding the direction of economic growth and the shape and organization of economic activity, even as they engineer the retreat of the state. And business interests still get their way, not only as in the past by exploiting intra- and inter-ministerial rivalries or trading on personal relationships, with the politics of accommodation and cooptation the norm, but now also through lobbying at the EU level.

Although most have welcomed these changes in business-government relations, not all remain convinced that the changes have been entirely positive, given recent history. By the last couple of years of Mitterrand's second seven-year term, as France suffered from prolonged economic recession while European integration appeared stalled, the demise of heroic policymaking no longer occasioned the same sense of relief as in 1988, when the economy was flourishing. Although the French would not necessarily have desired a return to the ideologically inspired heroism of the recent past, they nevertheless felt a sense of loss for what that heroism had represented in terms of forceful leaders with clear plans of action and political certainties about what was to be done to resolve French economic problems. This was expressed in a SOFRES survey just preceding the April 1995 elections, in which 64 percent of respondents wished for "a real leader who will bring back order and command" (by contrast with the 1981 survey results which emphasized promoting political and social change or those of 1988 which preferred maintaining established rights and consensus).[77] What is more, 67 percent recommended that the state intervene more in the economic life of the country (although, as to be expected, respondents on the Left were more interested in state intervention, at 74 percent, than those on the Right, at 61 percent). European integration and trade liberalization, interestingly enough, were not connected to this sense of loss: 63 percent of respondents actually called for an acceleration of integration (versus 25 percent against—significant in view of the nearly even split in the Maastricht vote), while 69 percent insisted on the continued acceptance of free-trade (versus 21 percent against).[78]

The sense of loss manifested itself in the increasing disillusionment with government officials who appeared unresponsive to citizen desires, incapable of solving the problems that the public cared about the most (for example, high unemployment), and increasingly corrupt, given the scandals related to corrupt election financing, insider trading, misuse of pubic funds, and the distribution of tainted blood.[79] The issue of corruption in particular has generated a crisis of confidence in the political class and in the integrity of the French political process more generally. The corruption first manifested itself in the scandals involving top Socialists: whether the tainted blood affair in which top ministers including Prime Minister Fabius were accused of unnecessarily allowing hemophiliacs to be infected with the HIV virus by delaying on ensuring the safety of the French blood supply in order to allow a French product to come to market; the corrupt election financing scandals that began in the 1980s with a number of scandals concerning kickbacks from construction contracts awarded in Socialist-controlled regions that found their way into party coffers and which, by the time it was over, had led to the trial and conviction in March 1995 of Socialist Party chairman, Henri Emmanuelli, and 16 other defendants for illegal party financing practices between 1988 and 1991 (Emmanuelli received a two year suspended sentence); or the game-fixing involving the football team owned by Socialist politician and entrepreneur Bernard Tapie, which left him facing 18 months in prison in 1995. The Right, however, has not been spared either. Three ministers in Balladur's government had to resign in 1994, implicated in scandals involving illegal election financing, as in the case of Foreign Aid Minister Michel Roussin, who was accused of syphoning money for the party from the Paris-region public housing authority; fraud and misuse of public funds, as in the case of former mayor of Grenoble Alain Carignon, who went to jail for this; and abuse of public trust, as in the case of Minister of Industry Gérard Longuet, who accepted favors from private building societies. It is telling that in the April 1995 SOFRES survey, 62 percent of respondents agreed that most political leaders were corrupt (versus 31 percent who disagreed).[80]

Lately, this crisis has even extended to business heads. Recent scandals affecting CEOs involve bad business decisions, as in the case of Jean-Yves Habérer's overly ambitious merger and acquisition program for the Crédit Lyonnais, which led to losses of 7 billion francs in 1993 and 12 billion in 1994; misuse of company funds and fraud, as in the case of Pierre Suard of Alcatel Alsthom, under investigation for over a year on such charges as billing home remodeling work to the company, involvement in a scheme to overcharge France Télécom by more than 100 million francs, and illegal channeling of upwards of 20 million francs to political parties before he was replaced as CEO in April 1995; or underhanded business deals, as in the case of the acquisition of two Belgian companies by the CEO of Schneider,

Didier Pineau Valencienne, which led to his brief detention in a Belgian jail. All together, these scandals suggest that public trust for business may also be hard to maintain. Because such scandals raise questions about business heads' probity and leadership capability, they undermine the legitimacy of business, thus adding to the overall crisis of leadership. If the scandals continue along with high unemployment rates, and if the economy does not have a full recovery from recession soon, then the end of traditional state dirigisme, although a boon in all sorts of ways, will itself represent yet another source of malaise for France and a major challenge for President Chirac and the Juppé government.

The answer to this malaise or to France's economic problems, however, cannot be a return to dirigisme. As events during the Juppé government's first year in office attest, although the dirigiste reflex has not disappeared the government's dirigiste ability to manage the economy has. Initially, it looked as if the new government had recognized that dirigisme was truly dead and had abjured dirigiste policymaking processes along with the heroic policies of the past in order to rely, instead, on consensus-building for everyday politics. This was epitomized by Prime Minister Juppé's firing of Finance Minister Alain Madelin in August 1995 because he advocated major cuts in social spending without prior consultation. But a mere three months later, the government demonstrated that it lacked policy autonomy, as the pressures of European Monetary Union forced it to renege on one of its main campaign promises and to raise taxes rather than lower them. It also demonstrated that the lesson learned from the changing relationship between business and government, in which everyday policymaking had replaced the heroism of the past, for the most part, had not carried over to the labor and social policy arena. The government's failure to seek some sort of consensus or consultation before announcing major changes in social security policies, layoffs, and cutbacks to railway workers was a throwback to the past. The public's response—in particular the widespread sympathy for the over three weeks of public sector strikes, despite the disruption caused by the lack of rail and other services as well as its general condemnation of the technocratic elites—suggests that dirigiste policymaking processes are no longer generally accepted even if nostalgia for dirigiste policies may remain. Moreover, the government's subsequent withdrawal of the reforms and its pledge to consult substantially on any revised version of them demonstrates that it, too, has recognized that dirigisme is no longer acceptable either as a set of policies or policymaking processes.

Notes to Chapter 5

1. John Zysman, *Political Strategies for Industrial Order: State, Market, and Industry in France* (Berkeley: University of California Press, 1977): 194.

2. David Wilsford, "Tactical Advantages versus Administrative Heterogeneity: The Strengths and Limits of the French State," Comparative Political Studies 21, no. 1 (April 1988). Wilsford enumerates these characteristics as: strong independent executive with proposal and decree powers that allow it to impose its program without debate in the National Assembly if it so chooses; a weak or "arena" legislature that does the majority government's bidding; an active, homogeneously-trained bureaucracy with a strong ministerial direction; a judiciary with limited powers and little tradition of judicial review; and ideological, fragmented societal interests.

3. Jack Hayward, "Mobilising Private Interests in the service of Public Ambitions: The Salient Element in the Dual French Policy Style?" in J. Richardson ed., *Policy Styles in Western Europe* (London: Allen and Unwin, 1982): 116. See also Peter Hall, *Governing the Economy* (New York: Oxford University Press, 1986), pp. 164-65. Hall attributes the French state's strength to its ideal-typical "elitism", which is derived from the state's cohesiveness, its insulation from the demands of other societal actors, its ability to speak for the public interest, and its capability to implement policy over the objection of social groups if necessary.

4. See the summary description of this model in Pierre Muller, "Entre le Local et L'Europe: La Crise du Modèle Français de Politiques Publiques," *Revue Française de Science Politique* 42, no. 2 (April 1992): 275-76.

5. Catherine Grémoin, *Profession, décideur: Pouvoir des Hauts Fonctionnaires et Réforme de l'Etat* (Paris: Gauthier-Villars, 1979).

6. Ezra Suleiman, *Politics, Power, and Bureaucracy in France: The Administrative Elite* (Princeton, N.J.: Princeton University Press, 1974), pp. 137-54. See also Vivien Schmidt, *From State to Market? The Transformation of French Business and Government* (New York: Cambridge University Press, 1996), chapter 7.

7. Ezra N. Suleiman, *Private Power and Centralization in France: The Notaries and the State* (Princeton, N.J.: Princeton University Press, 1987). On the differences between heroic versus everyday in the statist pattern, see Schmidt, *From State to Market?* chapter 2.

8. In recent years, French commentators have been especially critical of the state's inability to respond to such resistance creatively, complaining that the result is a powerless state, incapable of making the reforms necessary to the society with societal interests. See, for example, Denis Olivennes and Nicolas Baverez, *L'Impuissance Publique* (Paris: Calmann-Lévy, 1989). See also Michel Crozier, *Etat Modeste, Etat Moderne* (Paris: Fayard, 1987).

9. Andrew Shonfield, *Modern Capitalism: The Changing Balance of Public and Private Power* (Oxford: Oxford University Press, 1965), p. 389.
10. See: Schmidt, *From State to Market?* chapters 1 and 2.
11. I use the term liberalism here in the European sense, to denote an economic focus on free market economics and laissez-faire capitalism, rather than in the American sense, to suggest a center-left political orientation.
12. For a good summary of the history, see Zysman, *Political Strategies*. See also Richard Kuisel, *Capitalism and the State in Modern France* (New York: Cambridge University Press, 1981); Tom Kemp, *Economic Forces in French History* (London: Denis Dobson, 1971).
13. Peter A. Hall, "The State and the Market," in Peter A. Hall, Jack Hayward, and Howard Machin eds., *Developments in French Politics* (New York: St. Martin's Press, 1990), p. 174.
14. On the external constraints faced by all EC countries, see Wayne Sandholtz and John Zysman, "1992: Recasting the European Bargain," *World Politics* 42, no. 1 (October 1989): 95-128.
15. See Peter Hall, *Governing the Economy* (Oxford: Polity Press, 1986); Michael Loriaux, *France after Hegemony: International Change and Financial Reform* (Ithaca: Cornell University Press, 1991). On the history of planning and its problems, see Stephen S. Cohen, *Modern Capitalist Planning: The French Model* (Berkeley: University of California Press, 1977); Vera Lutz, *Central Planning for the Market Economy* (London: Longmans, 1969); Saul Estrin and Peter Holmes, *French Planning in Theory and Practice* (London: George Allen & Unwin, 1983); Jack Hayward, *The State and the Market Economy: Industrial Patriotism and Economic Intervention in France* (New York: New York University Press, 1986); and Hall, *Governing the Economy*.
16. See Jonah Levy, "Tocqueville's Revenge: The Decline of *Dirigisme* and Evolution of France's Political Economy" (Ph.D. Dis. Massachusetts Institute of Technology, 1993), p. 51; Christian Stoffaës, *La Grande Menace Industrielle* (Paris: Calmann-Lévy, 1978); Stephen S. Cohen, "Informed Bewilderment: French Economic Strategy and the Crisis" in Stephen S. Cohen and Peter A. Gourevitch, eds., *France in the Troubled World Economy* (London: Butterworths, 1982).
17. See Peter A. Hall, "Socialism in One Country: Mitterrand and the Struggle to Define a New Economic Policy for France," in P. Cerny and M. Schain, eds., *Socialism, the State and Public Policy in France* (London: Frances Pinter, 1985).
18. On the nationalizations, see André Delion and Michel Durupty, *Les Nationalisations* (Paris: Economica, 1982); W. Rand Smith, "Nationalizations for What? Capitalist Power and Public Enterprise in Mitterrand's France," *Politics and Society* 18, no. 1 (1990); and Vivien Schmidt, "Industrial Manage-

ment under the Socialists in France: Decentralized *Dirigisme* at the National and Local Levels," *Comparative Politics* 21, no. 1 (October 1988).

19. On the industrial policy and its results, see Schmidt, *From State to Market?* chapter 4; Schmidt, "Industrial Management"; Levy, "Tocqueville's Revenge," 65; Elie Cohen, *L'Etat Brancardier: Politiques du Déclin Industriel (1974-1984)* (Paris: Calmann-Lévy, 1989), pp. 230-31; Pierre Dacier, Jean-Louis Levet, and Jean-Claude Tourret, *Les Dossiers Noirs de l'Industries Française* (Paris: Fayard, 1985).

20. Lionel Zinsou, one of Fabius' advisors, did not go quite as far when he observed, "We went from the idea of a break with capitalism to the very different idea of a break with the failures of capitalism." Lionel Zinsou, *Le Fer de Lance* (Paris: Olivier Orban, 1985), p. 61. On the evolution of the Socialists' position with regard to the economy, see Schmidt, *From State to Market?* chapter 4.

21. Hall, "State and Market," 177-78. See also A. Fontaneau and P.-A. Muet, eds., *La Gauche Face à la Crise* (Paris: Presse de la Fondation Nationale des Sciences Politiques, 1985).

22. Pierre Favier and Michel Martin-Roland, *La Décennie Mitterrand* 1 (Paris: Seuil, 1990): 441. See also Philippe Bauchard, *La Guerre des Deux Roses: Du Rêve à la Réalité, 1981-1985* (Paris: Grasset, 1986).

23. *Rapport 1986 du Haut Conseil du Secteur Public* (Paris: Documentation Française, 1988); and Michel Durupty, *Les Privatisations* (Paris: Documentation Française, 1988), p. 23.

24. For a full discussion, see Michel Bazex "L'actualité du droit économique: La déréglementation," *L'Actualité Juridique. Droit Administratif* no. 11 (November 20, 1986).

25. Only Matra and Crédit Agricole were sold off after. On the details of the privatizations, see Michel Durupty, *Les Privatisations en France* (Paris: Documentation Française, 1988). See also Schmidt, *From State to Market?* chapter 5.

26. See Vivien Schmidt, "An End to French Economic Exceptionalism? The Transformation of Business under Mitterrand," *California Management Review* 36, no. 1 (fall 1993). On "protected capitalism," see François Morin, *La Structure Financière du Capital Français* (Paris: Calmann-Levy, 1974).

27. See Michel Albert, *Capitalisme contre Capitalisme* (Paris: Seuil, 1991); Philippe Delmas, *Le Maître des Horloges* (Paris: Odile Jacob, 1991); Jean-Louis Levet, *Une France sans Complexes* (Paris: Economica, 1990); Dominique Taddei and Benjamin Coriat, "Spécial: Made in France," *Industries* special edition (September 1992); Levy, "Tocqueville's Revenge"; and Schmidt, *From State to Market?* chapter 6.

28. See Schmidt, "End to French Economic Exceptionalism?"

29. Ibid; and Schmidt, *From State to Market?* chapters 6 and 13.

30. These are the research and development programs that promote technological cooperation in such areas as information technology (ESPRIT), communications technology (RACE), industrial technology (BRITE), advanced materials (EURAM), and high technology (EUREKA).

31. See Vivien A. Schmidt, "Loosening the Ties that Bind: The Impact of European Integration on French Government and its Relationship to Business," *Journal of Common Market Studies* (forthcoming June 1996).

32. See Vivien A. Schmidt, "A Profile of the French CEO," *International Executive* 35, no. 5 (September-October 1993): 413-30.

33. Shonfield, 139.

34. Charles Lindblom, *Politics and Markets* (New York: Basic, 1977), p. 183.

35. Jack Hayward, *The State and the Market Economy: Industrial Patriotism and Economic Intervention in France* (New York: New York University Press, 1986), p. 230.

36. See Schmidt, "Industrial Management"; Michel Bauer and Elie Cohen "Le politique, l'administratif, et l'exercise du pouvoir industriel," *Sociologie du Travail* no. 27 (March 1985); Claude Durand, Michelle Durand, and Monique VerVaeke, "Dirigisme et libéralisme: l'État dans l'industrie," *Sociologie du Travail*, 27 (March 1985); and Jocelyne Barreau, "Les Relations Etat-Groupes Nationalisés: Le Formel et l'Informel," in Barreau et al., eds., *L'Etat Entrepreneur* (Paris: L'Harmattan, 1990).

37. For France, this has been a problem especially with regard to European regulations and directives, which the French have had a tendency to treat as they have traditional French regulations, much to the consternation, and censure, of the European Court of Justice. See Schmidt, "Loosening the Ties."

38. Daniel Derivry, "The Managers of Public Enterprises in France," in Mattei Dogan, ed., *The Mandarins of Western Europe* (New York: John Wiley and Sons, 1975).

39. See Schmidt, "Profile of French CEO."

40. Raymond Vernon, "Linking Manager with Ministers: Dilemmas of the State-Owned Enterprise," *Journal of Policy Analysis and Management* 4, no. 1 (1984): 42-45. Anne Stevens, "'L'Alternance' and the Higher Civil Service," in Philip Cerny and Martin Schain, eds., *French Politics and Public Policy* (New York: St. Martin's, 1980), p. 144. See also Jacques Chevallier, "Un nouveau sens de l'État et du Service Public," in F. de Baeque and J.-L. Quermonne, eds., *Administration et Poltique*, (Paris: Presses de la Fondation Nationale des Sciences Politiques, 1981).

41. Claude Durand, Michelle Durand, and Monique VerVaeke, "Dirigisme et libéralisme: l'État dans l'industrie," *Sociologie du Travail*, 27 (March 1985); Philippe Messine, "Nationalisations, dénationalisations," *Le Monde Diplomatique* (March

1986) Jocelyne Barreau, "Les Relations Etat-Groupes Nationalisés," in Jocelyne Barreau et al., eds., *L'Etat Entrepreneur: Nationalisation, Gestions du Secteur Public Concurrentiel, Construction Européenne (1982-1993)* (Paris: L'Harmattan, 1990).

42. Shonfield, 128, 145.
43. Hall, *Governing the Economy*, 152-55.
44. Ibid, 169-71.
45. Hayward.
46. Harvey Feigenbaum, *The Politics of Public Enterprise: Oil and the French State* (Princeton, N.J.: Princeton University Press, 1985), p. 14.
47. Ibid., 94.
48. Ibid., 95.
49. Michel Bauer and Elie Cohen, "Le politique, l'administratif, et l'exercise du pouvoir industriel," *Sociologie du Travail* no. 27 (March 1985): 324-27.
50. Derivry, 217-18.
51. Lynne Krieger Mytelka, "In Search of a Partner: The State and the Textile Industry in France" in Stephen S. Cohen and Peter A. Gourevitch, eds., *France in the Troubled World Economy* (London: Butterworths, 1982), pp. 140-42; and Stephen S. Cohen, "Informed bewilderment: French economic strategy and the crisis" in Cohen and Gourevitch, eds., *France in Troubled World Economy* (London: Butterworths, 1982); Elie Cohen and Michel Bauer, *Les Grandes Manoeuvres Industrielles* (Paris: P. Belford, 1985).
52. Levy, "Tocqueville's Revenge," 51-52.
53. Cohen and Bauer, *Grandes Manoeuvres Industrielles*, 139.
54. Jean-Louis Beffa, CEO of Saint Gobain, interview by author, Paris, May 13, 1991.
55. Cohen and Bauer, *Grands Manoeuvres Industrielles*, 99-108.
56. Ibid., 258-68.
57. Testimony of Georges Pébereau, CEO of CGE up until a few months before privatization, *Rapport de la Commission d'Enquête sur les conditions dans lesquelles ont été effectuées les Opérations de Privatisation d'Entreprises et de Banques appartenant au Secteur Public depuis le 6 Août 1986* Assemblée Nationale no. 969, 3 vol's. Journal Officiel, October 29, 1989, 2, p. 717-18.
58. Ibid., 725.
59. Durand et al., 258-68.
60. Ibid., 257.

61. Francis Lorentz, former CEO of Bull (CEO at time of interview), interview by author, Paris, May 28, 1991.

62. David Wilsford, "Theories, Frameworks and Concepts: Disaggregating the French State and its Role in Industrial Policy," (paper prepared for presentation to the annual meeting of the American Political Science Association, Washington, D.C., August 30-September 2, 1991), pp. 20-23.

63. See *Rapport de la Commission sur les Opérations de Privatisation*, vol. 1.

64. See Eric Le Boucher, *Le Monde, Bilan Economique et Social 1986*, January 15, 1987.

65. Louis Schweitzer, CEO of Renault (number two at the time of the interview), interview by author, Paris, May 10, 1991.

66. *Les Echos*, April 8, 1991.

67. *L'Usine Nouvelle*, no. 2348, January 23, 1992.

68. *Wall Street Journal*, July 25, 1991.

69. *Le Monde*, April 9, 1991.

70. *Le Monde*, July 23, 1993.

71. See Schmidt, "Loosening the Ties."

72. As of September 1992, a majority (52 percent) of French CEOs were convinced that although the EC was less important than France, it would become more important than France by the year 2000 (by contrast with 24 percent who thought that the EC was and would stay less important, and 17 percent who thought that the EC was already more important.) *L'Expansion*, 3-10 September 1992, p. 57

73. J. François-Poncet and B. Barbier, *1992: Les Conséquences pour l'Economie Française du Marché Intérieur Européen* (Paris: Economica, 1989).

74. *Bruxelles mode d'emploi*–cited in T. Lefébure, *Lobby or not to be* (Paris: Plume, 1991), p. 113.

75. S. Andersen and K. Eliassen. "European Community Lobbying, " *European Journal of Political Research* 20 (1991): 173-87.

76. Elie Cohen, "Dirigisme, Politique Industrielle et Rhétorique Industrialiste," *Revue Française de Science Politique* 42, no. 2 (April 1992): 217-18.

77. *Le Monde*, April 11, 1995.

78. *Le Monde*, April 11, 1995.

79. See Yves Mény, *La Corruption de la République* (Paris: Fayard, 1992).

80. *Le Monde*, April 11, 1995.

Chapter 6

Does the French Labor Movement Have a Future?[1]

Mark Kesselman

A measure of how much the French labor movement has changed in the recent period can be gleaned from an article published by Jean Dubois in 1993.[2] What is most noteworthy about the transformation of the French labor movement, Dubois claims, is not—contrary to most other accounts—that French unions are in crisis. Although he admits that organized labor is experiencing a decline, more significant, in his view, is a strategic shift. Whereas in the past French unions typically sought to destroy the prevailing economic system, they now seek to participate with management in a joint effort to increase productivity.

This view is utopian, or, rather, ideological in Karl Mannheim's sense; the fact that the article was published in the official journal of the French National Association of Personnel Directors suggests the need for skepticism. However, the mere fact that it was published is noteworthy: it is unthinkable that such a position could have been expressed prior to the 1980s.

Contrary to Dubois, virtually all observers agree that the French labor movement faces a crisis of unprecedented proportions in the post-war period.[3] Indeed, one recent account speculates that the labor movement may be in its terminal stages.[4]

At first glance, the massive strikes of November–December 1995 contradict this grim analysis. Although it would be foolish to deny the magnitude or importance of the intensive strike wave in 1995, I question whether the strikes are a reflection of a strong, confident labor movement. Without question the strikes revealed the existence of widespread discontent, far beyond the sectors in which walkouts occurred. Yet, at the same time, the strikes were a reflection of the weakness of a labor movement that could not persuade the government to consult with it before announcing extensive cuts in social benefits, and which (despite the strikes) failed to prevent the government from reorganizing the public health system in a way that further weakens the labor movement. After analyzing the dimensions of the crisis of French labor in the body of this paper, I explore the significance of the strike wave of November–December 1995.

Although all labor movements in the industrialized countries are confronting severe challenges, why is French labor experiencing such an exceptionally deep crisis?[5] For over two decades, economic, political, and ideological changes have placed labor unions in all advanced capitalist countries on the defensive. But the French labor movement confronts an especially grave crisis, a product of its own particular character and specific features of the French context in which it has functioned. Why are recent developments, which pose a dramatic challenge to all union movements, especially threatening to organized labor in France?

The power of organized labor in France traditionally derived from two major sources, which set it apart from other labor movements. The magnitude of the crisis derives from the erosion of these two traditional sources of support. First, French trade unions typically sought to mobilize their members and sympathizers to engage in direct action in defense of labor's interests. Second, the labor movement exploited its mobilizational capacity to extract benefits from the formidable French state, notably via legislative and administrative regulation. Contestation and state support partially compensated for the inability of the labor movement to promote voluntarist negotiations between management and labor—the principal strategy utilized by the more powerful labor movements of northern Europe.

Although French labor was relatively weak throughout the post–war period, it has become a veritable paper tiger following the erosion of its two major strategic resources. Beginning in the mid-1970s, following the high point of direct mobilization in May 1968 and its aftermath, the labor movement's capacity to mobilize workers for direct action declined precipitously. The change was temporarily obscured by the "divine surprise" of May-June 1981 when the election of a Socialist president and legislative majority apparently offset labor's inability to mount direct protest. The Socialist government initially sponsored a range of redistributive measures that benefited its working-class supporters. However, its "right turn" in economic and social policy of 1983-84, which produced France's new-style "socialism without the workers," deprived organized labor of state support and the trend accelerated when conservative governments assumed office in the late 1980s. Since the mid-1980s the labor movement has been unable to mount an effective challenge to the state's conservative economic and social priorities, a trend that has continued since the election of Jacques Chirac in 1995.

This essay begins by reviewing evidence of labor's renewal in the 1980s. The following section describes more powerful tendencies that produced a crisis of organized labor; the third section seeks to explain labor's decline; and a concluding section assesses whether the strike wave of late 1995 suggests a reversal of the downward trend.

The Expansion and Institution of Organized Labor

In the post-war period, prior to the changes initiated by Socialist government reforms in the early 1980s, the French union movement displayed a highly bifurcated stance. At the local level, unions were forced to rely on their own efforts, principally direct action in the form of strikes and other kinds of protest, because employers and the state typically opposed the presence of organized labor in the workplace. Employer opposition and the absence of legal protections on the shopfloor that unions enjoyed in other advanced capitalist countries meant that union locals had a precarious existence. Relations between management and labor at the shopfloor and firm levels were far more chaotic and conflictual in France than in other advanced capitalist countries.

On the other hand, industrial relations at higher levels exhibited two tendencies. The first, consistent with the prevalent pattern locally, included intense rivalry among unions, and outbidding in their relations with management.[6] The second—and very different—pattern at higher levels was that unions were important participants in formal and informal regulatory institutions in the industrial, administrative, and political spheres. For example, representatives of the three major union confederations (including the ostensibly radical Confédération Générale du Travail—CGT) were members of the Economic and Social Council in the Fifth Republic, played a key role in administering the public health system (Sécurité Sociale), and served on official French delegations to international organizations like the United Nations. How did local contestation coexist with national participation? The answer was that important segments of the labor movement, especially the CGT, the largest and most influential union, which was closely linked to the Communist Party (PCF), engaged in a kind of conflictual participation. (The pattern was reminiscent of the PCF, which sought every opportunity to participate in order to express its opposition to the political system!)

The Auroux laws sponsored by the Socialist government in 1982-83 represented an attempt to bridge the gap between chaotic, voluntarist labor relations at the local level and more institutionalized labor relations at higher levels.[7] The reforms aimed, in the oft-quoted words of Minister of Labor Jean Auroux, to enable workers to become citizens in the firm. Some aspects of the reform package strengthened unions. For example, the state sought to ensure that all private sector workers would gain the protection of collective bargaining framework agreements negotiated by unions and employer associations at sectoral levels concerning minimum wage levels, skill classifications, and working conditions. Prior to the 1980s, many industries lacked such agreements and workers in these sectors were protected only by the more meager provisions of the Labor Code.

The Auroux legislation sought, with substantial success, to empower unions to represent workers. It required employer associations at industrial levels to bargain collectively with unions at least once every five years in order to establish or review a sectoral framework agreement regarding industrial standards of minimum wages, hours, working conditions, and skill classifications. (Employer associations, however, were not required to conclude agreements during these negotiations.) Since passage of the Auroux laws in the early 1980s, the number of employees not covered by a sectoral framework agreement declined from 3 million to 1 million.[8]

Another important provision of the Auroux reforms, which strengthened organized labor, required employers to bargain collectively with local unions. Although legislation passed after the May 1968 general strike recognized the legal existence of local unions, employers were not obligated to bargain collectively with them. The Auroux laws effected a minor revolution when, for the first time, employers in firms with at least fifty employees were required to bargain collectively over wages, hours, and working conditions. (As with sectoral bargaining, employers were not required to conclude agreements.) Along with other provisions, which granted local unions new rights and privileges, the reform in effect represented the French equivalent of the Wagner Act (passed in the U.S. nearly 50 years earlier!) A commission appointed by the government to evaluate the results of the Auroux laws reported in 1993 that the agreements negotiated since passage of the Auroux laws represent "the most extensive wave of negotiations in the history of French labor relations."[9] This was not mere hyperbole: the number of firms and/or plants in France which negotiated local bargaining agreements soared from 1,477 in 1981, prior to passage of the Auroux laws, to 6,750 in 1991, the high point of firm-level bargaining.[10]

Closer analysis suggests that the impact of the Auroux reforms was more limited and contradictory than its supporters claim. The reforms not only failed to guarantee legal representation for all workers but in part served to divide them. For example, nearly half of all private sector workers continue to be employed in plants that lack any representative institution, including a local union organization, works committee, or *délégués du personnel* (elected grievance committee representatives).[11] Despite the fact that employers in firms with over 10 employees are legally obliged to organize elections in which workers select *délégués du personnel,* only one-quarter of plants with 10-49 employees actually have one. Similarly, long after passage of the Auroux laws, only one-quarter of all private sector workers are covered by a firm-level collective bargaining agreement. Workers not covered are employed in firms whose small size exempts them from the requirement to bargain collectively, in firms where collective bargaining failed to produce an agreement, and in firms where, despite the legal injunction, employers violate the law by refusing to bargain collectively.

As in other countries with weak union movements, France exhibits the pattern of a dual labor market, with a substantial disparity between industrial relations patterns in the organized and unorganized sector. Most workers covered by annual enterprise agreements (accords), who enjoy more stable and regularized working conditions, work in large firms. In 1992, 70 percent of workers covered by an agreement worked in firms with over 1,000 employees; only 7 percent of workers covered by an agreement in 1992 worked in firms under 200 employees.[12]

In some respects, as Chris Howell has suggested, the Auroux laws actually weakened unions, for example, by authorizing unions to negotiate local agreements which eroded restrictions on employers' ability to deploy the labor force.[13] The legislation also created new channels for worker participation and representation, partially short-circuiting unions, by organizing shopfloor assemblies in which workers discussed working conditions directly with supervisors.

Overall, whatever gains the Auroux reforms may have produced for organized labor were more than offset by other developments in the French and global political economy. The fact that over 6,000 firm-level collective bargaining agreements are negotiated annually does not signify that the labor movement has developed a powerful grass-roots base. Indeed, it is doubtful that labor's organizational infrastructure is stronger following implementation of the Auroux laws. For example, although the percentage of plants employing at least fifty employees with at least one union delegate increased slightly, from 57-60 percent, between 1985 and 1989, there was a larger decline (from 76-70 percent) in the proportion of workers in plants employing over fifty employees without a union local. The explanation of this paradox is that the number of very large firms has declined and unions are less effective in organizing smaller plants. Whereas virtually all plants with over 500 employees have a shop steward, fewer than half the plants with 50-100 workers do.[14] In any event, the existence of a bargaining agreement need not necessarily signify an active union presence. Union locals may lead a precarious existence with a few leaders and a handful of members yet manage to go through the motions of collective bargaining.[15]

More generally, in part under the impact of the Auroux reforms, French unions have become far more institutionalized as a result of the legal mandates imposed on employers in the 1980s to bargain with unions at local and industrial levels, as well as to inform and consult with works councils (often controlled by unions) regarding social, economic, and technological issues. However, the more secure, institutionalized position that unions have achieved is a mixed blessing, for it has stretched unions' meager resources to the limit and further widened the gulf between union leaders and the workers they purport to represent.[16] Focusing on the Auroux reforms, as many studies do, may obscure more powerful developments in the recent period. The next section identifies some of the key factors that have plunged French unions into the most severe crisis since the World War II.

Contours of the Crisis in French Government

The French labor movement is in the throes of a crisis unprecedented in the post-war period.[17] Diverse elements have combined to produce this result.

Decline of union members. While membership statistics on French unions are notoriously unreliable, specialists agree that union membership—never very high in France—has plunged to under half the levels of the early 1980s.[18] Measured by the usual criterion of unions' ability to organize their potential constituency of wage earners, French unions have become a negligible presence: whereas unions organized 23 percent of the labor force in 1975, the proportion of union members declined to 19 percent in 1980, 12 percent in 1990, and under 10 percent in 1992.[19]

Decline in worker support for unions. It is often noted that membership figures underestimate the strength of French unions because far more workers support unions than belong to one. An important reason is the free-rider phenomenon: in most industries, there is no legal compulsion to join a union and benefits accruing from union activity (higher wages, better working conditions, etc.) are distributed to all workers in the firm. Moreover, there are strong disincentives to joining a union, notably, the relatively high cost of dues and the risk of incurring management sanctions.

In the past, unions could flourish despite a small membership base because so many non-unionized workers heeded union strike calls and voted for official union candidates in elections for works councils and other representative bodies. This is less true recently. Consider the dramatic increase in the number of non-union representatives elected to works councils. In firms with under 100 employees, the proportion of non-union members of works councils increased from half in the late 1970s to two-thirds a decade later.[20] In all French firms, non-union representatives on works councils nearly doubled, from 14.2 percent in 1968, to 26.5 percent in 1989-90. Whereas union-sponsored candidates received 63 percent of all votes in works council elections in 1968, they received only 47 percent twenty years later.[21]

The decline in unions' ability to garner support for their candidates in works councils not only illustrates unions' declining influence; it also further contributes to weakening organized labor. Controlling works councils provides unions with important resources; alternatively, works councils not controlled by unions represent potential rivals.

Declining support for shopfloor representative institutions. The unions' decreasing ability to control works councils is part of a larger failure to mobilize worker support for, as well as unify, the diverse network of legally prescribed representative institutions in the workplace. Declining support for union candidates in works councils elections has been accompanied by declining turnout in these elections. Between 1967-90, turnout for works councils elections fell from 73 percent to 63 percent.[22] Another example: the substantial decline in worker support for labor mediation tribunals, *conseils de prud'hommes,* which act as grievance mechanisms for 13 million French wage earners. Whereas turnout for worker representatives to labor tribunals was 63 percent in 1979, it declined to 58 percent in 1982 and slipped further to 46 percent in 1987.

The disappearing strike. The diminished support for unions and representative mechanisms might signify workers' greater willingness to act directly in defense of their interests. Quite the contrary: prior to the strike wave of 1995, strikes were at their lowest level in the post-war period. Whereas in 1970, there were 1,750,000 days of work stoppage due to strikes, by 1990 the comparable figure was less than one-third as high.[23]

A general decline in the strike rate does not signify total labor peace. In addition to the strike wave of 1995, there have been isolated and severe strikes in recent years in the aerospace, transportation, health, and administrative sectors. In the bulk of cases, strikes have occurred in the public sector, where the risks are less, and their principal target and interlocutor is the state. Rather than reflecting an aggressive (if beleaguered) union movement, however, such strikes further highlight unions' low standing. Most were defensive, seeking to prevent layoffs and block reductions in benefits. In several cases, they were initiated and led by strike committees *(coordinations),* not union leaders. Although many influential members of the strike committees were union militants or former militants, they often initiated strikes outside union channels and in some cases in defiance of union directives. The strike committees are an indirect indictment of unions' inability to represent workers.[24]

A shift in the focus of collective bargaining. Whereas collective bargaining traditionally involved unions' attempts to increase social benefits, collective bargaining now often involves the exchange of benefits between management and labor, that is, givebacks. The process was facilitated when the Socialist government issued an administrative regulation in 1982 authorizing local unions to negotiate agreements violating legislation on the scheduling of work. In 1987, the Chirac government sponsored legislation widening the scope for locally negotiated agreements to reduce legally mandated social benefits.[25] Under President Chirac, the government has sought to enlist unions in the search for flexibility.

Increased fragmentation of the labor movement. French unions have always engaged in fierce ideological and jurisdictional disputes, and such rivalries remain as intense as ever. Hence, the whole of the labor movement is less than the sum of its parts. Each of the three largest union confederations has developed a distinctive strategy which, if adequately tested in practice, might contribute to strengthening the labor movement as a whole. However, internecine strife has prevented unions from implementing any coherent strategy. The result is the chasm, common in other areas of French society, has widened between rhetoric and practice.

In addition to the typical pattern of inter-union strife, new conflicts have divided organized labor in the recent period. First, each of the major union confederations has experienced heightened internal cleavages.[26] In the mid-1990s conflict further increased within the Confédération française démocratique du travail (CFDT) and CGT. At the 1995 CFDT Congress, delegates took the unprecedented step of refusing to pass the traditional motion endorsing the current leadership, while several prominent CGT leaders criticized the union's undemocratic practices and were evicted from their positions at the Centennial Congress.

Tensions have also increased within each confederation between unions rooted in the private sector, whose members are especially vulnerable in the new situation of deregulated labor markets, and public sector unions, whose members are relatively more protected.[27] Another source of intra-union division involves local union leaders who oppose federation and confederal directives. As a result of changes in work organization and the legal framework of industrial relations, union locals at the plant and firm levels now enjoy considerably greater autonomy. Local unions are more inclined to go their own way, and leaders at the federal and confederal levels are less able to develop common policies and coordinate local unions' activities. Guy Groux claims that this development has produced a veritable rupture in the typical pattern of social regulation prevailing in France.[28] Whereas in the past, national-level collective bargaining agreements *(conventions collectives),* as well as state legislative and administrative decisions, shaped the industrial relations framework, the proliferation of firm-level collective bargaining agreements has eroded uniform national standards. One indication is that a significant number of recently concluded firm-level collective bargaining agreements involve the organization of the labor process, for example, the scheduling of work. In the past, this area was regulated by national legislation and collective bargaining.[29]

Low public support. Public opinion poll data suggest unions' general unpopularity. For example, when citizens were asked in 1985 to evaluate a range of economic institutions, including public and private firms, banks, and the stock market, unions received the lowest rating by a wide margin. Only 24 percent of those polled expressed even minimum confidence in unions; 61 percent expressed a total lack of confidence. (The next most unpopular institution, multinational corporations, had a confidence rating of 33 percent.)[30]

In 1993, unions enjoyed a modest rise in support, when 28 percent of the French reported at least some confidence in unions. The slight increase may represent a response to conservative government policies; it may also result from popular recognition of just how weak the labor movement (and, in particular, the CGT) has become.[31]

The evidence presented here points to a decline of historic proportions in the density, capacity, and influence of organized labor in France. What explains this fundamentally important shift in the French political economy?

Why Have Unions Declined? Toward an Explanation?

The crisis of the French labor movement is the product of a confluence of factors. While I distinguish in what follows between economic and political tendencies that have weakened unions, the two developments are often closely intertwined in the recent structural transformation of the French political economy.

The Brave New Political Economy

Structural changes in the French and world economy have been the primary cause of the decline of organized labor. Although our focus on organized labor precludes extended analysis of the changing global context in which the labor movement functions, several centrally important trends should be noted.

The sharply increased tendency toward the globalization of production and finance has enormously decreased labor's capacity. Within the sphere of production, employers have less latitude for concessions to labor, as a result of intensified competition and the demise of protected markets, as well as fewer incentives to make concessions, given greater capital mobility. French industry, which was traditionally reluctant to engage in direct foreign investment, has moved abroad with much greater frequency since the early 1980s. The labor movement has been left far behind. Increased international economic integration has also sharply reduced the French state's latitude for regulation and concessions. In particular, the constraints imposed by France's membership in the European Union (EU) have outstripped any possible gains that membership might provide French labor. As Streeck and Schmitter aptly note, the EU institutionalizes pluralism and deregulation, limiting the possibility for social regulation at the European level.[32] Moreover, the French labor movement is especially disadvantaged within the European Trade Union Confederation because the CGT, alone among major European unions, continues to be excluded from membership.[33]

Reorganizing production. Changes in technology and workplace organization have further weakened the power of organized labor. Throughout the twentieth century, the French labor movement has operated with an ideological and organizational map in which employers are responsible for directing production while unions contest the choices made and seek to maximize benefits for their members. Unions' strategies were directed to unifying their members on a class-wide or occupational basis, congruent with Fordist methods of mass production and consumption. In the post–Fordist era of dispersed and decentralized production, rapid technological change, and participatory management, unions no longer have a defined role.

The changes in the French political economy identified here provide a broad overview of the new context within which organized labor must operate. These changes underline the gravity of the challenge confronting labor.

Fewer jobs, more jobless. The transformation of the French economy represents a mortal threat to organized labor. The economy no longer produces an adequate number of stable, full-time jobs, and French unions have proved powerless to counteract this trend. Between 1980-90, the adult population in France increased by 2.15 million (+9 percent), while the number of wage earners increased by only 740,000 (+4 percent), and the number of unemployed increased by 1.8 million, that is, over double the number of newly created jobs. Moreover, the rate of unemployment nearly doubled during the decade.[34] The trend made a mockery of the Socialist Party's denunciation in 1981 of the conservative government's inability to contain rising unemployment. France's unemployment rate of over 11 percent in 1996 was the highest among the major OECD countries.

The greater severity of unemployment. Whereas in 1980 unemployed workers were jobless for an average of 240 days, the comparable figure a decade later was 361 days.[35] Youth are likely to be among the primary victims, with the unemployment rate among the young double that of older workers. When young people do obtain jobs, they are likely to be part-time or temporary. Fully two-thirds of those between 16-25 are unemployed, enrolled in vocational training programs, or are part-time or temporary workers. Although the French safety net is more extensive than in most countries (witness, for example, the creation of a minimum income program in 1988), rising structural unemployment has swollen the marginalized sector of society, what the French usually call "the excluded" and what Robert Castel describes as the victims of "social invalidation."[36]

Militants without jobs. When layoffs occur, union militants are often a particular target, which both directly damages unions and creates a chilling effect that deters others from participating. In a study of former union activists, Dominique Labbé and Maurice Croisat report that a major reason why militants abandoned union activity was the threat of reprisals. "The fear of job loss apparently played an important role in determining individual behavior in the industrial firms where layoffs occurred. Most workers claimed that union members were the first victims of job reductions."[37]

Sectoral changes. Since the early 1980s, industrial jobs have decreased by one quarter, with losses concentrated in union bastions such as metalworking, mining, steel, and printing.

Changing work organization. In addition to the shrinking pool of jobs, shifts in the composition of the work force have further weakened organized labor. One notable change is an increase in the proportion of part-time and temporary jobs. While the number of such jobs increased by 30 percent from 1988 to 1993, the number of stable, permanent jobs declined by 15 percent. In the current period, most newly created jobs are short-term.[38]

Composition of the wage earning population. Between 1982 and 1990, the number of higher-level managers, cadres, and professionals increased by 42 percent; technicians and middle level executives increased by 18 percent; employees increased by 10 percent, while manual workers decreased by 1.7 percent.[39] There is an inverse relation between the expanding occupational categories and those where unions are traditionally well entrenched.

Firm size. Similarly, shifts in the size of firms have been to the disadvantage of unions. The proportion of large firms, where unions are better organized, has significantly diminished. In 1974, about one-fifth of all firms had fewer than ten employees; by 1986 this figure had increased to one quarter. At the other end of the scale, 22 percent of workers worked in firms with 500 plus employees in 1974; only 15 percent did so by 1986.[40] The largest industrial firms, the sector of greatest union strength, were hardest hit: they shed 600,000 workers between 1982-92.[41]

Feminization of the labor force. There has been a sharp increase in the proportion of wage-earning women: the proportion of women aged 25-49 in the paid labor force increased from 59 percent in 1975 to 73 percent in 1991.[42] In France, as in other countries with weak labor movements, women are less likely to be recruited to unions: French women are half as likely as men to be union members. At the same time, the core constituency of organized labor has declined. For example, in the decade after 1980 the proportion of employed men over age fifty in the paid labor force diminished from 48 percent to 35 percent.

In sum, changes in the shape of the economy have dealt a mortal blow to French unions. This trend is not simply a result of impersonal economic forces; it is linked to political changes at many levels which further marginalize organized labor.

Less State, Weaker Unions

The transformation of the French economy has involved important changes in power relations in the workplace and at higher levels. In all countries, technological and economic changes since the 1980s have weakened organized labor, but the traditional orientation of French trade unions has made them especially vulnerable in the new setting.

The French labor movement was typically too weak to pressure employers into negotiating private deals. Advances achieved in other countries by collective bargaining between management and labor were often gained in France (if they were achieved at all) as a result of state legislation and administrative regulation. It is ironic that the French labor movement which, ever since the Charte d'Amiens in 1906, strongly opposed linking its fate to the actions of political parties and the political sphere, was forced to rely so heavily on the state for protection. The labor movement reflected an orientation consistent with dominant currents in French political culture, analyzed by observers from Tocqueville to the present. Patterns of French industrial relations were a product of close state regulation and unilateral action by business and labor. What was missing in the sphere of industrial relations, as in other areas of civil society in France, was effective self-regulation deriving from institutionalized relations between private social actors.

In the post-war period, state regulation of workplace relations was closely linked to the state's important role in steering the economy. The state pursued a vigorous industrial policy, allocated the bulk of industrial capital, and was a direct economic participant via the extensive public, industrial, and financial sectors. (Along with Japan, France is often cited as a prime case of state economic leadership.)

The Auroux laws represented, in part, merely the most recent expression of the labor movement's dependence on the state to achieve through legal mandate what it could not achieve on its own. At the same time, the reforms might have enabled the labor movement to free itself from state dependence by developing a more autonomous capacity. As described above, this has not occurred. The decline of state regulation and shift toward firm-level regulation has been especially disorienting for French unions.

Beginning with the Socialist Party's U-turn in economic affairs in 1983-84, the traditional pattern has been fundamentally transformed. Rather than full employment and wage gains being seen as contributing to economic growth, they are now widely regarded as a liability. Under Socialist and conservative governments alike, the new priorities in economic policy are a strong franc, low inflation, and reduced wage costs, all of which are antithetical to the interests of organized labor and its constituents.[43] While the Socialist government in 1981-83 pursued more redistributive policies than did other governments of this period, from 1984 the pendulum swung further to the right in France than elsewhere. Both Socialist governments, following the U-turn of 1983-84 and the collapse of the Communist Party, and, to an even greater extent, conservative governments in recent years have been single-minded in giving priority to economic modernization over social equity.

Since the onset of economic and social conservatism in the 1980s, the French labor movement has borne a disproportionately heavy share of the costs involved in rationalizing the French economy. Two notable examples: first, unemployment levels in France have been among the highest of the OECD countries for over a decade. Second, although the French economy expanded by 2.3 percent annually between 1980-91, the portion of the Gross

Domestic Product (GDP) going to wages in this period declined from 68.8 percent to 60.1 percent.[44] In other words, what is occurring in France does not merely reflect global shifts occurring throughout the world. Political factors help account for the fact that conservative trends occurring elsewhere have been especially pronounced in France.

Organized labor has been further marginalized by an effective strategic reorientation of French employers dating from the 1980s. In the past, the combination of high employment, state regulation, and arbitrary managerial practices increased workers' support for unions. French management has evolved in ways that pose difficult challenges for the labor movement. The new approach is reflected in the title of an article in the official journal of the French personnel directors association, "From labor relations to social regulation."[45] Consultative techniques have proliferated in French industry since the 1980s as management successfully regained the initiative after a labor offensive dating from the late 1960s and stretching through the Socialists' first years in office after 1981.

In the 1980s, modernist managers in France in large companies like BSN, Péchiney, and Rhône-Poulenc began to emulate participatory management practices that originated in Japan and the United States.[46] In the new credo, managers no longer coerce; they now seek to integrate workers on an individual basis. For example, rather than granting across-the-board wage increases on a collective basis, wage levels are determined selectively, on the basis of merit. The modernist approach was given important recognition when, in 1994, Jean Gandois, a prominent business executive who was one of its influential practitioners, was chosen to lead the major employers association, the Conseil National du Patronat Français (CNPF).

Contrary to the claims of some business leaders and scholars, it is questionable whether the modernist trend represents a genuine redistribution of power to shopfloor and office workers.[47] In any event, these developments do deprive unions of their legal and de facto monopoly of representation. For example, when asked how they pursue job grievances, the vast majority of workers (78 percent) reported that they addressed their supervisor directly. Only one-fifth enlisted the support of their shop steward or other representative (for example, the *délégué du personnel*).[48] Although comparable poll data from an earlier period are not available, it is doubtful that workers in the past typically engaged in this kind of face-to-face conflict regulation. Two specialists on French labor relations suggest the consequence of this shift for organized labor: "When workers gain the possibility for autonomous expression, the rationale for unions has disappeared."[49]

Under certain conditions, organized labor might preserve a favored place in the new situation. But it would require a labor movement far more closely implicated in day-to-day and long-run managerial decision-making, a movement able to demonstrate its value both to management by cooperating in the attempt to maximize economic competitivity and to workers by providing them with concrete benefits.[50]

In the past, French unions flourished primarily because, by demonstrating their capacity to initiate significant protest activity, they were an effective veto group and, by gaining institutional positions, they could extract benefits for their constituents and themselves. But this situation has changed: as workers fear the consequences of engaging in collective protest, unions cannot mount a credible threat. The state, especially in conservative hands following the electoral swings of 1993 and 1995, is less inclined to defer to unions. These trends produce a vicious circle of continued decline: as time passes, the phenomenon of "[institutionalized] unions without members" (in the apt phrase of Guy Groux and René Mouriaux) will likely further alienate workers from unions and thus accelerate the decline of the labor movement.[51]

The Strike Wave of 1995: Parenthesis or New Departure?

Until this point, save for the insertion of a few phrases foreshadowing the analysis to follow of the strike wave of November–December 1995, the paper was completed before the explosive opposition movement erupted in late 1995. On the one hand, the strikes apparently contradict the entire thrust of the paper. At least they represent a throwback to the earlier pattern, when labor successfully mobilized to press its claims. Most analyses of the strikes do in fact highlight how much they portend a reversal of recent trends.[52] On the other hand, I would suggest that the strikes resulted from unions' inability to negotiate satisfactory adjustment measures. Their outcome may slow the tempo but not fundamentally alter the trajectory of the labor movement, that is, continued decline.

The background to the strikes was Jacques Chirac's about-turn in October 1995. During the presidential campaign and in his first actions as president Chirac exploited the widespread discontent with an economic situation that had brought few benefits and imposed many costs. Moreover, Chirac's campaign represented a sharp break with the past. For the first time since the Socialist Party's U-turn of 1983-84, a candidate from one of the "big three" centrist parties challenged the fiscal orthodoxy, which had informed French policy under governments of the Left and Right alike. These policies promoted the intensive modernization of French industry but at the cost of soaring unemployment (among the highest in the OECD countries), a growing number of socially excluded, and intense discontent. During the campaign, Chirac claimed that these sacrifices were unnecessary. In a famous phrase, he opined, "the pay stub [i.e., an adequate wage] is not the enemy of employment."

Chirac's strategy was electorally successful and politically costly. Only months after he had aroused hopes that things could be different and that government policy would accord priority to reflation and social ends, he sharply reversed his position. The government's first major salvo was to announce a freeze of public-sector wages in September 1995. This was quickly followed by a large one-day strike of public-sector employees in October (the ministry of the interior conservatively estimated that 320,000 civil servants stayed away from work).

At this point, Chirac unleashed the blast that would nearly bring down his government and shake the entire political system. In a televised interview in late October he announced that his initial optimism about the possibilities for reflation was mistaken. The situation was more difficult than he had recognized and there was no alternative to additional austerity measures.

His words were quickly followed by actions when the Juppé government announced fundamental reforms, which struck at the heart of the social contract with labor and the French model of social benefits and industrial relations. A measure of how little unions counted in the new situation is that, contrary to past practice in such a situation, they were not consulted or even informed in advance about the details of the proposals. Both in form and substance the proposals virtually represented a declaration of war on unions and on public-sector workers—by far the better organized segment of the work force. Among the proposed measures were increased taxes, a public-sector wage freeze, reduced retirement benefits for civil servants (and notably for some of the best organized categories, especially the railway workers), and changes in the public health system that would reduce benefits and union influence in a sector where unions have traditionally derived enormous power and patronage.

The reaction to the proposed reforms was swift and harsh. Strikes immobilized railroads, the Paris metro, and urban transportation systems throughout France. Electrical workers, teachers, postal workers, garbage collectors, and others walked off the job. Organized labor played a prominent role in the 1995 strikes, unlike some earlier walkouts where unions trailed behind. The rhythm of protest reached its peak on December 7 when well over a million participated in demonstrations in cities and towns throughout France. Prolonged demonstrations of this magnitude and duration had not occurred since May 1968. The strikes began to wind down only when the government retreated on some key points.

It would be foolish to claim that nothing has changed as a result of the strike wave of late 1995. Yet, I would suggest that if the government lost the battle it won the war. The strikes slowed the tempo of retrenchment but did not reverse its direction. They have demonstrated that the state cannot ignore unions but the strikes have resulted neither in new policy initiatives favorable to labor's interests nor in a revitalization of the labor movement. Thus, the strikes reflect the crisis of French labor analyzed in this paper and they have not yet served to reverse labor's decline. Where it will stop, nobody knows.

Notes to Chapter 6

1. Earlier drafts of this paper were given at the Tenth Conference of Europeanists, Chicago, March 14-16, 1996, and the conference, "Chirac's Challenge: Public Policy and Protest in France," Center for West European Studies, The University of Washington, Seattle, April 12, 1996. I am especially grateful for the incisive comments of Amrita Basu.

2. Jean Dubois, "Crise ou declin du syndicalisme?" *Personnel* no. 341 (May 1993): 18-22.

3. For a review essay analyzing alternative approaches to the crisis of French trade unions, see René Mouriaux and Françoise Subileau, "La Crise syndicale en France entre 1981 et 1990: Analyses et interprétations globales" (paper presented to the 12th World Congress of Sociology, Madrid, 1990). See also Geneviève Bibes and René Mouriaux, eds., *Les Syndicats européens à l'épreuve* (Paris: Presses de la FNSP, 1990); Guy Groux and René Mouriaux, *La CFDT* (Paris: Economica, 1989); Groux and Mouriaux, *La CGT, Crises et alternatives* (Paris: Economica, 1992); Groux and Mouriaux, "The Dilemma of Unions Without Members," in Anthony Daley, ed., *The Mitterrand Era: Policy Alternatives and Political Mobilization in France* (New York: New York University Press, 1995); Mark Kesselman and Guy Groux, eds., *The French Workers' Movement: Economic Crisis and Political Change* (London: Allen & Unwin, 1984); Kesselman, "The New Shape of French Labor and Industrial Relations: Ce n'est plus la même chose," in Paul Godt, ed., *Policymaking in France: From de Gaulle to Mitterrand*

(London: Pinter Publishers, 1989): pp. 165-75; René Mouriaux, *Le Syndicalisme face à la crise* (Paris: La Découverte, 1986); Pierre Rosanvallon, *La Question syndicale* (Paris: Calmann-Lévy, 1988); Alain Touraine et al, *Le Mouvement ouvrier* (Paris: Fayard, 1984); Anthony Daley, *Steel, State, and Labor: Mobilization and Adjustment in France* (Pittsburgh: University of Pittsburgh Press, 1996); and Pierre Eric Tixier, *Mutation ou déclin du syndicalisme? Le cas de la CFDT* (Paris: Presses Universitaires de France, 1992).

4. Dominique Labbé and Maurice Croisat, *La fin des syndicats?* (Paris: L'Harmattan, 1992).

5. For accounts of difficulties in labor movements in western Europe and the United States, see Miriam Golden and Jonas Pontusson, eds., *Bargaining for Change: Union Politics in North America and Europe* (Ithaca: Cornell University Press, 1992); Peter A. Hall, ed., "European Labor in the 1980s," *International Journal of Political Economy* 17 (fall 1987); Horst Kern and Charles F. Sabel, "Trade Unions and Decentralized Production: A Sketch of Strategic Problems in the West German Labor Movement," *Politics & Society* 19, no. 4 (December 1991): 373-402; Kern and Michael Schumann, "New Concepts of Production in West German Plants," in Peter J. Katzenstein, ed., *Industry and Politics in West Germany: Toward the Third Republic* (Ithaca: Cornell University Press, 1989); Charles F. Sabel, "Bootstrapping Reform: Rebuilding Firms, the Welfare State, and Unions," *Politics & Society* 23, no. 1 (March 1994): 5-48; Peter Swenson, *Fair Shares: Unions, Pay, and Politics in Sweden and West Germany* (Ithaca: Cornell University Press, 1989); Swenson, "Labor and Limits of the Welfare State: The Politics of Intraclass Conflict and Cross-Class Alliances in Sweden and West Germany," *Comparative Politics* 23, no. 4 (July 1991): 379-99; Kathleen Thelen, "West European Labor in Transition: Sweden and Germany Compared," *World Politics* 46, no. 1 (October 1993): 23-49; Richard M. Locke and Kathleen Thelen, "Apples and Oranges Revisited: Contextualized Comparisons and the Study of Comparative Labor Politics," *Politics & Society*, 23, no. 2 (September 1995):337-67; and Lowell Turner, *Democracy at Work: Changing World Markets and the Future of Labor Unions* (Ithaca: Cornell University Press, 1991).

6. See Martin A. Schain, "Relations between the CGT and the CFDT: Politics and Mass Mobilization," in Kesselman and Groux, eds., 257-76.

7. For analyses in English, see Bernard E. Brown, "Worker Democracy in Socialist France" Occasional Papers, no. 7 (Center for Labor-Management Studies, the Graduate School, The City University of New York, 1989); Brown, "The Rise and Fall of *Autogestion* in France," in M. Donald Hancock et al, eds., *Managing Modern Capitalism: Industrial Renewal and Workplace Democracy in the United States and Western Europe* (New York: Praeger, 1991), pp. 195-214; Duncan Gallie, *"Les lois Auroux:* The Reform of French Industrial Relations?" in Howard Machin and Vincent Wright, eds., *Economic Policy and Policy-making under the Mitterrand Presidency, 1981-1984* (New York: St. Martin's, 1984), pp.

205-21; Chris Howell, "The Dilemmas of Post-Fordism: Socialists, Flexibility, and Labor-Market Deregulation in France," *Politics & Society* 20, no. 1 (1992); Howell, *Regulating Labor: The State and Industrial Relations Reform in Postwar France* (Princeton: Princeton University Press, 1992); Bernard Moss, "After the Auroux Laws: Employers, Industrial Relations and the Right in France," *West European Politics* 11, no. 1 (January 1988): 68-80; W. Rand Smith, "Towards *Autogestion* in Socialist France? The Impact of Industrial Relations Reform," *West European Politics* 10, no. 1 (January 1987): 46-62; and Frank L. Wilson, "Democracy in the Workplace: The French Experience," *Politics & Society* 19, no. 4 (1991).

8. Michel Coffineau, *Les Lois Auroux, dix ans après, Rapport au premier ministre* (Paris: La Documentation Française, 1993), p. 48.

9. Ibid., 23.

10. However, the number has declined since then as a result of the recession of the early 1990s. For example, according to figures from the Ministère du Travail, *La Négociation collective en 1993*, vol. 1 (Paris: La Documentation française, 1993), p. 12, the number of enterprise-level agreements declined by 12 percent between 1992 and 1993.

11. Coffineau, 77. Other figures in this paragraph are from the Coffineau report.

12. Ministère du Travail, 34.

13. Howell, *Regulating Labor*, and Howell, "The Dilemma of Post-Fordism."

14. Coffineau, 64.

15. This point is made by Guy Groux, "Le Syndicalisme d'enterprise: Lieu commun ou notion ambigue?" *Raison Présente* no. 111 (third quarter, 1994): 61-80; and corroborated by research reported in Mark Kesselman, "French Labour Confronts Technological Change: Reform That Never Was?" in Daley, ed., *The Mitterrand Era:* 161-71.

16. See the references cited in the previous note, as well as W. Rand Smith, *Crisis in the French Labour Movement: A Grassroots Perspective* (London: Macmillan, 1987).

17. For some accounts of the shift in class relations, see Commissariat Général du Plan, *Négociation collective, Quels enjeux?* Report of the commission "Evolution de la Négociation Collective" (Paris: Commissariat Général du Plan, 1988); GRECO, *L'Etat de la négociation collective. Les Cahiers du GRECO*, no. 3. (July 1990); François Lagandré, *Nouvelles relations de travail: Pratiques contractuelles et perspectives* (Paris: L'Harmattan, 1990); Dominique Martin, ed., *Participation et changement social dans l'enterprise* (Paris: L'Harmattan, 1990); and Renaud Sainsaulieu, ed., *L'Enterprise, une affaire de société* (Paris: Presses de la FNSP, 1990).

18. Groux, "Le Syndicalisme d'enterprise"; Clisthène, "Quel avenir pour le syndicalisme?" *Esprit* no. 189 (February 1993): 132-41.

19. Coffineau, 87.
20. Ibid., 63.
21. Ibid., 151. This comparison, however, is somewhat misleading, in that the size of the potential constituency significantly increased in the interim with the legally mandated creation of works councils in small firms, where unions are poorly organized.
22. Ibid., 63.
23. Groux, 64.
24. Danièle Kergoat, "L'infirmière coordonnée," *Futur Antérieur*, no. 6 (summer 1991): 71-85; and Patrick Rozenblatt, "La forme coordination: Une catégorie sociale révélatrice de sens," *Sociologie du Travail* 33, no. 2 (1991): 239-54.
25. See part 3 in Howell, *Regulating Labor*; and Guy Caire, "Négociations collectives en France: Evolution avant et après les lois Auroux," *La Revue de l'économie sociale* 27-28 (1992): 407-26.
26. For a review of the situation in the early 1990s, see Clisthène.
27. For a review of how this cleavage divides unions elsewhere, see Swenson, *Fair Shares*; and "Labor and Limits."
28. Groux, "Le Syndicalisme d'enterprise."
29. Ministère du Travail.
30. Annie Sinclair, "Les Valeurs dans la société française," in SOFRES, *L'Etat de l'opinion 1994* (Paris: Le Seuil, 1994), p. 226.
31. The decline of the CGT, both in absolute size and relative to other union confederations, is a key element in the recent trajectory of the French labor movement. One illustration of the shift is that, in elections to works councils between 1981-91, the vote for CGT candidates declined from 32 percent to 20.4 percent. The major beneficiary was not other sections of the union movement. For example, the CFDT vote also declined, from 22.3 percent to 20.5 percent, while Force Ouvrière (FO) support increased modestly, from 9.9 percent to 11.7 percent. The significant increase was achieved by candidates not sponsored by unions, whose vote increased from 22.2 percent to 30.9 percent. (Figures from Coffineau, 87.)
32. Wolfgang Streeck and Philippe C. Schmitter, "From National Corporatism to Transnational Pluralism: Organized Interests in the Single European Market," *Politics & Society* 19, no. 2 (June 1991): 133-64.
33. Guy Groux, René Mouriaux, and Jean-Marie Pernot, "L'Européanisation du mouvement syndical: la Confédération Européenne des Syndicats," *Le Mouvement Social* no. 162 (January-March 1994): 41-67.

34. Jean-Michel Fourniau, "Point de Repères," *Société Française* 38 (1991), p. 14.
35. Ibid.
36. Robert Castel, *Les métamorphoses de la question sociale, Une chronique du salariat* (Paris: Fayard, 1995), p. 22.
37. Labbé and Croisat, 89.
38. Philippe Chevalier and Daniel Duré, "Du chômage à l'exclusion, pourquoi licencie-t-on?" *Problèmes économiques* no. 2.396-2.397 (November 2-9, 1994): 25.
39. Coffineau, 82.
40. UNIDEC, *Bulletin de Liaison* (September-October 1987): 90-91.
41. Coffineau, 86.
42. Ibid., 83.
43. For accounts of the shift, see David R. Cameron, "Exchange Rate Politics in France: The Regime-Defining Choices of the Mitterrand Presidency," in Daley, ed., *The Mitterrand Era*; Cameron, "From Barre to Balladur: Economic Policy in the Era of the EMS," in Gregory Flynn, ed., *The New France in the New Europe* (Boulder: Westview, 1995), chapter 7; W. Rand Smith, "Industrial Crises and the Left: Adjustment Strategies in Socialist France and Spain," *Comparative Politics*, 28, no. 1 (October 1995): 1-24; Peter A. Hall, "From One Modernization Strategy to Another: The Character and Consequences of Recent Economic Policy in France," paper presented to the Tenth International Conference of Europeanists, Chicago, March 15, 1996; and Hall, *Governing the Economy: The Politics of State Intervention in Britain and France* (New York: Oxford University Press, 1986), chapter 8.
44. Coffineau, 81.
45. Gérard Donnaieu et Gérard Layole, "Des relations du travail à la régulation sociale," *Personnel* no. 341 (May 1993).
46. For an early and influential statement of the new approach, by one of its leading practitioners, see Antoine Riboud, *Modernisation, mode d'emploi* (Paris: Editions 10-18, 1987).
47. For some contrasting views, see Lagandré; Martin; and Danièle Linhart, *Le Torticolis de l'autruche. L'éternelle modernisation des enterprises françaises* (Paris: Le Seuil, 1991).
48. Coffineau, 90.
49. Annie Borzeix and Danièle Linhart, "Droit d'expression directe: la boule de cristal," *Les Temps Modernes* no. 476 (March 1986): 91.

50. For a somewhat utopian analysis along these lines, see Sabel. Rosanvallon proposes a different but also quite unrealistic direction for French unions.
51. Groux and Mouriaux, in Daley, ed., *The Mitterrand Era*.
52. See, for example, Bernard Moss, "The French Strike and Social Divide: The End of Consensus Politics?" unpublished paper (Birmingham, England: Aston University, 1996).

Part III

Politics of Social Policy

Chapter 7

The Immigration Debate and the National Front

Martin A. Schain

Nothing has symbolized the malaise of French politics during the past decade more than the growing electoral support for the National Front. In the first round of the presidential elections in April 1995, the longtime leader of the party, Jean-Marie Le Pen, attracted more than 15 percent of the vote, just three points less than Edouard Balladur who ran as an incumbent prime minister. Perhaps more important, the National Front was able to capitalize on the momentum established in the presidential race in order to make significant breakthroughs in the municipal elections in June 1995. By contrast, the Chirac victory seemed to establish a reverse momentum: barely a month after Jacques Chirac's presidential victory, the governing parties of the Right were dealt a severe blow in the municipal elections both from the opposition Socialists and from the National Front.[1]

Among political commentators, there seems to be little doubt that this new electoral breakthrough will increase the influence of the National Front over the policy agenda, but, at least in the area of immigration policy, this influence has been growing for a decade. The FN (National Front) has strongly influenced the emergence of the issue, the way it has been defined, the willingness of various governments to deal with this issue, and the growing concern about immigration (or at least immigration as it has been defined within the political process) among voters of all political persuasions.

The influence of marginal political parties over agenda formation has generally been understood from the perspective of coalition politics. Thus small parties influence the development of the policy agenda in a cabinet system through their ability to provide the necessary votes to one of two parties with a plurality in Parliament, especially in the process of government formation. However, little attention has been given to the influence of marginal parties over the political agenda when they are not needed for coalition formation. In the case of the French National Front, the party was represented in the National Assembly for only a brief period of two years (1986-88). Before that and since, although its electoral support has grown, the electoral law has more or less assured that the party would have virtually no national representation.

This leaves us with two related puzzles. Why does the party seem to have considerable influence over the policy agenda, and why have voters continued to support a party that appears to have little hope of actually entering government? There is no obvious reason why FN should have significant influence over agenda formation on immigration, since, at least in principle, the major parties reached a general understanding on immigration policy over a decade ago with the passage of the Law of July 17, 1984, which established the equivalent of a French "green card."[2] On the most fundamental aspects of immigration policy there has been a sustained agreement since that time: the continued ban on non-EU immigrants (balanced by a policy of family unification); the encouragement of voluntary repatriation; and the incorporation of existing immigrant groups into French society. For its part, the Left no longer focuses on multiculturalism, as it did before 1984, and the Right has generally avoided references to repatriation of resident, legal immigrants.

Despite occasional acknowledgements of this broad area of agreement, however, both the Left and the Right have tended to develop very different portrayals of the immigration issue, and have focused on policy differences that derive in part from these divergent portrayals. Moreover, the political issues of immigration have considerably exaggerated the policy differences. How can we understand this tendency to focus on differences and to increasingly politicize immigration issues, and how can we understand the role that the National Front has played in this process?

We will focus here on are the strategic behavior of party leaders and policymakers, and their attempts to manipulate the terms of the political debate on immigration. Seen in this way, the substance of the issues involved in the immigration debate can be best understood as a part of a more general strategy of political competition. The importance of immigration issues on the political agenda, and the way that these issues have been portrayed, has had little to do with either how much opposition there has been to immigration or the potential impact of the policy proposals. As Frank Baumgartner argues,

> The degree of conflict surrounding an issue, and therefore the incentives for the adoption of different strategies of policy-making, is not determined simply by the content of the policy. On the contrary, certain environments are much more likely than others to lead to conflict, no matter what the content of the policy.

The content of the issue or the policy proposal may limit strategic possibilities, argues Baumgartner, but, as he has also demonstrated in this volume, an issue is defined and determined by policymakers and policy proposers in the context of political conflict.[3]

The political importance of some issues is sometimes clear and evident, and in those cases the problems cannot be denied, but most often policymakers pick and choose issues around larger strategic considerations. Moreover, the way an issue is defined and portrayed determines who will become involved in the debate, what E. E. Schattschneider calls the "scope of conflict," and in which political arena the issue will be decided. Schattschneider contended that the result of the struggle to expand or contract the scope of conflict is the most important determinant of its outcome.[4]

The impact of this struggle can be seen in the evolution of the question of immigration issues in France. The party struggle has revolved around issue portrayal, the result of which has effectively expanded the arena of conflict; within the expanded arena of conflict, in turn, it has become more difficult to maintain the general agreement that was reached in the late 1980s. The success of the National Front has been more than electoral. Through the dynamics of party competition and policy formation, the party has succeeded in changing the terms of the debate on immigration in a way that favors its own electoral success. In the remainder of this chapter, I will analyze the dynamics of this success.

The Emergence of Conflict and Issue Portrayal

From the perspective of 1996 it is difficult to remember that conflict over immigration policy in France emerged relatively recently. One measure of this is that, with the exception of the 1972 legislation against racial discrimination, no laws on immigration were passed by the French Parliament between the end of the World War II and January 1980. Since then, as Alec Hargreaves has accurately noted, every new French government has proposed important new legislation.[5]

The lack of attention to questions of immigration at the parliamentary level under the Fifth Republic is in part a consequence of the reduced powers of Parliament under the Fifth Republic Constitution, and the ability of the executive to act without the parliamentary approval (see Chapter 2). However, Parliament refrained from acting during the entire period of the Fourth Republic as well. In fact, the lack of legislative action can be attributed to the relatively uncontroversial nature of immigration policy during the long period of economic expansion and labor shortages. As long as immigration policy was portrayed in terms of labor recruitment there was little conflict among the diverse administrative agencies responsible for developing and monitoring this recruitment.

By the late 1960s, however, economic expansion had begun to slow down in France, and conflict began to emerge over how to deal with immigrants as "problematic" residents rather than necessary labor. Government reports issued after 1969 favored the restriction of immigration, especially immigration from North Africa, presuming that such immigrants constituted an "inassimilable island."[6] There was no significant conflict around the idea of immigration restriction, but there was also no agreement on how to implement these ideas. Throughout the decade of the of the 1970s, governments attempted to use the same administrative approach that they had used to recruit immigrant labor in order to both impose restrictions and create processes through which resident immigrants could be more easily integrated into the society and economy. Here the consensus which had supported recruitment broke down.

The first indication of the breakdown was the reaction of the Left to two ministerial circulars issued in 1972: The Marcellin Circular, issued by the Ministry of the Interior, stipulated that the well-established practice of regularizing illegal immigrants must be linked to a one-year work contract and proof of adequate housing; The Fontanet Circular, issued by the Ministry of Labor, was intended to improve housing conditions for immigrant workers. As was usually the case, neither of these directives was issued with either the consultation or the approval of labor or employer organizations. The result was a somewhat strange explosion of conflict and opposition. The directives served to mobilize the support of the Socialists and Communists—as well as the trade unions, CGT, and CFDT—in favor of the rights of immigrants in France.

The Council of State struck down the Fontanet/Marcellin Circulars in 1975 (their implementation had been delayed as opposition to them increased), but this did not deter the government from making even more rigorous proposals a few years later. By the end of the decade it was no longer possible to limit consideration of immigration policy to a small group of administrators, or even to the executive alone. Consequently, when the president decided to deal with problems of immigrant labor in 1979, two of his ministers proposed legislation *(projects de loi)*. Interior Minister, Bonnet, proposed broader police powers to deal with illegal immigrants, and authorized those accused of illegal entry to be detained for up to a week; Labor Minister Stoléru proposed the abolition of permanent labor permits, and the limitation of new permits to three years, only where jobs actually existed. But Bonnet and Stoléru were in disagreement; Bonnet felt that his colleague's bill was too weak, and forced it to be withdrawn, while large chunks of the Bonnet law, finally passed in 1980, were declared unconstitutional by both the Council of State and the Constitutional Council.[7]

The Bonnet/Stoléru proposals dealt primarily with relatively narrow questions of entry and expulsion, but nevertheless provoked serious disagreements among policy actors. However, as the initiatives of the state moved from frontier control to intervention both against and on behalf of immigrants already in France, conflict among policymakers—as well as political parties and interest groups—became more widespread and more intense. Conflict tended to follow changes in the policy arena, and the arena expanded as a result of the way in which the definition of the immigration issue evolved during the 1970s.

At the national level, efforts to expel migrants in the country were opposed by the parties and unions of the Left; at the local level, however, elected officials of the Left cooperated with the government. The development of programs to incorporate and integrate migrants increasingly involved many local political officials from the Left, as well as administrative decision-makers. Thus a 1974 amendment to the finance law that required that a portion of the employer salary tax be set aside for immigration housing programs, ultimately required collaboration between national and local housing officials (OHLM), who in many cases were (and are) local elected officials. Similarly, the language classes for immigrant children, provided for in decrees by the Ministry of Education in 1970 and 1975, and other efforts to deal with the education of immigrant children involved similar collaboration, despite the fact that local governments have only limited involvement in education matters.

In this new and more complex decision-making arena that dealt with policies of integration the commitments of representatives of the Left became more ambivalent. During the 1970s numerous Communist and some Socialist-governed municipalities began to portray the immigration issue in terms of a dispute over limited social resources between native French and immigrants. Communist mayors, who had previously (1969) publicly protested the inequitable distribution of immigrant workers and their families in Communist-governed towns, reiterated their position in stronger terms in 1972 and 1974, and sent delegations to the prefectures to underline their differences with national administration at the local level.[8] By the late 1970s it had become commonplace in Communist and Socialist-governed municipalities to exclude immigrant families from housing, schools and even social services, actions often justified by notions of a "threshold of tolerance."[9]

In some cases these actions were taken in concert with national administration, while in others they represented a challenge to established practice. As conflict among decision-makers developed, however, local elected authorities tended to expand the arena of politics through public statements and public meetings, using a negative portrayal of immigrants and a general portrayal of the dangers of immigration as mobilizing devices. This conflict at the local level spread to the national level during the presidential campaign in 1980-81 when the Communist Party engaged in a more generalized anti-immigrant campaign, which related immigrants not only to housing problems, but to crime as well.[10]

The expansion of the decision-making arena was given greater impetus by urban riots involving immigrant youth during the "hot summer" of 1981. The organization of two major commissions to deal with urban problems not only assured broader participation and consultation on problems of integration, but also further transformed the portrayal of immigration by expanding the number of policy areas to which it was related.

Thus, by the time of the electoral breakthrough of the National Front in 1983-84, not only were immigration issues on the political agenda, but their portrayal had changed fundamentally as compared with a decade earlier. As a result of efforts to deal with questions of integration, especially after the suspension of most legal, non-European immigration in 1974, local officials were brought into the policy-making process. Within this larger arena, local officials (especially those in left-governed municipalities in which there were large concentrations of immigrants) in conflict with the some of the policies imposed or permitted by central authorities, further expanded the scope of conflict by going public, in order to mobilize support, with a portrayal of immigration as an ethnic danger. This portrayal was further accentuated when issues of immigration were injected into the presidential campaign in 1980-81, and the scope of conflict was further widened as a result of the urban riots during the summer of 1981 and other incidents during subsequent years.

Even without the National Front, by 1983-84 the portrayal of immigration issues had ensured a broad scope of participants in the decision-making process at several levels of the French governmental structure, all of them periodically tempted to expand the scope of the political debate from time to time. In this context, I would argue that a party agreement on immigration issues would be difficult to maintain even under the best of circumstances. Furthermore, the electoral breakthrough of the National Front at this point becomes more understandable in a context in which the scope of conflict had been expanding for some time, and in which the portrayal of the issues by some of the participants had approached the portrayal that FN had been advocating at least since after the 1978 legislative elections.[11] Two trends support this conclusion.

First, although dissatisfaction with the Socialist-Communist government developed rapidly in 1983-84, voters need not have expressed this dissatisfaction by voting for the National Front; after all, they had the obvious option of voting for the established opposition, which is exactly what voters had done in 1981. The National Front and its precursor, *Ordre Nouveau* (New Order), had been preaching an anti-immigrant theme for a decade, without any significant electoral response. By the early 1980s, however, the restructured policy arena, and the conflict within the arena, not only provided the dynamic to expand the scope of conflict, but also changed the political opportunity structure for a marginal party such as the National Front. The mobilization efforts initiated by local officials worked to FN's benefit by reinterpreting the core issue of the extreme Right in terms of the rhetoric of the Left. Second, what most differentiated the FN electorate from the electorate of the established Right, from the very beginning of the breakthrough, was its opposition to immigration and its commitment to voting in terms of fears about *sécurité* (see table 7.1).

The initial electoral breakthroughs of the party assured that the pattern that had developed in the late 1970s would continue; that is political party conflict would continue to generate conflictual (rather than consensual) portrayals of immigration (and integration) issues, even when divergence on policy was relatively narrow. This was true, first, because the challenge of the National Front brought increasing numbers of anti-immigrant voters into the arena of conflict, even when they tended to support other political parties; second, because electoral support for the National Front grew, even when the party lost elections, posing a challenge to the electoral, if not the representational balance between Left and Right. Finally, the electoral success of the National Front has been sufficient for the party to gain representation below the national level, and to create considerable policy pressure.

The Voters and the Agenda

The primary influence of the National Front on the political agenda derives from its ability first to attract and then hold voters, and second from its ability to influence the priorities of voters who support other political parties. As the party has attracted and held voters, it has posed a strategic problem primarily for other political parties of the Right, but increasingly for parties of the Left as well for somewhat different reasons.

The electoral emergence of the National Front in 1983-84 has been well documented and analyzed: from the sudden breakthrough in the European elections in 1984 with over 11 percent of the vote (2.2 million), to the 14.4 percent of the vote that Jean-Marie Le Pen attracted in the first round of the presidential elections in 1988 (4.4 million votes), to the record 15.1 percent (4.6 million votes) vote for Le Pen in the first round of the presidential elections in 1995.[12] The structure of that vote has changed somewhat over the years. However, from the point of view of its influence on agenda formation, what is most important is first that the overwhelming majority of National Front voters in 1984 "converted" from the established parties of the Right (see table 7.1); since then, the growth in the FN electorate can be attributed to its ability to attract a large percentage of new voters (and former abstainers), while holding on to its old voters better than any other party in France.

Half of those voters who supported Le Pen's list in the European elections in 1984 had "converted" from one of the two major political parties of the established Right, while another 19 percent had been mobilized from the ranks of new voters and abstainers. The remainder had either voted for François Mitterrand in 1981 or had voted for one of the lesser candidates of the Right or Left. Clearly, in 1984, these were not party loyalists for the most part, since three-fourths of these voters identified with a party other than the National Front (see table 7.1).

Between 1984 and 1986 this electorate gradually solidified. Surveys indicated that 65 percent of those who had voted FN in 1984 voted for the party once again in the 1986 legislative election. Although almost 30 percent of this electorate did "return," to the RPR/UDF, FN continued to attract a proportion of former abstainers and new voters that was larger than the proportion of the party vote in the election, and its "loyalty" rate was far higher than that of other protest parties, such as the Ecologists (with a 20 percent level). It was argued at the time that the temporary impact of proportional representation had encouraged the electorate to vote FN in this "serious" election (as compared with the European elections four years earlier, which were deemed to have no serious consequences).

When proportional representation was abandoned for the 1988 legislative elections, the percentage of the vote remained about the same as in 1986, but the proportion of voters remaining loyal between 1986 and 1988 rose to that of the established parties (see table 7.2). Moreover, FN continued to attract a disproportionate share of new voters and former abstainers. These new recruits, combined with defectors from the established parties of the Right, made up for those who had returned to the Right. Some softness in FN electoral support was signified by the fact that Le Pen, the candidate for the presidency in 1988, had attracted 5 percent more than National Front, his party, with most of the losses in the legislative elections going to support candidates of the established Right. Nevertheless, by the 1993 legislative elections, FN candidates (none of whom won a seat) attracted 89 percent of the voters that had voted for the National Front in 1988, as well as a significant number of new voters from the Right, the Left, new voters and former abstainers, to increase its legislative showing by 25 percent (see table 7.3). The loyalty rate among FN voters greatly exceeded that of all established parties in 1993.

Thus during the past decade the National Front has become established and stabilized as an electoral party, largely, though not entirely, at the expense of the more established parties of the Right. But, in a more subtle way, the establishment of the FN has also come at the expense of the Left. One of the most striking aspects of the electoral growth of the party has been its spread to current and former "bastions" of Communist strength.

If we consider 23 towns (with a population of more than thirty thousand) in which the Communists dominated from at least 1947 until at least the early 1980s, in all of these towns the National Front has attracted an

TABLE 7.1
THE POLITICAL ORIGIN OF THE 1984 NATIONAL FRONT ELECTORATE (%)

Vote in the first round of the 1981 Presidential Elections:	
G. Marchais (Communist)	1
A. Laguiller (far left)	—
F. Mitterrand	24
B. Lalonde (environmentalist)	2
V. Giscard d'Estaing (UDF-Centrist)	23
J. Chirac (RPR-Gaullist)	27
M. Debré-M-F Garaud (div. right)	4
Abstainer, no response or new voters	19
Party Preference in 1984:	
Communist	1
Socialist	9
MRG	1
Ecologists	2
UDF	12
RPR	33
FN	24
No response	18
TOTAL	100

Source: From a SOFRES survey in Edwy Plenel and Alain Rollat, *L'effet Le Pen* (Paris: Editions la Découverte/Le Monde, 1984), p. 130.

electorate well above its national average, and in some it has become the second party to the Communists (PCF). In 1986, when the party gained less than 10 percent of the vote nationally, it attracted more than 13 percent in these bastions. In 1993, with 12.5 percent of the vote nationally, the party attracted 17 percent of the vote in these towns. In the 1995 municipal elections FN demonstrated its ability to field attractive local candidates by gaining 11.6 percent of the vote in the 226 cities with more than thirty thousand people, but a record 19 percent in the PCF bastions.

There is no evidence of which I am aware that there has been any substantial direct transfer of votes from former Communist voters to the FN, although there is evidence of a transfer of Socialist voters to Le Pen in the first round of the 1995 presidential elections.[13] Perhaps more important, the FN seems to have succeeded in mobilizing the *kinds* of voters that used to be mobilized by the Communists: young and working class. This is probably what accounts for the sharp rise in the proportion of working-class votes going to the National Front, as well as the fact that FN has become the number two party in a third of the old PCF bastions (see table 7.4).

TABLE 7.2
VOTE TRANSFERS FROM 1986 TO 1988 LEGISLATIVE ELECTIONS
VOTE IN 1988 LEGISLATIVE ELECTIONS, FIRST ROUND

Vote/86	COM	SOC	ECO	RT.	FN	
COM	85	15	0	0	0	100%
SOC	8	84	0	5	3	100%
RPR/UDF(RT)	1	5	1	86	7	100%
FN	0	0	0	19	81	100%
ABSTENT/NEW	12	34	1	38	13	100%

Source: SOFRES, *Les Elections du printemps 1988* (Paris: SOFRES, 1988), p. 36.

TABLE 7.3
VOTE TRANSFERS FROM 1988 TO 1993 LEGISLATIVE ELECTIONS
VOTE IN 1993 LEGISLATIVE ELECTIONS, FIRST ROUND

Vote/88	COM	SOC	RPR	UDF	FN	
COM	78	4	1	5	2	100%
SOC	7	50	8	6	7	100%
RPR-UDF	1	2	39	35	8	100%
FN	1	2	2	4	89	100%
ABSTENT/NEW	6	15	21	19	13	100%

Source: J. Jaffré, "Legislatives, 93 . . . ," SOFRES, *L'Etat de l'opinion 1994* (Paris: Seuil, 1994), p. 145.

Thus, in important ways, the National Front has become an established political competitor, and this role has been stabilized not only at the national level, but within the constituencies and subnational politics as well. With both the Right and the Left, the FN is seeking to expand its influence by competing for similar voters. This process seems to have had the impact of changing the political agenda for voters, not only for those who have voted for the National Front, but for voters who have supported other parties as well. One possible indication of this impact is the priority that voters have given to various issues from election to election.

In 1984, what most clearly differentiated the voters for the National Front from those of the more established Right (as well as other parties) was the priority that they gave to the issue of immigration. Of the subsample who voted for the National Front, 26 percent cited "immigrants" as their primary concern, and 30 percent cited "law and order," compared with 6 percent and 15 percent for the entire sample (see table 7.5). By 1986, as the FN electorate began to solidify, the priorities of party voters also

TABLE 7.4
PERCENTAGE OF BLUE AND WHITE COLLAR WORKERS VOTING FOR THE
NATIONAL FRONT: 1984-95

	1984E	1986L	1988P	1988L	1993L	1995P
BL. COL	10	11	18	11	15	27
WT. COL	11	12	13	10	16	17

Sources: Elisabeth Dupoirier, "L'Electorat français, le 17 juin 1984," in SOFRES, *Opinion publique 1985* (Paris: Gallimard, 1985), p. 209; SOFRES, *Les Elections du printemps 1988*, pp. 4 and 34; Jérôme Jaffré, "Législatives 93: l'alternance inéluctable," SOFRES, *L'Etat de l'opinion 1994* (Paris: Seuil, 1994), p. 144; *Liberation*, April 25, 1995, p. 8.

solidified, with 50 percent giving priority to law and order and 60 percent to immigration (several responses were possible).

What is more striking, however, is how the issue priorities of the National Front and its voters have influenced the priorities of those voting for other political parties. In 1984, relatively few voters aside from those that supported the National Front considered either immigration or law and order to be a strong priority. Now, the importance of these issues ranks with such issues as social inequality, and far higher than concerns about the environment, corruption, and the construction of Europe; only concern with unemployment ranks higher.[14]

We can look at the relationship between the rise of the National Front and the evolving priorities of voters in a somewhat different way. In 1993 fewer than half of the voters who identified themselves ideologically as "centrist" said that they had voted for a candidate of the established Right— RPR-UDF— (most of the others had voted for the Left), compared with 63 percent in 1986; on the other hand, 63 percent of those who identified as "extreme Right" (now a larger group) voted for the established Right in 1993, compared with 55 percent in 1986. By 1993, "We find ourselves... in the presence of a political radicalization of the moderate Right electorate [that is, those who vote for the moderate Right], probably linked to the increase of its audience among working-class categories."[15]

Thus, the emergence of the National Front in electoral politics in the early 1980s at first reflected the preceding weakening of the party system, as well as conflict about the political agenda on integration and incorporation among political actors involved in the policymaking process across the political spectrum. Later, the ability of FN to build an electoral following, and its increasingly important role in the political debate, had an impact on the priorities of all voters. In a little more than a decade, the National Front appears to have played a key role in the development of the political agenda

TABLE 7.5
THE MOTIVATIONS OF VOTERS: 1984-93*
(Percentage of Party Voters Voting for These Reasons)

	Law and Order				Immigrants				Unemployment				Social Inequality			
%:-->	84	86	88	93	84	86	88	93	84	86	88	93	84	86	88	93
PC	9	13	19	29	2	7	12	16	37	59	59	77	33	30	50	52
PS	8	10	21	24	3	8	13	19	27	40	43	71	24	25	43	40
Rt	17	31	38	37	3	16	19	33	20	50	41	67	7	8	18	23
FN	30	50	55	57	26	60	59	72	17	35	41	64	10	10	18	26
TT	15	24	31	34	6	17	22	31	24	46	45	68	16	17	31	32

*Since several responses were possible, the total across may be more than 100%. For 1988, the results are for supporters of presidential candidates nominated by the parties indicated.

Sources: Exit Poll, SOFRES/TF1, June 17, 1984; *Le Nouvel Observateur*, June 22, 1984; and SOFRES, *État de l'opinion, Clés pour 1987* (Paris: Seuil, 1987), p. 111; Pascal Perrineau, "Les Etapes d'une implantation électorale (1972-1988), in Nonna Mayer and Pascal Perrineau, eds., *Le Front National à découvert* (Paris: Presses de la FNSP, 1988), p. 62; Pascal Perrineau, "Le Front National la force solitaire," in Philippe Habert, Pascal Perrineau and Colette Ysmal, eds., *Le Vote sanction* (Paris: Presses de la FNSP/Dept. d'Etudes Politiques du Figaro, 1993), p. 155.

by effectively challenging the Communist Party in mobilizing young working-class voters, and by moving the priorities of the voters on the moderate, established Right further to the Right (that is, the extreme Right).

The Party System and the Political Agenda

The changing priorities of the electorate, however, both reflected and supported the dynamics of the party system, with the National Front as an emerging player. Once immigration became an issue in party politics, the dynamics of the party system gradually served to change its portrayal to that of an ethnic danger to the French nation. In fact, in the 1980s a significant gap emerged between the political portrayal of immigration and the principal aspects of immigration policy. The role of the National Front assured that conflict over policy portrayal would continue to dominate the essential agreement about immigration policy among the established parties. In the context of French party politics, the National Front has succeeded in expanding the terms of the political debate from specific issues of immigrant integration to broader questions of French national identity.

Through the dynamics of party competition it has forced other political parties, especially those of the Right, to address these issues and to place them high on their political agendas. The story of immigration politics after 1983 is less about the struggle over policy than about the struggle by political parties on both the Right and the Left to undermine the ability of the National Front to sustain the initiative in portraying these issues. Jacques Chirac's center-right Rassemblement Pour la République (RPR) has been deeply divided in its competition with FN for voters who are frightened by the problems of a multi-ethnic society either by cooperating with FN and accepting their issues in more moderate terms, or by attempting to destroy their rival on the Right through isolation and rejection of their portrayal of the issue altogether. Each time that RPR feels it has succeeded in outmaneuvering the National Front (the legislative elections of 1988, the municipal elections of 1989, and the immigration legislation of 1993), the party is reminded that the challenge will not disappear (the by-election victories of the FN in Marseilles and Dreux in December 1989, and the presidential and municipal elections of 1995). In the end, the electorally weak parties of the Right frequently need the 10-15 percent of the electorate that has voted FN.

As for the Socialists, through 1993 they struggled to defuse the rhetoric of the National Front with a variety of approaches: by policy initiatives (strengthening border controls, at the same time that they tried to develop a policy of integration) when they controlled the government; by agreeing with the established Right when they were electorally threatened by the opposition, as did Socialist Prime Minister Laurent Fabius by agreeing with Jacques Chirac in 1985 that "the National Front poses some real questions..."; and, more generally, by alternating between the pluralist rhetoric of a "right to difference" approach to immigrants and an individualistic "right to indifference."[16]

Despite the confusion, the dynamics of party competition have resulted in a redefinition of the issue of immigration in national politics, from a labor market problem, to an integration/incorporation problem, to a problem that touches on national identity, to problems of education, housing, law and order, to problems of citizenship requirements. A reasonably clear consensus among the established parties of the Right and Left developed between 1984 and 1985, if not about the details of policy, then about a general approach to policy, that goes back to the consensus vote in July 1984 on legislation to establish a single ten-year residency card (a French Green Card), and the Fabius-Chirac debate in 1985: a policy of integration "... respecting our laws, our customs and our values," that limits any substantial increase in immigrants, but that also excludes recourse to forced return.[17]

However, within the relatively open national party arena it has been difficult to relate the general consensus on policy to the details on application and (most of all) to the public portrayal of immigration issues. The National Front has maintained pressure on other parties of the Right, while the Socialists in government were challenged both by the Right and by more politicized and organized North Africans born in France ("beurs"), as well as Moslems who have been less hesitant about questioning French laws, customs and values.

Thus, the Rocard government wanted to downplay the issues of immigration when it first arrived in office in 1988. Nevertheless, it found that, because of the challenge of the "Islamic scarf" crisis in the fall of 1989, as well as subsequent electoral victories of the National Front, it was unable to avoid the pressure that moved immigration to center-stage. The "foulard affair," (scarf affair) very quickly became the concern of the minister of education, as well as an issue of parliamentary debate.[18] A decade earlier, such incidents might have been dealt with more quietly within the local arena, in the same way that decision-makers had dealt with housing and other school problems. By 1989, however, local school problems that involved integration could no longer be contained by the local political-administrative system, and were rapidly translated into the vocabulary of national political issues. In the context of party competition, new incidents are thus redefined in terms of the existing debate.

The importance of the struggle over issue portrayal is illustrated well by events in the spring of 1990, when the Rocard government attempted to develop a consensus about the portrayal of the immigration problem. Using as a pretext a disturbing report by the National Consultative Committee on the Rights of Man, the prime minister called a meeting of all political leaders, except those of the National Front, to develop a program to combat racism. The RPR-UDF opposition, however, rejected this definition of the problem, and organized their own meeting (March 31–April 1) the weekend preceding the meeting with the prime minister to discuss problems of immigration. When they met with the government, the opposition came armed with four propositions for changing immigration policy. They were able to extract from the Rocard government a commitment to a second meeting that would deal with RPR-UDF opposition initiatives, preceding a general parliamentary debate on racism and immigration in May 1990.[19]

Behind most of this activity was the continuing pressure of the National Front, which was holding its National Congress while the government and the center-right opposition were developing their positions. The opposition groups (that is the Right) had never come closer to agreement on a unified approach to the politics of immigration, and their propositions represented a way of differentiating themselves from the government while tentatively approaching some of the ideas of the National Front. The clearest statement was made by former president Valéry Giscard d'Estaing, who was quoted as saying: "The foreigners can live in France with full rights [dans le respect des droits de l'homme] but they cannot change France." Giscard promptly launched a national petition to hold a referendum to make naturalization legislation more restrictive (one of the proposals agreed to by the opposition and eventually passed in 1993).

Not all the actions of the Socialist governments emphasized consensus. Both Michel Rocard and Edith Cresson also attempted to portray their approach to immigration as "hard" and decisive. Thus, after the Socialists returned to power in 1988 there was a steady increase in the number of foreigners detained because of invalid documents: the number of foreigners detained rose two and a half times from 1989 to 1991, but the percentage of those actually expelled (some after hearings) declined from over 60 to 18 percent of those detained.[20] The government was clearly making a point at a time when it was under considerable pressure from the opposition, and when the National Front was doing well in by-elections.

So, the struggle to maintain a core consensus among the established parties was undermined in important ways by the electoral success of the National Front (mostly in by-elections during this period), which exacerbated divisions between the government and the opposition over immigration—or rather over how to define and treat foreigners on French soil. The far Right benefited from growing national concern about immigration (between September 1989 and February 1990, the issue moved from seventh to second place among the concerns of French voters), but also mediated and defined that concern within the party system. In this kind of environment, it seems unlikely that any kind of *expression* of consensus could develop, despite the more general agreement on policy. As *Le Monde* noted several years ago, "... political leaders are convinced that the issue is too important for partisan quarrels.... They vie with each other to accentuate their divergences as if to mask their agreements."[21]

These divergences were further accentuated after the return of the Right to power in 1993. The victorious coalition of the Right made immigration/integration policy a centerpiece of their campaign, but this did not prevent the National Front from increasing its percentage of the vote by 25 percent over 1988 (but with no victorious candidates).

As the platform of the Right coalition had already announced, the new government resuscitated and passed legislation that modified the nationality code to make it more difficult for children born in France of non-French parents to obtain French citizenship: the resuscitated proposals also gave mayors the right to block family reunification, and facilitated the jailing and expulsion of undocumented foreigners. In addition, the 80 percent majority in the National Assembly permitted the government to amend the constitution, and to severely restrict asylum applications.[22] All of these moves certainly made life more difficult for resident foreigners (and non-white citizens as well). Indeed, their implementation produced results that should have broadened the electoral attraction of the establish Right.

The conflict between consensus-building on immigration policy and political pressures to focus on party differences is also evident from the way policymaking structures were organized and used by different governments. The emphasis by the Cresson government on border controls in 1991-92, as a way of expressing concern over questions of immigration, was decided in a well publicized meeting of a *comité intérministériel* (a meeting of a group of ministers called and chaired by the prime minister) on immigration. The report issued at the end of the meeting accentuated the government's commitments to focus on border controls.[23] *Comités intérministériels* have been relatively infrequent in recent years, and have been used as an arena for a public shift in the political agenda.

This focus was a change from that of the previous Rocard government (1988-91), which had been reacting to a series of incidents that began with the "foulard affair" in the fall of 1989. Rocard, who had been forced to give more weight to problems of integration because of the "foulard affair," attempted to circumscribe and contain these issues in a different way. He first created a new framework for political decision-making: a High Commission on Integration under the auspices of the same director (Marceau Long) whom the previous conservative government had named to head *their* commission to study the naturalization and citizenship aspects of immigration in 1987; and a special secretary-general (Hubért Prévot) who operated out of the prime minister's office and, in effect, establish a direct link with him.

With the support of the commission, the government attempted to redefine the portrayal of the problem of integration, with a much stronger focus on immigrants as only one of several groups on the margins of urban society. In its first report to the prime minister, the High Commission, rejected notions of *insertion* that were current in the early 1980s as too close to *le droit à la différence* (the right to be different), and ideas of assimilation as too close to a narrow Jacobin notion of cultural unity. Instead, borrowing from the work of Jacqueline Costa-Lascoux, the commission chose to define its policy recommendations in terms of *intégration,* a dynamic, reciprocal process, which, while recognizing the importance of cultural differences, stresses the importance of those cultural elements shared by the entire community.[24]

In fact, the report reflected policy choices that were well underway by the time it was published. Since 1989, the Rocard government had been increasingly portraying immigrant problems as part of a broader urban agenda, and highlighting the need for equal treatment for immigrants in many sectors of French social and economic life. This policy orientation picked up and emphasized aspects of policy development that had begun in the early 1980s in housing and education. In practical terms, this seemed to mean a portrayal of the immigration issue in terms that could defuse those aspects that were most effective for electoral mobilization.[25]

The Cresson government made a different policy choice, which was related to a different way of organizing decision-making. It downgraded consideration of integration questions altogether by removing responsibility for these issues from the prime minister's office, and by naming a secretary of state for integration of African origin (Kofi Yamgnane) attached to the Ministry of Social Affairs. The new secretary of state had been mayor of a small French town, and had little political weight. Secretary-General Prévot remained, but he too was now attached to the Ministry of Social Affairs. While he continued to attend some meetings, the office no longer played any role in coordinating immigration policy.[26]

Yamgnane might have replaced him in this role but his position was too weak, and the mandate of his office reflected the new thinking about immigration to a far greater degree than had that of his predecessor. All of the top civil servants in the secretariat were experts on urban problems (indeed almost all of them had come from the Minister of Urban Affairs), and none had any experience working on immigration problems.[27] The projects in which the secretariat was involved included those related to immigrants, but most dealt with more general considerations of "the excluded": poverty, prostitutes and battered women, young workers and job training.

Thus, under Cresson, between electoral cycles, integration policy was moved from the more public political arena back to the administrative arena, constrained by what the administrators refer to as a "general political line" that emphasized "integration" in the ways defined above. However, as we have seen, the dynamics of the party arena created a volatile situation, and, with the onset of yet another electoral cycle in the fall of 1992, integration policy was "politicized" once again.

The organization of the new government under Balladur in April 1993, reflected its intention to move in a clear and aggressive way to attract the electorate of the extreme Right by raising the stakes of the immigration debate in a way that would differentiate it from the previous Socialist government. The powerful Ministry of the Interior was given to Charles Pasqua, who had held the same post during the period of 1986-88. Pasqua, strongly committed to such changes, would be the chief government spokesman for this high-profile effort. At the same time, Pierre Méhaignerie, whose position on immigration and integration was far "softer" than that of Pasqua, was given the ministry of justice, and Simone Veil, who was an open opponent of the National Front and its hard line towards immigrants, became minister of social and urban affairs. Thus, Veil would be the effective spokesman for integration policy, while Méhaignerie would attempt to soften the rough edges of the Pasqua hard core policies.[28] The focus on new departures in immigration policy had been organized into the Ministry of the Interior, while lower priority management of integration policy had been left with the Ministry of Social and Urban Affairs. In both cases, policymaking remained in the public arena, centralized in the office of each minister, and arbitrated through the office of the prime minister through public and well-publicized moves.[29]

Initially, these bold and open moves seemed to produce real results. "Agreement with the ideas supported by J-M Le Pen" fell by 40 percent, (and even more among the electorate of the Right) during the year after the conservative victory in 1993 and opposition to his ideas as "a danger to democracy" increased to record levels.[30] In addition, by 1995 it was clear that the new legislation was producing desired results by dramatically reducing immigration by 30 percent in 1994.[31] However, support for Le Pen had been falling rapidly since 1991, but neither this nor the success of the new legislation produced the desired *political* results. The support for Le Pen's ideas began to rise once again in 1994: between January 1994 and April 1996 this index rose from a low of 19 percent to 28 percent, with almost half the sympathizers of the Right supporting these ideas.[32] It was this environment that enabled Jean-Marie Le Pen to top his previous record in the Presidential elections in April 1995 and the National Front to deepen its local roots two months later.

It is hardly surprising that the electoral success of the National Front has served to define and drive agenda formation of successive governments. What has been more surprising is how shocked established political leaders always seem to be when the FN is successful. One conclusion we might draw is that portrayals of immigration/integration issues that are meant to mobilize a broad scope of participation for established parties seem only to increase FN support. However, governments, driven by the dynamics of party competition, seem incapable of eluding the pressure to recapture a volatile electorate by engaging with the National Front.

The difficulty of the FN challenge was demonstrated well by the end of the electoral cycle in 1995. Immigration themes played almost no role in the presidential election campaign. Both Balladur and Chirac appeared to presume that the legislation passed in 1993 would defuse the issue, while Jospin, in a brief paragraph in his election program, indicated that he would ease the requirements on the children of immigrant parents born in France imposed by the 1993 legislation. Only Le Pen spoke of going further.[33]

After Le Pen's impressive showing in the first round, however, both Chirac and Jospin attempted to attract FN voters without making obvious overtures to Le Pen. Jospin spoke approvingly of proportional representation, while both Chirac and Juppé (who would be named prime minister) spoke darkly of problems of law and order and "... the confiscation of the maintenance of order by ethnic or religious groups."[34]

The campaign and results of the municipal elections in June 1995 once again focused attention on immigration issues. Le Pen promised to use the new local power of the FN to emphasize "national preference" in all policy areas. Clearly, like problems of unemployment, this new tilt of the immigration issue has posed a challenge for Chirac, a challenge that spills over into other issues. The president created a full ministry to deal with questions of immigration and integration, with the awkward name of the Ministry of Integration and the Struggle Against Exclusion.

In one of his first moves, the new minister, Eric Raoult announced a program to move "delinquent families" (generally considered a code word for immigrant families) out of slum neighborhoods, presumably into other slum neighborhoods. At the same time, Minister of the Interior Jean-Louis Debré began an intensive crackdown on undocumented aliens, sending two plane-loads home during the first weeks of July. He noted that the only way to integrate legal immigrants was to clamp down on illegal immigrants.[35] Finally, in reaction to the victories of the National Front in the municipal elections, as well as to a new wave of bombings by Algerian dissidents, the president suspended the implementation of the Schengen Accords in July.[36] In an interview with a German newspaper, one of Chirac's chief aides argued that "Europe works for Le Pen," and he suggested that the Le Pen challenge might be met by derailing Schengen and returning to a hard-line Gaullist portrayal of the nation-state.[37]

The massive strikes in December 1995 (see chapter 6), and the losses of by-elections in large numbers, kindled fears within the Chirac government and majority that the Right would lose the 1998 legislative elections.[38] Such fears were fed by the increased influence of the National Front in public opinion, by new FN organizational initiatives that were linked to the December strikes, and by a change in FN party strategy.

In the early months of 1996 the National Front sought to capitalize on widespread worker disaffection (as well as the weakness of established trade union organizations). In rapid succession, the party organized its own police union, its own union of Paris transport workers, and its own association of small and medium enterprises.[39] At the same time, the FN developed a strategy—which they dubbed *dissuasion du faible au fort* (deterrence of the strong by the weak)—that would challenge the established parties of the Right more directly. The party leadership ordered its followers to oppose candidates of the majority Right in by-elections with the objective of forcing the government to pass a new electoral law that would reestablish proportional representation for the 1998 legislative elections.[40] In addition, the party began to develop a "social" rhetoric to attract recruits into its new union organizations. Although the success of the new strategy has been mixed and is weakly supported by National Front voters,[41] the pressure on the government and the majority seems clear.

In April 1996 thirty members of a National Assembly committee recommended new immigration legislation that would limit undocumented immigrants' access to hospitals and schools and that would facilitate expulsion of minors from French territory. The recommendations were widely opposed even within the majority; opposition included former hard-line interior minister, Charles Pasqua.[42] Nevertheless, immigration legislation was now back on the political agenda, placed there by committee members who were particularly vulnerable to the new FN strategy. In the districts of 9 members of the committee the National Front was the second party in the 1993 legislative elections; and in 22 of 30 districts of members the FN vote was well above the 1993 national mean for the party.[43]

The Dynamic of Alliance Formation

This reminds us that the dynamic of competition is also evident in alliance formation at the subnational level. Alliance formation in regions, departments, and communes takes place at two levels: that of electoral alliances, and that of governing. In general, established political parties would prefer not to engage with the National Front in the formation of alliances either explicitly or implicitly. Nevertheless, from the very earliest days of the electoral breakthrough, this became a position that was almost impossible to maintain. In the municipal elections of March 1983, local RPR and UDF politicians in Dreux decided to form a joint electoral list with the FN, a decision that was approved by the national leadership of both parties. That decision was reversed when irregularities forced a second election in September. Unable to secure an absolute majority in the first round of the election, the RPR-UDF would have been forced to pay an unacceptable price if they continued to ignore FN in the second round. In the end, they decided to form a joint list with the FN, which was victorious. As a result, three National Front councilors were named assistant mayors in the new local government.[44]

Since then, the ability of the party to win elections at the subnational level, where there is some dose of proportionality, has increased with its ability to field candidates. In 1986, FN lists were presented in each of the 22 regions in France. With almost 10 percent of the vote, the party elected 137 (out of 1682) regional councilors; not a lot, but enough to exert strategic influence over coalition formation in 12 of the 22 regions. In six regions their votes were needed to elect a council president from the established Right. In Languedoc-Roussillon the Gaullist president reached a formal accord on a "Program of Action" with FN; in five other regions FN was able to negotiate important positions in the regional government, and in five additional regions it gained some lesser positions.[45] Six years later, the FN increased its regional representation to 239, with representation in every region. In 14 of the 22 regions, the Right now depended for its majority on the councilors of the FN, who carefully demonstrated their ability to arbitrate in the election of regional presidents and the selection of regional executives.[46] The influence of FN elected representatives on agenda formation is still unclear, but the expanding implantation of the party at this level will probably have an impact on the day-to-day operation of government and on the construction of alliances for future elections. We find a similar pattern at the local (commune) level.

With little presence at the local level (despite the victory in Dreux), the National Front benefited from some conversions of local notables from the established Right during the decade of the 1980s. By 1989, FN was able to present lists in 214 of the 392 cities with more than twenty-thousand people. In other cases, candidates of the FN joined with others in lists simply dubbed *divers droite* or *extrême droite*. Well over a thousand FN municipal councilors were elected in 143 towns with more than twenty-thousand people, 478 on lists with the FN label and 621 on alliance lists or as individual candidates. Here too, the agenda-setting role of these municipal councilors was unclear. What has been clear is that, at least in the larger towns in France, the National Front has been engaged in day to day politics, and has been in a position to build support on the basis of its local *notabilité* in much the same way that it did after its success in Dreux.[47]

The 1995 municipal elections, therefore, both confirmed the effective presence of the FN at the local level and demonstrated its ability to build on that presence. For the first time, the party won outright victories in three large towns and expanded its presence (thanks to proportional representation) in many others. Of particular importance was the victory in Toulon, where FN captured 41 of the 56 municipal council posts. In Marignane, the party won control from the UDF, gaining 27 of the 39 council seats; and in historic Orange, FN won 24 of the 35 seats by edging out the Socialist in the second round. In at least four other towns—Vitrolles, Noyon, Dreux, and Mulhouse—only "republican front" (Left/Right) alliances in the second round prevented FN from taking control. In all of these towns, however, the National Front had been building support for a decade, and, in this sense, the breakthrough was the result of a long and successful effort.

All in all, the National Front fielded almost 25 thousand candidates in 1995, which enabled it to more than double the number of municipal councilors directly or indirectly affiliated with the party.[48] Perhaps the best measure of its growing influence was the fact that, with almost 12 percent of the vote in towns with a population of more than thirty thousand the National Front gained sufficient support to remain in the second round in more than half of them (119), and then win seats in most of the towns (101) in which it ran. The FN became the key arbitrator of the second round. Although it certainly failed to provoke the parties of the established Right to form common coalitions (despite some initial successes that were later withdrawn[49]), its presence in the second round had a strong influence on outcomes for both the Left and the Right.[50]

The results of the municipal elections of 1995 are important because local electoral success in France is frequently the key building block for national success. They are also important because thousands more FN elected officials are now in place and prepared to trade their votes for influence over the policy agenda. Finally, municipal elections are important because of their influence over the policy agenda at the local level. By November 1995, mayors from the parties of the conservative majority were reporting that they were cutting back on programs against "exclusion" and in favor of immigrant integration. Voter distrust of such programs, they argued, "... explains the rise of the National Front".[51]

Conclusion

Now we can return to some of the questions with which we began. The National Front has been a major force in agenda formation essentially because of its ability to attract large numbers of voters away from other parties. The electoral breakthrough of FN can be attributed in part to electoral volatility and the willingness of voters to reject the established parties of the early 1980s, but also because of what had happened to the core issue represented by the National Front. During the period of the 1970s, governments had shifted the focus of policymaking to problems of integration/incorporation, which in turn brought large numbers of elected local officials and administrators into the policymaking network. The expansion of the this network also served to increase disagreement about policy choices and conflict about policy tempted those in disagreement to expand the scope of conflict by portraying immigration issues in terms that would bring them new allies. This process then created an environment favorable to the National Front.

In the cauldron of party competition the National Front proved adept at altering the political agenda: first, by actually winning some elections; second, by threatening to deprive other parties of winning elections; and, finally, by winning enough electoral contests at the subnational level to engage in alliance-building (often unacknowledged) and/or political blackmail. In either case, the FN gained influence over agenda formation. One major result of this process was to convince increasingly large numbers of voters that, whichever party they supported, questions of immigration were an important priority.

What is most striking about the process we have analyzed here is, first, the extent to which issue portrayal has been dominated by the concerns of the National Front; second, the gap between the conflict over portrayal and a broad area of agreement among political parties on policies of immigration; and third, the extent to which portrayal appears to be different from what we know about immigrant integration. The National Front taps deep fears about national identity and the ethnic danger posed by large numbers of North African immigrants of the Islamic faith, fears that have been fed for decades by leaders of all major political parties, as well as by administrative reports. Nevertheless, the most recent study of Algerians in France indicates a steady process of quiet integration: a high level of intermarriage (50 percent for men born in France) and a low level of religious practice rivaling that of the "native" French population.[52] While such data are important to integrate into our analysis, they do not necessarily have an impact on the political debate, since political issues and political reality are constructed through dynamics that tend to mold new facts into old political categories.

Notes to Chapter 7

1. In fact, the political balance of power among the 226 cities with a population of over 30 thousand remained more or less stable, compared with 1989. However, the governing parties, having won a massive legislative victory in 1993 and the presidency in 1995, were expected to make major electoral inroads among the cities governed by the Left. Their failure to do so, combined with several important victories by the Socialists and three victories by the National Front, were widely interpreted as a real lack of an *effet Chirac*. See, for example, *Le Figaro*, June, 20, 1995, p. 6; and *Liberation*, June 19, 1995, p. 3.

2. See Patrick Weil, *La France et ses étrangers* (Paris: Calmann-Lévy, 1991), Chapters 6 and 7.

3. Frank R. Baumgartner, *Conflict and Rhetoric in French Policymaking* (Pittsburgh: University of Pittsburgh Press, 1989), p. 6.

4. E. E. Schattschneider, *The Semi-Sovereign People* (New York: Hold, Rinehart and Winston, 1960), p. 4.

5. Alec Hargreaves, *Immigration, "Race" and Ethnicity in Contemporary France* (London: Routledge, 1996), p. 177.

6. See the best known report written by Correntin Calvez, "Le Problème des travailleurs étrangers," *Journal Officiel de la Republique Française, Avis et Rapports du Conseil Economique et Social*, 27 March 1969.

7. See the account in Douglas E. Ashford, *Policy and Politics in France: Living With Uncertainty* (Philadelphia: Temple University Press, 1982), chapter 7.

8. See André Vieuget, *Français et immigrés: le combat du P. C. F.* (Paris: Editions Sociales, 1975)

9. I have previously explored this process in Martin A. Schain, "Immigrants and Politics in France," in John S. Ambler, ed., *The French Socialist Experiment* (Philadelphia: Institute for the Study of Human Issues, 1985).

10. I have analyzed this campaign in Martin A. Schain, "Immigrants in the Town: Communism and Urban Politics in France," in Ida Simon-Barouh and Pierre-Jean Simon, eds., *Les Etrangers dans la ville* (Paris: L'Harmattan, 1990).

11. The anti-immigrant theme had been part of the FN rhetoric from the very beginning. However, after 1979 the party strongly emphasized the danger of immigrants and immigration as a way to establish a clear demarcation with the established Right.

12. See my article, Martin A. Schain, "The National Front in France and the Construction of Political Legitimacy," *West European Politics* 10, 2 (April 1987); and the excellent collection by Nonna Mayer and Pascal Perrineau, *Le Front National à découvert* (Paris: Presses de la FNSP, 1989).

13. See Pascal Perrineau, "La dynamique du vote Le Pen: le poids du gaucholepénisme," in Pascal Perrineau and Colette Ysmal, *Le Vote de crise* (Paris: Presses de la FNSP, 1995), pp. 243-261. Also see *Le Monde*, February 1, 1996.
14. See Pascal Perrineau, "Le Front National la force solitaire," in Philippe Habert, Pascal Perrineau and Colette Ysmal, eds., *Le Vote sanction* (Paris: Presses de la FNSP/Dept. d'Etudes Politiques du Figaro, 1993), p. 155.
15. Jean Chiche and Elisabeth Dupoirier, "Les Voies contrastées de la reconquête électorale. L'électorat de la droite moderée en 1993," in Philippe Habert, Pascal Perrineau and Colette Ysmal, ed., *Le Vote sanction* (Paris: Presses de la FNSP/Dept. d'Etudes Politiques du Figaro, 1993), p. 133.
16. *Le Monde*, February 11 and December 7, 1989; See Judith Vichniac, "French Socialists and *Droit à la différence*," *French Politics and Society* 9, 1 (winter, 1991).
17. See Leveau, "Les partis et l'intégration des beurs," 258-261; and Weil, 181-185 and Chapter 7.
18. See David Beriss, "Scarves, Schools and Segregation: The Foulard Affair," *French Politics and Society*, 8, 1 (1990).
19. The initiatives of the government and the opposition are reported in *Le Monde*, April, 3 and 4, 1990.
20.

ARTICLE 22 EXPUSIONS ("RECONDUITES À LA FRONTIÈRE")

	Detained for Expulsion	Expelled	Percentage
1988	8992	5863	65.2
1989	7669	4808	62.7
1990	9641	4567	47.4
1991	32673	5867	18.0

Source: Ministry of the Interior, Fichier GASCH3

21. *Le Monde*, April 3, 1990, p. 12.
22. The constitution was officially amended on November 19, 1993. The procedure was necessitated by the decision of the Constitutional Council of August 13, 1993 (confirmed by the Council of State a month later), which had declared eight articles of the immigration legislation of July 13 unconstitutional. Many of the provisions of the new immigration legislation, including those that deal with family unification, stricter rules regarding marriage, the deportation of undocumented aliens, and new judicial procedures would not have been possible without this amendment.
23. *Comités intérministerials* are infrequent formal meetings initiated by the prime minister around a specific subject. More frequent, regular contacts among ministries dealing with a particular problem are *réunions intérministérielles*, usually attended by high civil servants. For the results of the July 1991 meeting, see *La Maitrise de l'immigration*, Premier Ministre, Service de Presse, July 11, 1991.

24. Haut Conseil à l'Intégration, *Pour un modèle français d'intégration* (Paris: La Documentation Française, 1991), pp. 18-19; Costa-Lascoux, *De l'immigré au citoyen*, (Paris: La Documentation Française, 1989) pp. 11-12.
25. Costa-Lascoux, 77-114.
26. Hubért Prévot, interview by author, Paris, June 4, 1992.
27. Secretariat d'Etat de l'Intégration, interviews by author, Paris, May 27, 1992.
28. *Le Monde*, April 2 and June 20-21, 1993.
29. *Le Monde*, June 22, 1993.
30. *Le Monde*, February 4, 1994.
31. *Le Monde*, February 12-13, 1995.
32. *Le Monde* April 3, 1996.
33. See *Le Monde*, September 20, 1994.
34. *Le Monde*, April 27, 1995. On these questions, see James G, Shields, "Le Pen and the Progression of the Far Right in France," *French Politics and Society*, 3, 2 (spring, 1995): 34-35.
35. These, and other early moves by the government are documented in *The European*, July 21-27, 1995.
36. Implementation of the Schengen Accords was formally delayed until the end of the year, a procedure that was permitted under the accords. See *Le Monde*, July 18, 1995. Implementation was then further delayed with the French government citing as its reason the inability of the Benelux states to control the movement of drugs across their frontiers, and has now been only partially implemented. *Le Monde*, March 26, 1996.
37. Ibid; See also *The European*, July 28-August 3, 1995.
38. *Le Monde*, April 6 and 10, 1996.
39. See *Le Monde*, February 13, March 24-25, and April 3, 1996.
40. *Le Monde*, March 26 and April 3, 1996.
41. *Le Monde*, April 3 and May 3, 1996.
42. *Le Monde*, April 17 and 19, 1996.
43. *Le Monde*, April 19, 1996.
44. I have explored the Dreux election in Martin A. Schain, "The National Front and the Construction of Political Legitimacy."
45. See Guy Birenbaum, *Le Front National en politique* (Paris: Balland, 1992), pp. 79-80.

46. See Claude Patrait, "Pouvoirs régionaux en chantier...," in Philippe Habert, Pascal Perrineau and Colette Ysmal, eds. , *Le vote éclaté* (Paris; Presses de la FNSP/Dept. d'études politiques du Figaro, 1992), p. 311.
47. See Birenbaum, 162-170.
48. Exact numbers are hard to verify, since many FN candidates—as in previous elections—presented themselves as "divers droite or "indépendants. " See *Le Monde*, June 21, 1995 and *Liberation*, June 19, 1995.
49. See *Liberation*, June 1 and 4, 1995.
50. In the second round, the presence of the FN resulted in 97 three-way races and 20 four-way races, almost all in large towns and cities. See *Liberation*, June 19, 1995.
51. *Le Monde*, November 12-13, 1995.
52. These are results of a study by INED, the initial results of which were published by Michèle Tribalat, *Faire France: Une enquête sur les immigrés et leurs enfants* (Paris: La Découverte/Essais, 1995). Excerpts from this volume were cited in *Le Monde*, March 31, 1995, p. 8.

Chapter 8

Conflict and Consensus in French Education

John S. Ambler

French education is often characterized as stalemated, deadlocked, and incapable of adapting to its changing environment. In fact, French education has been transformed in recent decades, although there are specific policy areas in which change has been difficult. The most striking change has been from elite to mass education at the secondary and higher levels, a process that has created a new set of issues and controversies superimposed upon the old ones. Policy has also responded to changing ideas and preferences with regard to democratization, decentralization, and government subsidies to private schools. The evolution of policy in these areas will be examined in search of an understanding of the conditions which inhibit or facilitate policy change.

Michel Crozier, the prominent theorist of bureaucratic stalemate in French society, has often cited education as one of those sectors that remains deadlocked, impervious to all serious reform, except when forced to change in response to a crisis.[1] Indeed, with respect to the most sensitive issues—church schools and student rights—the education minister's margin for maneuver is very limited. Even reforms designed to change pedagogical methods are likely to meet with resistance from powerful unions that, like the majority of their members, tend to view the imposition of new and different duties for teachers as a violation of their rights. Olivier Guichard, who had the misfortune of being appointed minister of education not long after the social and political upheaval of May 1968, complained that any change proposed in educational structure or content (he sought to delay the introduction of Latin from the sixth grade to the eighth) seemed sure to set off "a war of religion."[2] A few months later, in 1970, Guichard described his job as impossible: "There is no political or administrative post in France that is as monstrous as that of national education minister. The notion that a politician can supervise 811,000 civil servants and a budget of 17 billion francs with the help of a skeletal headquarters staff is far-fetched."[3] François Bayrou, writing just three years before he himself was given the job, described the typical minister of education as arriving in office with "reforming zeal," "certain of engraving his name in the marble of another reform"; later, having met with insults, protest demonstrations and collapse of support, "the minister, or what is left of him, climbs back into his ivory tower and awaits his successor. He has done nothing. He is worn out."[4]

Education, more than most policy areas in France, carries the potential for arousing enormous passion. Each new minister of education either knows, or soon learns, that the education policy arena is littered with minefields. Any proposed change in the delicate balance between public schools and subsidized private schools, any threat to the established rights of university students, may well detonate a political explosion capable of blowing the minister away. A massive demonstration of private school supporters in June 1984 resulted in the resignation of both the minister of education, Alain Savary, and of the prime minister, Pierre Mauroy. In the fall of 1986, angry student demonstrations against a bill that would have given French universities the right to select their own students resulted in the withdrawal of the bill and the resignation of Deputy Minister for Higher Education and Research Alain Devaquet. Other massive student demonstrations threatened to overturn the entire Fifth Republic in May 1968, forced the government to increase funding for secondary schools in late 1990 and for universities in 1995, achieved the withdrawal of a government proposal allowing reduced salaries for young job-seekers in the spring of 1994, and persuaded the government to abandon its proposed reform of technical university programs in February 1995.

The Transition to Mass Education: Successes and Unanticipated Consequences

Despite the hazards of reform, it would be grossly misleading to label as "deadlocked" an educational system that has expanded the proportion of the age group completing a full secondary school program from under 5 percent in 1950 to 34 percent in 1980, and to over 60 percent in 1990, en route to what now appears to be a realistic goal of 75-80 percent by the year 2000.[5] The Organization for Economic Cooperation and Development (OECD) reports that as of 1992, the proportion of seventeen-year-olds in school full time stood at 87.2 percent in France, compared to 72 percent in the United States and to 55.3 percent in the United Kingdom.[6] Total enrollments in institutions of higher education soared from 310,000 in 1960-61 to 1,840,000 in 1991-92.[7] Over the past four decades, France has moved from elite to mass education at the secondary and tertiary levels, while also becoming a world leader in preschool education. Between 1960-61 and 1990-91, the proportion of children in preschool rose from 9.9 percent to 34.4 percent for two-year-olds, from 36 percent to 98.8 percent for three-year-olds, and from 62.6 percent to 100 percent for four-year-olds.[8]

In France, as in most of Western Europe, the prosperity of the post-war years created both the wealth and the incentives necessary for the expansion of secondary and higher education. On the demand side, French families have urged their children to seek more and higher diplomas in order to compete effectively in a changing job market. On the supply side, government officials, whether conservative or Socialist, have expanded secondary schools and universities at a rapid pace, not only to satisfy the expectations of their electorates, but also in the hope of strengthening the national economy in an era of high technology and fierce global competition. In a policy area often marked by bitter conflict, a broad consensus has emerged in support of mass secondary education. When in 1985 the Socialist minister of education, Jean-Pierre Chevènement, launched the slogan, "80 percent of the age group to the level of the baccalauréat by the year 2000," the goal was thought by many to be unrealistic. Chevènement's conservative successor, René Monory, pared the objective back to 74 percent, but pledged that the government would continue to expand access to full secondary education. By the time the conservatives came to office again in 1993, the goal, now variously defined as 75 percent or 80 percent, was so broadly accepted that it was not seriously called into question.

While apparently irreversible, the trend toward mass secondary and higher education has created new social tensions and raised new issues. These will be considered under three headings. First, the expansion of education has failed to solve the problem of unemployment among youth. Second, keeping young people in school longer has not greatly facilitated upward social mobility for children from the working class. Third, the stresses of expansion have created anxiety and frustration among students and teachers and within the public at large.

Rising Unemployment Among Youth

Contrary to the expectations of the many partisans of the manpower theory of economic growth, the French economy performed more erratically in the 1980s and early 1990s than in the 1960s, even though educational levels were rising rapidly. During the recession of the early 1990s, the unemployment rate among those 15-29 years of age on the job market (those employed or seeking employment *not* including those in school) rose from an already high 14.9 percent in March 1991 to 20.7 percent in March 1994. Young people without a diploma did worse, with an unemployment rate of 34.6 percent in March 1994; yet even among those with the full secondary diploma, the *baccalauréat,* or *"bac,"* the unemployment rate rose from 12.5 percent to 18.4 percent over this same three-year period.[9] Obviously there are forces far more powerful than education that shape the French job market. Among these, most likely, are labor laws and labor unions which tend to protect the jobs of experienced workers at the cost of inhibiting the creation of new jobs.[10] A new social schism has emerged in French society in an era of chronic youth unemployment: that between young people and their more privileged elders.[11]

Growing unemployment among high school and university graduates has been added to the many problems for which French schools are blamed by their critics. A recent book by a longtime critic of French schools, Maurice T. Maschino, is entitled *L'Ecole, Usine à Chomeurs, (The School: Unemployment Factory).*[12] There is little agreement among the critics, however, as to whether the problem is too much vocational training, too little, or simply the wrong kind. A more fundamentally pessimistic assessment is now being heard even from supporters of the schools like René Rémond, former president of the University of Paris-Nanterre and head of a government planning commission for education. Rémond told an interviewer,

> ... if educational qualifications no longer protect the degree holder from loss of employment, if relocation of even the most sophisti-

cated economic activities toward other parts of the globe take away the principal argument for the development of education, what is the purpose of dedicating a large part of the country's resources to it?[13]

Similar disillusionment with mass education was heard during the recession of the 1970s. Whether or not it will spread depends now, as it did then, upon the future performance of the French economy.

The Deceptions of Democratization

The French educational system, in theory equally open to talent from all social classes, has been widely criticized since the 1960s for being largely a "reproducer" of existing social elites.[14] In 1959-60 industrial workers made up approximately 37 percent of the work force, but their children composed less than 4 percent of all French university students.[15] Upward mobility through education was discouraged by a dual educational system—one school for the masses, another for elites—and by early selection for entry into the elite sector. More affluent families often sent their children to the "little classes" of the *lycée,* from the age of six onward, while the children of industrial workers and farmers attended primary schools. Movement from primary school to the *lycée* was possible, but it normally took place at age eleven, or not at all. Children of modest social origin usually stayed in the elementary school for the "higher primary" certificate, or transferred to short-cycle vocational programs.

One strategy used by reformers from the 1960s onward to increase equality of opportunity was to generalize preschool education, usually beginning at age three. Like head-start programs in the United States, preschool programs were widely believed to be an effective means of reducing the social and cultural handicaps of children of parents with limited education and income as well as those of immigrant background. Subsequent research indeed demonstrated that performance in elementary school was positively correlated with the number of years a child had spent in preschool programs; yet the extent of improved performance (measured in terms of failure rates) was even greater for middle-class children than for working-class children. Preschool improved the subsequent academic performance of all social classes, but had the ultimate effect of increasing the gap between them rather than narrowing it.[16]

Following another track, reformers from the end of World War I onward had proposed that dual, socially segregated schools be replaced by the comprehensive "single school." The Socialists adopted this goal in the 1930s, but were unable to implement it, either in the Third or the post–war Fourth

Republic. The Left failed to overcome resistance to reform, not only from political conservatives, but from many in their own camp, including powerful teachers unions. Any proposal of a "single school" beyond the primary level pitted elementary teachers against *lycée* teachers, each group fearful that the other sought to assert total control over post-primary education.[17] When the single middle school finally emerged in the 1960s and 1970s, it was under the political leadership of the conservatives who dominated French politics from 1958 until 1981.

In early 1959, only a few months after the creation of the Fifth Republic, the legal school-leaving age was extended from 14 to 16. The single middle school was established in 1963 in the form of the *Collège d'Enseignement Secondaire* (CES), covering grades six through nine. The conservative reform movement culminated in the Haby Law of July 1975, which surpassed in its egalitarianism the comprehensive schools emerging in other European countries by ordering the elimination of ability tracks within the *collège*.

It is not surprising that in practice the Haby injunction against tracking was sometimes evaded, nor that the "single school" varied dramatically from *collège* to *collège*, depending upon the social background of its students and its origins, either in a former higher primary school or a *lycée*. Nonetheless, the institutional structure of French education by the late 1970s offered far fewer obstacles to equal opportunity than did the old dual system. The proportion of university students from families headed by an industrial worker crept up from under 4 percent at the end of the 1950s to approximately 13 percent in the 1980s and early 1990s. At the beginning of the 1960s, a child from a family headed by a member of the liberal professions or by a senior manager was 41 times more likely to go to the university than a child from a family headed by an industrial worker; by 1989, a child from a professional family was less than six times as likely to be a university student as a child from a working-class family.[18]

Despite the rapid expansion of enrollments in secondary and higher education, democratization proved to be an elusive goal. Working-class students tended to set low educational goals for themselves, taking short, technical programs or dropping out before completing longer programs. They were poorly represented in the "noble" programs of the bac (particularly those heavy in science and math), in the highly selective *grandes écoles* ("great schools"), which lead toward prestigious positions in higher management in both the public and private sectors, and in university programs leading to the professions.[19] In 1987-88, students of working-class origin represented 15.4 percent of all regular university students in the first two-year cycle of the university program, but only 10.8 percent in the second, full-degree cycle, and 6.7 percent in the third, or doctoral cycle, which includes medicine, law and pharmacy, as well as science and letters.[20] Among students in the second cycle in 1978-79, 55 percent of those from working-class families were enrolled in relatively unselective and unprestigious general programs in letters and science, compared to 33 percent of those from families headed by senior managers or members of the liberal professions.[21] By 1992-93, when non-selective programs had absorbed a much higher share of rapidly growing university enrollments, 70 percent of second-cycle students from working-class families were in these programs, compared to 57 percent of students from professional families.[22] The long jump from the working-class into the liberal professions in one generation, while no longer as unthinkable as it was forty years ago, is still difficult and relatively rare.

Those working-class students who do push on toward the bac and beyond find that the flood of degree-holders on the job market has depressed the value of their diplomas. In France, as in other industrialized countries, mass secondary and higher education have produced a "credentialing revolution," in which employers constantly raise the amount of education that they require for particular jobs as more well-educated candidates become available. One of the forces driving the demand for secondary and higher education no doubt is students' perception that, in an era of high youth unemployment, they must stay in school longer and longer, pursuing higher degrees, simply to keep up with the pack.

The Strains of Educational Expansion: Students

The transition from elite to mass education has produced additional student anxiety that is periodically expressed in political protests. Faced with a rapidly expanding pool of degree holders, many young people see the expected fruits of their labors disappearing in front of them as they approach their educational goals. Over the past three decades the growing numbers of students entering the *lycées* and universities have also found themselves confronted with overcrowded facilities, programs seemingly in constant flux, and, in the first cycle of the university, failure rates often above 50 percent. Anxiety over career prospects has been one of the underlying sources of student discontent at least since 1968. In a national survey of students in September of that year, respondents were asked to rank in order of importance three possible reasons for the dramatic demonstrations of the previous May; 56 percent gave first-place ranking to anxiety over jobs, 35 percent to the inadequacy of the universities and only 7 percent to the most commonly stated objective of protest leaders—"rejection of the consumer society."[23] A subsequent SOFRES poll of students in 1973 concluded that ". . . the major concern of students was their professional future. They reproached the present system for not giving them real professional training."[24] Further evidence of student anxiety is found in a 1994 government survey of 15-25 year-olds designed to initiate a dialogue with French youth. The results are suggestive, even though they are based, not on a representative national sample, but on mail-in questionnaires, with the unavoidable self-selection bias that this method entails. An initial analysis of 800,000 of the 1,539,000 questionnaires returned showed that 72 percent of the respondents declared little or no confidence in the future, 78 percent believed that schools do not prepare well for the working world, and 87 percent felt that employers do not have confidence in young people.[25]

The most common breeding ground of student protest from the 1960s through the 1980s was among the many anxious students in nonselective programs in the social science and humanities, particularly in large, bureaucratized universities.[26] Large numbers of *lycée* students, now increasingly anxious about their futures, joined demonstrations in 1986 against the Devaquet Bill, which would have allowed individual universities to set admissions requirements beyond the *bac*. *Lycéens* took to the streets again in large numbers in 1990, this time against a Socialist government, to demand more funds to staff and maintain overloaded secondary schools.[27] Students in specialized post-bac programs participated en masse in the successful demonstrations of March, 1994 against the *Contrat d'Insertion Professionnelle* (CIP), a bill that would have allowed employers to pay substandard wages to young people entering the work force. A government proposal to limit the number of students in University Technical Institutes (IUT) permitted to continue university studies beyond a two-year diploma was greeted with angry student demonstrations in February 1995. With presidential elections rapidly approaching, the government promptly withdrew its proposal. Career anxiety, along with unemployment, had now extended into the ranks of advanced technical students.

As the grandiose, if ambiguous, ideological goals of the *soixante-huitards* (the "sixty-eighters") have given way to the protection of existing rights in the student movements of the 1980s and 1990s, education policy has been caught up in a vicious cycle. With the notable exceptions of the demonstrations of *lycéens* in 1990 and university students in 1995, student protest has become essentially a negative restraint on policy innovation. The ability of universities to control intake is inhibited by fierce student hostility to any innovation that seems to sanction "selection" of incoming students. The result is overcrowding, high failure rates, and more student anxiety that feeds further protest. Even holders of the new "professional" *baccalaureat,* who were intended to go directly into the work force, have begun to enroll in non-selective university programs for which they have little background and slight chance of success.

In the fall of 1995, student discontent with overcrowded classes was expressed in a series of strikes and demonstrations that began in provincial universities and spread to Paris. Confronted with over 100,000 angry students on the streets in late November, the government found 396 million francs above budget to provide some 1,200 additional instructors and 1,700 new support personnel for higher education. While these concessions succeeded in quieting the storm of student protest, they seemed unlikely to cure the underlying causes of university unrest.

One unintended consequence of unrestricted access of holders of the *baccalauréat* to the university is a widening of the status gap between selective and non-selective programs. In an era of mass higher education, it would seem the highly selective *grandes écoles* are major beneficiaries of open enrollment in the universities. Even in the universities there is a trend toward creeping selection. Medicine, dentistry, pharmacy, management, political science, engineering, and advanced technical programs (the University Institutes of Technology) all select their students carefully. In the absence of university admissions requirements other than the *bac* for study in the humanities or the social sciences, the first two years of university work in these fields has become a brutal selection cycle. Students in letters were no more numerous than those in the health fields (medicine, dentistry, and pharmacy) in 1960; by 1993 the ratio of letters students to health students was three to one and growing rapidly.[28] New "professionalized" programs that have been introduced at the second (upper division) cycle are all selective.

Open enrollment has the virtue of allowing even marginal students a chance to show that they can do university work. Its disadvantages include high failure rates, intense student anxiety, and devaluation of non-selective programs.

The Strains of Educational Expansion: Teachers

In 1951-52, there were 27,800 public secondary teachers in metropolitan France, of whom almost 19 percent were holders of the prestigious *agrégation*.[29] By 1991-92, the ranks of public secondary teachers had swelled to 351,800, of whom less than 8 percent were *agrégés*.[30] It is not surprising that teachers perceived a sharp decline in their status over this period in which secondary education ceased to be an elite phenomenon. Indeed, in the 1980s the press was full of reports of the "malaise" of *collège* and *lycée* teachers purportedly confronted with undisciplined, poorly prepared, and virtually unteachable classes of mixed ability.[31] The reality is more complex. An unpublished SOFRES survey of teachers' attitudes commissioned by the Ministry of National Education in April 1991, found that, while 83 percent of the 809 respondents were unhappy with "the place given to them in society," 66 percent believed their salaries to be inadequate, and 63 percent thought that their working conditions were bad, 80 percent were either "satisfied" or "very satisfied" to be teachers and over two-thirds would without hesitation choose teaching again if they had it to do over.[32] The picture that emerges from this survey, as well as from an earlier SOFRES survey,[33] is of teachers who are generally happy with their profession but bitter over their declining status in society, hostile to the educational bureaucracy, annoyed with constant government attempts to reform the schools, and hurt by the barrage of public criticism to which they are subjected. *Lycée* teachers are particularly suspicious of pedagogical innovations like team teaching, individual tutoring, or teaching outside one's field of expertise—all of which are perceived as demeaning attempts at "primarization" of secondary education.

The rise of mass secondary education has been accompanied by the decline and eventual schism of what was once one of the most powerful unions in France: the Federation of National Education (FEN). In 1952, 77 percent of all employees of national education (including non-teaching personnel) belonged to the FEN. Known sometimes as the Second Ministry of National Education (MEN Bis), the FEN exercised extensive power over personnel policies and decisions, commanded the Right to be consulted on all policies, and once claimed to have "had the skin" of at least one minister.[34] At a time of declining union membership throughout the

French economy, the FEN's proportion of potential membership remained far above the average even for public sector workers, but still dropped to 62 percent in 1970 and 48 percent in 1985. Its total membership rose from 173,000 in 1952 to 550,000 in 1978, then began a decline to under 400,000 by the end of the 1980s.[35] The declining attraction of the leading teachers' union was no doubt a reflection, in part, of the general deunionization of French labor in the 1980s, when total membership levels dropped below 10 percent of the work force (see chapter 6). The gradual increase of the number of middle-class women among teachers also undermined the appeal of unions which identified closely with parties of the Left and with the working-class.[36] The proportion of women among all secondary school teachers rose gradually from 47 percent in 1950-51 to 56 percent in 1991-92.[37]

The FEN also suffered from two forms of intense internal conflict: among organized Communist, Socialist, and Trotskyist "tendencies," which it tolerated as the price of nominal unity, and between elementary and secondary teachers. The FEN's national organization was dominated by the largest component union, the National Union of Elementary Teachers (SNI); both were led by the socialist faction, "Unity, Independence and Democracy" (UID). In 1967 the National Union of Secondary Education (SNES) came under the leadership of the rival faction, Unity and Action (UA), many of whose leaders were close to the Communist Party. Despite their often conflicting political rhetoric, the SNI and the SNES were divided much more by the perceived interests of their teacher clienteles than by the difference in their ideological perspectives.

By the late 1980s, the FEN leadership felt increasingly threatened. For more than two decades before 1981 the FEN had played the role of critic and political opponent of conservative governments, rejecting most proposed initiatives and calling constantly for more funds. In national elections it worked actively for the Left, and particularly for the Socialist Party. With the victory of the Left in the presidential and legislative elections of 1981, the FEN at last had friends, indeed many fellow teachers, in the National Assembly and in key ministries. The results were devastating for the Socialist leadership of the FEN. Teachers received modest salary increases in 1982, but soon thereafter the government initiated what became a long-term policy of budget austerity. The FEN was even unable to achieve the promised integration of subsidized private schools into the public system.

While membership continued to drop, polls of teachers revealed growing dissatisfaction with a FEN leadership perceived to be ineffective, overpoliticized, and too closely tied to the Socialist government.[38] Even more alarming was the continuing decline in the relative strength of elementary teachers (the SNI), who made up 80 percent of Federation membership in 1949, but only 50 percent in 1985. The rapid expansion of secondary education guaranteed that the future would belong to secondary teachers, whose union was led by the communist faction. Fearing total and permanent loss of control of the FEN, the UID leadership group considered a variety of strategies. In its national congress of 1988, the FEN sought to overcome the divisions among teachers by proposing the elimination of the multiple grades, salaries, and workloads of teachers at various levels and with various diplomas.[39] The proposed slogan "for a single school, a single corps of teachers," could only confirm the fears of certified secondary teachers and *agrégés* in the ranks of the SNES that elementary teachers sought to reduce all teachers to their level. In his preparatory report for the 32d National Congress of the FEN in 1990, Secretary-General Yannick Simbron took a different tack; he recognized that young teachers were repulsed by the ideological quarrels within the FEN and called on the union to take a more constructive, cooperative stance in adapting education to the changing needs of society.[40] Three months later Simbron was removed by the Federal Bureau of the FEN for policies which they perceived to be too soft on the SNES and its UA leadership.[41] The new leadership, under Secretary-General Guy Le Néouannic, decided to force out the SNES in hopes of establishing direct FEN control over all teachers. In April 1992, the two largest unions controlled by the communist tendency—secondary teachers (SNES) and physical education teachers (SNEP)—were asked if they were willing to "submit to federal discipline."[42] They agreed to respect their obligations to the Federation, but rejected any attempt to supress the sovereignty enjoyed by national unions within the FEN. Judging this reply to be inadequate, the Federal Council of the FEN expelled the SNES and the SNEP on May 6, 1992. The expelled unions successfully appealed to the courts to declare that the Council had no power to expel them under FEN bylaws. A special meeting of the FEN Congress legalized the expulsion in October 1992.

It soon became apparent that the FEN leadership had overestimated its capacity to draw secondary teachers away from the SNES and underestimated the negative reaction of teachers to the purge. Membership continued to decline, despite a broad restructuring in which the FEN was renamed the "Union of Teachers" (SE). The expelled unions joined with the National Union of Technical Education (SNETAA) and several smaller unions to create a broadly based rival, the Federation of Unified Unions (FSU), which appealed to elementary as well as secondary teachers with a relatively non-ideological message, then proceeded to win 190,000 votes, compared to 110,000 for the former FEN, in the elections of teachers' representatives to various official councils in December 1993.

Until the split in 1992, the great majority of organized French teachers had been represented by a single federation, even if component unions often spoke with different voices. Now they suffered the same malady that has weakened French unions in most sectors since the schism of the General Confederation of Labor (CGT) in 1947: rivalry between ideologically based federations. It is ironic that the breakup of the FEN took place at a time of declining ideological conflict in French society, when the Communist Party was rapidly losing support and the Communist group in control of the SNES was de-emphasizing ideology in favor of vigorous defense of the interests of its members. Now, as in the past, the real conflict between the SNI and the SNES appears to have been based less on ideology than on the very different perceived interests of elementary and secondary teachers. The Socialist group in control of the FEN, largely representing elementary teachers, was unable or unwilling to share power with the growing mass of secondary teachers arising out of the movement toward mass secondary education.

The Strains of Educational Expansion: Public Opinion

The transition from elite to mass secondary education has been accompanied in the 1980s and 1990s by a constant stream of books and articles decrying the "decline" of discipline and standards in the *collège, lycée,* and university. The shelves of French bookstores have abounded with titles like *Education in Distress* (Romilly, 1984), *Do You Really Want Idiot Children?* (Maschino, 1984), *The Massacre of the Innocents* (Jumilhac, 1984), *Lycées, State of Urgency* (Berland, 1991), *The Management of Ignorance* (Bartholy and Despin, 1993), *Pedagogical Chaos* (Nemo, 1993), and (by a future conservative minister of education) *1990-2000: The Decade of the Poorly Taught* (Bayrou, 1990).[43] Newspapers and magazines frequently called the attention of their readers to school violence in working-class suburbs, to the demoralization of teachers, and to the pitiful state of knowledge among secondary students.[44] Occasional voices raised to argue that young people today actually know more than did their predecessors, particularly about science and math,[45] were largely drowned out by a chorus of skeptics.

Simply reading the press, one might easily reach the conclusion that the French are so dissatisfied with the performance of public schools that they have lost confidence in them, just as they have lost faith in political parties and politicians. In fact, the general public, like the teaching profession, is less cynical about the educational system than the media.[46] A study examining SOFRES survey results over time reaches the conclusion that public confidence in elementary teachers, secondary teachers, schools, and universities rose steadily from 1981 to 1993.[47] In a February 1993 survey, 86 percent of respondents expressed confidence in elementary teachers and 82 percent in secondary teachers, compared to 27 percent in politicians and 21 percent in political parties in general.[48] Teachers received more expressions of confidence than any other profession except for firemen (99 percent) and physicians (90 percent). In the same survey, when respondents were asked if they had confidence in a series of values, more expressed confidence in education (86 percent) than in any other value mentioned except for the family (93 percent), with only 31 percent expressing confidence in a political ideal.[49] Confidence levels in educational institutions, as shown in table 8.1, are somewhat lower, but still substantial. Other attitude surveys, both of the general public and of parents of school children come to similar conclusions.[50]

In an era when diplomas have become critical to economic survival, the French public places high value on the ideal of education, continues to have confidence in teachers, and generally trusts its schools. This trust is higher at the preschool and elementary levels than at the secondary and higher levels and declines as one moves from the ideal of education to the practical functioning of the educational system as a whole.[51] Just as the 1993 SOFRES poll found that the public is much more likely to have confidence in mayors (73 percent) and deputies (51 percent) than in "politicians in general" (27 percent), so a survey of parents found that 42 percent were "very satisfied" with their child's school, but only 6 percent believed the whole educational system to be "very good."[52] This is a pattern that should be familiar to observers of American politics, who have long noted that citizens can condemn Congress while retaining confidence in their own congressman. To the extent that French parents are unhappy with the way their children are being educated, their discontent tends to focus primarily on secondary schools and universities, which have been most affected by

TABLE 8.1.
PUBLIC CONFIDENCE IN INSTITUTIONS
IN GENERAL DO YOU HAVE CONFIDENCE OR NO CONFIDENCE IN THE FOLLOWING INSTITUTIONS? (IN PERCENTAGES)*

	December 1985 Confidence	No Confidence	February 1993 Confidence	No Confidence	Change in Confidence Index**
The "Great Schools"	71	9	78	13	+3
Schools	74	19	73	23	-5
Universities	63	15	72	20	+4
The Police	74	20	70	27	-11
Laws	56	33	56	40	-7
Parliament	42	30	53	36	+5
The Justice System	44	47	46	50	-1

Notes: * "Avez-vous plutôt confiance ou plutôt pas confiance dans les institutions suivantes?"
**The confidence index is the difference between positive and negative responses. This column represents the change in that index from 1985 to 1993.
Source: Anne Sinclair, "Les Valeurs dans la société française," in SOFRES, ed., L'Etat de l'opinion 1994 (Paris: Seuil, 1994), p. 221, chapter 11.

expansion and increased heterogeneity. Despite the particular grievances of teachers and of secondary and university students, French education has been spared the general loss of public confidence suffered in recent years by political parties and political institutions.

Conflict and Consensus in an Era of Mass Education

Even if the general public remains generally supportive of education, and if the effective role of student demonstrators and teachers' unions is to inhibit change, partisan debate suggests that the Left and Right are fundamentally at odds on education. Listening to party rhetoric, one might expect that every change in party control of government should produce major policy innovations. In order to evaluate the impact of parties on education policy, their positions on major issues must be examined, as well as their behavior when in power.

Private Schools

Education is the last major battleground in the longstanding war between supporters and critics of the Catholic Church. Even in an era of declining church attendance, a voter's relationship to the Church is the best predictor of whether he/she will vote for the Right or the Left.[53] Conservative parties, encouraged by their many Catholic voters, have been consistent supporters of government subsidies to Catholic schools from 1951, when the first indirect subsidies were introduced, to the Debré Law of 1959, which allowed private schools under state contract to pay for some 90 percent of their costs with government funds, to the aborted attempt in 1993-94 to eliminate restrictions in the Falloux Law on the right of local governments to fund construction of new private schools. For parties of the Right, private schools are "free schools"; defense of their interests is often equated with defense of freedom itself.

For the Left, anticlericalism has been a core value since the French Revolution, and particularly since the bitter church-state battles of the late nineteenth and early twentieth Centuries. The expansion and rationalization of the public school system in the 1880s was intended to strengthen republican loyalties against the Church and its royalist friends.[54] To defend the public school was (and still is for many supporters of the Left) to defend the Republic itself. When the National Assembly debated the Debré Law in December 1959, former Socialist prime minister, Guy Mollet, warned that the Left would return to power and, when it did, it would carry through the logic of subsidies by simply absorbing all subsidized schools into the public system.[55] Presidential candidate François Mitterrand seemed to incorporate this vow into his platform prior to the 1981 election: once in power, he promised, the Left would create "a great public service of National Education, unified and secular."[56]

The growth of subsidies to private schools serves as a dramatic example of the power of political parties to impose new education policies—particularly when no change is required within the public education establishment. Yet despite the continuing battle of rhetoric over private schools, both the Right—and more particularly the Left——have moved a long distance toward a compromise position. The Debré Law allowed private schools to survive and expand, but it also restricted their autonomy by requiring that schools receiving subsidies accept students without regard to religious beliefs and refrain from teaching religion to nonbelievers. It required that schools receiving the most lucrative "contract of association" follow the curriculum of public schools. In consequence of these restrictions, and of the preferences of the many parents who choose Catholic schools for purely educational rather than religious reasons, subsidized schools (90 percent of which are Catholic) have become much more like public schools.[57]

The Socialist Party, which came to power in 1981 enjoying full control of both the executive and legislative branches of government for the first time in French history, was expected by many of its supporters—and particularly by the major teachers unions—to simply integrate subsidized private schools into the public system. In fact Mitterrand chose as minister of education a skilled diplomat, Alain Savary, who recalled that his president had pledged to "convince, not compel" in achieving the goal of school integration.[58] Over the next two and a half years, Savary came very close to reaching a compromise solution acceptable to Catholic education.[59] In the process, he made concessions to the autonomy of private schools that alienated the secularist lobby, which in turn counterattacked with tough amendments added to the bill by their friends in the National Assembly. As Savary had warned, the amendments destroyed any chance of a compromise with Catholic education. It took a million supporters of private schools marching through the streets of Paris on June 24, 1984 to persuade President Mitterrand to withdraw the amended Savary bill. Savary resigned and was replaced by Jean-Pierre Chevènement, who was instructed to "restore peace."[60] The Socialist Party leadership—unlike many of its secularist militants—had concluded that, with a strong majority of public opinion clearly favoring subsidized private schools, the political costs of integrating them into the public system were too great. A subsequent socialist minister of education, Jack Lang, gave further evidence that the Socialists had accepted the status quo when in the spring of 1992 he reached an accord with Catholic education over outstanding disagreements on financing. The passionate battle in 1993-94 against repeal of the Falloux Law (which restricts local government funding of private school construction) demonstrated that the private school issue was far from dead. This time, however, before the Constitutional Council declared the government's bill unconstitutional, the Left was seeking simply to defend the status quo, not to change it.

Autonomy and Competition

The Left has historically taken the Jacobin position that only a highly centralized educational system is capable of defending the public interest and maximizing equality. With a national curriculum, national diplomas, national bac examinations, and teachers who are national civil servants, it is argued, students in all parts of the country are protected against the inequities of funding and standards found in a decentralized system like that of the United

States. Conservative parties talk more of the advantages of competition among relatively autonomous schools and universities. De Gaulle contributed to the student unrest expressed in the demonstrations of May 1968 when he proposed to allow universities to select their students. The Devaquet Bill of 1986, which provoked massive student demonstrations, would have given individual universities this right, among others.

When in power, neither the Right nor the Left has acted consistently in accordance with these expressed beliefs. As minister for the universities in the late 1970s, Alice Saunier-Séïté exercised central controls over programs and funding to punish and restrain universities controlled by elected councils of leftist persuasion. Conservative governments of the 1960s and 1970s took only modest steps toward deconcentration of authority to the academy and department levels in order to deal more efficiently with a rapidly growing bureaucracy. Christian Beullac, minister of education under President Valéry Giscard d'Estaing, was a particularly strong partisan of decentralization, believing that it was one of the few ways in which traditional barriers between the school and the business community could be broken down.[61]

Once in power after 1981, the Socialists embarked on a far more ambitious program of decentralization of education within the framework of the Defferre Law of 1982, which called for broad enhancement of the powers of regional and local governments.[62] The "self-management" wing of the Socialist Party, supported in education by the General Union of National Education (SGEN), an affiliate of the reformist French Conferation of French Labor (CFDT), prevailed over the party's Jacobin loyalists. Rectors in the 25 academies of metropolitan France, assistant rectors in the country's 96 departments, and principals of individual schools were given enhanced authority at the expense of the central bureacracy. Individual schools, in consultation with school councils representing parents and community leaders as well as teachers, were encouraged to select unique school projects, to experiment with new teaching methods, and to establish cooperative relations with local businesses and industries. On January 25, 1985, the third series of decentralization laws transferred responsibility for maintaining and constructing schools to elected councils at the level of the region (for the *lycées*) and of the department (for the *collèges*).

Even though primary control over teaching personnel and curriculum remained in the hands of the central government, teachers (especially at the secondary level), central administrators, and their unions were alarmed at the prospect of sharing power with representatives of parents and with elected local officials. Organized to mirror the centralized structure of the Ministry of Education and thus fearful of a loss of influence in a decentralized structure, the FEN became the principal defender of the traditional Jacobin creed.[63] Decentralization, it warned, would open the schools to political interference from local officials who had no competence in educational matters. Jacky Simon, who negotiated the major decentralization provisions for the Ministry of Education, recalls leaving for the Ministry of Interior amid calls of "You are going off to betray us."[64]

In terms of funding, decentralization has generally been successful. The contribution of departments to maintenance and construction rose from 3 billion francs in 1986 to 6 billion in 1988, while expenditures by the regions increased from 3.3 billion in 1986 to 12 billion in 1989.[65] By 1992, local and regional governments were paying 19.1 percent of the total costs of French education.[66] It seems unlikely that maintenance and construction expenditures would have risen so rapidly without decentralization.[67] Decentralization (or deconcentration) within the structure of national education has produced more mixed results. Many elementary schools and some *collèges* have taken advantage of their expanded autonomy to experiment with new teaching modes, to draw parents closer to the school, and to generally open up the school to the community. There has been greater resistance to change in the *lycées,* where a centralized curriculum and standardized work requirements are widely viewed as important means of protecting teachers from outside interference, whether from parents, local officials, or even the school principal.[68] Decentralization is gradually changing attitudes, even if it has not yet produced the great increase of effort and innovation that the reformers expected. The decentralization program conceived of and carried through by the Left, in a dramatic break with its intellectual heritage, represents one of the most important institutional changes in French education in recent decades. Decentralization now enjoys support across the political spectrum, although the Left conceives of it largely in terms of democratic self-governance, while the Right stresses the potential benefits of competition between autonomous units.

Equality

There is perhaps no theme more closely associated with the tradition of the French Left than that of equality.[69] From the 1930s onward, as noted earlier, the Left has proposed the ideal of the comprehensive school *(école unique);*

that is, mixing the children of all classes in the same school, and thereby encouraging children of the working-class to move upward in society through education. In order to assist children of poorly educated parents—particularly those of immigrants—the Left has called for more "modern," progressive teaching methods that rely less on homework and an authoritarian classroom atmosphere and more on small-group tutoring and team teaching. The rhetoric of the Right, in contrast, has a more elitist ring. François Bayrou, who became minister of education in 1993, argued that standards can be maintained, and students properly taught, only with traditional teaching methods and through placement of children in appropriate tracks, from the middle school onward. The *collège unique*, he argued, was in fact the *collège inique*—the iniquitous or unjust college, for it failed to distinguish pupils according to ability.[70] In a similar vein, Michèle Alliot-Marie, secretary of state in the Ministry of Education under the Chirac government from 1986-88, told the National Assembly in July 1989: "... our present system is very egalitarian. It levels and excludes, in some way, both those who are failing and those who should be progressing faster."[71]

Once again reality is more complex than rhetoric would suggest. It was a conservative, not a Socialist, government which established the *collège unique*, as its creator, René Haby, indignantly pointed out to Bayrou.[72] Although the Left has often been more open to progressive teaching methods than the Right, one of the most traditionalist of all groups in French education is the SNES, the secondary teachers' union led since 1967 by Communists. Traditional pedagogical views are quite compatible with leftist, even revolutionary, political views. Even among Socialist ministers of education, a clear split is evident between Alain Savary, who favored new methods in decentralized schools, and Jean-Pierre Chevènement, who championed an ideal of "republican elitism," built upon traditional methods within a centralized system.[73] The Educational Priority Zones (ZEP), developed by Savary to pour extra resources into poor, heavily immigrant districts, were largely ignored by Chevènement and his conservative successor, René Monory, before being revived after 1988 by a new Socialist minister, Lionel Jospin. They have survived two periods of conservative government, although funding has been more generous under socialist leadership.[74]

Rhetoric and policy diverge as well with regard to the education of immigrant children. While the Socialist governments of the 1980s and early 1990s often spoke sympathetically of cultural pluralism, the conservative wing of the Gaullist RPR sought to undercut the appeal of Jean-Marie Le Pen and his National Front by insisting that French education had to be French. The debate eventually focused on whether Moslem girls should be allowed to wear head scarves to school. This issue emerged in 1989, when Ernest Chénière, the principal of a *collège* in Creil, expelled a girl from school on grounds that her head scarf was a violation of the traditional secularism of French schools. On appeal, the *Conseil d'Etat* ruled that the head scarf, or any other religious symbol, was acceptable, except when the school principal judged it to be disruptive. In October 1993, following the conservative victory in the legislative elections of the previous spring, Chénière, now a Gaullist member of Parliament, urged Minister of Education François Bayrou to take stronger action. "Mister Minister, this cannot go on," he insisted. Bands of Moslem youth in the schools, he argued, were conducting an "insidious jihad," intimidating fellow students.[75] In his response, Bayrou simply recalled the 1989 ruling of the *Conseil d'Etat*.[76] He then sought to quiet the right wing of his parliamentary majority by urging principals to act quickly in cases where school is disrupted. In his first eighteen months in office, Bayrou's policy diverged only slightly from that of his socialist predecessors. Then, in September 1994, a new Ministry of Education circular outlawed the wearing of "ostentatious signs" of religious affiliation in the schools.[77] Around the country, schools proceeded to expel girls who insisted on wearing the scarf. Bayrou's circular came in the wake of a series of government measures, sponsored by Minister of Interior Charles Pasqua, designed to limit immigration and to prevent the spread of Islamic fundamentalism from Algeria to the French Moslem population. Sharp debate continues over the relative importance in education of protecting cultural pluralism as opposed to making Frenchmen. In this debate, many of the strongest proponents of traditional, secular French education are teachers, intellectuals, and activists (including the leadership of *SOS Racisme)* who support parties of the Left.[78]

In brief, as an increasingly large proportion of French students remains in school through the full secondary cycle and beyond, the partisan debate over equality continues, but with few clear-cut effects on policy. One of the few unambiguous policy differences between governments of the Left and Right is the repeated failed attempts of the latter to allow universities to choose their own students. Even on this contentious issue one hears a growing number of voices from the Left—including that of Lionel

Jospin—calling for more systematic selection as the only way to decrease failure rates and to improve the prestige of the universities.[79]

Education and Business

When a conservative government proposed in 1976 that outside businessmen and professional people be consulted in the design of new professionalized university programs, leftist students denounced this policy as an attempt to turn the universities over to the capitalists.[80] Again, in objection to the Devaquet Bill, students denounced the government's presumed intent to create a climate of "jungle capitalism" in competition among "Americanized," "Coca Cola" universities.[81] Judging from the views of protesting students and teachers unions, one might have thought that in 1986 the battle between the Left and big business over control of the universities was in full swing. In fact, by 1986, despite its long history of defending the autonomy of public education against the influence of business, the Socialist Party had made peace with the private sector to the point of enlisting the cooperation of professionals and businessmen in the design of technical and vocational programs, encouraging the development of internships, soliciting experts to assist teachers in the school, and looking favorably on school field trips to local businesses, all in the interest of "opening schools to life."[82] This historic reconciliation between public education and business was one facet of a more general transformation of Socialist Party views toward the private sector during its first few years in power in the 1980s. When the Socialists returned to power in 1988, they encouraged the expansion of contractual agreements, which were already developing between universities on the one hand and both private corporations and local governments on the other. Although a nuance of difference remains between the Left and the Right, with the latter still more consistently sympathetic to business interests, the great chasm that separated the two camps as recently as the 1970s, when Mitterrand wrote that "big capital . . . has measured out general education and oriented it to its fancy,"[83] was reduced in the 1980s to a shallow furrow.

There are many factors that help to explain why education policy does not swing wildly when party control of government changes. As French education specialists like to explain, the Ministry of Education, with over a million employees and 11 million students, is like a giant tanker; it can be turned, but only very slowly. With an average longevity in office of only 19 months, education ministers in the Fifth Republic seldom stay long enough to see policies through to completion. Moreover, they must deal with powerful forces resistant to change, including bureaucrats, students, and teachers unions. In recent years, the minister has been obliged to consider the Constitutional Council, which nibbled at several education laws in the 1980s, establishing grounds for broader rulings in the process, then struck down two laws in July 1993 and January 1994, both before the Balladur Government had been in office for a year. Soon after conservative parties swept the March 1993 elections, a bill with strong backbench support was rushed through Parliament to allow universities the option of choosing their own form of internal governance, thereby avoiding the requirement of three broadly representative elected councils prescribed in the Savary Law of 1984. The Constitutional Council promptly rejected this law on grounds that Parliament has an obligation to establish rules for the functioning of public institutions, or, at the very least, to establish guidelines for local experimentation.[84] In January 1994, the Constitutional Council declared unconstitutional a government bill which relaxed limitations of the Falloux Law on local government funding of private schools. The government's proposal, the Council held, would allow citizens in some communities to receive benefits that citizens in other communities would be denied. Indeed, policymakers are learning that they must anticipate the likely reaction of the Council.[85]

The relative continuity in education policy is attributable not only to powerful obstacles to change, but also in part to a growing consensus between moderate leaders of both conservative and Socialist governments. In each camp, pragmatic leaders have had trouble controlling "true believers." Mitterrand, Mauroy, and Savary all knew in the spring of 1984 that most French voters wanted subsidized private schools to survive. Mauroy gave in to the demands of the hard line secularists in his National Assembly group in order to avoid a bitter fight within the party. Alain Devaquet did not want to abrogate the Savary Law on universities and substitute a law of his own in 1986,[86] nor did Prime Minister Balladur seek legislation in the summer of 1993 to restructure university governance to favor conservative faculty. Each felt compelled to accept legislation proposed by party militants who sought relief from what they perceived to be unfair and ill-advised Socialist policies. Edouard Balladur did not initiate the attempt to amend the Falloux law for the purpose of allowing more local government funding of private school construction.[87] He merely accepted the initiative of strong private school supporters within his parliamentary majority. In all of these cases the proposals set off major political confrontations, and in all four the proposed legislation failed, either by withdrawal after protest with respect to the amended Savary Bill and the Devaquet Bill, or after a ruling of unconstitutionality by the Constitutional Council in the case of the other two. The problem is a common one in democratic governments, for example in the British Labour Party: party activists and parliamentary backbenchers, who have relatively little to lose, often support proposals which party and government leaders know to be politically dangerous.

The political and bureaucratic obstacles to policy change appear to be insurmountable on certain issues and within certain time frames, yet French education as a whole has responded effectively to a rapid and massive increase in demand by expanding its facilities and teaching staff. Although there have clearly been tensions as a result of expansion, public funding per pupil rose in constant 1992 francs from 19,800 in 1975 to 28,100 in 1992, while from 1970-71 to 1991-92 the average class size actually declined at the *collège* level (from 26.4 to 24.7) and rose only slightly at the *lycée* level (from 28.1 to 30.3).[88] Government has not always simply responded to demand. The extension of compulsory education to age 16 after 1959 and the 80 percent goal launched by Jean-Pierre Chevènement in 1985 are examples of government leadership effectively spurring on demand.[89] The decentralization policies of the 1980s, like the closer linkage of schools with the economy, are striking examples of the ability of government to initiate change, even against the resistance of teachers and bureaucrats. Lastly, and despite resistance from *lycée* teachers and some administrators, government initiatives have made significant progress in adapting the curriculum and teaching methods to an expanding clientele. The rapid creation of the *bac professionel* (the vocational *bac*) in 1985 and 1986, the revamping of many technical secondary school programs, and the creation of a host of new professionally oriented programs within the universities are examples of the capacity of French education to adapt to changing social and economic demands.[90]

As many an education minister can attest, it is difficult to predict the extent of opposition which a proposed reform will encounter; yet it is possible to discern certain conditions which support or undermine the likely success of policy change. The best facilitator of change is strong and consistent popular demand, as seen in the expansion of preschool, secondary, and higher education. When public opinion is supportive and the parties are in general agreement—as on decentralization—innovation is possible even against the strong opposition of teachers unions. On more controversial issues, success typically depends upon the ability of leaders (often the president) to unify the governing majority. In the early 1960s, the principal proponent of the single middle school, Jean Capelle, director general of the Ministry of Education, lacked the full support of his own minister. Skeptical conservatives, including Prime Minister Georges Pompidou, no doubt would have diluted or killed the CES had President de Gaulle not made it clear that he wanted the reform enacted.[91] De Gaulle's strong support was the major reason for the passage of Edgar Faure's Higher Education Orientation Law of 1968.[92] The Haby law of 1975, which called for the elimination of tracking in the CES, would have had little chance against its critics, both on the Left and the Right, without President Valéry Giscard d'Estaing's determination to establish his credentials as a social reformer.[93] Alain Savary's failure to achieve a settlement of the private school question in 1984 is attributable in large part to President Mitterrand's reluctance to aid him by insisting that the Socialist Party unify in support of the government's bill.

The reformer must also know, as Michel Crozier phrases it, that "One does not change society by decree," or at least not by decree alone.[94] The history of French education is filled with circulars, decrees, and even laws that have been implemented only partially or not at all. The problem of implementation, while common to all policy areas, is particularly acute in education, for ultimately teachers are the master in their classrooms. The easiest policy innovations to implement are those which do not require major changes in teacher behavior, for example, subsidies to private schools, expansion of preschool education, and the creation of new vocational schools and programs. Attempts at the *lycée* level to introduce new teaching methods, to establish close collaboration among teachers of different disciplines, or to extend the duties of teachers to include work with parents and community representatives, are unlikely to succeed unless teachers can be persuaded to cooperate. Teachers, however, are unlikely to be persuaded to accept changes that might further undermine their traditional status as *professeurs de lycée* unless the Ministry adheres firmly to its policy over a number of years, under conservative as well as under Socialist leadership.

Despite continuing conflict between elementary and secondary teachers, recurring tension over subsidized private schools, high failure rates and low morale in non-selective university programs, and a nonstop public debate over the "failure" of the schools, from a comparative perspective the French education system has adapted surprisingly well. It has opened up access to secondary and higher education without destroying the legendary *lycée*. Students in France rank near the top among industrialized nations in international tests on reading and mathematics.[95] Between periodic outbursts of student protest, there are signs of a growing consensus on major educational issues. In education, as in French politics more generally, the strength of that consensus will be determined in the future less by specific policies chosen than by the ability of the economy to grow and to create jobs for young people who count on education, probably more than ever before, to secure for themselves a stable position in society.

Notes on Chapter 8

1. Michel Crozier, *The Bureaucratic Phenomenon*, (Chicago: University of Chicago Press, 1963), pp. 238-44; and M. Crozier, *On ne change pas la société par décret*, (Paris: Grasset, 1979).

2. *Le Monde*, December 3, 1969.

3. Jack Hayward, *Governing France: The One and Indivisible Republic*, 2nd ed. (New York: W. W. Norton, 1983), p. 215.

4. François Bayrou, *1990-2000, La Décennie des mals-appris*, (Paris: Flammarion, 1990), pp. 124-25.

5. Direction de l'Evaluation et de la Prospective (DEP)/ Ministère de l'Education Nationale (MEN), *L'Etat de l'école*, no. 2 (October 1992), p. 21.

6. Organization for Economic Cooperation and Development (OECD), *Education at a Glance: OECD Indicators*, 3d ed. (Paris: OECD, 1995), p. 135.

7. MEN, *Repères et références statistiques sur les enseignements et la formation, 1993* (Paris: MEN, 1993), p. 27.

8. MEN, *L'Etat de l'école*, No. 3. (Paris: MEN, 1993), p. 37.

9. Antoine Reverchon, "Les diplômés s'en sortent mieux," *Le Monde de l'Education*, no. 217 (July-August 1994), 25.

10. Bruno Jobert, "Democracy and Social Policy: The Example of France," in John S. Ambler, ed., *The French Welfare State: Surviving Social and Ideological Change* (New York: New York University Press, 1991), pp. 248-52.

11. Jean-Michel Normand, "Une génération déclassée," *Le Monde*, March 18, 1994, p. 17.

12. Maurice T. Maschino, *L'Ecole, usine à chomeurs* (Paris: Robert Laffont, 1992).

13. *Le Monde*, June 15, 1993, p. 2.

14. Pierre Bourdieu and Jean-Claude Passeron, *Les Héritiers* (Paris: Editions de Minuit, 1964); Bourdieu and Passeron, *Reproduction in Education, Society and Culture* (London: Sage, 1977); C. Grignon and J.-C. Passeron, *Innovation in Higher Education: French Experience before 1968* (Paris: O.E.C.D., 1970), chapter 4; and Antoine Prost, *L'Enseignement s'est-il démocratisé?* (Paris: Presses Universitaires de France, 1986).

15. Institut Pédagogique National (IPN), *Informations statistiques: supplément au Bulletin Officiel de l'Education Nationale* (Paris: IPN, 1960), p. 300.

16. Alain Norvez, *De la Naissance à l'école: santé, modes de garde et préscolarité dans la France contemporaine* (Paris: Presses Universitaires de France/Institut National d'Etudes Démographiques, 1990), pp. 406-13.

17. Antoine Prost, *Histoire de l'enseignement en France, 1800-1967* (Paris: Armand Colin, 1968); A. Prost, *Education, société et politiques: Une histoire de l'enseignement en France, de 1945 à nos jours* (Paris: Seuil, 1992); John E. Talbott, *The Politics of Educational Reform in France, 1918-1940* (Princeton: Princeton University Press, 1968); Luc Decaunes and M. C. Cavalier, *Réformes et projets de réforme de l'enseignement français de la Révolution à nos jours (1789-1960)* (Paris: IPN, 1962); and Jean-Marie Donegani and Marc Sadoun, "La Réforme de l'enseignement secondaire en France depuis 1945. Analyse d'une non-décision," *Revue française de science politique* 26, no. 6 (December 1976), pp. 1125-46.

18. MEN, *Note d'Information*, (1979), no. 42, p. 1; MEN, Service des études informatiques et statistiques, *Etudes et Documents*, no. 2, (1980), p. 120; and Gabriel Languoët, "Les Années 80-90: quelle démocratisation?" *L'Orientation scolaire et professionnelle*, 22, no. 1 (1993): 11.

19. MEN, *Note d'Information*, no. 39 (1992), tables 2 and 4.

20. MEN, *Repères et références statistiques sur les enseignements et la formation, 1989* (Paris: MEN, 1989), p. 193.

21. MEN, *Note d'Information*, no. 42 (1979), table 3.

22. Direction de l'Evaluation et de la Prospective, MEN, unpublished survey results, 1993.

23. SOFRES, "Les Etudiants et la nouvelle université," *Réalité*, (November, 1968).

24. SOFRES, *Les Français et les problèmes de l'éducation nationale: études auprès des étudiants* (Montrouge: SOFRES, 1973).

25. *Le Monde*, September 25-26, 1994.

26. John S. Ambler, "Why French Education Policy Is So Often Made on the Streets," *French Politics and Society*, 12, nos. 2 and 3 (spring-summer, 1994): 41-64.

27. See chapter 9 in Antoine Prost, *Education, société et politique.*

28. Catherine Bédarida, "Les universités craquent," *Le Monde de l'Education*, no. 219 (October 1994): 31.

29. Antoine Prost, *Histoire*, 462.

30. MEN, *Repères, 1993*, 205.

31. Louis Pinto, "Le 'malaise enseignant.' Réflexion sur la construction d'un problème journalistique." *Politix* 3, no. 23 (1993), 102-12.

32. *Le Monde*, November 21, 1991, p. 15.

33. SOFRES, *Opinion Publique 1985* (Paris: Gallimard, 1985), p. 272.

34. John S. Ambler, "Neocorporatism and the Politics of French Education," *West European Politics* 8 no. 3 (July 1985): 23-42; Véronique Aubert, Alain Bergounioux, Jean-Paul Martin, René Mouriaux, *La Forteresse enseignante: La Fédération de l'Education National* (Paris; Fayard, 1985), pp. 96-97; and Hervé Hamon and Patrick Rotman, *Tant qu'il y aura des profs* (Paris: Seuil, 1984), p. 228.

35. Aubert et al., *Fortress...*, 96-97; and René Mouriaux, "Syndicalisme enseignant: une lente redéfinition," *Etude*, 372, no. 2 (February 1990): 185.

36. Claude Thélot, "L'Origine sociale des enseignants," *Education et Formations* no. 37 (March 1994): 19-21.

37. Prost, *Histoire*, 455; and MEN, *Repères, 1993*, p. 194.

38. Mouriaux, "Syndicalisme," 186-187.

39. Véronique Aubert and René Mouriaux, "Trois Chapitres sur le Syndicalisme Enseignant en France depuis 1968," *Document de travail* no. 56 (Paris: FNSP-CEVIPOF, 1993), 71.

40. *L'Enseignement Public*, March 1991, p. 5

41. Aubert and Mouriaux, *Fortresse...*, 71.

42. Ibid., 73.

43. Jacqueline de Romilly, *L'Enseignement en détresse* (Paris: Julliard, 1984); Maurice T. Maschino, *L'Ecole, usine à chomeurs* (Paris: Robert Laffont, 1992); Michel Jumilhac, *Le Massacre des innocents* (Paris: Plon, 1984); Jean-Pierre Berland, *Lycée, état d'urgence* (Paris: Lattès, 1991); Marie-Claude Bartholy and Jean-Pierre Despin, *La Gestion de l'ignorance* (Paris: Presses Universitaire de France, 1993); Philippe Nemo, *Le Chaos pédagogique: Enquête sur l'enseignement des collèges et lycées de la République* (Paris: Albin Michel, 1993); François Bayrou, *1990-2000, La Décennie des mals-appris* (Paris: Flammarion, 1990).

44. Pinto, *Malaise*.

45. Christian Baudelot and Robert Establet, *Le Niveau Monte* (Paris: Seuil, 1989); and Jean-Michel Croissandeau, *Les Bonnes notes de la France: Trente Ans d'Education* (Paris: Seuil, 1993), pp. 104-5.

46. Pinto, *Malaise.*
47. Anne Sinclair, "Les Valeurs dans la société française," in SOFRES, ed., *L'état de l'opinion 1994* (Paris: Seuil, 1994), p. 224.
48. Ibid., 230 and 235.
49. Ibid., 221.
50. Hélène Riffault, *Les Valeurs des français* (Paris: PUF, 1994), p. 222, and Frédéric Gaussen, "Les Parents sont satisfaits des enseignants," *Le Monde de l'Education,* no. 208 (October, 1993): 40-41.
51. Gaussen, 40-41, and SOFRES, ed., *L'Etat de l'opinion, 1991* (Paris: Seuil, 1991), pp. 264-65.
52. Sinclair, *Valeurs,* p. 236, and Gaussen, *Parents,* p. 40.
53. G. Michelat and M. Simon, "Religion, Class, and Politics," *Comparative Politics,* 10 (1977), pp. 159-84; and Daniel Boy and Nonna Mayer, *The French Voter Decides* (Ann Arbor: University of Michigan Press, 1993), table 1, p. 174.
54. Prost, *Histoire* 192-203; William Bosworth, *Catholicism and Crisis in Modern France* (Princeton, N.J.: Princeton University Press, 1962); and Joseph N. Moody, *French Education Since Napoleon* (Syracuse, N.Y.: Syracuse University Press, 1978)
55. *Journal Officiel, Assemblée Nationale, Débats,* December 23, 1959, p. 3608.
56. Alain Savary, *En Toute liberté* (Paris: Hachette, 1985).
57. Marie Zimmermann, *Pouvoir et liberté: clés pour une lecture des rapports église-état de Bonaparte à Mitterrand* (Strasbourg: Cerdic, 1981), pp. 74-77; and Robert Ballion, *Les Consommateurs d'école* (Paris: Stock/Laurence Pernoud, 1982), pp. 255-285.
58. Savary, *En Toute libérté,* p. 16.
59. Pierre Daniel, *Question de liberté* (Paris: Desclée de Brouwer, 1986); and Gérard Leclerc, *La Bataille de l'école* (Paris: Denoël, 1985).
60. Jean-Pierre Chevènement, interview by author, Paris, May 23, 1986.
61. Christian Beullac, "Pour une éducation nationale," *Paradoxes,* no. 42-43, (winter 1980), 67; and Beullac, interview with the author, May 9, 1986.
62. Claude Durand-Prinborgne, "La déconcentration," in Institut Français des Sciences Administratives (IFSA), ed., *L'Administration de l'éducation nationale* (Paris: Economica, 1992), pp. 43-84; Durand-Prinborgne, "Acteurs, processus, leur interrelations: état des lieux," *Savoir, Education, Formation* 5: 4 (October–December, 1993), pp. 593-621; Louis François, *Décentralisation et autonomie des établissements* (Paris: Hachette, 1994); Lionel Jospin, *L'Invention du possible* (Paris: Flammarion, 1991), chapter 9; Jacky Simon, "Décentralisation territoriale et système éducatif," IFSA, ed., *L'Administration de l'éducation nationale* (Paris: Economica, 1992), pp. 27-37; Simon, "La Décentralisation du système éducatif—six ans

après," *Savoir, Education, Formation,* 4, no. 2 (April-June, 1992), 223-37; Georges Solaux, "Politiques éducatives et conditions de l'objectif 80 percent d'une classe d'âge au niveau IV," *Orientation scolaire et professionnelle,* 22, no. 2 (June 1993): 121-45; Solaux, "Les Décisions de gestion dans l'Education Nationale," *Savoir, Education, Formation,* 5, no.1 (January-February 1993): 47-67; Bernard Toulemonde, "L'Autonomie des établissement scolaires et universitaires," in IFSA, ed., *L'Administration de l'éducation nationale* (Paris: Economica, 1992); Toulemonde, "Education Nationale: peut-on faire mieux encore?" *Savoir, Education, Formation* 5, no. 4 (October-December 1993): 575-91.

63. Alain Savary, "Une Ecole pour les élèves: Entretien avec Mona Ozouf," *Débat* no. 32 (November 1984): 9.

64. Simon, interview by author, Paris, April 8, 1994.

65. Michel Bart, "Discussion," in IFSA, ed., *L'Administration* 40.

66. MEN, *Repères, 1993,* 231.

67. Simon, "La Décentralisation," 33; and Cour des Comptes, *La Décentralisation et l'enseignement du second degré* (Paris: Direction des Journaux Officiels, 1995), pp. 52-54.

68. MEN, *Propositions du Conseil National des programmes sur l'évaluation du lycée* (Paris: MEN and Centre National de Documentation Pédagogique, 1991), p. 21; and Jospin, *L'Invention,* pp. 276-77.

69. See, for example, Parti Socialiste, *Libérer l'école: plan socialiste pour l'Education Nationale* (Paris: Flammarion, 1978), p. 12.

70. *Le Monde,* September 7, 1993, p. 12; and Bayrou, *1990-2000.*

71. *Journal Officiel, Assemblée Nationale* (1989), p. 2964.

72. *Le Monde,* October 21, 1993.

73. Jean-Pierre Chevènement, *Apprendre pour entreprendre* (Paris: Librairie Générale de France (Livre de Poche), 1985), pp. 39-42.

74. MEN, *Note d'Information* 1991, no. 36; Inspection Générale de l'Administration de l'Education Nationale (IGAEN), *Rapport 1993* (Paris: Ministère de l'Education Nationale/La Documentation française, 1993), pp. 35-58; Inspection Générale de l'Education Nationale (IGEN), *Rapport de l'Inspection Générale de l'Education Nationale 1993* (Paris: Ministère de l'Education Nationale/La Documentation française, 1993), pp. 13-38; Bruno Liensol and Françoise Oeuvrard, "Le Fonctionnement des Zones d'Education Prioritaires et les activités pédagogiques des établissements," *Education et Formation* no. 32 (November 1992): 35-45; Agnès Henriot-Van Zanten, *L'école et l'espace local: les enjeux des Zones d'Education Prioritaires* (Lyon: Presses Universitaires de Lyon, 1990); Viviane Isambert-Jamati, *Les Savoirs scolaires: enjeux sociaux*

des contenus d'enseignement et de leurs réformes (Paris: Editions Universitaires, 1990), chapter 7; Christine Garin, "La Grande désillusion," *Autrement* no. 136 (March 1993): 95-101.

75. *Le Monde*, October 22, 1993.

76. *Le Monde*, October 28, 1993; and Jacques Minot, "Législation et jurisprudence: Droits de l'homme et neutralité de l'état," *La Revue Administrative* 43, no. 253 (January–February 1990): 32-39.

77. *Le Monde de l'Education* no. 219 (October 1994): 13.

78. David Berris, "Scarves, Schools and Segregation: The Foulard Affair," *French Politics and Society* 8, no. 1 (winter 1990): 1-13; and *Le Monde*, October 27, 1994.

79. Jean-François Held, "La Sélection existe mais en dépit du bon sens," *L'Evénement du Jeudi* June 28, 1990, pp. 62-63.

80. Chris Rootes, "Student Activism in France: 1968 and After," in Philip G. Cerny, ed., *Social Movements and Protest in France* (New York: St. Martin's Press, 1982), pp. 27-34.

81. Paul Masson, for the Commission Sénatoriale sur les Manifestations, *Etudiantes, etudiants, police, presse, pouvoir* (Paris: Hachette, 1987); Julien Dray, *SOS génération* (Paris: Editions Ramsay, 1987); Daniel Gluckstein, *Qui dirige? Personne, on s'en charge nous-même* (Paris: Selio, 1987); Alain Devaquet, *L'Amibe et l'etudiant* (Paris: Editions Odile Jacob, 1988).

82. Bernard Toulemonde, *Petite histoire d'un grand ministère: l'Education Nationale* (Paris: Albin Michel, 1988), pp. 287-90.

83. Parti Socialiste, *Libérer*, 16.

84. *Le Monde*, July 30, 1993, p. 7.

85. Jean-Michel Blanquer, "Les Freins constitutionnels aux politiques publiques: les politiques publiques d'éducation," (DEA thesis, Paris: Institut d'Etudes Politiques, 1989).

86. Devaquet, *L'Amibe*, 47-52; and Toulemonde, *Petit*, 139-42.

87. *Le Monde*, August 20, 1993, p. 7.

88. MEN, *Repères, 1993*, p. 39; MEN, *L'Etat, 1993* 13; and MEN, *Note d'Information* no. 10 (1981), p. 5.

89. Georges Solaux, "Les Décisions de gestion dans l'Education Nationale," *Savoir, education, formation*, 5, no. 1 (January–February 1993): 47-67; Yves Bruchon and Georges Collonges, "Objectif 80 percent: bilan à mi-parcours," *Autrement* no. 136 (March 1993): 59-73; Bernard Charlot, "80 per cent niveau bac: derrière le symbole, quelles politiques?" *Education Permanente* no. 92 (March 1988): 91-108; and Paul Esquieu, "La Vague lycéenne: un défi pour les années

quatre-vingt-dix," in INSEE, *La Société française: Données sociales 1993* (Paris: INSEE, 1993), pp. 84-90.

90. Jean Lamoure and Jeanne Lamoure Rontopoulou, "The Vocationalisation of Higher Education in France: Continuity and Change," *European Journal of Education* 27, no. 1/2 (1992): 45-55; and Jean-Claude Guérin, "La Métamorphose du technique, *Autrement* no. 136 (March 1993): 102-8.

91. Jean Capelle, preface to *Le collège après la décentralisation*, 2nd ed., by Jean Ferrez and Pierre Scalabre, (Paris: Berger-Levrault, 1988); and Prost, *Education*, chapter 5.

92. Jacques Fomerand, *Policy Formulation and Change in Gaullist France: The 1968 Orientation Act of Higher Education* (Ph.D. Diss., City University of New York; Ann Arbor: University Microfilms, 1973), pp. 162-72.

93. René Haby, *Combat pour les jeunes français* (Paris: Julliard, 1981), chapters 3 and 4; and Valéry Giscard d'Estaing, *Démocratie Français* (Paris: Fayard, 1976), pp. 81-82.

94. Crozier, *On ne change*.

95. OECD, *Education*, 151-65.

Chapter 9

Reforming French Health Care Policy

David Wilsford

In this chapter, I will first lay out the current features of the French health care system, discussing both the institutions and culture that give it context. I will then turn to my central argument: as in many developed countries, economic pressures have been bearing in on French health care policymakers for many years and, recently, increasingly so. But also, as in other countries, policymaking—and especially reform efforts—are tied to history. In important ways, French health care policy in the 1980s and 1990s is path dependent. The main problem is clear: how can policymakers overcome the structural impediments of the past in order to strike out on a much-needed new policy trajectory, especially in ambulatory care? Overall, significant tensions push toward reform; important inertia constrains reform. So, in spite of politically effective institutions which successfully provide comprehensive health care coverage to virtually the whole French population, these very institutions are paradoxically ineffective in reorganizing significantly suboptimal elements of the system.

Institutions in Place

The main contours of the current health system were put into place in the period from 1945 to 1950, when national health insurance was extensively reformed and generalized. The ordinance of October 19, 1945 instituted a new and expanded social security system in three parts: retirement, family allowances, and sickness. This ordinance completely replaced the significantly less extensive social security system that had been established in 1930. The political impulsion for this new system came from the widespread feeling that the French prewar record of social services was indeed a dismal one compared to France's western European competitors (especially Germany) and from the widespread suspicion that this state of affairs had a great deal to do with the 1939 defeat to the Nazis. Mutual dependence and national obligation were important subtexts in this era of big reform, especially against a backdrop of extreme national imperatives for economic and social reconstruction.

Key decisions were made during this conjunctural moment that would affect the functioning and dysfunctioning of the system for many years to come. These decisions set the French health care system upon its particular post–war policy path: unlike the British, who established a national health service to be financed directly from tax revenues, the French chose to base their system on obligatory employer-employee contributory insurance. And, unlike the British, who nationalized the whole of the medical corps, the French left private practitioners in place. And unlike the British, who established a strict hierarchical referral system between general practitioners who delivered ambulatory care and hospital-based specialists who delivered non-ambulatory care, the French left in place the generalist-specialist overlap in ambulatory care, just as they left in place the uncoordinated links between the ambulatory and hospital sectors.

La médecine libérale

The French think of their medical system as a treasured mix of socialized access to health care, which fulfills important goals of national solidarity, and the private practice of medicine, which preserves the freedom and independence of the physician and patient. This latter aspect is known as *la médecine libérale* (liberal medicine). *La médecine libérale* in France rests upon four sacred principles of medicine first set forth in the 1927 manifesto known as the Medical Charter, or *Charte médicale*: (1) freedom of physician-choice by the patient, (2) freedom of prescription by the physician, (3) fee for service payment, and (4) direct payment by the patient to the physician for services rendered. These principles apply to the organization of health care delivered by private practitioners, both generalists and specialists, constituting the whole of the ambulatory sector. Private practitioners constitute 57 percent of the medical corps in France.

As the social security system was extended and generalized in the years after World War II, this system of liberal medicine as it applied to virtually all ambulatory care was incorporated almost wholesale into the new national health insurance system. For ambulatory care, patients in France may choose their physician freely (and may change as often as they wish), may seek care directly from general practitioners or specialists, and are reimbursed at fairly generous specified levels for payment of physician fees and for the cost of laboratory tests and prescription drugs. The physician, for her or his part, is free to prescribe any treatment she or he deems medically suitable. However, fee levels are strictly regulated through regular fee agreements that physician unions negotiate with the sickness funds. Victor Rodwin, in particular, has been quite critical of the suboptimality of this system.[1]

This relatively uncoordinated ambulatory care system resides uneasily alongside the French national hospital system that is, by contrast, centrally directed from the Ministry of Health in Paris. "Private" practitioners (all those in the ambulatory sector) do not enjoy admitting privileges to French hospitals as their American counterparts do. When patients are admitted for hospital care, the medical dossier passes from the private practitioner—generalist or specialist—to the full-time hospital medical staff. These hospital doctors are paid on a salaried basis and are considered professional civil servants of the French state. Hospital budgets are fixed by the Ministry of Health on a prospective global envelope basis with little connection to the type or quantity of services that a given hospital medical staff might think it medically appropriate to deliver.

Clearly, therefore, in the ambulatory sector there are few if any incentives to economize, as there are no central controls on patients or doctors. A true and striking anecdote illustrates that this system can indeed function perversely: a regional sickness fund discovered—quite by accident—that a patient had visited five psychiatrists in the span of *one* day. Moreover, as was the patient's legal right, she turned in a receipt for each consultation for full reimbursement, as well as for the drugs prescribed by each psychiatrist. The sickness fund could not legally refuse to reimburse this patient. "Perhaps the really amazing thing," remarked the associate director of the fund, "is that she's still alive!" Clearly, the ambulatory sector in France is user-driven, contributing greatly to its subobtimality.

By contrast, there are strong incentives to economize in the hospital sector under the centrally directed global budget procedure. Since that procedure was adopted in 1983, growth rates of hospital expenditures have stabilized and even dropped significantly. In 1992, hospital expenditures as a percent of total health care expenditures in France had dropped from 51.8 percent to 46 percent (a decrease of 11.2 percent). Ambulatory care expenditures, however, as a percent of the total had increased from 24.7 percent to 28.8 percent, and pharmaceutical expenditures had increased from 17.3 percent to 17.8 percent of the total. Overall during this period from 1982 to 1992, total French health care expenditures increased from 7.4 percent of GDP to 9.1 percent, putting France in a middle-range for OECD countries, performing a little worse than Germany (8.5 percent), a little better than Canada (10.0 percent), much better than the United States (13.4 percent), but much worse than Britain and Japan (both spending 6.6 percent of GDP on health care).[2]

The Sickness Fund

The administrative focal point of the French health care system under national health insurance is the national sickness fund (Caisse nationale d'assurance maladie des travailleurs salariés, or CNAMTS). This fund, however, is not the only one comprising the whole system. Separate funds for agricultural workers, independent professionals, government employees, merchant marines, and so on, cover altogether about 20 percent of the French population. But, since it alone covers 80 percent, the national sickness fund is clearly the dominant player and sets the tone for the other funds in negotiations with providers in particular. Virtually the entire population of France—over 99 percent—is covered by national health insurance.

At the national level, the CNAMTS governs a system of 16 regional funds and 129 local funds. The regional sickness funds coordinate preventive health care measures and capital development, in particular of hospital facilities. The local sickness funds, generally corresponding to departments, oversee the enrollment of those covered by the system and the collection of the employee-employer contributions. They are also charged with the reimbursement of claims. The national sickness fund fixes all general policy—often at the direction of the central government—regarding levels of contribution, levels of reimbursement, and levels of charges and fees. It also generally oversees the administration of this vast system. In 1985, there were over 100,000 administrators, agents, clerks, and physician-inspectors employed by the CNAMTS. Of these, 76,000 worked in the local funds. In 1984, 393 million payment operations were executed. In 1984, the CNAMTS administered 267 billion francs in payments. Yet, while vast, it is relatively efficient administratively: in 1990, only 1.5 percent of total health care expenditures in France went to administrative costs, compared to 5.9 percent in the United States (where total health care expenditures as a percent of GDP are also far higher).[3]

The national sickness fund is also responsible for the general financial equilibrium of the system, a task that has become increasingly difficult with each year. Given that French health care is an employer-based insurance system, revenues are generated by employer and employee payroll taxes, which are determined as a proportion of salaries. In 1994, the levels of payroll withholding *(cotisation)* for national health insurance were respectively 12.8 percent of the salary from the employer and 6.8 percent from the employee. Retirees are subject to lower levels of withholding on their pensions. Overall, national health insurance directly covers about three-fourths of personal health expenditures in France.

A Strong, Autonomous Bureaucracy in Health Policy

But while the administrative focal point of the French system is the national sickness fund, the decisional focal point is not. Rather, the centralized French bureaucracy continues to exert almost total control over each aspect of the health care system. In this, the French state acts principally through two ministries, social affairs (which includes health) and finance.

In France, the state structures that govern the health care sector are relatively homogeneous with clearly defined agendas. They also benefit from clear, effective policy instruments which give them a certain number of "tactical advantages" against actors from society, especially organized medicine.[4] By contrast, state structures in a country such as the United States are much more dispersed and heterogeneous, and operate upon less well-defined policy agendas. In addition, broad consensus over the health care agenda has been far clearer in France than in the United States.

Health care institutions in France are clearly characterized by what Michael Atkinson and William Coleman have called state autonomy at the sectoral level.[5] Important conditions for autonomy include a clear and consensual conception of the state's mandate in the policy arena, especially within the bureaus that are most intimately charged with decision-making in that arena and a functional mandate for the state agencies involved rather than a clientele mandate. The activities of the state agencies center around the execution of long-standing, clearly defined laws and regulations that are not subject to constant negotiation with societal groups; and the agencies have the in-house capacity to generate, use, and evaluate technical and scientific information independent of the societal associations.

The whole French health care system is, at least in theory, quite rationally organized with elaborate hierarchical structures, deliberate planning procedures, and clear lines of responsibility and mission. Formally, the central government assumes responsibility for general public health, such as prevention, planning and preparedness, and the fight against widespread socio-medical problems (for example, drug addiction or alcoholism). It organizes the training of health care personnel, participates in the regulation of their practice conditions, and serves as a watchdog over the quality and security of health care establishments and pharmaceutical production. It also ensures that health care services, including prevention, are provided at an adequate level and regulates the volume of available health care services: personnel, establishments, medical equipment, and marketing authorization for drugs. Of utmost importance, the state exercises regulatory authority over social protection, intervening actively in the means and methods of finance (assessment and rates of contribution), in the rules that govern the coverage available to the population, in its relations with the producers of health care services, and in the levels of coverage of health care services (prices and levels of reimbursement). The central government also tries to ensure the financial equilibrium of social welfare programs.[6]

At the national level, the Ministry for Social Affairs and Health is the most important government actor in the health care system. Three divisions within this ministry are especially important: the Division of Social Security, the Division of Hospitals, and the Division of Health. But other French ministries also regularly intervene in health care: the Ministry of Finance is of primary and regular importance when the budget is being drawn up and when social security deficits are being confronted. The Ministry of National Education controls medical training, including the number of physicians permitted to graduate from French medical schools and in what specialties. The Ministry of Industry plays an important role in setting drug prices.

At the local level, there are Regional Bureaus of Health and Social Affairs (DRASS), which report to the regional prefect, as well as Departmental Bureaus of Health and Social Affairs (DDASS), which report to the departmental prefect.

The DRASS coordinate planning regarding medical equipment in the region. They also provide an administrative liaison with the health professions. The DDASS are responsible for the smooth functioning of all health care delivery services, prevention, and local health promotion. They regularly build on the work of the Regional Health Observatories (ORS) whose mission is to evaluate the needs of the population and promote the improvement of available health care services.

Planning is implemented at the regional level and is especially critical to hospital policy. The two principal planning instruments are the Health Map *(la Carte sanitaire)* and the Regional Schema of Health System Organization *(le Schéma régional d'organisation sanitaire)*. The Health Map was established in 1970 and is especially important in specifying how much high technology medical equipment a hospital can have and in defining hospitals' in-patient bed capacity. It also regulates the utilization of costly medical technology. The Regional Schema organizes the geographical distribution of medical equipment and activities within each region. In some cases, a regional schema and an inter-regional schema may be simultaneously specified.

This description of the French state in the health policy domain clearly points to a state whose structures are strong, whose mandate and agenda are clear, and whose civil servants pursue their mission with zeal and coherence. This pattern remarkably resembles what Atkinson and Coleman defined as the "state-directed" policy network. In this network,

> with little warning and sometimes with little explanation, the state embarks upon economic projects that have serious repercussions for the investment decisions of business. Business is typically divided and, in any event, considered untrustworthy by officials. Politicians and bureaucrats are often self-righteous and manipulative. Officials are not in the mood for concertation, and they are by no means neutral with respect to outcomes and instrumentalities. The political-administrative style is one of managerial directive followed by a polite briefing. Business-state relations are barely cordial.[7]

Nonetheless, we will subsequently see that these state structures, as autonomous as they may be, are definitely not omnipotent. In particular, policy decisions in the past that have laid out suboptimal structural arrangements constitute a powerful drag on reform efforts designed to create new, more optimal policy paths, and some social forces—like organized medicine— are effective at blocking important change.

The Underpinning of National Solidarity: Health Care as a Public not a Private Good

These bureaucratic capacities, which, we will see, often face societal fragmentation in the health policy domain, are powerfully assisted by a strong societal consensus in France that health care is and ought to remain a public good, not a private one. Historically, this has often been expressed through the philosophy of national solidarity *(solidarité nationale)*.

By "national solidarity," I mean the agreement by all elements of an otherwise highly divided French society that social assistance is necessary to the strength and well being of France—both to its internal cohesiveness and to its power in the international order. This unity of purpose is focused around the concepts of both mutual dependence and national obligation, and in the immediate post-war period it was directed toward social welfare goals concerning unemployment, family allowances, retirement pensions, and health care. The theme of national solidarity dates at least to the French Revolution and has historically attracted all shades of French intellectual thought, ranging from radical Socialists of Blanc's time to the Gaullists and neo-Gaullists of the Fifth Republic.[8] This sentiment was particularly strong in France at the close of World War II. It was a crucial element in the coming together of *all* ideological factions in favor of an extensively reformed social security system.

To this day, virtually all French question incredulously the American frontier view that health care is and ought to be a private good instead of a public one. In the language of public choice theory, the French have always regarded health care in the same way that they view other public goods, that is, as the responsibility of the state to provide because it cannot be provided efficiently or equitably on a purely private basis. In the French view, the state is the juridical personification of the nation, and as such it must see to the nation's health, just as it must see to the provision of other public goods, such as roads and bridges, national defense, and a host of other goods and services that, because of their very nature, cannot be adequately provided at the individual level.

Interests at Play

As with any issue, the state and its institutions interact more or less aggressively with interest groups from society, who press (more or less effectively) their policy demands upon the state. In order to consider the society end of the equation, we will concentrate here on the providers of health care services—physicians and hospitals—and the consumers, the French public.

Doctors as Medical Corps and as Organized Medicine

As in any developed country characterized by increasingly complex and sophisticated health care systems, the medical profession in France has evolved into a highly heterogeneous mix of private practitioners, specialists and generalists, civil service hospital staff, biomedical researchers, older and younger generations of doctors, and increasing numbers of women. In general, French medical doctors, like other French labor groups, are not highly unionized. Most are apathetic to political organizing, although, like most French, this does not mean that they do not have distinct political opinions.

In general, French physicians feel underappreciated and underpaid in a society that regards them as nonetheless privileged and in a health care system that does its best to remunerate them stingily. By international comparison, French doctors are far less prestigious societally than their German, American, or Japanese counterparts; they are also remunerated less well than most of their OECD counterparts except the British and the Italians. I will return to this issue subsequently.

Abetting the state's dominance in making health care policy in France is the historical weakness of organized medicine. It has been weak since the earliest days of the nineteenth century because medicine, except for the occasional moment, has been deeply fragmented organizationally and poorly mobilized politically. These organizational variables cut across the generic characteristics of the "professions," such as technical expertise, which establishes the doctor as the strategically key figure in the health care system. Organizational variables are particularly important when professionals must mobilize politically, especially in the face of strong, focused opposition, such as the politically strong French state. Therefore, in the French case, fragmentation and poor mobilization have weakened the influence of organized medicine, and by extension the profession as a whole, in the health policy universe. What is worse, organized medicine in France is riven by internal conflicts that manifest themselves in competing professional associations that are in turn plagued by very low membership levels.[9]

Both division and divisiveness, we will see, are deeply rooted in the history of the medical profession in France. I will refer to these two dimensions together under the rubric of "interest mobilization." To what extent are the interests in the sector under study characterized by unitary organization ("peak association"?), high rate of membership, sufficient resources for collecting and analyzing political and technical information, and the ability of the organization to speak authoritatively with the government on behalf of its members? This last characteristic means that the association can effectively negotiate with the government because it can ensure the cooperation of members in implementing any accord that it reaches with the state authorities.[10]

Along these dimensions, the fragmentation of the French medical profession and its organizational weakness are striking. The first form this fragmentation takes is a splintering of organized medicine into competing medical unions, as well as into functional divisions. There are today three major medical unions that compete with each other to represent private practitioners—both generalists and specialists. A number of minor unions exist as well. In addition, there are several other unions representing the hospital and salaried sectors. These unions often compete with each other. The fragmentation is both political and ideological and is characterized by much intense polemic all around.

The oldest and largest medical association representing private practitioners in France is the Confédération des Syndicats Médicaux Français (CSMF). It was founded in 1928 and had momentarily consolidated a tenuous preeminence by 1930. One of the most persistent problems facing the CSMF is how to handle the competing pressures, both internally and externally, of forces within the medical profession that oppose it. By the 1980s, the CSMF had managed to consolidate a truce with its main rival, the Fédération des Médecins de France (Federation of French Physicians—FMF), enabling it to cooperate, or at least coordinate its activities with the rival group. Yet by the end of the 1980s, an antagonistic sentiment among general practitioners within the CSMF had grown so strong that a new rival union split off and regrouped under the label MG France, for Médecins généralistes de France (General Practitioners of France). This group began in a small number of provincial departments, but within two or three years had gathered great strength and was represented in most departments nationally. In the universe of medical profession forces, MG France was considerably reinforced when in 1989 the minister of social affairs designated it a "representative" union, that is, granted it official status for fee negotiations. The government regularly pursues this sort of divide-and-conquer strategy in the guise of providing interlocutor status to representative social groups. Such a strategy is only plausible, of course, against a backdrop of highly politicized social groupings.

In France, there are additional dimensions of fragmentation that characterize the medical corps. The first is common to all advanced health systems: the segmentation of the medical corps into general practitioners, various and diverse medical specialties, hospital staff and the biomedical research community. This functional segmentation is one centrifugal force damaging to the unity of the medical corps. In some countries, like Germany, Japan, or the United States, the profession's political structures have done a better, but not perfect, job of containing these centrifugal forces.

The second dimension of fragmentation is also "functional," but in a different way. Namely, ethical responsibilities and accountability have been the preserve of an organization entirely separate from "organized medicine," the Ordre des Médecins (Order of Physicians). Insofar as ethics and ethical questions could potentially serve as a powerful unifying force within the profession, its organizational isolation from the profession's political structures deprives the profession of an important source of unity and cohesion.

Moreover, the French medical profession is also fragmented demographically. Generational fragmentation—young versus old—pits older, more established doctors against young, struggling doctors in a resource environment characterized by extreme scarcity. Young doctors in France face great difficulties establishing a practice. Moreover, all doctors, young and old, compete with each other for patients who are perfectly willing to "shop around." Patients look for a physician who will provide the desired treatment—the right prescription drugs, the authorized medical leave from work, the better bedside manner, and so forth. French physicians also operate within a fee-for-service structure characterized by very low fees. Data on comparative incomes show that French physicians make notably less than their American and German counterparts. According to OECD health data for 1986 (the most recent year in which German figures were reported), the average income of a German physician was PPP$86,704.[11] By contrast, the average income of a French physician was only PPP$42,512 in that year and of a British physician PPP$41,615, while the American physician made PPP$119,500.[12]

A revealing and true anecdote illustrates the prevalence of this fragmentation within organized medicine, as well as the French tendency, first identified by Tocqueville, to organizational hyperfractionalism. On a consulting basis, an American social scientist was invited to give a policy seminar in Paris to a group drawn from one of the major medical unions representing general practitioners. After lunch, as the American was preparing to take the floor for his presentation, the leader of the union loudly confronted grievances with the assembled group. He then dramatically resigned from office and walked out! (The policy seminar then went on just as planned.)

Local Interests and the Hospitals

Other structural interests at play clearly work against the collective optimality of the French health care system in spite of its highly rational structure on paper. While in theory the hospital system is centrally directed from the Ministry of Health in Paris through the division of hospitals, in reality each individual hospital also occupies the corner of an iron triangle that includes the local municipality (usually the mayor) and the electoral-bureaucratic pork-barrel process in Paris. This triangle often works to protect the interests of the hospital in the individual locality, even when the collective interest is not served by bed or medical equipment overcapacity. Frequently, the mayor or his agent chairs the local hospital's administrative council. This mayor is also often a deputy in Parliament, especially if it is a medium or large city. Longstanding, complex patterns of patronage work to secure the local hospital's position with the health bureaucrats in Paris, who otherwise might not favor that local hospital in terms of bed or equipment capacity.

However, this portrait has been changed somewhat by recent reforms introduced in the period since 1993, which have given the management of individual public hospitals much greater flexibility and autonomy. In particular, the government's regulatory oversight in daily hospital management (for example, regarding loans, markets, personnel recruitment) is now exercised retrospectively by means of simple legal checks. Only hospital development programs, all budgets and the creation of new medical positions are subjected to prospective control by the government. Hospitals may now invest on their own and form "common interest associations."

The French Public: Consumers of Health Care

Finally, as we have alluded to above, the French health care system awards a remarkable degree of freedom of choice to patients regarding ambulatory and hospital care—between doctors, generalists and specialists, the ambulatory sector and the hospital sector, hospitals overall, as well as public hospitals and private hospitals.

In such a system, there are no controls over the amount of health care services consumed, much less over the level of service that would be medically appropriate. From 1981 to 1991, the number of office and home visits per capita increased from 5.5 to 8.0. From 1983 to 1989, the number of pathological and biological tests performed per capita increased from 78.8 to 145.4. And from 1982 to 1990, the amount of prescription drugs consumed per capita rose from 29 units to 38.[13]

The Policy Path:
Path Dependency—Structures and Conjunctures

Elsewhere I have explored cross-nationally the path-dependent character of most policymaking in health care (and indeed in other policy domains).[14] A path-dependent sequence of political changes is one that is tied to previous decisions and existing institutions. In path dependency, structural forces dominate, and, therefore policy movement is most likely to be incremental. Strong conjunctural forces are required to move policy further away from an existing path onto a new trajectory. It is the combination of path-dependent limits and occasional windows of exceptional opportunity, or conjunctures, that determine the way in which a political system responds to policy imperatives.

I have borrowed the notion of path dependency from economic history and, in particular, leaned heavily on the work of Paul David.[15] In economics, path dependency describes the interaction of state-dependent individual decision-making in a decentralized decision-making network. This interaction leads to path-dependent collective decision outcomes. Individual decision-making early on in the path may lead to "lock-in" of a pattern that is collectively suboptimal. Each decision-making moment constitutes a powerful focusing device for subsequent decision making. As time unfolds, the probability of continuing along the same path increases, while the probability of significantly deviating from the established path, or even striking out upon a new path, decreases.

While very early on a number of different paths may be equally plausible and probable, once a given path has been laid out—perhaps as the result of random variables initially—each subsequent decision-making episode at the individual level in this decentralized decision-making network reinforces the path, characterizes collective decision outcomes. These collective decision outcomes are as likely to be suboptimal as anything else because the initial conditions conspiring to lay out one particular path instead of another are random.

The notion of path dependency is especially useful in explaining long periods of essentially incremental policymaking, or policymaking without big change. On the other hand, path dependency alone is unable to explain the frequent importance of unpredictable contingency in bringing about crucial moments of big change that depart significantly from the path. The key, I argue, lies in the interplay of ongoing, long-term institutions with a conjuncture, the distinctive short-term mix of contingency with structure.

A conjuncture is the fleeting coming together of a number of diverse elements into a new, single combination. Because they are fleeting, in the grand scheme of history, conjunctures may change quite rapidly. By the same token, while the effects of structures are predictable (given their long-term character), the effects of conjunctures are unpredictable. The actual coming together of a propitious conjuncture is itself perhaps the most highly unpredictable element of all—not only as to when it will occur (timing) but whether it will occur at all (actuality).[16]

The framework enveloping a network of decision agents is specified by structures that grow up over time. As time unfolds, these structures channel decision-making along certain paths. The decision-making framework specified by structures sets out both impediments to certain kinds of decisions, as well as an incentive structure that incites certain decisions over others. This structural framework then interacts with conjunctural factors to influence individual agents at their decision-making moments.

Put another way, structures are the institutions and processes that form the infrastructural framework for policy (decisions). Dynamic events unfold over time within this framework. This may be thought of as an endogenous universe, which then may be subject to exogenous shocks, that is, conjunctures (either positive or negative) that are comprised by a distinctive mix of contingency and structure.

History of French Health Care Structures: Path Development

We may divide the post–war history of French health care policymaking into two periods: In the first, from the 1950s through the early 1960s, the state's dominance was established and reinforced. In the second period, from roughly the 1970s to the present, the state's attempts to control expenditures and the medical decisions that ultimately determine expenditures have been stymied. This period is characterized by persistent suboptimality, especially in ambulatory care: no gatekeeping to control access to the more expensive specialists, continued reliance on a fee-for-service system to remunerate private practice doctors, high levels of prescription drug consumption, and multiplication of consulations, tests, and other fee-for-service acts.

As it established the modern French social security system, an early goal of the French government was to implement a binding fee system on all physicians. In the French system of *la médecine libérale*, patients paid physicians directly and were later reimbursed specified amounts by the sickness funds, usually from 75 to 80 percent of the scheduled fees. (Hospitalization, however, was covered in total and paid directly by the funds.) Because the scheduled fees were not binding, however, reimbursements to patients actually varied widely—sometimes as low as 30 percent of the fee charged. Without a binding schedule, physicians could charge what they wished—and they did.

Responding to public discontent, successive governments, with the support of the sickness funds and both labor and management, sought a binding fee schedule. Two rationales advanced by the government proved to be equally compelling. First, as we have seen, the principle of solidarity was both widely shared in society and deeply perceived. This sentiment cut across traditional ideological cleavages and traditional economic class divisions. Second, as physicians raised fees beyond those specified by the reimbursement schedules, the public put pressures on the sickness funds and on successive governments to raise the fees specified in the schedules so as to maintain the 75 to 80 percent reimbursement rate.

Throughout the 1950s, physicians fought these government attempts to establish binding fee schedules. In particular, the project Gazier, a comprehensive reform initiated by the minister of social affairs in 1956-57, was barely stopped by the CSMF; in the end, the project definitively forced French medical syndicalism into a highly reactive political position. As the conflict developed, tensions and two tendencies within the medical profession became more apparent. The CSMF leadership moved toward a policy of relative conciliation, while a large and growing dissident movement favored non-cooperation with the government and the sickness funds. The difference between these two tendencies may be thought of as the difference between remaining within normal negotiating channels and contesting the government from outside.

The controversy simmered—never too far below the surface—as the government persistently tried to circumvent organized medicine's resistance to reforming the health insurance system. The growing political crisis in France in 1958 over the Algerian question, the fall of the Fourth Republic, de Gaulle's return to power, and the creation of the Fifth Republic worked to distract the state authorities momentarily from domestic battles. But by 1960, the state had returned to business and with a vengeance. The decree of May 12, 1960 imposed binding fee schedules on all physicians. Further, it required physicians, rather than the mediating institutions of organized medicine, to adhere individually to the negotiated agreements. Individual physicians who did not sign agreements to abide by these fee schedules lost their patients' right to be reimbursed by the sickness funds. This constituted an extraordinarily effective wedge, driven by the state between, first, the patient and the physician and, second, the physician and organized medicine. In the face of this thorough defeat, the French medical profession formally splintered; several dissident movements broke off from the CSMF to form their own groups.

Since the 1970s, however, the French state has been largely stymied (with one important exception to be examined below) in its attempts to force structural change in the health care system. While we have seen that the French do far better than the Americans in the amount they spend on health care and their general coverage of the population, they, like the Germans, believe that they are still spending too much and that total expenditures cannot continue growing at rates far higher than general inflation. Moreover—and against the backdrop of worldwide recession—it is the legal duty of the government to insure that social security accounts are balanced. When the employer-based insurance funds run deficits, they must be supplemented by general tax revenues.

For many years, French governments of both the Left and the Right have grappled with this vexing problem.[17] In 1983, for example, under the Socialist government, the Plan Bérégovoy froze physician fees and pharmaceutical prices and put into place the global budgeting method for hospital financing. In 1986, under a conservative government the Plan Séguin instituted a variety of measures mostly designed to exact more copayments from patients for hospital stays and drug reimbursements.[18] (It also eliminated the franking privilege that all French citizens enjoyed when sending in reimbursement forms to the sickness fund!) Moreover, throughout the 1980s and 1990s the sickness fund has been extremely stingy with fee increases for private practitioners, who work on a fee-for-service basis, while the government has been equally stingy regarding approved prices for prescription drugs. Yet year after year, after momentary stability, high growth in total expenditures resumes and the social security accounts dive back into the red.[19]

The results of reform have been so poor in France because most reform has been tied closely to the habitual path of French health policy, in which the structures of the system allow uncontrolled use of the system, which leads in turn to higher, uncontrollable expenditures. For example, in the ambulatory sector, every reform effort left intact the fee-for-service system of physician remuneration. And while the sickness fund has been stingy with increases, the medical corps has responded by increasing the number of services rendered. Equally important, there is no gatekeeping in the ambulatory sector; French citizens are free to consult with any and as many doctors as they wish. Therefore, a patient, through a crude understanding of his or her own symptoms, may go directly to specialist X, only to find out that (a) a general practitioner (paid less) would have been just as or more than medically adequate or that (b) in fact, it is specialist Y or Z who is most medically qualified to treat such a condition. In all this, the patient has the legal right to be reimbursed at the specified levels for each and every consultation and for all the drugs prescribed.

But with Conjuncture Come Non-Incremental Hospital Reforms

However, one example of truly big change within the French system was the reform of hospital financing in 1984. And it was the only reform able to meet the goal set for it, that is, stabilization of hospital expenditures. What enabled this non-incremental reform to set hospital financing onto a trajectory far from its habitual path? Here, precisely, the crucial variable was conjunctural. Social security deficits were nothing new, but they became a particularly salient target when the leftist government in power executed an economic policy U-turn in 1983. After two years of disastrous experimentation—during which France alone, of all European countries, tried to spend its way out of an American-led global recession—the government announced a severe new austerity policy in 1983.

Within the social security system, the health accounts constitute by far the largest component, and they tend to run in the red more often than the other social security accounts (pensions, unemployment, and family allocations). Within the health accounts, the hospital sector presents a particularly inviting target. In the early 1980s, hospital expenditures had been growing at a particularly alarming rate under a per bed, per day financing mechanism (incentives that clearly drove hospitals and their doctors to fill as many beds as possible with as many patients as possible for as long as possible). In the period from 1975 to 1982, French hospital expenditures as a percentage of total medical consumption had risen from 46.0 percent to 51.8 percent.

At the time of the 1983 austerity policy, a new director of hospitals was also named by the government. Jean de Kervasdoué, a civil administrator sympathetic to the Socialists, took over the post from a Communist, Jack Ralite. Kervasdoué proved to be an especially tenacious reformer. Completely revamping the hospital financing system, he instituted a policy of anticipatory global budgeting: each hospital was given an "envelope" for the year, a fixed lump sum out of which it had to pay all of its operating and capital expenses.

The hue and cry from the largely conservative hospital medical corps was loud and long. But with the unwavering support of a Socialist government (which did not care much for conservative doctors anyway) preoccupied with digging the country out of near financial ruin (and therefore willing to be severe with measures that would reduce and control expenditures), Kervasdoué (with extraordinary determination) succeeded where others had feared to tread. In this story of successful departure from a traditional but suboptimal path, Kervasdoué benefitted from a favorable conjuncture and was smart enough to make the most of his structurally strategic position atop the centralized national hospital system.[20] The results were impressive: from 1984 to 1988, French hospital expenditures as a percentage of total medical consumption fell from 50.8 percent to 46.9 percent. From 1988 to 1992, they have continued to decline slightly, from 46.9 percent to 46.0 percent.[21]

However, Hospitals Act II: Still Tied to a Suboptimal Policy Path

Nonetheless, there is still substantial fragmentation of the hospital sector as a whole in France, and this works against the aggregate rationality of the system in spite of Kervasdoué's impressive reform success in modes of financing. As of 1992, France had 546,500 hospital beds, or 9.5 beds per

1,000 inhabitants (5 of these are short-stay beds). Just under two-thirds of these beds are in the public sector, the remainder in the private sector. Just over half of the private-sector beds are found in for-profit hospitals *(cliniques)*. The rest are in private-sector non-profit hospitals which are governed by the same regulations as the public sector. (For the same year, 945,000 people, or 4.2 percent of the active work force in France, were employed in the hospital sector either full- or part-time. Of this total, non-physician care-giving personnel accounted for just under two-thirds and medical doctors accounted for a tenth.)

These two hospital sectors—public and private—differ along certain lines: breadth of mission, ways they function, medical infrastructural endowment, type of clientele, and method of compensation. For example, teaching and research are part of the specific functions of public hospitals, which are also morally charged with providing care to all patients, especially in hospital emergency rooms as opposed to private hospitals. In the public hospitals, all personnel, including doctors, are salaried civil servants. By contrast, most doctors in the private hospital sector are private practitioners and generally have a practice outside the hospital.

Public sector hospitals include both general and specialized facilities, ranging in size from the 29 prestigious "Regional Hospital Centers" to the very modest local hospitals with an average of just 59 beds. Other than providing medical care services, the regional hospitals enjoy a greater endowment of medical equipment and are also responsible for research and the training of medical students and other medical personnel. In 1992, public hospitals represented 64.6 percent of total hospital beds. Public hospitalization, accounting for 63 percent of short-term beds, is relatively more important to general medicine (77 percent of beds) and in psychiatry (70 percent) than in surgery (49 percent of beds) or maternity (59 percent).

Private non-profit hospitals with public sector obligations *(établissements privés assurant le service public hospitalier*—PSPH) represent 30 percent of the beds in the private sector. These hospitals are subject to the same public service obligations as public sector hospitals (that is, they may not dump patients) and are governed by the same rules of operation and payment.

Private sector hospitalization, overall, includes acute care facilities, medium- and long-term stay facilities, and psychiatric hospitals. This sector includes about 35 percent of hospital beds generally, but a bit less than half of the beds in surgical services and 65 percent of the beds in medium- and long-term stay facilities.

Private sector hospitalization covers hospitals of varying legal statute, ranging from the for-profits to the non-profits. The for-profits are oriented mainly to short-term stay patients, who account for more than two-thirds of private beds. In recent years these for-profit hospitals have experienced a consolidation of the very small into the larger units, and they have gone through a period of technical development. Private non-profit hospitals provide relatively more care for medium and long-term stay patients.[22]

So while Kervasdoué benefitted from a propitious conjuncture to enact non-incremental financial reforms in the hospital system, no one to date has been able to enact substantial structural reforms within this very complex, very fragmented mix of public and private hospital facilities. The main problem left unresolved is that there are so few disincentives for patients seeking treatment in the more expensive private hospital sector, which the state nonetheless finances.

The Policy Prognosis

Since the mid-1970s, France like many other countries has experienced a slowing of economic growth and an increase in levels of unemployment. Both phenomena have affected contributions to the social security system because these are based on workers' incomes. Assuring the financial equilibrium of the various health care regimes is therefore a primary preoccupation of the public authorities. We have seen that the various reform attempts made up to the present have done little so far to introduce major changes in the organization of health care in France. These measures have heretofore only touched on the margins of the fundamental structural elements of the system: the preponderant role of national health insurance, the coexistence of public and private sectors, widespread private-practice medicine, unlimited patient choice in ambulatory medicine, the doctor's total clinical autonomy in the ambulatory sector and virtual clinical autonomy in the hospital sector, and fee-for-service remuneration in ambulatory care.

Other policies have reduced the level of collective coverage for different areas of medical consumption. These measures aim to restrain the demand for health care services by increasing the financial participation of the patient. Among these measures are the increase in copayments for certain pharmaceutical products, physical therapy, and laboratory tests, the implementation of a hospital day charge to be paid by the patient, the extension of fee exemptions to private practitioners in sector two (not subject to the negotiated fee schedules), and a limiting of special illnesses that qualify for 100 percent coverage. It is, however, impossible to quantify the exact impact of these various policies or to estimate whether or not they have worked to avoid unnecessary medical consumption without, at the same time, limiting access to justifiable care.

While national health insurance legally covers virtually the entire population of France, it does not cover about a quarter of all expenditures for medical consumption. To cover this difference, a growing number of French—87 percent in 1992—have resorted to supplementary insurance, such as that provided by mutual aid societies and non-profit and for-profit private insurers. These organizations offer a variety of supplemental programs. Overall, for 1992, mutual aid societies financed 6.2 percent of medical care expenditures while private insurers paid about 3 percent. Supplementary coverage is sometimes sought by the individual, but is most often offered on a group basis at the workplace. In the latter case, the firm contracts with an insurance organization for coverage of all of the firm's employees or for an entire occupational category. Insofar as increasing copayments has been a consistent strategy of French governments in their struggle to contain health care expenditures, widespread supplementary insurance renders this strategy rather ineffective.

Other policies have had mixed results. For example, the adoption of the global budget system for public hospitals has greatly slowed the growth of hospital expenditures. Negotiations between national health insurance officials and representatives from the health care professions have contained the growth of medical fees to the levels of general inflation, but aggregate remuneration of the medical corps as a whole has risen as a result of the multiplication of medical services. Likewise, pharmaceutical prices in France have been kept very low, but overall pharmaceutical consumption is up. Agreements for "moderation" have been signed with nurses, biological laboratories, and private clinics, but enforcement of moderation is not specified and the agreements themselves amount to little more than general statements of good intentions. Recent national agreements (conventions) have also set annual targets for medical services. If these targets are exceeded, the agreements provide for reimbursement to the national health insurance system or for downward adjustments in allowable fees.

Nonetheless, in spite of all these measures, the financial difficulties of the national health insurance system that have resulted from the poor economic situation remain. According to social security accounts, national health insurance ran a 26 billion franc deficit in 1993 and a 30 billion franc deficit in 1994. More new measures aimed at health care cost containment are still being studied.

The new medical convention signed in December 1993 contains, among other things, three significant new provisions, although implementation and enforcement remain open questions: (1) The application of utilization guidelines *(références médicales)* aiming to help the physician use the most appropriate health care services; (2) The implementation of a permanent patient file—to be carried on credit-card size health cards containing a computer chip—allowing the treating physician to avoid contradictory or redundant prescriptions; (3) The setting of a preliminary annual target (+3.4 percent in 1994) for growth in total private practice fees and prescriptions.

It remains to be seen, however, whether these new measures will be sufficient in slowing the growth of health care expenditures or if, to the contrary, additional measures will be necessary in order to attain an equilibrium between the receipts of national health insurance and the benefits it pays out.

In addition, the framework agreement signed at the beginning of 1994 by the government and the pharmaceutical industry provides for the setting of an annual national target for the growth of health care expenditures on drugs. The sales volume of a reimbursable drug that exceeds the conditions specified for "sound medical use" *(bon usage des soins)* will be subject to sanctions, either by lowering the approved price proportional to the abnormally high sales volume or, in the extreme, "de-reimbursement," that is, removing the drug entirely from the approved list of reimbursable drugs.

Clearly, structural changes in the delivery of ambulatory care services are currently the most pressing need. Unrestricted freedom of choice for the patient and unrestricted freedom of prescription for the doctor (clinical autonomy) mean that a third of total expenditures escape all regulation or control. The entrenched character of the ambulatory sector—widely supported by both patients and doctors—weighs very heavily against non-incremental reform efforts, in spite of a virtual consensus among bureaucratic elites that non-incremental change is very long overdue. Reform has been ineffectual because it has been tied so closely to history, and because it has been so dependent upon the previous policy path.

A New Conjuncture?

Let us define the optimal policy solution in health care to be one which works more or less to assure (a) relatively high access to (b) fairly comprehensive coverage while (c) not breaking the bank. For the OECD countries, generally, this constitutes (a) covering about all of the population with (b) major ambulatory, hospital, and prescription drug benefits, while (c) spending about 6 to 9 percent of GDP on health care with (d) rates of growth in expenditure that are fairly flat as percentages of GDP.

Compared to the United States, of course, France has done fairly well in reaching these goals, but it has not done as well as the United Kingdom, Germany, or Japan. Moreover, doing as well as France has involved a constant and intense struggle for French policymakers who face, on the one hand, fiscal imperatives of growing proportions and, on the other hand, entrenched societal interests that support the most suboptimal parts of the system.

In France, in the absence of a powerful, compelling conjuncture, private practitioners are still paid on a hopelessly suboptimal fee-for-service basis. Worse, there is still no gatekeeping of patients seeking treatment and no overall coordination of treatment patterns for ambulatory medicine. Even in the highly centralized French system, where strategically placed bureaucrats execute their health care mission with great determination and zeal, the hand of history is noticeable and makes a difference. Yet the financial basis of the hospital system was changed in a big way, even if some of the structural peculiarities of the triangular relationship between individual hospitals, local municipalities, and the electoral-bureaucratic pork barrel universe in Paris have hardly changed at all.

The health care policy arena in France exemplifies some important elements of the overall argument developed in this book: the state is powerful but paradoxically ineffective. It is ineffective because, in spite of its political powers, the state is tied to path dependency, especially when powerful social interests are involved. Equally paradoxical, organized medicine is politically weak when it comes to improving its own economic lot, while it is at the same time structurally powerful in defending the status quo of clinical autonomy and its traditional fee-for-service remuneration system.

What conjuncture might come together to permit non-incremental change in the ambulatory sector and among hospital structural relationships? Clearly, in the face of widespread support for the current system among both patients and doctors, the French government will have to invest a great amount of political capital in order to achieve health care reform. As the long Mitterrand reign drew to a close in 1994 and 1995, and as a sharp battle developed on the Right between Chirac and Balladur during the presidential campaign of 1995, conditions were clearly not propitious for politically costly health care reform.

In the event, Jacques Chirac prevailed to win the French presidency. Would conjunctural conditions now prove sufficiently different to provide Chirac with fresh, strong leverage for a fundamental overhaul of the system? That, of course, is the question.

In a policy domain as volatile as welfare reform, any political analysis is forced to follow a target that moves quickly. Upon assuming office in May 1995, Chirac appointed Alain Juppé, (a long-time confidant and "politico-technocrat") as prime minister.

In the fall of 1995, Juppé unveiled a proposal for vast reform of the social welfare system. In addition to targeting health care reform he also proposed to reign in the generous retirement benefits of public-sector workers. This latter proposal ignited a dramatic three week period of nationwide strikes in December 1995, which were especially concentrated in the transport sector and that paralyzed Paris and other major regional centers.

The Juppé government backed down on pension reform, but held firm to the health care proposals. They were passed into law in April 1996. They called for the total social security budget to be fixed annually in advance by parliamentary vote, removing this prerogative from the sickness funds. In the ambulatory sectors, patients who accept new gatekeeping powers of their general practitioner will be reimbursed at higher levels than those who go directly to specialists or who frequently change general practitioners. And for private practitioners, financial penalties will be imposed if overall spending targets are exceeded in a given year. Finally, hospitals will have to undergo stricter accreditation procedures designed to reinforce quality and, especially, to eliminate waste.

Three of the main doctors' unions—the CSMF, FMF, and SML— opposed the government's reforms and organized a number of public demonstrations, including a "strike," in April 1996. Their efforts were to little avail, however, for the major union representing general practitioners (MG France) pointedly supported the government. Furthermore, French public opinion showed little support for the medical unions opposing the reforms in part because the transport strike of December had vented much of the available anti-government steam, and in part because the French have never widely supported doctors' protest movements.

Why so little support for doctors? On the one hand, the medical corps is still widely regarded as a privileged, white-collar class. On the other hand, doctors themselves have never presented a united front that could have provided leverage for stirring up public opinion. Finally, media attention in France concentrated conspicuously on the pension issue and glossed over the health care issue.

Will Juppé's reforms succeed where others before him have failed? Tellingly, his attempt for structural reforms are greater than any ever before. The key unknown element may be the French patient's reaction when the reforms are actually implemented, since the traditional freedom of the patient to choose his or her doctor is, under the reform measures, restricted for the first time. If French patients accept this change, the doctors will have no choice but to accept it too. If patients rebel, doctors will have a valuable ally in compromising the reforms during the implementation process. This part of the conjuncture is still unknown, so the prognosis for dramatic change in French health care policy is not yet certain.

And during all of this, the target keeps moving.

Notes to Chapter 9

1. See Victor G. Rodwin, "Management without Objectives: The French Health Policy Gamble," in Gordon McLachlan and Alan Maynard, eds., *The Public/Private Mix for Health* (London: The Nuffield Provincial Hospitals Trust, 1982).
2. Centre de Recherche et de Documentation en Economie de Santé (CREDES), *Eco-Santé France* (Paris: CREDES, 1993); Organization for Economic Cooperation and Development (OECD), *OECD Health Data* (Paris: OECD, 1993).
3. OECD.
4. See David Wilsford, "Tactical Advantages versus Administrative Heterogeneity: The Strengths and the Limits of the French State," *Comparative Political Studies* 21, no. 1 (April 1988): 126-68.
5. Michael M. Atkinson and William D. Coleman, "Strong States and Weak States: Sectoral Policy Networks in Advanced Capitalist Economies," *British Journal of Political Science* 19 (1989): 47-67.
6. Marc Duriez and Simone Sandier, *The French Health Care System: Organization and Functioning*, (trans. David Wilsford) (Paris: Ministry of Health, 1994).
7. Atkinson and Coleman, 59.
8. Douglas Ashford, "The British and French Social Security Systems: Welfare State by Intent and by Default," in Douglas Ashford and E. W. Kelley, eds., *Nationalizing Social Security* (Greenwich, Conn.: Jai Press, 1985).

9. David Wilsford, "The State and the Medical Profession in France," in Frederic W. Hafferty and John B. McKinlay, eds., *The Changing Character of the Medical Profession: An International Perspective* (New York: Oxford University Press, 1993), 124-37.

10. Atkinson and Coleman.

11. These figures are net gross incomes after expenses but before taxes expressed in OECD purchasing price parity dollar units. These units wash out both differences in purchasing power and exchange rate fluctuations.

12. See David Wilsford, *Doctors and the State: The Politics of Health Care in France and the United States* (Durham N.C.: Duke University Press, 1991).

13. OECD, *OECD Health Data*.

14. David Wilsford, "Path Dependency, or Why History Makes It Difficult but Not Impossible to Reform Health Care Systems in a Big Way," *Journal of Public Policy* 14, no. 3 (1995): 251-83.

15. Paul A. David, "A Paradigm for Historical Economics: Path Dependence and Predictability in Dynamic Systems with Local Network Externalities," (Center for Economic Policy Research, Stanford University, 1989).

16. David Wilsford, "The *Conjoncture* of Ideas and Interests," *Comparative Political Studies* 18, no. 3 (1985): 357-72.

17. Wilsford, *Doctors and the State*.

18. Copayments are a questionable strategy, at best, for restraining overall expenditures. Evidence is mixed on whether copayments work to restrain consumption on the part of those who must pay them. Especially in systems such as the French, where many supplementary insurance regimes are in place to cover the difference between that which is paid out-of-pocket and that which is reimbursed by the sickness fund, copayments do not constitute any special disincentive to consumption. At best, in such systems, copayments merely constitute a one-time shift in spending from the public accounts to private individuals.

19. Wilsford, "The Medical Profession in France."

20. Wilsford, "Path Dependency."

21. CREDES.

22. Duriez and Sandier.

Chapter 10

Sexual Harassment, Gender Politics, and Symbolic Reform

Amy G. Mazur

1992 was a pivotal year for the development of sexual harassment policy in France. In July, new legislation reforming the penal code included a section on *harcèlement sexuel* (sexual harassment).[1] In April, the Council of Ministers approved a bill presented by the *Secrétaire d'Etat aux Droits des Femmes et à la Consommation* (deputy minister of Women's Rights and Consumption) on sexual harassment in the work place. Parliament adopted the bill on November 2, 1992. The specific legislation did not come into effect until February, 1993[2] and the implementation of the article in the penal code reform was delayed.[3] These new laws introduce for the first time a legal definition of sexual harassment which covers direct harassment of employees by superiors, but does not cover indirect harassment caused by a hostile environment.

The new legislation establishes sanctions for offenders (up to 100,000 francs and one year in prison) in the public and private sectors, allow organizations registered with the government to plead harassment cases, and stipulate that court proceedings may take place in closed sessions if requested. Witnesses within the firm are also protected from retaliatory action by the employer under the new law. Without specifying how businesses should develop prevention programs, the specific legislation (#92-1179) recommends that firm-level safety committees propose such programs. Neither law places responsibility for harassment on management. As many French observers argue, these laws present a very limited approach to sexual harassment in the firm.[4]

In comparison to sexual harassment policy in other post-industrial democracies, French policy differs in content, timing, and approach. Policy in the United States, the United Kingdom, Ireland, Canada, and at the European Union level, for example, has defined sexual harassment in terms of indirect as well as direct sexual harassment.[5] In France, sexual harassment in the workplace was not defined as a public problem until the mid 1980s, nearly ten years later than in many other post-industrial democracies. French policy also takes a different approach to sexual harassment since the state has addressed these issues through legislation rather than through executive orders or case law.

This chapter will argue that these divergences are a product of the combined effect of three aspects of French politics and society: statist policy formation, legal culture, and attitudes about sexual relations between colleagues. First, although not operative in all policy sectors, French statist policy formation has been characterized by the interplay between a strong (though structurally fragmented) state and weak, ideologically divided groups in society with little influence over government policy. As a result, state actors tend to dominate policy formulation and implementation, favoring input from the interests they perceive to be most legitimate.[6]

This statist dynamic has structured the formation of women's policies in France for some time.[7] Presidents, since 1974, and Prime Ministers, since 1986, have formally charged cabinet level offices with the advancement of women's rights and status. Using the placement of women's rights issues on the chief executive agenda as a power base, these ministerial offices have sought tight control over the elaboration of most feminist-oriented policies,[8] while a fragmented and protest-oriented feminist movement has stayed away from lobbying for women's rights reform. In general, few organized interests have influenced women's policy formation. The statist nature of women's rights policymaking has contributed to the late recognition of sexual harassment as a public problem and the recalcitrance of Socialist and right-wing governments to take concrete steps against sexual harassment in the workplace, particularly because, within this statist logic, the priority given to a particular policy item by the president and/or prime minister determines how it will be treated by policy actors. In general, chief executive decision-makers have given women's rights policies a very low priority on the greater policy agenda. As a result, these policies tend to consist of weak efforts with little real enforcement power.

The second aspect that has influenced the formation of sexual harassment policy involves the legal system. The Romano-Germanic legal system in France excludes the threat of expensive lawsuits (individual and class action) from the calculations employers make about dealing with real discrimination against women in the firm.[9] Unlike the United States, Great Britain, and Canada, employment discrimination law in France has not been a focal point for intense and effective litigation by interest groups, trade unions, or government agencies. The dearth of case law in this area was instrumental in developing support for specific legislation to formally define sexual harassment. French legal culture reinforces statist policy formation by diluting the ability of activists to become important players in the enforcement of new sexual harassment law.

A third influence is that a certain level of acceptance of consensual sexual relations between colleagues makes it difficult to draw a clear line between sexual relations that are generally perceived to be normal and sexual harassment. For example, a 1992 cover story in the weekly magazine, *Le Nouvel Observateur,* entitled "L'amour au bureau" ("Love at the Office") suggests that the French accept that employees in the same firm date, sleep together, and get married.[10] As a consequence, many policy actors, including judges, upper-level civil servants in the women's ministries, and members of Parliament see the regulation of sexual harassment, especially hostile environment harassment, as a potential infringement on individual liberty. In other countries like the UK, Canada, and the United States, where puritan values tend to discourage consensual sexual relations between colleagues, the regulation of indirect as well as direct sexual harassment is more acceptable. This chapter will show how these three factors influenced the different content, timing, and approach of French policy by tracing the 1992 legislation through the following stages of the policy formation process: problem definition, agenda-setting, formulation, and implementation.

Defining Sexual Harassment as a Public Problem

Unlike in the United States, where sexual harassment was identified as a problem in the mid-1970s by feminist consciousness-raising groups,[11] feminists in France during this period did not identify sexual harassment in the work place as a result of women's inferior status in society. In fact, it was not until the new feminist movement of the 1970s was in decline that feminist activists turned to the issue of sexual harassment in the work place.[12]

Compared to second-wave feminist movements in other countries,[13] the French feminist movement of the 1970s, the *Mouvement de libération des femmes* (MLF), was more anti-system and, with the exception of abortion reform, more removed from policy reform efforts.[14] Even though the MLF and the abortion rights group, *Choisir,* thrust the legalization of abortion onto the public agenda through collective action and high-profile court cases, the right-wing Parliament would not have adopted the controversial legislation without President Valéry Giscard d'Estaing's support. This dynamic reflects the statist pattern of weak interest group involvement and a high degree of chief executive control over policy formation. Moreover, the 1979 legislation was very restrictive, and, as a result, it was only adopted for an initial five-year experimental period.[15]

Two new feminist pressure groups were created outside of the MLF in the 1970s: *Choisir,* a single-issue group involved with the campaign to legalize abortion, and the *Ligue du Droit des Femmes* (LDF). Reflecting the general orientation of second-wave feminism in France, neither group concentrated its activities in the 1970s on issues—like sexual harassment—that were related to gender-based inequities in the workplace. The LDF was founded in 1972 by women in the MLF who did not like the insular nature and the anti-reform position of the movement. In 1979, a highly publicized legal battle over control of the MLF label demonstrated the deep divisions within the movement. After the breakup of the MLF in 1979, the LDF remained active well into the 1980s.

Since its creation, the LDF has pushed for anti-sexist legislation. In 1982, the LDF was instrumental in convincing the minister of the rights of woman *(Ministre des Droits de la Femme),* Yvette Roudy, to place an anti-sexist bill at the top of her legislative agenda. Broad-based opposition to the bill, however, led the Socialist government to drop the proposal from its legislative agenda that same year.[16] Following this failure, the LDF increasingly turned its attention to sexual violence against women in the home and in the workplace.

By 1985, Yvette Roudy had exhausted her list of reforms and was looking for new feminist policy issues. The successful adoption of a toned-down version of the anti-sexist law in 1985, which allowed associations registered with the government for five years or more to plead discrimination cases, gave feminist interest groups a new organizational impetus to get involved with gender-based discrimination cases such as sexual harassment. Thus, it was during 1985 that sexual harassment became a central issue for feminist action in both the state and society.

In the early 1980s, as many activists argued, *harcèlement sexuel* was still considered a private issue attached to personal sexual preferences and hence not an object of public scrutiny or policy.[17] In 1979, for instance, a government report on women's inferior status in the work force did not include sexual harassment in the workplace as a cause of gender-based inequities in employment. In 1985, Socialist Party (PS) campaign organizer, Jacques Seguéla, was quoted as saying,

> Of course, I have had occasion to hump cute chicks on my office carpet. Sexual harassment is the demeanor of all Latin men towards women. In my country, we call that courtship. It is French men's needs to seduce at work as well as in the subway. But be careful, in the final analysis, it is the woman who decides.[18]

The LDF and the *Association européene contre les violences faites au femmes au travail* (European Association Against Violence Against Women at Work—AVFT) lead the campaign to publicize the problem of sexual harassment. Founded in 1985 by a group of reform-oriented feminists, including a CNRS researcher and a member of European Parliament, the AVFT's goal was to create an atmosphere in firms in which victims of sexual harassment could come forward and in which their complaints would be taken seriously by union delegates, employers, and labor inspectors.[19] As an officially registered group, in addition to funding from the MDF, the organization received subsidies from the European Community (EC). After 1990, the AVFT helped victims of harassment take their cases to court. With its team of jurists and researchers, the AVFT was the first association in France to systematically examine how current labor and penal law could be used in cases of sexual harassment.[20]

In 1985, the LDF organized the first National Colloquium on Sexual Harassment.[21] The organizers invited feminists, victims of harassment, employers, and representatives of political parties, trade unions, and employer associations to discuss the problem of sexual harassment. With funding from the *Ministère des Droits de la Femme*, the LDF was able to publicize the conference. This was the first time the French media systematically treated the issue of sexual harassment. That same year, the LDF cosponsored with BIBA (a women's magazine for young professionals) a survey of 960 women on sexual harassment. The survey found that 36 percent of the respondents had been victims of unwanted sexual advances in the workplace.[22]

While the conference drew unprecedented attention to sexual harassment in the workplace, organizers were disappointed with the level of conference participation from trade unions (with the exception of the *Confédération Française Démocratique du Travail*—CFDT), political parties, employer associations, public and private sector management, and the Ministry of Labor. Many of whom refused invitations to attend. The week after the Colloquium, the *Confédération Générale du Travail* (CGT), which had refused to attend, held a confederal conference on women in the work force. The issue of sexual harassment was briefly mentioned at a meeting in one session, but no concrete measures to help victims of sexual harassment were put forward.[23]

The CFDT has been more involved than the CGT in addressing sexual harassment in the workplace and calling for government policy. The CFDT union participated in the 1985 colloquium, taking an active role in the discussion of sexual harassment. Union representatives argued that sexual harassment contributed to women's overall inferior position in the labor force, while a union lawyer made significant contributions to the discussion of problems experienced by women victims at the firm-level.[24]

Even though key policy actors in state and society continued to ignore calls for solutions to the problem, the 1985 conference defined sexual harassment in the workplace for the first time in a public forum as an unacceptable society-wide problem. Participants maintained that apathy towards sexual harassment at work contributed to women's increasingly precarious position in well-paid full-time jobs and that women's inferior position in the labor market made them more likely to be targets of sexual blackmail by their male superiors. They also emphasized that sexual harassment was linked to all violence against women in French society. Participants asserted that, when left unpunished, sexual harassment decreased productivity and increased costs to the firm.

The colloquium produced a list of solutions which included the need to better differentiate between sexual relations in the office and sexual harassment. Once this difference was established, it was argued, employees in the firm would be less willing to accept sexual harassment. Trade unions were encouraged to sensitize representatives in the firm to sexual harassment, and employers were reminded that it was their responsibility to promote an environment in which such behavior would not be tolerated. Calls were made for the creation of a coalition to further promote anti-sexual harassment efforts. Women were encouraged to seek help from associations like the AVFT and the LDF as well as the territorial delegates of the women's rights ministry.[25] With the new 1985 law, women's groups were urged to take an active role in applying anti-discrimination law to cases of sexual harassment.[26]

Conference participants emphasized that current law was unsatisfactory for effectively trying sexual harassment cases. Lawyers involved with these cases argued that it was impossible to have favorable decisions without a specific legal definition of sexual harassment. Although several cases had been won on the basis of unfair firing practices, many more cases were lost. Reflecting the general attitude of the French about sexual relations in the workplace, jurists also maintained that judges were reluctant to rule in favor of victims because many judges felt that sexual harassment was related to actions of a highly personal nature and hence not within the court's jurisdiction. For example, one victim of sexual harassment had taken her employer to court. Although the plaintiff had a signed medical certificate attesting to harassment, the judges ruled that the employer's actions were within the bounds of normal conduct, stating, "... the action [the harassment] did not go beyond what a certain familiarity, born from a daily work place relationship, could allow."[27] The relative freedom given to judges to apply the anti-discrimination laws by the Romano-Germanic legal system was instrumental in the outcome of this case.

Those who advocated for sexual harassment legislation at the 1985 conference asserted that not only did the legal vacuum make it difficult to get favorable rulings, but it also created an atmosphere that discouraged victims from coming forward. Moreover, they maintained that the lack of a clear legal definition of sexual harassment indicated to employers and potential harassers that sexual harassment would not be taken seriously. It was this practical need for an official policy statement from the government which underscored the strong call for specific legislation at the end of the 1985 conference.

Thus, the dynamics of problem definition were driven by the combined effects of the statist dynamics of women's rights policy formation, the Romano-Germanic legal culture, and social attitudes about sex between work colleagues. While the fragmented nature of the feminist movement meant that sexual harassment did not become a public issue until after the movement dissipated, the Ministry of Women's Rights played a pivotal role in that process. Likewise, the late appearance of this issue may also be attributed to the inflexibilities of the Romano-Germanic legal system in the sense that judges refused to allow plaintiffs to use already existing legislation. Underpinning the judicial resistance to punishing sexual harassment and the manner in which this issue became salient, were the broader social mores that condoned amorous relations between men and women working in the same establishment and, hence, made defining unacceptable sexual advances at work a highly thorny enterprise.

Placing Sexual Harassment Legislation on the Decision Agenda

Despite the public attention drawn to the issue and Yvette Roudy's promise at the 1985 colloquium to immediately draft a bill proposal on sexual harassment, it took another seven years before the Council of Ministers, under Socialist Prime Minister Pierre Bérégovoy, approved draft legislation on April 29, 1992.[28] Thus, while sexual harassment legislation had been placed on the "government agenda" (the list of policy items up for serious government discussion) in 1985, it was not placed on the "decision agenda" (the actual list of policy items that the government plans to act on)[29] until 1991 when the *Secrétaire d'Etat aux Droits des Femmes et à la Consommation,* Véronique Neiertz announced to the *Conseil Supérieur de l'Egalité Professionnelle* (the High Council for Equal Employment) that her ministry would produce a bill.[30] Indeed, political forces did not converge to create a political opportunity—what Kingdom (1984) refers to as an open policy window—for sexual harassment legislation until 1991. What explains this six-year delay in decision agenda status for a new policy that seemed to have an unprecedented amount of public support? The answer lies, once again, in the combined impact of statism, legal culture, and social attitudes.

With the defeat of the Socialists in the 1986 legislative elections, the new right-wing government under Gaullist prime minister, Jacques Chirac, from 1986 to 1988 neither formulated new women's rights policy nor implemented policy that had been promoted by the Socialist Ministry of Women's Rights. Jacques Chirac demoted the *Ministère des Droits de la Femme* (MDF) to a *Délégation à la Condition Féminine* (a delegation of women's status) attached to the Ministry of Labor with no position in the cabinet. It was within this new political context that sexual harassment was removed from the government agenda.

After the reelection of François Mitterrand and the return of a Socialist government under Michel Rocard in 1988, women's policy in general was still given a much lower position on the government's agenda than during President François Mitterrand's first term from 1981 to 1988. Although the DCF was restored to a *Secrétariat d'Etat aux Droits des Femmes* (Deputy Ministry of Women's Rights), it was a deputy ministry and therefore not given full ministerial status. Rocard's decision to appoint Michèle André to the Minister's position, rather than Yvette Roudy, further accentuated the lower priority given to women's policy issues during the Rocard administration. Unlike Roudy, André had little experience in promoting women's rights policy. Many observers in the women's ministry, the PS, feminist groups, and trade unions agreed that André had been appointed more for her loyalty to Rocard in the PS than for her interest in improving women's societal status.

In 1989, in the context of the government's refusal to take any decisive action on sexual harassment, the AVFT organized a second colloquium, *Violences, Harcèlement Sexuel et Abus du Pouvoir au Travail*.[31] With funding from the European Commission, the conference was oriented towards an international as well as a French audience. The AVFT invited policy experts from all 12 member countries, Canada, Quebec, and the United States. Despite this international exposure, the conference received less attention in the French media and less support from the government than had the 1985 colloquium. Unlike the active participation and support of Minister Roudy in the first conference, *Secrétaire d'Etat* André took little initiative in the second conference.

In a 1989 interview with a national weekly magazine, André expressed doubts about the effectiveness of any specific legislation on sexual harassment. In the interview, she insisted that her staff did not have any clear ideas on how to deal with a problem that needed to be approached in "a prudent and wise manner."[32] Immediately following the 1989 conference, André formally assembled a working group on sexual harassment under the aegis of the *Conseil Supérieur de l'Egalité Professionelle* (CSEP).[33] However, the group did not meet until March 1990, it met three more times before André was replaced by Neiertz in 1991.[34] Staff of the CSEP stated that, in 1990, they had elaborated draft legislation on sexual harassment;[35] however, André refused to present these proposals.

Rocard's decision to appoint the inexperienced André to the women's rights post meant that her inaction on this issue could effectively block the formulation of a new policy in this area until 1991. Because of the statist way that feminist issues had been bureaucratized into a single ministerial structure, the women's ministries had acted as a pressure group within the French state for women's rights policy issues. As a consequence, the government was reluctant to take action on feminist issues without cues from the Ministry of Women's Rights. Furthermore, apart from the less powerful feminist groups such as the AVFT and the LDF, few mainstream interest groups articulated demands for government action on sexual harassment. While the CFDT continued in the late 1980s to support harassment victims and sensitize union members to sexual harassment, the CGT was still ambivalent about taking a strong position on the subject. For instance, the confederation did not send a representative to the 1989 colloquium.

The appointment of Edith Cresson to head the Socialist government in May 1991 opened a policy window for sexual harassment legislation in France. Although not a feminist activist, Cresson had tacitly supported efforts of women's rights activists within the PS to place feminist issues on the party agenda. As minister of european affairs, Cresson had been an advocate of French compliance with European policy directives and the new European social policy, which included actions against sexual harassment policy. Cresson's nomination of a new *Secrétaire d'Etat aux Droits des Femmes et à la Consommation* (SEDF) represented this more favorable stance on feminist issues.

The new SEDF, Véronique Neiertz, according to members of the team responsible for drafting the 1992 legislation, was more interested in sponsoring sexual harassment legislation than had been her predecessor. In an interview in July 1993, Neiertz stated that she had immediately discovered that trade union representatives and employers identified the need for law in this area, albeit a highly limited legal framework. She saw her role as that of a policy entrepreneur who negotiated a compromise between opponents to legislation and what she labeled the "extremist" position of feminist groups who wanted an authoritative law that covered direct and hostile environment harassment with stiff penalties.

In 1991, she formally funded a Louis-Harris poll on the incidence of sexual harassment.[36] This poll was an important tool for the SEDF to develop support for the 1992 bill. One of the survey's major findings was that 21 percent of men and women interviewed claimed to have either been sexually harassed in the work place or to have witnessed such harassment.[37] Also, in November 1991, a 1990 European Community Council resolution on "the protection of women's and men's dignity," was given further authority by a Commission recommendation with an attached code of practice for reducing the incidence of sexual harassment at work.[38] In the context of the Maastricht Summit on European integration in December 1991, the French government was interested in demonstrating its support for European Community policy and, therefore, in promoting legislation that would have brought French policy more favorably in line with EC standards. The femocrats, feminist-oriented bureaucrats, in the SEDF also invited Michael Rubinstein, an EC expert on the new sexual harassment policy, to speak to the CSEP working group in May 1991.

In the summer of 1991, the Socialist parliamentary group in the National Assembly, led by Yvette Roudy, proposed an amendment to ongoing penal code reform being debated in the National Assembly.[39] The "Roudy" Amendment became part of the new penal code reform that was adopted that year and implemented in 1994. This amendment introduced the legal definition of sexual harassment into the penal code. A partial product of wider EC pressures, this bill put more weight on Neiertz to produce her own bill. Neiertz herself stated that PS sponsorship of the amendment indicated that the Council of Ministers would not oppose draft legislation on sexual harassment.

In 1992, the Socialist government agreed to sponsor sexual harassment legislation elaborated by Veronique Neiertz's office. Supported by the relatively marginalized deputy secretary, neither the president, prime minister, nor PS leadership made a public statement on the bill. As the final content of the law demonstrates, the low priority given to the 1992 bill proposal contributed to generating a law that did little to concretely address sexual harassment in the workplace. Statist patterns of policymaking were crucial in this stage, because, while on the one hand the presentation of sexual harassment legislation was purely a function of the state feminist minister's decisions and not any interest group input, on the other hand, the low priority of that bill was determined by the apathy of decision-makers in more powerful positions than Deputy Secretary Neiertz. Indeed, without any broad-based support outside of the Ministry of Women's Rights, the content and implementation of the bill would also be a product of the top-down intra-governmental politics that had determined most women's rights policy under the Fifth Republic.

Formulating the 1992 Sexual Harassment Bill in Parliament

In the context of the low placement of the sexual harassment legislation on the PS government agenda, the demands for stronger legislation, articulated by feminist groups, were closed out of the formulation process. The lack of political influence of the LDF and the AVFT made it nearly impossible for advocates of an authoritative policy to convince mainstream policymakers in the SEDF, the PS government, and the parliament to accept feminist recommendations for the new policy. Furthermore, without any widespread public support for strong sexual harassment reform non-feminist interest groups, political parties, and state actors were not compelled to take action. Consequently, as Véronique Neiertz, and members of parliament openly admitted, the new legislation was a modest attempt to deal with sexual harassment.

Throughout the formulation process, it was clear that state actors sought to produce symbolic policy statements rather than authoritative policy designed to effectively reduce the incidence of sexual harassment in the firm. For instance, throughout the debates of the bill, members of parliament questioned the relevance of the legislation in the context of what they saw as more pressing problems and a lack of public interest. In her opening remarks in the senate debate on the sexual harassment bill, *Secrétaire d'Etat* Neiertz expressed the commonly held hostility towards what many referred to as Anglo-Saxon puritanism in the American-derived two-pronged approach to direct and indirect sexual harassment.

> At the same time this bill proposal attempts to simultaneously respond to the preoccupations of social partners and to the European imperatives, we seek to avoid falling into the situation of American repression which, in my opinion neither corresponds to our culture, nor to the realities of our country.[40]

Similar concerns were expressed by a senator during the parliamentary debates.

> In the USA, for example, the situation is excessive. In effect, the slightest look or smallest normal invitation to have a friendly work discussion—we have seen the Thomas Affair—can be sanctioned.[41]

The Clarence Thomas hearings had thrust sexual harassment into the French public's purview in a very critical light. As one member of the AVFT asserted, linking French sexual harassment legislation to United States policy may have worked against public support for the legislation given French fears of a United States-based policy being far too restrictive. Eric Fassin's analysis of French attitudes towards the Thomas hearings shows that the French were astonished at how far American policy went in regulating sexual harassment at work.[42]

Most policymakers, therefore, perceived the regulation of sexual harassment as a potential threat to personal freedoms. Hence, they refused to support the inclusion of hostile environment harassment in the bill. When asked by senators about the impending reform, employers also voiced their opposition to the broader definition of sexual harassment, arguing that such intervention in the workplace would be an impediment to effective management of a firm.[43] Even though Neiertz had originally supported the inclusion of colleague harassment,[44] the general opposition to a restrictive sexual harassment regulation forced the SEDF team to drop it from the final bill proposal.

In addition to defining sexual harassment in terms of direct and indirect harassment, advocates of authoritative sexual harassment policy had sought to compel employers to take responsibility for sexual harassment, arguing that employers should confront the issue because of the potential cost reduced productivity could bring to a firm. However, since in the French Romano-Germanic legal system law suits in general are less frequently filed and, when damages are awarded, they are not as large, French businesses have no real financial incentive to take action against harassment.

Conversely, in common law countries, public policy has placed the burden of responsibility for sexual harassment on management. In the United States, for example, Equal Employment Opportunities Commission (EEOC) regulations and court decisions have presented large corporations with million dollar sexual harassment suits. As a result, many businesses have invested resources into confronting sexual harassment within the firm. A few companies, such as Dupont, have developed in-house prevention programs and 24 hour victim hotlines. Several consulting firms near Washington D.C. were recently created to help smaller firms deal with harassment suits and design prevention programs.[45]

Although French employers admit that sexual harassment does occur, they have generally maintained that the problem of sexual harassment can only be addressed through a long-term evolution in social attitudes and not through employer initiative. French businesses in general have not been attentive to gender-based discrimination in the firm. For instance, the 1983 equal employment law instituted voluntary firm-level programs that could be partially funded by the state. These equality plans were intended to provide a framework in which employers and workplace committees *(comités d'entreprise)* could promote female employees within the firm. Without any effective incentives, however, few firms have taken advantage of these programs.

In this atmosphere, weak feminist demands for employer responsibility in sex equity matters have little political saliency. The absence of any significant pressure for an employer-centered policy clearly underpinned the formulation of the 1992 sexual harassment legislation. Throughout the parliamentary debates, there was little discussion about the responsibility of management to deal with the issues of sexual harassment within the firm. Indeed, the new sexual harassment legislation makes no direct reference to employer responsibility.

Prevention has also been a major demand of sexual harassment advocates. In both the 1985 and 1989 conferences on sexual harassment, advocates had argued that sexual harassment contributed to an unhealthy work environment and, from this perspective, should be dealt with by firm level institutions such as the *comités d'entreprises*, the work inspectorate, or workplace health committees *(Comité d'hygiène de sécurité et des conditions de travail*—CHSCT), especially in light of employer reluctance to adopt prevention programs. The original 1992 bill proposed by the SEDF included an article suggesting that the worker-run CHSCT could develop ". . . information and prevention programs on sexual harassment (Article 5);" this article was eliminated during the senate debates. Members of several CHSCT interviewed by the senate had objected to this unwanted task since they were not sure what would be expected of them. The Communist parliamentary group in the senate had also argued that any additional duties given to the already overloaded CHSCT would be too many. The CHSCT clause, however, was reintroduced during a second reading of the bill in the National Assembly and included in the final legislation.

The legislation on "abuse of authority in sexual matters in work relations" was voted into law on October 24, 1992.[46] Neither this law nor the penal code reform used the term *harcèlement sexuel*. The final vote reflected the broad partisan support for weak sexual harassment policy in both houses. Only the Communists abstained, most likely because the CHSCT clause in Article 5 mentioned above was included in the final version. Although France was the first member of the European Community to adopt specific legislation on sexual harassment,[47] the highly restricted scope of the law will limit the new policy's effect on the incidence of sexual harassment in the workplace. Moreover, specific legislation does not necessarily mean an active and effective policy, particularly given the poor implementation of the new law.

As with the preformulation stages, the formulation of the 1992 law was guided by the statist dynamic of policymaking, with low interest group influence and state feminist offices supporting a policy that responded to the wishes of the governing majority more than feminist groups in society. Even more so than the agenda-setting stage, the parliamentary debates of the law reflected the extent to which fears of infringing on what were perceived by many as normal relations at work limited the scope of the legislation. The absence of a legal culture giving employers and victims incentives—such as large settlements—to take cases through the legal system allowed recalcitrant parliamentarians to support a law that provided no authoritative means for preventing sexual harassment in the firm or pursuing cases of sexual harassment.

Implementing Sexual Harassment Policy

As of the summer of 1995, it is still impossible to systematically evaluate the implementation of these new laws. As in the case of past equal employment policy for women, the absence of mainstream concern for effective policy will mean that few actors will be interested in the implementation and enforcement of the new legal provisions. If future sexual harassment cases are similar to past cases of gender-based discrimination in employment, they will be rare, difficult to win, and receive little public attention. According to a French government report to the European Union, there have been only ten cases of sexual harassment taken to court from 1972 to 1989 on the basis of already existing equality law. Nine out of the ten cases were decided in favor of the victim, with only one judgment defining the "motives for dismissal" as "real and serious." Nevertheless, even when decisions are in favor of the plaintiff, the report states that "very few people are granted damages for sexual harassment."[48]

It will be important to monitor the number of sexual harassment cases in the future to determine whether the laws have any concrete impact. Also, it would be interesting to examine whether the new penalties for sexual harassment deter potential harassers. Collecting this data may prove to be difficult, however, because there is no specific administrative agency, like the EEOC in the United States, that systematically oversees employment discrimination cases.

The right-wing government in office since the 1993 elections has given little support to the implementation of the new policy. The connection between the Socialist Party and the ministerial level office was demonstrated when the SEDF lost its position following the landslide victory of the Right in the 1993 legislative elections. Between April 1993 and June 1995, under Gaullist Prime Minister Eduard Balladur and President François Mitterrand, the administrative services were left in place without a separate ministry. The national women's rights administration (the *Service des Droits des Femmes*—SDF), was formally attached to the Ministry of Social Affairs through an upper level civil servant in the minister's cabinet. The SDF was one level below a delegation, consisting of one department among 19 attached to a ministry that is simultaneously in charge of social affairs, health, and urban issues.

While the minister, Simone Veil, was known to be a supporter of women's rights, these issues constituted a minute part of her agenda. Nonetheless, Veil reactivated the High Commission for Equal Employment in the spring of 1994 after the commission had been virtually ignored by Neiertz and mobilized the SDF to begin preparing a report for the United Nation's Conference on Women in Beijing in 1995. In the summer of 1994, many observers asserted that the right-wing government attention to women's rights issues stemmed primarily from a desire to prove to the international community that France was taking the upcoming UN conference on women seriously. For most advocates of feminist policy—such as that addressing sexual harassment—the precarious position of the state feminist structures will mean, even more than in the past, limited agency in implementing policies.

Nonetheless, femocrats in the *Services* attempted to sensitize the public and key policy actors to the new laws. For instance, a new brochure on sexual harassment was distributed in 1993, while in June of the same year, the SDF sponsored an implementation workshop on the new laws in Paris.[49] The day-long session brought together women's rights administrators from the regions and the departments, labor inspectors, members of the AVFT, and trade union representatives from the CFDT to educate sectoral actors about the new laws. Run by ministry femocrats, the workshop emphasized the symbolic nature of the new laws, while simultaneously stressing the importance of the new legal definition of sexual harassment as a tool to encourage prevention programs in firms.

Much of the workshop covered the process by which firms—with the help of trade union delegates, women's rights and labor administrators— could develop prevention programs, rather than how victims of sexual harassment could seek potential redress under the new laws. As one femocrat announced during the workshop, "we do not want to stress sanctions but prevention."[50] Also, it was made clear that the government officials in the women's rights administration would increasingly look to the already overloaded and underfunded AVFT for advice and initiatives in implementing the new policy at the local level. Despite these efforts, the French policy on sexual harassment was very limited, essentially because no one saw the enforcement of these new laws as an effective deterrent. The dynamics of the Romano-Germanic law system minimize the punitive damages and overall deterrent potential of the new laws on future sexual harassment cases.

In fact, enforcement through the courts has proven to be complicated. In 1993, employers were pursuing a new strategy of taking women who had accused management of sexual harassment and the AVFT for helping these women to court for libel. In both of the cases I followed, neither of the victims had actually taken their employers to court, only formal letters had been sent asking that employers do something about the intolerable situation for the alleged victims of the sexual harassment. During the courtroom proceedings of these two cases, judges and prosecutors appeared unfamiliar with the notion and repercussions of sexual harassment, tending to talk about the libelous actions of the alleged victims in more serious terms than the sexual harassment.

Since the election of Gaullist, Jacques Chirac to the presidency, the *Services* remain attached to the ministry responsible for family and social affairs, under Minister Colette Codacionni. Given the record of Codacionni in this area as the regional delegate of women's status in the department of the Nord under *Cohabitation I*, it is highly unlikely that she will actively pursue implementation of the new laws.

Conclusion

The limited nature of French sexual harassment policy can only be understood in the context of the interplay between the mode of state-society relations, legal culture, and societal attitudes about sexual relations. As this chapter has suggested, the unique combination of these three factors found in the French case—a statist pattern of policy formation, a Romano-Germanic legal culture and a general acceptance of sexual relations between colleagues—provides a plausible explanation for the apparent exceptionalism of French policy.

At the same time, the French experience might not actually be so exceptional when compared with post-industrial democracies, like Spain or Italy, with similar state-society relations, legal cultures, and social attitudes. Still, the hypothesis about environmental effects and policy outcomes posited by this chapter indicates that countries with a common-law legal culture, a policy process dominated by powerful interest groups, and dominant attitudes which are less accepting of sexual relations at work might formulate policy that is less symbolic. Therefore, before any conclusions can be reached about the impact of these three environmental variables and the exceptional nature of sexual harassment policy formation in the French case, a more systematic comparative study of government responses to sexual harassment at work needs to be undertaken.*

---

*I would like to thank Indiana University-Purdue University at Indianapolis, the Center for West European Studies at Indiana University, Bloomington and the American Political Science Association for grants which allowed me to make two research visits to Paris in the summers of 1993 and 1994 to conduct the research for this chapter. Also, Laura Levine Frader, as editor of *French Politics and Society*, gave me useful comments to strengthen the argument of an earlier version of this chapter published in that journal.

Notes to Chapter 10

1. Parti Socialiste deputy, Yvette Roudy, introduced these provisions into penal code reform in June 1991. The new penal code reform (no. 92-684) was adopted by Parliament on July 22, 1992 *(Le Monde,* 24 October 1992). For more on the penal code reform see Sylvie Cromer, "Histoire d'une loi: La Pénalisation du harcèlement sexuel dans le nouveau code pénal," *Projet Féministes* 1 (March 1992): 108-17.

2. *Circulaire d'application du 11 février 1993* cited in *Journée Harcèlement Sexuel* Service des Droits des Femmes (June 22, 1993): 9.

3. Although government officials had predicted that the penal code reform would be in effect by 1993, the implementation of the reforms was officially delayed until March 1994.

4. This evaluation was partially drawn from open-ended interviews conducted in 1988-89 and the summers of 1993 and 1994 with policy actors involved in the formation of sexual harassment policy including representatives of femi-

nist organizations, policymakers in the women's ministry, labor ministry, women's ministers, trade union representatives, policy experts, political party activists, and work inspectors. A list of these interviews is available on request.

5. For sexual harassment policy in the United States and Sweden, see R. Amy Elman, "Feminism, Public Discourse and Social Policy: Sexual Harassment in Sweden and the United States" (paper presented at the International Conference of the Council for European Studies, Chicago, March 1992). For European Community policy in this area see Victoria A. Carter, "Working on Dignity: EC Initiatives on Sexual Harassment in the Workplace," *Northwestern Journal of International Law and Business* 12, no. 431 (1992): 431-60 and chapters 2 and 3 in R. Amy Elman, ed., *Sexual Politics and the European Union: The New Feminist Challenge* (Oxford: Berghahn Books, 1996).

6. For more on statist patterns see, for example, David Wilsford, *Doctors and the State* (Durham, N.C.: Duke University Press, 1991), chapter 2; Ezra Suleiman, *Elites in French Society: The Politics of Survival* (Princeton, N.J.: Princeton University Press); and John Dunn, Jr., "The French Highway Lobby: A Case-Study in State Society Relations and Policymaking," *Comparative Politics* 27, no. 3 (summer 1995): 275-96.

7. For analyses of women's policy formation in France see, for example, Amy Mazur, *Gender Bias and the State: Feminist Policy at Work in France* (Pittsburgh, Penn.: University of Pittsburgh Press, 1995); Jane Jenson, "Changing Discourses, Changing Agendas: Political Rights and Reproductive Policies in France," *The Women's Movements of the United States and Western Europe*, Mary Katzenstein and Carol McClurg Mueller, eds., (Philadelphia: Temple University Press, 1987), p. 64-88; or Dorothy Stetson, *Women's Rights in France* (Westport, Conn.: Greenwood Press, 1987).

8. For more on the evolution of these women's policy machineries see Amy Mazur, "State Feminism in Fifth Republic France: Strong State, Weak Society and Symbolic Reform," In Mazur and Stetson, eds., *Comparative State Feminism* (Newbury Park, Calif.: Sage, 1995), pp. 76-94.

9. For a discussion of the Romano-Germanic family see, Henry W. Ehrmann, *Comparative Legal Cultures* (Englewood Cliffs, N.J.: Prentice-Hall Inc., 1976), pp. 13-15.

10. L'Express, February 7, 1992.

11. Rosemarie Tong, *Women, Sex and the Law* (Totowa, N.J.: Rowman and Littlefield, 1984), p. 66.

12. For background on the evolution of this issue see O. Dhavernas, "L'harcèlement sexuel," *Actes* no. 57/58 (winter 1985); Zelensky and M. Gaussot, *Le harcèlement sexuel scandales et réalités* (Paris: Garancière, 1986); "Interview with Annie Sugier and Ann Zelensky, co-founders of La Ligue du Droit des Femmes," *Actes* no. 57/58 (winter 1985); "Rapport Fait au nom de

la commision des affaires sociales sur le project de loi relatif a l'abus d'torité en matiere sexualle dans les relation de travail et modifiant le code de travail et le code de procedure penale no. 350. 1992." Senate Report no. 350 for the 1992 draft legislation; Janine Mossuz-Lavau, *Les Lois de l'amour Les Politiques de la Sexualités en France (1950-1990)* (Paris: Documents Payot, 1991), pp. 226-230; Dorothy Stetson, *Women's Rights in France* (Westport, Conn: Greenwood Press, 1987), p. 149; and Sylvie Cromer and Marie-Victoire Louis, "Existe-il un harcèlement sexuel à la française?" *French Politics and Society* 10, no. 3 (1992); AVFT, *De l'abus de pouvoir sexuel: Le harcèlement sexuel au travail* (Paris: La Découverte, 1990).

13. See for example, Drude Dahlerup, ed., *The New Women's Movement: Feminism and Political Power in Europe and the USA* (London: Sage Publications, 1986); and Mary Katzenstein and Carol McClurg Mueller, eds., *The Women's Movements of the United States and Western Europe* (Philadelphia: Temple University Press, 1987).

14. For analyses of the French feminist movements see, for example, Claire Duchen, *Feminism in France From May 1968 to Mitterrand* (London: Routledge, Kegan and Paul, 1986) or Jane Jenson, "Ce n'est pas un hasard: the Varieties of French Feminism," Holyworth and Ross, eds., *Contemporary France* (London: Frances Pinter, 1989), pp. 114-143.

15. Janine Mossuz-Lavau, "Abortion Politics in France Under the governments of the Right and the Left (1973-1984)," J. Lovenduski and J. Outshoorn, eds., *The New Politics of Abortion* (London: Sage, 1986), pp. 86-104; and Anne Batiot, "Radical Democracy and Feminist Discourse: The Case of France," D. Dahlerup, ed., *The New Women's Movement* (London: Sage, 1986), pp. 85-102.

16. Stetson, *Women's Rights*, 183-190.

17. Zelensky and Gaussot, 10.

18. Ibid., 138. All translations are by the author.

19. Although the AVFT explicitly seeks to help women, the AVFT has helped male victims of harassment.

20. The AVFT published a quarterly journal from 1986 to 1992 called *Cette Violence dont nous ne voulons plus* ("This Violence which we no longer want") and beginning in 1992 a more academically oriented journal called *Projet Féministe*.

21. For a written report on this meeting see Zelensky and M. Gaussot, *Le harcèlement sexuel scandales et réalités* (Paris: Garancière, 1986).

22. Ibid., 10-11.

23. *CGT Conférence: Des femmes salariées*, (CGT: Nanterre, October 9-10, 1985), p. 46.

24. Zelensky and Gaussot, 15.

25. Since 1978, the women's rights ministry has developed a network of women's rights offices at the regional and departmental levels (Mazur, 1995).

26. The most frequently cited legal provisions were the 1975 equal treatment law, the 1983 *égalité professionnelle* (equal employment) law, certain articles of the *lois Auroux* and the 1985 anti-sexist law. For a complete analysis of applicable law in the civil, penal and work codes by jurist Patrick Nicoleau see Zelensky and Gaussot, 155-160.

27. Ibid., 155.

28. *Le Monde* April 30, 1992.

29. John W. Kingdon, *Agendas, Alternatives and Public Policies* (Boston: Little Brown, 1984).

30. Minutes of the meeting of the Conseil Supérieure de l'Egalité Professionelle (CSEP), July 11, 1991.

31. I attended this two-day conference. For a written report on this conference see AVFT, *De l'Abus de Pouvoir Sexuel: Le Harcèlement Sexuel au Travail* (Paris: Editions La Découverte/Boréal, 1990).

32. *Le Nouvel Observateur*, March 2-8, 1989.

33. This Council had been created by the 1983 equal employment law to oversee the implementation, evaluation, and future redefinition of equal employment policy for women. The law did not give the Council any enforcement powers and, as a consequence, its influence on equal employment policy for women has been minimal.

34. Minutes from the working group meetings, March 16, 1990; April 16, 1991; May 27, 1991 and June 18, 1991.

35. *Projet de Loi Rélatif au Harcèlement Sexuel* (draft legislation), November 19, 1990.

36. Louis Harris, *Le Harcèlement Sexuel: Enquête des Français Perceptions, Opinions et Evaluation du Phénomène*, December 1991.

37. Ibid., 10.

38. Evelyn Collins, "European Union Sexual Harassment Policy," R. Amy Elman, *Sexual Politics and the European Union*, 23-34; and Parlement Européen, *Combattre Le Harcèlement Sexuel sur les Lieux du Travail: L'action Menée dans les Etats Membre de la Communauté Européene* Document de Travail (working document), pp. 8-14.

39. Cromer, 1992.

40. *Débats Parlementaires*, Sénat, Journal Officiel (May 21, 1992): 1326.

41. Ibid., 1328.

42. Eric Fassin, "Pouvoirs Sexuels: Le Juge Thomas, la Cour Suprême et la Société Américaine," *Esprit* 12 (December 1991): 102-3.

43. See for example the positions of the major employer organizations articulated in the senate report (Rapport du Sénat) on the 1992 draft legislation, p. 20.
44. See interview with Neiertz in *Le Monde*, June 28, 1991.
45. *New York Times*, November 8, 1992.
46. Law no. 92-1179 of November 4, 1992.
47. *Le Monde*, October 24, 1992.
48. Florence C. Hubert,"Enforcement of the EC Discrimination Law in France," Internal Report to the French Government, pp. 10-13.
49. I attended the workshop. For a written report of the proceedings see, *Journée Harcèlement Sexuel*, Service des Droits des Femmes, June 22, 1993.
50. Ibid.

Chapter 11

The Limits of Malaise in France

Marie-France Toinet

According to historian and sociologist Pierre Rosanvallon, French "politics has been in crisis for two centuries! One could even say that democracy has always disappointed those most hopeful in its virtues."[1] It is undeniable that a malaise, a feeling of crisis, a sort of anxiety, periodically overtakes the French. These times are marked by a general feeling among the French that the political system neither adequately represents them nor responds to their demands and needs and by the perception that the system is globally corrupt. Of course, there is nothing new in this situation. From Baron Haussmann, the urban planner who built the modern Paris[2] to the *Affaire des piastres* (a currency scheme between France and Indochina under the Fourth Republic, by which many public officials, including General Salan of Algerian putsch fame, became rich); to the Gaullist scandals (generally in the building trades), to Giscard's diamonds, scandal has followed scandal. Financing of the parties[3] in the past was an even worse mess than it is now. This is known only, and only partially, through the satirical newspaper *Le Canard Enchaîné*. In that respect, the legal obligation (1970) of the *"chèque barré"* (only the person to the order of whom a check is written can cash it—and only by putting it in a bank account) made the most convenient instrument of corruption identifiable, all the more so with computerized accounting.[4]

In the past voters kicked "rotten apples" out of office. In the most famous of these cases, Georges Clemenceau was defeated in the election of 1893 because of his role in the Panama Canal affair. (That scandal arose because the Panama Canal Company bought off not only the generally conservative press but also Clemenceau's own newspaper, *La Justice,* which went bankrupt in 1889.) He was reelected in 1902 only because he redeemed himself in the public's eye during the Dreyfus affair by publishing Emile Zola's "J'accuse," thereby reestablishing his political credentials. Often, public opinion went from decrying the rotten apples to declaring the whole apple barrel rotten: this meant a change of majority or even a change of regime, notably from the Fourth to the Fifth Republic.

There are always specific features to each political crisis, and the present one—if it actually is a crisis—is no exception, though it seems more ideological and less "systemic" than preceding ones. First and foremost, there is what might be called an identity crisis: the French seem to doubt their "Frenchness." At the elite level, French identity seems to be threatened through the development of the European Union. "Brussels" decides everything at the expense of French sovereignty and national institutions (particularly in the judicial domain). At the grassroots level, the most recent arrivals (Blacks and Arabs) seem to integrate less easily than did their predecessors from Europe. The French look back at the past and long for times when France was a great power and thus able to decide for itself as it pleased. Looking toward the future, they worry that labor conditions will never be the same and unemployment will never be reduced.

Of course, none of this is entirely true. Since the constitutional reform of 1992, for example, the French government at last has given a significant amount of control over European policy to the French parliament. Furthermore, Italians[5] and Portuguese, not to mention East European Jews, were never considered easy to integrate. It has been a long time since France was a superpower (one could argue that it stopped being one in 1866 when its policy of neutrality permitted Prussia to defeat Austria at Sadowa). And last but not least, the composition of the work force and the general organization of the French economy have not been stable, but have profoundly changed in the past. Most recently, this change occurred in the 1950s when France completed its transformation from a peasant society to an industrial one (the farming population went down from 31 percent of the active population in 1954 to 20 percent in 1962).

"Crisis" and Malaise

But is there a political crisis, in the sense that Charles S. Maier[6], Samuel Huntington[7] and many other analysts refer to crisis? Is it disabling the western world with electoral convulsions, conflicts of civilization, and a skeptical and ontological despair, so that politics and politicians have become unable to define and achieve *le bien commun* (the common good)? We submit that at least in France this is not presently the case. The constitutional system is infrequently questioned, certainly less so than it was in the 1950s. The Fourth Republic (1946-1958) was never popular and it paid for its difficult beginnings;[8] it was seen as inefficient, which was hardly true, but true enough for public opinion, which is what counts. I still remember as a 10-year-old child the 13 ballots needed to elect René Coty, president of the Republic in 1953 and the scorn my family heaped on a system producing such an outcome. The French felt their country was the sick man of Europe—a feeling they no longer have today, even if they do have their gripes.

But politicians these days, from Valéry Giscard d'Estaing to Edouard Balladur, from Jacques Chirac to Jack Lang, from Charles Pasqua to Charles Millon, all want to tinker with the constitution—to no avail. Even the primary system that Charles Pasqua persisted in trying to introduce in the electoral arena in 1994 backfired, thanks to the sane reaction of public opinion.[9] The more the public knew about it, the less they were convinced that it was as good a device or better than the existing two-round French electoral system.

The present constitution and the way it works suits the French well. Certainly, discontent does exist, but the French are discontent with corruption, with *cumul des mandats* (holding several elected offices at the same time) and with failed promises rather than with the constitution itself. This type of discontent clearly involves the political class, not the political framework that has so frequently failed in the past.

One should not exaggerate the "populist" reaction to the malfunctioning of the representative system. No demagogue, whether Jean-Marie Le Pen or Phillipe de Villiers (who both claim to have come from purer stock, a claim that makes them targets for the satirical press) or even Bernard Tapie, is any more likely to succeed than Pierre Poujade did under the Fourth Republic or Boulanger under the Third. And some politicians as a group remain surprisingly popular. In an poll of *Le Courrier des Maires*, 73 percent of the sample "trust" their mayor (22 percent "distrust" him or her); indeed, even the least "trusted" official, the European deputy, is still trusted by 44 percent of the public (42 percent "distrust" him or her).[10]

All things considered, we submit that France does not suffer from a crisis, but rather from *malaise*. As the word itself entails, the French are "ill at ease" with the present situation, but this has not (yet) reached a critical stage—the crisis stage. If there is malaise, it is not limited to France alone. In fact, in many respects this malaise might be less intense in France, where malaise is still channelled through traditional electoral outlets, as well as through new political formats which run parallel to *and* are connected with elections than in other western countries.

As one analyst tells us, "The malaise that currently sows public opinion... reveals itself most saliently in tremendous electoral volatility."[11] This undoubtedly appears to be the case if one considers Japan, the United States, Canada, Germany, or Italy; France has also experienced such tremendous electoral volatility. In the last legislative election in 1993 the Socialist Party lost 75 percent of its parliamentary group (it went from 269 to 55 members), and in that election 43 percent of incumbent candidates were defeated. Incumbent vulnerability, however, is nothing new in France. Traditionally, incumbent parties have faced difficulties in elections, though the results were somewhat more severe in 1993 than is customary. Rather than a sign of malaise, we consider this phenomenon to be an indication that the French electorate still basically believes there are political alternatives to the status quo within the general political framework.

Conversely, this belief in political alternatives does not seem to prevail—despite what has been said and written—in the United States, especially when one considers the results of the 1994 congressional elections. As usual, due in part to high abstention (62 percent), incumbent candidates were reelected to the House of Representatives in more than 90 percent of the cases. Electoral competition was somewhat limited as there was no contest to speak of for 12 percent of the House seats (37 seats were uncontested and there was only one major party candidate in 16 cases). In another 24 percent of House constituencies (105 cases), the winner was elected with 70 percent or more of the votes.

This does not occur in France where competition remains high even in local elections. There is never a seat in the National Assembly that is not contested in the first round, and if a candidate is uncontested in the second round (one must attract 10 percent of the registered voters in the first round to remain for the second), then abstentions as well as blank and void ballots immediately increase. Even municipal elections are competitive; over 3 percent of French voters have been candidates in political elections at some time, and over 1.5 percent have been elected (there are half a million municipal councilors). In addition, there are hundreds of thousands of French citizens who volunteer to work at the polling stations on election day, who are elected (without compensation) to school boards and *comités d'entreprises* or *prud'hommes* (labor courts), and who lead the 700,000 national associations, many of which are involved in humanitarian and charitable tasks.[12] Even more striking is the fact that 23 percent of a representative sample of French citizens over 18 state their willingness to be elected municipal councillor. Among men, the number reaches 41 percent.[13]

According to Maier: "the moral crisis of democracy ... comprises a flight from politics ... : weariness with its debates, disbelief about its claims, skepticism about results, cynicism about its practitioners."[14] We do not find this to be happening in France or, for that matter, anywhere else. In every western country, there are cyclical crises and persistent underlying currents, different of course in each country, but nowhere is there an end of ideology, an end of history: that myth is as old as political science.

In the early 1960s, the Fondation Nationale des Sciences Politiques organized a workshop on *"depoliticization"* and *"de-ideologization,"* themes that were debunked by Georges Vedel, Georges Lavau, Jean Touchard, and René Rémond. In particular, Touchard argued that the myth of the end of politics was politically motivated and was the perennial hope of the conservatives. He quote Michel Debré to the effect: "The number of citizens involved in public affairs is limited, and all for the better. The city, the nation where, every day, great numbers of citizens would talk politics, would be close to ruins."[15]

Concepts of the Left and Right are not old-fashioned in France, as research by CEVIPOF (the French research organization) has convincingly demonstrated.[16] There is no weariness of public debate, as is evident by the pervasiveness and quality of the debates on such issues as the Maastricht Treaty (Europe Union), unemployment, social protection, GATT, primaries, Bosnia, or church-state relations. In fact, there is a general dissatisfaction among the French because there is too *little* public debate. And there is no cynicism (in the sense of impudence and immorality) about politicians, but rather a legitimate (though exaggerated) worry about corruption.

The issue of corruption has gnawed at politicians' reputations: 39 percent of a sample in a recent SOFRES poll feel that politics is "not very" or "not at all *honorable*," and that feeling is shared by 63 percent of young people (aged 16-24). A majority considers office holders to be "ambitious and manipulative liars."[17] But, as stated earlier, this changes strikingly if one compares mayors (who are probably as "tainted" or even more tainted by corruption than are deputies, considering the former's direct involvement with money) with other elected officials. During the period around 1968 one of the favorite mottos of young people was "*Elections, piège à cons*" ("Elections, traps for fools"); nowadays, only the primaries are thus described, and by politicians as distinguished as Raymond Barre and Phillippe Séguin.

This distrust of politics, particularly sharp among young people, is a distrust of *established* politics and therefore does not mean people in general are apolitical or alienated from the political process. There is a search for new forms of politics—which of course are not very new—or even for "new" politicians such as Tapie, whose incredible popularity, particularly among young people, can be witnessed in his rating in the European elections of June 1994 (he received 12 percent of the vote). "New" politicians are successful because they are not considered part of the elites or the mainstream.

Thus, during the period of the Balladur government, we saw widespread and successful participation among young people in the struggles against university reform, for secularity, against the lowering of the minimum wage and for modification of the agricultural and fishing policies. Even more interesting have been the "new" forms of militancy, again, particularly among young people described in *Le Monde* by Philippe Bernard:

> From student associations helping with homework in the [ghettos] to the *Restos du Coeur* [feeding poor people], from Bosnia committees to *Act-up*, from associations against homelessness to *SOS-racisme*...this generation learns politics in associations.[18]

Of course, this frustration with "traditional" politics can also lead to less pleasant forms of militancy: 18 percent of 18–24 year olds voted for the National Front in the legislation elections of 1993, compared with 13 percent of all French voters, as many as voted for the socialists. In the presidential elections of 1995, about as many young people voting for the first time voted for Le Pen (21 percent) as voted for Chirac (21 percent) or Jospin (23 percent).[19] But the young always select the fringes, whether the extreme Right or Left, the Greens or Tapie.

To be sure, compared to 15 or 20 years ago, there are fewer (or rather, generally less well-attended) public demonstrations, fewer acts of terrorism, fewer political assassinations, and fewer strikes. This is true in all Western democracies, but this does not prevent analysts—always concerned with malaise—from believing that citizens are less ready to act politically and more prepared to act violently.

Yet, until now at least, there have been no *jacqueries*, and there has been no luddism, even though France, like the other Western democracies, is undergoing a true technological revolution which has enormously increased unemployment (due neither to higher social protection nor to better salaries, but to a tax system bearing more heavily on labor than on capital investment and machines). Such developments are very hard on society, particularly when compounded with greater inequalities than 20 years ago: whereas salaries have gone up only slightly, capital gains have increased tremendously. This has frayed social cohesion, though less in Germany and France than in Britain and the United States, thanks to the maintenance of a social safety net and the reassertion of national identity. Contrary to some analyses, French identity has been expressed less by a chauvinistic or xenophobic movements (despite the upsurge of support for Le Pen in 1995), than by a reassertion of republican values: *laïcité* (for which there is no proper word in English, but that translates roughly as "secularity"), integrity (hence the revulsion with political scandals), tolerance, solidarity, not to mention liberty and equality.

Except for the racists, integration of the foreign-born, after years of calls for multiethnicity and multiculturalism, is now back on the agenda, and public opinion is reverting to a very traditional, and perhaps peculiarly French, vision of the state.[20] The French melting pot is still working well.[21] At least up to now, "Citizens do not confront their states with demands as they back away in disillusion." French citizens have had a very secular view of the state best characterized by the biblical sentiment: "Give unto Caesar what belongs to Caesar, and to civil society what belongs to civil society." They believe the public sphere is essential to the functioning of society and reject the notion of the "invisible hand," "laissez-faire" or "laissez-passer" vision of society: they are convinced that public regulation and protection is indispensable. After all, they are not beyond measuring the baneful effects of a misunderstood, unregulated "market," such as scandals, corruption, and private enrichment of public officials.

Conversely, the French erupt in laughter at the notion that the state should impose public prayer or censorship in schools (not to mention creationism) or criminalize sexual behavior or obscene publications. More specifically, French public opinion is convinced that the Islamic veil (as well as the Kippah and the cross) are better left out of (public) schools and worn in private or church.

France is supposed to be the epitome of a very inefficient type of statism. But, as Alain Minc has reminded his audience on (private) television,[22] France has the highest level of exports per capita *in the world;* its GDP has increased more than any of its European neighbors in the last 10 years, and its inflation was less than 2 percent last year; its standard of living (in real terms) has gone up 40 percent in the last 20 years and its privately-held wealth has doubled during the same period. True, unemployment has been hovering around 13 percent for several months. Nonetheless, as a recent OECD study has shown, the actual rate of unemployment in the United States, if calculated with European norms, is currently "significantly above" 10 percent.[23] Moreover, as the *Wall Street Journal* recently stated, it is better to be unemployed in Europe than "working poor" in the United States.[24]

Expressing Dissatisfaction

There are many ways in which French citizens can show their dissatisfaction with the way their political system works without overthrowing it: electoral registration, electoral participation (voting, but also militancy and candidacy) or abstention, blank or void ballots, votes in favor of fringe parties, and changing the presidential or parliamentary majorities. They have been as adept and as subtle as American citizens (with the split ballot, for instance) in using any and all of these instruments. Of course, their choices mean different things as far as both type and level of dissatisfaction are concerned. It is clear that non-registration indicates the lowest degree of satisfaction with (or interest in) politics, and the highest degree of alienation and/or apathy. Undoubtedly, kicking out a majority (not to mention voting for a fringe candidate) is much less a sign of malaise, disinterest, apathy, or alienation; political hope is still there.

The first sign of interest in politics is registration, which in France (as in the United States) is the individual responsibility of each citizen, and a process generally more difficult there than in the United States. In France, one has to go to city hall, produce identification, and prove legal residence (a telephone bill is enough), and one must register the year before the election to be able to participate.

Despite these difficulties, only about 10 percent of eligible voters are not registered in France, compared to about a third of those eligible in the United States. There are slight variations from year to year: the sophisticated French voter tends to register when he or she knows an election is upcoming. This tactic may backfire, as it did in 1974 when Pompidou died, because unplanned elections may preclude voters from registering in time. Thus, about two-thirds fewer voters registered in 1993 (there were no elections in 1994 except the European elections, which are not considered to be very important) than in 1992 (there were legislative elections coming up in 1993, not to mention an unexpected referendum). There has been no recent movement (from 1955 to 1992) towards non-registration, indicating that the impact of malaise is not as widespread and as deep, even among young people, as critics suggest. The young display much lower levels of registration than middle-aged voters: for the legislative elections of 1988, 29 percent of 19-year-olds were not registered compared to 5 percent of 60- to 65-year-olds.[25] But this has always been true—and in fact it is remarkable that so many young people (71 percent) are actually registered at age 19.

Non-voting in France is both generally and individually cyclical. There are times—that are difficult to date precisely—when non-voting is quite low. One such time was during the Fifth Republic, from the legislative elections of 1973 (when only 18.7 percent did not vote in the first round) to the presidential election of 1981 (when only 14.1 percent failed to vote in the second round). At other times abstention has been high, as it was, for instance, in legislative elections in 1946 (22 percent) and 1962 (31 percent). Still, there is no doubt that since the first round of the legislative elections of 1981, there has been an increase in nonvoting. The highest abstention rate ever recorded since the introduction of universal suffrage in France was reached in the referendum on New Caledonia in 1988 (in which 63 percent of the electorate did not vote). The years 1988 and 1989 have registered perhaps the lowest rate of electoral participation in recent times: in the legislative elections of 1989, non-voting reached 34 percent, the highest percentage since 1857; in the 1989 municipal elections, 27 percent stayed away from the polling booths, the most since World War II; and in the 1989 European elections, less than one voter out of two went to the polls.

But is this a sign of malaise or is it sign of greater impending political crisis? It is worth noting that low rates of participation draw more attention in France than in America. In the United States, low rates of voter turnout have characterized midterm congressional elections for most of the century, with no one paying much attention. In France, when elections to the 159 Chambers of Commerce and Industry took place on November 21, 1994, both the national and regional press reported the next day the precise number of potential voters and the rate of participation (23.72 percent). I have been vainly looking for the same basic information for the November 8, 1994 American midterm elections and have found only estimates of voting by age (in *Le Monde!*) and turnout.[26] Official figures, very imperfect, appear at the end of December in *Congressional Quarterly*, which is not exactly a mass circulation publication. The French press deplored the low, mediocre, unsatisfactory rate of participation in the United States' elections.[27]

On an individual basis, participation is also cyclical. Studying the same individuals' electoral participation over time, Françoise Subileau and I have demonstrated[28] that among those who remained on the electoral registers for more than ten years, only *one percent* never voted—and most probably, they either were deceased or had moved. This means there is no "party of the non-voters" in France and that non-voting has not become a structural phenomenon but remains conjunctural and highly strategic.

The best index of the crisis "du politique," and of the disinterest for politics, we are told, is that young people vote less than ever, as witnessed in the 1993 legislative election where one-third of those 18- to 24-year-old registered voters stated they did not vote, compared to a 24 percent abstention rate for the whole electorate.[29] In fact, in our sample of Paris polling stations sample, 38 percent of the young did not vote compared to 33 percent for the whole Parisian electorate.[30] But this does not represent any kind of dramatic change: in the 1981 legislative election, 41 percent of 20-24 year-olds did not vote, while in the 1981 presidential election, for which there was a high level of voter turnout, only 28 percent of this age group failed to vote.[31]

In fact, we argue that voters decide whether to participate in elections according to the stakes involved. Thus, as would be expected, they vote more on important ballots (presidential and legislative) than on minor ones (departmental or municipal). Furthermore, while participation is always high in presidential elections (because the stakes are high everywhere in the country), it varies tremendously in local elections according to the size of the town: in the more rural areas the participation is high (because each vote counts, the stakes are higher); in the more urban areas the participation is lower (each vote counts less, so the stakes are lower). In 1988-1989, for instance, the abstention rate (second rounds) tumbled from 81 percent (in departmental elections) to 16 percent (in presidential elections) in the same urban canton of Bourges 3 (Cher) but remained strikingly similar (and low) in the rural canton of Vigeois (Corrèze): 9 percent in the presidential and 12 percent in the *cantonales* ("departmental") elections.

There is another type of national consultation in which the participation rate varies tremendously from one to the next, because the stakes themselves vary tremendously: referendums. Participation went down from 76.5 percent in the 1961 referendum on Algeria (the importance of which no one could ignore), to 37 percent in the 1988 referendum on New Caledonia (which everyone knew was superfluous and even manipulative).

What is new, or rather what has intensified, in recent years is strategic voting (contrasting one's participation in the different ballots), particularly in "minor" elections. Our "rural" polling stations show that two-thirds of the voters abstained at least once in the *municipal* and departmental elections of 1988-1989, as opposed to less than a quarter in the "major" legislative and presidential election of 1989. Voting was probably more systematic in previous years, though non-voting increased from 22.4 to 31.1 percent between the two rounds of the 1969 presidential election, the only time this has ever occurred. This 1969 increase was certainly an example of strategic voting, as voters from the Left did not have a candidate in the second round and did not want (a willful act) to choose between *la peste et le choléra* ("the plague and cholera").

Voters appear to act strategically in every election. Whatever the national rate of participation, abstention shoots up when there is only one candidate remaining in the second round. For instance, in the 1993 legislative elections in the town of Mâcon (Saône-et-Loire), the UDF-PR candidate was the only one to go on to the second round. Between the two rounds, abstention went up from 34 percent to 56 percent, and blank or spoiled ballots increased from 4 percent to 13 percent.

To measure precisely the importance of strategic abstention (which is hidden in general results), one has to go to the registration files and check individual participation. Thus, in one of the polling stations of our Parisian sample (the 18th *arrondissement)*, in the legislative election of 1993, there were 637 non-voters among 1367 registered voters in the first round and 529 in the second—a decrease of 0.5 percent in the abstention rate. In fact, 102 first round participants did not vote on the second and 110 first round abstentionists participated in the second: 212 voters (17 percent) participated selectively, or in other words, politically.

TABLE 11.1
PARTICIPATION IN LEGISLATIVE ELECTIONS ACCORDING TO
THE POLITICAL ORIENTATION OF POLLING-STATIONS
(FIRST BALLOT, PERCENT OF REGISTERED VOTERS)

Polling-stations	1978	1986	1993
Communist-oriented	76	66	59
Socialist-oriented	80	75	65
RPR-oriented	78	74	68
UDF-oriented	78	79	68

Source : Subileau-Toinet (Parisian sample)

The really striking change on the non-voting front in recent years has been in the social composition of the abstaining group. It used to be that rich and poor voted or abstained more or less in the same proportions. Before 1974, for instance, there was hardly any difference in Paris between bourgeois and working-class polling stations. Since 1981, however, significant differences between rich and poor voters have appeared, though in France the gap in favor of the bourgeois voters is far smaller than it is in the United States where, as Walter Dean Burnham states, "The rich vote and the poor do not."[32] Those differences are up to 10-15 points nowadays according to our FNSP-CSA poll of 1992.[33] These social differences are basically parallel to political differences. There, too, prior to 1978 little difference existed in abstention rates between voters of left-wing and right-wing parties. From 1978 until 1993, this difference in abstention rate due to political inclination has consistently increased (table 11.1), according to our sample of 40 Parisian polling stations.

Even more striking is the persistent decline of electoral participation in communist and socialist polling stations, which started as early as 1981 for the Communists and as 1986 for the Socialists. This does not mean that abstentionists *belong* to the Left: no one *owns* non-voters and every party at one time or another is struck by non-voting. But since 1978, the rate of abstention has been higher among left-wing voters.

For the Communists, the gradual demise of communism has left their electors who did not want to vote communist anymore but could not switch to socialist (or to the National Front) only one option: the "refuge" of non-voting. In the most communist-oriented polling stations of our Parisian sample, non-voting in legislative elections (first round) has gone up 17 points between 1978 and 1993.[34] For the Socialists (whose abstention rate increased ten percent between 1978 and 1993), disappointed and dispirited because they felt, rightly or wrongly, that the socialist governments had become as conservative as their conservative opposition, abstention was a way to show dissatisfaction, to give a lesson to the Socialist Party without actually voting for the Right. Non-voting is so political in France that parties will sometimes recommend it, as did the Gaullists in 1946 (the referendum on the constitution) and in 1988 (New Caledonia), the Socialists in 1972 (the entrance of Great Britain into the European Union), and the Communists in 1969 (the second ballot of the presidential election).

The "blank and void" votes—another form of electoral protest very similar to non-voting—signify a refusal to choose between the existing alternatives because they are not enticing. This is only different from non-voting in that one actually goes to the polls to register one's discontent, to mark a deliberate choice of "none of the above". Because they are accounted for in the official results, such votes are an institution peculiar to France. Not only are they accounted for but, contrary to popular belief, they do count. Even a candidate who has gathered over 50 percent of the vote cannot be elected on the first round if at least 25 percent of the registered voters have not bothered to go to the polls: "blank and void" votes count with the *votants* (those who voted) and not with the *abstentionnistes* (those who did not).

"Blank and void" voters are considered more civic-minded. After all, if it is only to express a refusal of the choices offered, "blank and void" voters have bothered to go to the polls rather than playing truant. But if there is a civic dimension in this vote, it coexists with the will to preserve the secrecy of the vote. For ten days after an election, by law, each citizen can go and check the voting registers[35] to see who has or has not voted: in small towns, people do not necessarily want to appear to be following that party's line, if there has been a party call for abstention. Thus, in the presidential election of 1969, in which the Communist Party encouraged its voters not to participate, Jean Ranger has demonstrated that, the smaller the town, the higher the percentage of "blank and void" votes; conversely, the larger the city, the higher the percentage of non-voting.[36]

"Blank and void" voting varies, as does non-voting, according to the stakes. Under the Fifth Republic, it went from a minimum 0.9 percent in the first round of the 1965 presidential election (the first with direct popular suffrage) to 7.1 percent in the referendum of 1972 on Great Britain's entrance into the EEC (in which the Socialist Party had asked "its" voters not to participate). In a legislative election in individual districts, blank and void ballots can reach very important proportions in the second round,

TABLE 11.2
RESULTS OF ELECTIONS (FIRST BALLOTS)
IN PERCENTAGE OF REGISTERED VOTERS

	1978	1986	1993	1995*
"Parties of government"	74%	56%	45%	54%
Non-voting	17	22	31	21
"Blank and void" votes	2	3	4	3
"Fringe parties"	7	19	20	22
Total "refusal"	26	44	55	46

* Candidates from "parties of government" etc.

Source : Subileau-Toinet and Le Monde, *L'Election presidentielle 23 Avril-7 Mai 1995*, (Paris: *Numero Spécial des Dossiers et Documents du Monde,* May 1995), p. 36.

when the political choice becomes limited: in 1993, for instance, it reached 19.5 percent in Bergerac (Dordogne), 19 percent in St. Claude (Jura) and 16 percent in Montbazon (Indre-et-Loire). But this is nothing new: in 1978, in Georges Marchais' district, the leader of the Communist Party saw "blank and void" votes go up to 25 percent on the second round.

Very striking also, in recent years, is the flight away from the "parties of government," that is, parties that have held ministerial positions in the government at one time or another and towards the fringe parties, particularly in recent elections: 53 percent of the "expressed" votes (excluding abstainers) for the European election (1994) and 29 percent in the first round of the 1993 legislative elections were cast for fringe parties. In the first round of the 1995 presidential elections, the three top candidates attracted only 68 percent of the (expressed) vote. In other words, the refusal to vote for the "parties of government" (reached by adding abstentions and "blank and void" votes to votes for "fringe parties") added up to 46 percent of registered voters in 1995 and 55 percent in 1993, versus 26 percent in 1978 (see table 11.2).

For the Left in particular, the results were catastrophic: the Left vote went down from 37 percent to 19 percent of the registered voters between 1978 and 1993. The Socialist Party, paid dearly. It was held responsible—and rightly so as it was in power most of the last 12 years—for unemployment, and, since the Left is held to higher ethical standards than the conservatives, perhaps even more for corruption. In addition, the Communist Party was still paying the price of the failures of communism in eastern Europe and its unwillingness to admit it.

TABLE 11.3
NUMBER OF SEATS PER PARTY UNDER THE FIFTH REPUBLIC

Parties	Nov. 1958	Nov. 1962	March 1967	June 1968	March 1973	March 1978	June 1981	March 1986	June 1988	March 1993
Comm.	10	41	72	34	73	86	44	35	27	23
Soc. & MRG	88	106	121	57	102	115	283	216	275	55
Center	182	91	85	94	119	123	61	131	131	214
Gaull.	201	233	200	293	183	154	83	155	130	259
FN	-	-	-	-	-	-	-	-	1	-
Ind.	-	-	-	-	-	-	-	35	-	25

Author's Data

Nevertheless, it cannot be said that the Right took advantage of the Left's downfall. The enthusiasm in its favor was limited: it was more the Left that bled (to "abstention") than the Right, which won by default. The Left lost votes, but the conservative "parties of government" did not win them. Though the electoral system for national legislative elections basically makes it impossible for fringe parties to win seats, the vote for these parties does influence the often steep variations in the number of seats for each "party of government" (table 11.3). There, the manifestation of malaise is clear (see chap. 7).

Malaise and Democracy

Could this "malaise," ambiguous and undefined, become a full-fledged crisis? As Maier rightfully states: "Moral crises do not necessarily doom liberal regimes, but they provide a powerful opportunity for political outsiders to capitalize on the perceived defects and corruption of "the system."[37] Interestingly enough, at present there is no Ross Perot or Silvio Berlusconi in France: electoral support for Le Pen, though it increased impressively during the last elections, is limited by the violent opposition to his ideas, and de Villiers, whatever his eagerness, attracted few votes in the presidential elections and, moreover, does not fit the bill.

Moreover, a political crisis is not necessarily resolved through the appearance of a populist phoenix; it can also translate into an implosion of society, a slow process which, I fear, we are witnessing in the United States: when 4.6 million adult men (more than those looking for work) are under (as the *International Herald Tribune*[38] puts it) "state supervision" (prison, parole, or probation); when schools let half the adult population go illiterate; when Michael Eisner of Disney fame takes home about $100,000 an hour ($216 million total in 1993), while the minimum-wage worker takes home less than $5 an hour[39]; when 35 million Americans (out of 255 million) cannot afford to go to the doctor or to the hospital; when intolerance gnaws at civilized discourse; when "abortion" doctors are killed; and when multiculturalism, clerical in its nature, denies the common roots of the "American" people; a collapse of society is not far off, and its causes are deeply political, mainly in the frayed relationship between those who govern and those who are governed.

Even though France is less "advanced" on that road, there are problematic signs that it has started down it. That is, when a large majority (60 percent) of the people believe than democracy is "not working very well"

(37 percent) or "not at all" (23 percent)[40] or when, on both the Left and Right, people start to believe that the Socialist Party is just as *"neoliberal"* (in the French meaning of the term) as Jacques Chirac, Edouard Balladur and Co., or that it has favored the rich more than the poor, or that it is just as corrupt as the Right and that in a word, there is no difference (except verbal) between the *parties* of the Right and of the Left, they may be half wrong—but they are half right, and that is what counts.

The responsibility of political leaders, in that respect, is preeminent. Valéry Giscard d'Estaing bemoaned on the eve of his 1981 defeat, "une France *coupée en deux* (cut in two)," as if a total consensus was the ideal to emulate. Consensus, as we know, does not necessarily mean a more democratic society. Far from it. We submit that the decline of a political party even as undemocratic as the French Communist Party (which still garnered 20 percent of the vote in the difficult legislative elections of 1968 and 21.5 percent in the 1969 presidential election, but has barely reached 10 percent in recent elections) has undermined the working of the French democratic system. The decline has produced both a lower quality of public and programmatic debate and more abstention. In the long run, if non-voting becomes epidemic and structural, non-voters will not be truly represented anymore—and will thus be excluded.

Politicians have also become less convinced of the necessity of a strong opposition, or less ready to accept being reduced to "shadow cabinet" status, as if it were useless and unworthy. We submit that the Left in particular, when it is a strong opposition and seems to be on the verge of reaching power, might be at least as successful, if not more successful, in implementing its program as when it is in the majority. This was often true under the Fourth Republic, and until 1981 under the Fifth Republic.

Parties in France are despised by the Gaullists and the Conservatives: so-called "direct" democracy (referendums, primaries, polls) are supposed to be superior to "smoke-filled" rooms. Thus, one of the first acts of the new president, in July 1995, was to submit to parliament an amendment to the constitution that would expand the areas for which the government can propose referendums; the amendment passed easily over the opposition of the Socialists and Communists. In following the results of polls (for which France is one of the biggest, if not the biggest, consumers among western democracies), they pretend to be following *vox populi*. In fact, they are trying to please, or rather not to displease, each and every voter. This is no way to govern. Polls and referendums are essentially reactive; only mass parties (democratic and open to any voter who wants to belong) can define policies, aggregate demands, and hierarchize priorities. The voter then can select and elect. Presently, voters seem less volatile than disoriented: they cannot choose among different visions of the public interest, because none are offered. Instead they must make up their mind among competing private interests (or obsessions), all made to appear equal, but not necessarily important to the whole of society.

In the last analysis, western democracies, France and others, are not suffering of an *excess* of *Etat* (state, in the European meaning) but from a *lack* of *gouvernement* (government, in the American meaning). They are suffering not from their leaders being too daring and public-minded but from their being too shy and privately oriented. They have too often been told that civil society should replace the state, whereas each has its rightful sphere of action—including in foreign affairs: armies cannot be responsible for humanitarian tasks; this is the proper task of non-governmental organizations, as we verified in Somalia, and perhaps in Bosnia.

Maier writes that:

> [e]lectorates today remain poised between contending visions of political communities. If the traditional parties that speak for reenergizing the public sphere can produce plausible and attractive leaders, they can channel public dissatisfaction into an era of renewed reform. This was the American outcome in the 1930s and the early 60's [I would say the 1950s], and I, for one, hope that the United States shall later be able to claim it was the results of the 1990s.[41]

I hope so too: for the United States, for France, for the rest of the world.

Notes to Chapter 11

1. Pierre Rosanvallon, in *Libération*, August 16, 1994, p. 9.

2. His wife is supposed to have said, "I don't understand why, but each time we move, we are expropriated by the building authority."

3. See Pierre Assouline, *Une éminence grise: Jean Jardin, 1904-1976* (Paris: Balland, 1986).

4. See "Le prix de la démocratie," France 2 TV, November 28, 1991.

5. One can read further on the subject and with great pleasure in Cavana, *Les Ritals* (Paris: Belfond, 1978).

6. Charles S. Maier, "Democracy and Its Discontents," *Foreign Affairs*, (summer 1994): 48-64.

7. Samuel Huntington, "The Clash of Civilization," *Foreign Affairs*, (summer 1993): 22-49.

8. The Fourth Republic came into being after a first constitutional project was rejected (May 1946) and the second (October 1946) accepted narrowly in referendums. In October, as de Gaulle (who was opposed) wrote, "One-third of the French electorate submitted *(résignés)* to it; one-third opposed it *(opposés)* and one-third ignored it *(ignorée)*."

9. In the SOFRES polls, approval for primaries went constantly down, from 53 percent approval in late September 1994 to 23 percent in late November (and from 61 percent to 33 percent among RPR-UDF sympathizers).

10. "Sondage: Les Français jugent les maires," *Le Courrier des Maires,* September 9, 1994, pp. 14-22.

11. Maier, 48.

12. See the special section of *Le Monde* on associations, November 24, 1994.

13. Poll of *Le Courrier des Maire,* September 9, 1994, p. 22.

14. Maier, 59.

15. Georges Vedel, ed., *La dépolitisation: mythe ou réalité?* (Paris: Armand Colin, 1962), p. 28.

16. Guy Michelat, "A la recherche de la gauche et de la droite," in CEVIPOF, ed. (Centre d'Etudes de la Vie Politique Française), *L'électeur français en questions* (Paris: Presses de la FNSP, 1990, pp. 71-103).

17. In Olivier Duhamel and Jerôme Jaffré, eds., *L'état de l'opinion 1994* (Paris: Le Seuil, 1994).

18. Philippe Bernard, "Les nouveaux territoires des jeunes II. La politique sans les politiciens," *Le Monde,* May 28, 1994.

19. See the survey in *Le Monde, L'Election presidentielle, 23 avril/7 mai 1995* (Paris: Numéro spécial des Dossiers et Documents du Monde, May 1995), p. 47.

20. Stewart Toy, "Privatization is unpopular: only 11 percent of the French want less government control of business," *Business Week,* December 12, 1994, p. 29.

21. See Emmanuel Todd, *Le destin des immigrés: assimilation et ségrégation dans les démocraties occidentales* (Paris: Le Seuil, 1994). See particularly, Michèle Tribalat, *Faire France: une enquête sur les immigrés et leurs enfants* (Paris: La Découverte/ Essais, 1995).

22. "L'heure de vérité," TF1, November 6, 1994. See also Alain Minc, ed., *La France de l'an 2000* (Paris: Odile Jacob, 1994).

23. "Selon une étude de l'OCDE ... ," *Le Monde,* November 26, 1994.

24. See Tony Horwitz, "Minimum-wage Jobs Give Many Americans Only a Miserable Life," *Wall Street Journal,* 12 November 1993; and David Wessel & Daniel Benjamin, "Work Ethic," *Wall Street Journal Europe,* March 14, 1994.

25. INSEE, *Premiers résultats,* April 1988.

26. *Le Monde,* November 1994 and the *International Herald Tribune,* November 11, 1994.

27. *Le Figaro,* November 23, 1994 and *Le Monde,* November 22 and 23, 1994.

28. See Françoise Subileau et Marie-France Toinet, *Les chemins de l'abstention: une comparaison franco-américaine* (Paris: La Découverte, 1993) p. 157. For this study, we selected four polling stations: two in Paris (one bourgeois and one working class); one in Normandy (in a small town close to its industrial neighbor); and one in l'Orléanais (very rural). In each of these we studied, voter after voter, turnout for all elections in the last 15 years (1978-1992), up to 21 votes (13 consultations, with one or two rounds).

29. SOFRES, *Post Election Polls,* March 1993.

30. Among those aged 18 to 25, the 18-19 year-olds, who have just bothered to register, are the most participant group.

31. Subileau-Toinet, 110.

32. Walter Dean Burnham, "Fighting the Image War," *New Republic,* October 20, 1976, p. 21.

33. See Subileau-Toinet, 115 and 119.

34. One has to remember, to put things in context, that Paris has become more bourgeois and has voted less on the Left ever since the sixties.

35. This is how Françoise Subileau and I have been able to work on individual electoral participation, preserving, of course, the total anonymity of the voters.

36. See Jean Ranger, "L'électorat communiste dans l'élection présidentielle de 1969," *Revue Française de Science Politique,* (April 1970): 282-311.

37. Maier, 60.

38. Sylvia Nasar, "Blue Collars Become Scarce," *International Herald Tribune,* December 3-4, 1994.

39. John Byrne, "That Eye-Popping Executive Pay," *Business Week,* April 25, 1994.

40. FNSP-CSA Poll (June 1992), in Subileau-Toinet, 213.

41. Maier, 60.

Part IV

The Challenges of Europe and the World

Chapter 12

The Maastricht Referendum and the Party System

Andrew M. Appleton

Introduction

On June 3, 1992, President François Mitterrand announced that the French ratification of the Maastricht Treaty on European Union[1] would be subject to approval in a general referendum. At the time most observers predicted that the French public would overwhelmingly vote in favor of the Treaty. The European Commission's own data supported this optimistic outlook; a Eurobarometer survey conducted in France between March 18 and April 5 revealed that 72.1 percent of the sample viewed the Treaty as either very important or important. A majority (58 percent) thought that it would have a positive effect on the European Community, 48 percent thought that it would have a positive effect on France (with only 13 percent expecting a negative effect), and 26 percent thought that it would have a positive effect on their own life (8 percent responded negatively).

On September 20, 1992, just under 51 percent of valid ballots were cast in favor of treaty ratification, far short of the resounding "yes" that had been anticipated a few months before. Furthermore, the narrow passage of the Maastricht Treaty at the poll had been preceded by a nerve-racking period for the political class advocating its ratification; several indicators had shown mass public sentiment to be leaning dangerously towards a "no" outcome in the run-up to the vote. The outcome appeared to reveal a number of fault lines in French political life that were exposed to lengthy analyses by leading commentators, such as the reemergence of a center-periphery cleavage, class-based differences, secular-religious divisions, the gap between the mass public and the political class, a generational phenomenon, and simply the widening gulf between the "haves" and the "have-nots."

More strikingly, the outcome of the referendum seemed to pit one section of the mass electorate against the established political elite. The anti-Maastricht sentiment was not confined to supporters of the Parti Communiste Français (PCF) and the Front National (FN), which both campaigned against it; large blocks of those on both the moderate Left and Right also defected from their party positions. Why is this significant? The argument of this chapter is that the European integration issue, placed under the political spotlight in the referendum campaign, has peeled away the somewhat fleeting and illusory impression of firmness of the French party system to reveal that the core is weak. While I will argue that this was in part due to Mitterrand's choice of the referendum as an institutional device to split the parties of the Right, I will also show that the phenomenon is more enduring than just the Maastricht campaign. In other words, the outcome of the referendum was not an anomaly from which the party system will quickly recover, but part of an underlying trend that portends significant problems for the "established" parties in France in the coming years.

The early months of the Chirac presidency and the Juppé government seem to confirm this situation. On the one hand, the first act of the new president was to visit Helmut Kohl and reassure him as to the solidity of the Franco-German relationship. On the other, the French government has signalled a change of course in some crucial areas of integration, notably monetary policy and immigration. Without full French support for the single currency as outlined in the Maastricht proposals, it is unlikely that even the "slow track" to a common currency is viable. On immigration, the Juppé government has pulled back from implementation of the Schengen accords, retaining border controls that were due to be eliminated. The fine line that has appeared between the elite-driven commitment to Europe and the demands of the significant anti-European element in the electorate is one that will prove difficult to maintain in the coming years.

Why the Referendum?

Officially, the recourse to ratification of the Maastricht Treaty by popular referendum was supposed to confirm the support of the French populace for the integration process and to give the Treaty a boost at a time when it had run into some trouble, notably in Denmark, Britain, and even (for a while) Germany. Given the preoccupation of Helmut Kohl with the problems of unification in Germany, it was an opportunity for France and for François Mitterrand personally to seize the initiative and assume the mantle of leadership in a critical period of institution-building at the European level. Expansion (both with the European Free Trade Area [EFTA] nations and to the east), economic and monetary union (EMU), and world trade (the completion of the Uruguay round and the transformation of the General Agreement on Tariffs and Trade [GATT]) were all major challenges facing the European Community at the time; a categorical vote in favor of Europe by the French public would bolster France's claim to leadership at this important moment in European history. Given the state of public opinion in early 1992, there seemed no reason to believe that the Treaty would not be overwhelmingly approved.[2]

But was this the only reason to choose a referendum as the path to Treaty ratification? The choice of this mechanism placed France in the minority amongst its fellow members; only two other countries held similar tests of public opinion, Denmark (twice!) and Ireland. Given that the referendum seemed almost certain to pass by a large majority,[3] was there any particular reason to go ahead with it, beyond the general argument of the government presented above? In fact, as I have argued elsewhere,[4] there was a strategic incentive for Mitterrand to pursue popular ratification arising from domestic concerns. With the government trailing badly in the opinion polls in the run-up to the 1993 legislative elections, a referendum would achieve three related goals just six months before the renewal of parliament.

First, it would give the government a badly needed victory on a popular issue. Furthermore, the government would likely garner the support of at least the centrist elements of the Union de la Démocratie Française (UDF), thus providing some evidence of the politics of *l'ouverture* (centrism) to the public. Second, the campaign would serve as a rallying cry to the Socialist Party, badly divided and already fractured over the "after Mitterrand?" question. The referendum would be a chance for the party to place its internal divisions behind it and to mount a united campaign on a winning issue.

Third, and perhaps most importantly, the referendum route would expose divisions on the Right that had seemingly been overcome with the negotiation between the UDF and the Rassemblement Pour la République (RPR) of a common election platform for the 1993 elections. This latter point is perhaps the key to explaining the domestic concerns for Mitterrand and the government that mitigated in favor of a referendum.

It was no secret that the RPR was badly divided over the question of Europe, a situation reflecting the Gaullist heritage of the party and the durability of the *l'Europe des patries* sentiment among party supporters. Particularly since the emergence of the markedly anti-European FN as a significant electoral force, the leadership of the RPR was forced to consider the nationalist, conservative wing of the party. For example, the RPR had experienced a significant hemorrage of party activists in the mid-1980s to the FN, perhaps greater than has yet been recognized. Despite Chirac's warning in January 1992 that Europe must not become a subject causing division on the Right, the issue placed severe internal constraints on his freedom of action in the negotiations with the pro-Europe, pro-Maastricht UDF. Thus, until the referendum was announced, the issue had been left largely untouched in the elaboration of a common program by the two major political parties in the opposition.

But a referendum, with its attendant public campaign, would force the hand of Chirac and potentially place a wedge between the RPR and the UDF. Since it was virtually inconceivable that the latter party would oppose ratification of the Maastricht Treaty (Giscard d'Estaing had already firmly endorsed it on several occasions), the leadership of the RPR would have to find some way of reconciling the divisions within their own party in order to maintain an alliance strategy with the UDF. Chirac had studiously avoided organizing the (announced) *états généraux* (general conference) on Europe with the UDF throughout late 1991 and early 1992, evidently hoping that the press of domestic issues would quietly drown the troublesome issue of integration. A referendum would mean that the RPR could no longer avoid the issue; better still, it would place it in the political spotlight and highlight the divisions on the Right in contrast to the (hoped-for) new-found unity among the Socialists.

Thus there were compelling domestic reasons to seek ratification by referendum. Mitterrand's assertion in his May 1 address, prior to the referendum announcement, that "this is not a matter of clans, this is not a matter of parties, this is a matter that concerns all French people, both partisans and adversaries..."[5] no doubt dissimulated exactly the contrary. As long as the government could garner the committed support of the UDF in the campaign, the procedure would provide an invaluable opportunity to bolster the sagging fortunes of the Socialists in the run-up to the 1993 legislative elections. Given Mitterrand's reputation as a master tactician, this was not an opportunity that he would likely pass up.

The potential of the referendum to achieve these goals was amply quantified during the parliamentary debates in May, prior to the announcement of the referendum by Mitterrand on June 3, 1992. The obligations imposed by the Maastricht Treaty necessitated the passage of a constitutional amendment, the preparatory legislation for which was introduced by the government in the National Assembly in late April. After conceding to some slight amendment of the original text, the government's bill passed the National Assembly by an overwhelming margin of 398 votes to 77. Having been conceded these amendments, the UDF voted in the majority for the text, whereas the leadership and the majority of the RPR opted for abstention. But a sizable minority of Chirac's party (31 deputies in all) chose to oppose the bill, while five deputies voted with the government.[6] Chirac's hopes that the opposition could abstain as a bloc had been undone; according to the centrists and the Giscardians, they could "justify their positive vote by explaining that it was they who had remained faithful to the principle of unity and it was the RPR that had broken it."[7] Just three weeks later, Mitterrand announced the popular plebiscite, with the date to be fixed at a later cabinet meeting.[8]

The Parties and the Campaign

The behavior of the parties during the campaign itself cannot be understood without reference to two important linked events in the then near future; the legislative elections of 1993 and the presidential elections of 1995. In turn, the significance of each of these events was tightly meshed with the personal ambitions of several of the leading protagonists. The legislative elections provided the center-right with the common goal to become once again the majority in the National Assembly; however, the office of prime minister would no doubt go to the party with the largest number of seats, thus ensuring an element of competition within coalition. Equally so, the election of Mitterrand's successor, though still nearly three years off, was the event on which many had their eyes firmly fixed, thus determining an element of competition within the parties. While the PS was less hopeful of retaining a majority after March 1993, there was still much talk of a possible centrist coalition, perhaps with the renegade Union des Democrates du Centre (UDC) parliamentary group; just as much for the center-right, the prospective presidential elections were already stirring the ambitions of more than one leading figure in the party.

Within the RPR, there was a genuine fear that the UDF and its centrist allies were capable of supplanting the neo-Gaullist movement as the major force on the Right and that the Maastricht debate provided the occasion for this to take place. Thus leading pro-Maastricht RPR figures such as Edouard Balladur had been quietly trying to persuade the centrist parties to abstain from voting on the constitutional amendment. When this failed, and when it became obvious that other leading RPR figures such as Phillipe Séguin and Charles Pasqua were prepared to break ranks over the issue, the leadership of the party was placed in a quandary. Chirac could not legitimately oppose the referendum process (and thus call for abstention), for it had been he who had initially called for just such a consultation. The dilemma facing the leadership was to try and maintain some semblance of unity within the opposition, while allowing the anti-Maastricht forces to campaign against the referendum without demobilizing the entire RPR as an effective electoral force.

To comprehend the full complexity of this dilemma, the Séguin-Pasqua axis must also be understood. For Séguin, opposition to the Maastricht Treaty was a matter of principle, and he "picked up with pleasure the role of the concerned national guardian played by Michel Debré in former times."[9] Though Séguin's views placed him at odds with the declared official position of the RPR leadership, it made his reintegration into the party following the campaign less problematic. Pasqua, on the other hand, may not have been guided by such deeply held convictions; for example, he is supposed to have remarked during the constitutional debates that he was in fact for the Treaty and only opposed to the matter of constitutional revision.[10] At the time, it was alleged that Pasqua saw this moment as an opportunity to weaken Chirac's leadership and to move towards the creation of a new conservative party with the presidency in 1995 as the ultimate prize.[11] While Séguin seemed content to avoid direct confrontation with other members of the center-right leadership in 1992, Pasqua appeared intent on provoking it following his June 14 announcement that he would campaign against the Treaty. This assertion takes on all the more cogency in the wake of Pasqua's subsequent decision to back Edouard Balladur for the presidency against the official RPR candidacy of Jacques Chirac in 1995.

Fairly quickly, Chirac's worst-case scenario unfolded. In the name of union, he had demanded that members of the center-right opposition refrain from participating in pro-Maastricht meetings where members of the PS or the government were present. His request was met with indifference; the next day, Giscard d'Estaing himself attended a rally alongside the minister for european affairs, Elisabeth Guigou, one of the major government spokespeople on the issue. Four days later, François Léotard (UDF) appeared on a platform with Prime Minster Bérégovoy, the two warmly shaking hands. At the same time, the UDF leadership made public a statement demanding that Chirac clarify both his party's and his own personal position on the referendum.

Chirac's response was to publish a communiqué on June 12 in which he demanded "an attitude of reserve" from members of the RPR, specifically requesting that they make no public statement on the issue until the party had adopted an official line. Yet two days later, Pasqua's announcement that he would join Séguin in campaigning against the Treaty effectively put an end to this attempt to buy time. Immediately, the leadership of the UDF let it be known that they would not back any candidate for the presidency in 1995 who had not given a clear and precise commitment to European integration.[12] In the face of this mounting pressure, Chirac leaned on RPR parliamentarians not to attend the June 23 extraordinary constitutional congress at Versailles.

The fissure within the RPR was sealed on July 4 with Chirac's announcement that he would be voting for the yes position in September. Addressing an audience of party *cadres* at a party congress, he announced that he would "vote yes without enthusiasm but without any complexes." This declaration was greeted by jeers and whistles from his listeners. Continuing, he declared that the party would not seek to impose any discipline upon its members and that individuals would have to make up their own minds on the issue.[13] This formula avoided a complete rift with the UDF and preserved the presidential ambitions of Chirac himself; on the other hand, it placed pressures on the party organization that others such as Balladur and Nicholas Sarkozy have argued could have been avoided by promoting abstention as the official party line.[14]

However, the other major parties in France were not immune to internal divisions stemming from the referendum. While the elite of the UDF (across its different constituent parties) was almost uniformly pro-Maastricht, the sentiment was not necessarily shared by all of its members. In particular, there was hostility to integration among some of the more locally well-implanted notables, a traditional bastion of the UDF. This reaction to the Maastricht Treaty and to the extremely pro-Europe stance of Giscard d'Estaing, Léotard, and others, was personified by the opposition of Philippe de Villiers. De Villiers had formed his own movement, *Combat des valeurs* (Fight for Values) and was arguing that the only reason to hold a referendum was as a plebiscite on Mitterrand's presidency. According to de Villiers, if "the no to Maastricht wins, Giscard should watch out, as the UDF will fall into my hands."[15] De Villiers announced that he would campaign for the no, although not officially joining the Séguin-Pasqua sponsored movement *Rassemblement pour le "non" au référendum* (Movement for the "no" in the referendum).

The green movement also experienced internal dissension. Antoine Waechter, leader of the *Verts* (Greens), and Brice Lalonde, founder of *Génération Ecologie* (Ecology Generation—GE), were both pro-Maastricht in their orientation. However, the uncertainty of the green electorate in France (being a relatively new phenomenon), made any official party position difficult to formulate. Lalonde was the less constrained of the two leaders as a consequence of both the more hierarchical organization of the GE and the less-developed membership at the local level; he announced that he would campaign for ratification of the Maastricht Treaty. Waechter, on the other hand, found himself confronted by significant opposition within the *Conseil national interrégional* (CNIR), the governing body of the *Verts*. A final decision was deferred until August, when the CNIR split almost equally on the issue, the no faction being led by Dominique Voynet and Alan Lipietz. Thus the party did not elaborate any official position on the referendum, although Waechter himself continued to campaign for it *à titre personnel* (on a personal basis).

The PS, purportedly the beneficiary of Mitterrand's strategy, did not escape its own rift, albeit less dramatic than those recounted above. It was not surprising that Jean-Pierre Chevènment chose to defy the government over this issue, as he represented a wing of the party that had traditionally been hostile to European integration. Chevènment was also in a state of virtual rupture with the party leadership at this moment, and the Maastricht debate was merely the catalyst in an ongoing discussion about the direction of the socialist movement. However, Chevènment was a figure of some stature in the party whose reputation exceeded the 7.43 percent of the party membership that was ascribed to his faction, *Socialisme et République,* at the party conference in July. It was at that moment that

Chevènment announced his resignation from all leadership functions within the PS to concentrate on campaigning against the Treaty.

Not surprising was the decision of both the PCF and the FN to oppose the Maastricht Treaty. Both parties had consistently opposed it since the original negotiation, and had already begun to wage a public campaign against this next step in the integration process even before the announcement of the referendum. However, the PCF in particular took its opposition to Maastricht to a degree that was unprecedented, opening the pages of its official organ *l'Humanité* to almost anyone hostile to the yes position, including a prominent RPR senator from the Dordogne, Yves Guéna. Other left wing groups were formed to promote the no, by those such as Max Gallo (a former spokesperson for the PS) and Daniel Bensaïd, member of the extreme-left Ligue Communiste Révolutionnaire (LCR). More ecumenical was the *Comité pour une autre Europe* (Committee for a Different Europe), led by a curious alliance of left-Gaullists, Socialists, and ex-Communists.

The campaign itself was marked initially by the failure of the government to become fully engaged. Indeed, the early strategy was to leave any pro-Maastricht campaigning to individual leaders and their party organizations until the opening of the official campaign on September 7. The splits within the RPR, the defection of de Villiers, and the party conference of the PS in mid-July kept each of the major pro-Maastricht forces from assuming any great role in this early period. Thus momentum lay with the opposition forces throughout June and July. By mid-summer, it was becoming clear to Mitterrand and his close advisors that the referendum was in trouble. Despite earlier more optimistic forecasts, two successive polls conducted by IFOP (in June) and IPSOS (in July) cast doubt upon the outcome. These surveys indicated that the yes vote had not gained any ground since the announcement of the referendum, in contrast to the no. According to Jean-Marc Lech, president of IPSOS, the yes vote would not progress beyond the 52 percent that it was then showing in the two polls, despite more favorable showings in other surveys of public opinion.[16]

The response of the government was to launch a hastily coordinated campaign under the guidance of the charismatic and popular Jack Lang. In mid-August Lang announced the formation of a *Comité national pour le oui* (National Committee for the Yes) and also succeeded in persuading Mitterrand to do a live interview on television on September 3. However, Lang's leadership was criticized within the government as opinion polls continued to show a deterioration of the yes position through August. For example, Jean Le Garrec denounced what he saw as the "gimmicky" side of Lang's initiatives, arguing that it was necessary to inform the public and debate the issues, rather than relying on media-oriented slogans.

The errors of the campaign bordered on the comic, as I have described elsewhere.[17] The late entry of both Giscard and Chirac reflected the growing alarm amongst the pro-Maastricht political class that the unthinkable could happen and that the referendum could produce the defeat of the treaty. Suddenly it was not enough to watch the government being embarrassed by a close vote, for a defeat of the treaty would signal a defeat of the pro-integration position shared by the majority of that elite. The discourse became more threatening; to vote no would be to dismantle Europe, to reject the past forty years, to destabilize the French franc and the economy, to undermine the international credibility of the country, and to throw the party system into chaos. It may well be that this element of fear was reinforced at the last moment by the turmoil in the currency markets. Similarly, the eleventh-hour announcement of Mitterrand's ill-health may have neutralized the proclivity of some potential voters to use the referendum as a vehicle to attack his presidency. The extraordinarily close outcome left the political elite relieved but nervous.

Integration and the Bifurcated French: Anomaly or Trend?

A second question posed at the beginning of this chapter was to what extent the Maastricht referendum was revelatory of wider trends in public attitudes towards European integration? Was the vote an anomaly or part of a trend? Clearly the outcome (while positive) contradicted the optimistic assessments heard at the end of May. Yet it is possible that the vote reflects a more profound bifurcation in the French electorate, one that transcends the Maastricht Treaty and that encompasses conflicting views of the national state in the modern integrative environment. The availability of opinion poll data allows for a careful examination of this question that has profound implications for governance in the post-industrial world. In particular, three opinion polls will be analyzed in detail here: the first is the Eurobarometer survey EB37.0 compiled by INRA at the request of the Commission of the European Community; the second is a pre-referendum, post-announcement poll carried out by BVA on June 5-6, 1992; and the third source is a post-referendum survey also conducted by BVA between May 1-15, 1993 in the wake of the March 1993 legislative elections.[18]

TABLE 12.1
SOLIDITY OF VOTING INTENTIONS FOR DECLARED POSITIONS

	Definite	Could Change	Total
Yes	n=264	152	416
	63.5%	36.5%	64.8%
No	133	93	226
	58.8%	41.2%	35.2%
Column	397	245	642
Total	61.8%	38.2%	100.0%

Source: BVA

As mentioned above, initial opinion poll data seemed to show that a majority of potential voters would endorse the Maastricht Treaty. In the pre-referendum BVA poll, 45 percent of respondents said that they would cast a yes vote, while only 24 percent replied that they would vote no. Of the rest, an additional 24 percent declared that they were undecided. However, indecision over voting choice was not a reflection of apathy; only 19 percent of the whole sample said that they would not be participating in the plebiscite (almost perfectly matching the actual participation rate). Of the 82 percent who reported that they would vote, only 3 percent (of the total sample) thought that their turnout was uncertain.

As far as the stability of the declared vote both for and against the Treaty is concerned, table 12.1 shows that probable yes voters appeared to be slightly more definitive about their decision, although not to a significant degree.

Thus we can discount the notion that the Maastricht debate was a product of voter apathy that later turned to resentment, for voting intentions were high from the start. We can also discount the notion that the outcome represented a massive sanction against Mitterrand, although some voters were no doubt motivated by this position; in the post-referendum poll, only 18 percent said that opposition to Mitterrand had played a significant role in their decision. So, if voters were neither apathetic and mobilized late nor simply anti-Mitterrand, were they drawn to the voting booths by deeper, more underlying forces? In order to examine this hypothesis, it is useful to refer to three different models of electoral participation that each make some claims about the nature of attitudes in the electorate towards European integration. These models are often referred to as the *sociological*, the *new politics*, and the *partisan identification* models.

The first is derived from the processes of party system formation described by Seymour Martin Lipset and Stein Rokkan.[19] In that classic study that spawned the development of political sociology in the study of European party politics, it was argued that two revolutions had effectively established the parameters of political participation in modern European states. Each of those revolutions was responsible for the creation of two cleavages. The national revolution produced a dichotomy between center and periphery, and between church and state; these were termed *segmental* cleavages. The industrial revolution engendered deep-rooted cleavages between landed and industrial interests, and between owners and workers (capital and labor); these were labeled *economic* cleavages.

Thus, according to the dictates of the model, modern European party systems are based on cleavage structures that are in turn a product of sequential interactions along these four dimensions. The timing and character of the two revolutions along with the divergences in the nature of cleavages generated can account for a high proportion of variance observed across party systems when engaged in comparative analysis. Most important, however, is the notion that these cleavage structures in most cases preceded the establishment of modern party systems, and remained the basis of party politics in the post–war era. In Lipset and Rokkan's own words, "... the party systems of the 1960's reflect, with few but significant exceptions, the cleavage structures of the 1920's."[20]

At the level of the individual voter, the sociological model predicts that voting choices will be determined on the basis of the hierarchical ordering of cleavage effects. A succession of studies showed that the two most salient cleavages in explaining voter preferences in Europe have been class and religion. The former has often been replaced in the analysis by left-right location as measured by expectations for government intervention in the economy. The latter is to be understood less in terms of confessional differences (that do exist) than in the degree of religiosity as measured, for example, by the frequency of participation in services. Other cleavages are still salient for some categories of voters; for example, the center-periphery cleavage has been seen as a major explanatory force in Norway, Great Britain, and recently Italy.[21]

While Lipset and Rokkan established the taxonomic power of the cleavage model, additional scholarship has suggested that these "frozen" cleavages may be giving way or evolving in a manner that is contributing to the turbulence in party systems mentioned above. Erik Allardt argued that post–war European societies are witnessing a third upheaval, which he termed the educational revolution.[22] In the mid-1970s, empirical evidence was assembled that provides support for Allardt's identification of a new emerging cleavage structure. Ronald Inglehart identified a set of core "quality of life" values that cut across old cleavage structures and that have given rise to the material/post-material divide.[23] Younger voters, socialized into the political process during the material prosperity and high growth of the post-war years, are much less likely to adopt orientations based on class or religion; instead they are, according to Inglehart, more concerned with quality of life issues that do not fall on the Downsian left-right scale. This new type of citizen he termed post-materialist. Inglehart has argued that the sociological predictors inherent in the Lipset and Rokkan framework are losing salience in comparison to new predictors based on the properties of post-materialism.

The most recent developments in political sociology suggest the presence of two new cleavage structures.[24] The first may be termed an establishment/anti-establishment cleavage. This "aligns various establishment institutions, such as the bureaucracy, the police, and occasionally the clergy, against new agents of social change such as radicals, student protesters, the women's movement, and minority groups."[25] The second new cleavage involves 'quality of life concerns"; the environment, anti-nuclear orientations, sexual equality, human rights, consumer advocacy, and 'the new morality." However, the same evidence also points to a persistence of the older left-right economic cleavages; furthermore, some have argued that the resurgence of ethnic and regionalist movements in the past two decades indicates a renewed salience of segmental cleavages that were not resolved prior to the twentieth century. Kitschelt and Hellmans have suggested that Inglehart's notion of the transformation of the meaning of left and right into a new dimension of post-material value orientations is better understood as a pluralization of the meanings of left and right.[26] Nonetheless, these approaches, despite differences in nuance, can be collectively labeled *new politics* models.

The two models of participation described above share a common assumption, namely that partisan preferences are structured at the individual level by independent sociological or value-based effects, and that the accumulation of preferences then determines the strength of party support. However, the *partisan identification* model emphasizes the importance of the enduring quality of voters' attachments to party positions. The critical difference is that according to this model, voters look to parties for cues in determining their positions on issues.[27] Thus individual orientations are dependent upon party identification and party position. This does not contradict the importance of the cleavages in the structuring of the party system, but the model underscores the freezing detected by Lipset and Rokkan since the 1920s.

What do each of these models inform us about European integration? The sociological model highlighted the importance of the national revolution in the development of modern European polities, and the structuring of church-state and center-periphery relations. It could be assumed, as did Roy Pierce, Henry Valen, and Oleg Listhaug in their study of referenda voting on the EC issue in Britain and Norway,[28] that voters in the periphery would be less supportive of European integration than those in the center. Presumably this would be explained by the image of the European Community as an artifact of national state governments. However, developments in European integration since the early 1970s, including the growth in structural and cohesion funds and the establishment of a Committee of the Regions, could have served to gain the support of those in the periphery seeking to loosen the effects of centralized national state control.

Similarly, it could be argued that the gradual transfer or pooling of sovereignty to the supranational level would engender the hostility of more religious sectors of the population. In Britain, for example, the Church of England is a national institution, and it would be logical to assume that the erosion of the Church of England's power implied in the process of integration would be opposed by the most religious elements within its ranks. Similarly, events surrounding the abortion issue in Ireland have shown how Catholic hostility towards the European Union can be stirred up. Yet Emmanuel Todd explained what he saw as the predisposition of Catholics in France to support the Maastricht Treaty as a function of ultramontanism, Catholic loyalties to the national state in France having been historically weaker than other groups.[29]

Clearly logical deductions can be used to predict both support for and rejection of European integration from peripheral and religious groups. However, it is clear that integration to some degree undoes the national revolution in the modern European polity, and that this should have discernible consequences for the sociological model. The same point can be made about economic structures. To the extent that the Single Market is a vast exercise in deregulation (the Thatcherian vision), support should be found on the Right where there is a desire for less government intervention in the economy. However, the European Union of Jacques Delors is also one that promotes the social dimension of integration and that has sought the transfer of certain economic policymaking functions to the center, which could garner the support of those on the Left who are historically wedded to more government intervention in these areas.

Work on the new political cleavages has indicated that those with postmaterialist value-sets are more informed and more participatory than materialists. In addition, they are less attached to the traditional political institutions and intermediary organizations of the liberal democratic state. Postmaterialists are more supportive of European integration and more willing to abandon nationalist positions, a finding reproduced in several recent studies. Assuming that the new politics model of citizen participation and voting behavior has a high degree of explanatory power, it would be safe to assume strong support for the Maastricht Treaty should be within the postmaterial cohort, with the materialists being somewhat opposed.

The partisan identification model would predict that, where political party elites have taken a cohesive position towards the integration of European countries, their supporters would be likely to adopt the same position. However, where parties have been split or unable to clearly define their position, loyal party followers will be similarly divided in their positioning on the issue. The history of European integration has exposed the difficulties facing national political parties in elaborating clear and consistent positions; the Danish "earthquake" election of 1973 was but one dramatic example of a party system fractured by the issue of national sovereignty versus closer integration.

Pierce, Valen, and Listhaug argued in their analysis of the referenda in 1973 in Norway and 1975 in Britain that the central explanatory factor in determining voter positions was partisanship, with a lesser left-right effect evident and a still weaker center-periphery relationship detected, thus giving partial confirmation to two of the three models discussed above. The post-referendum survey in France affords the opportunity to partially reproduce the Pierce, Valen, and Listhaug study for the Maastricht referendum, as it contains left-right, urban-rural, and partisan identification items.

In fact, careful analysis of the data indicates limited support for each of these three models. Using techniques of multivariate analysis, both the urban-rural cleavage and partisan identification were shown to have an impact upon vote choice in the referendum. Voters in more urban communes and those who had previously voted for parties promoting Maastricht tended to be more pro-treaty. Neither left-right orientation nor religiosity had any significant impact upon vote choice in this test. In addition, the information contained in the pre-referendum Eurobarometer survey

TABLE 12.2
CROSS-TABULATION OF VOTE DECISION WITH VOTE IN THE 1993 LEGISLATIVE ELECTIONS

	Yes	No	Spoiled	Abstained
Parti Communiste	25	61	6	22
Parti Socialiste	65	18	2	12
Génération Ecologie	55	26	4	15
Les Verts	53	19	7	21
UDF	58	30	2	11
RPR	51	41	1	7
Front National	26	59	0	16

Note: all figures are percentages within rows.

indicated that there was a positive correlation between post-material value sets and a pro-Maastricht orientation, controlling for the other variables discussed above. This evidence is important, for it demonstrates that voters were behaving in predictable and understandable ways according to models of participation developed in a broader context.

Moving away from the determinants, what are the consequences of the Maastricht referendum, in particular for the party system? Does the continued salience of partisan identification provide cause for comfort to party leaders in an era of high levels of apathy and distrust? It must be recalled that European integration had an explosive effect on the Danish party system in the early 1970s and has continued to pose challenges to parties across the continent from the British Conservatives to the Greek Socialists.

Polls in France showed that a remarkable proportion of the electorate was prepared to "disobey" party leaders in the referendum. Table 12.2 gives the cross-tabulation of reported voting in the 1993 legislative elections with vote position drawn from the post-referendum sample. These figures reveal the degree to which partisan loyalties were strained by the Maastricht referendum process. But was this unusual? Put in a broader context, these figures actually demonstrate a remarkable stability when matched with prior attitudes towards European integration. Table 12.3 shows the support for either the Treaty or the European Community in general, broken down by declared partisan identification. The patterns revealed in these data are quite extraordinary. Between the announcement and the actual vote, voting positions (reported in the June 1992 and May 1993 samples) for parties that were not split barely moved. However, the three partisan groups that show large movement were those that were deeply split over the referendum (les Verts, the UDF, and the RPR).

TABLE 12.3
CROSS-TABULATION OF POSITIVE ATTITUDES WITH PARTISAN IDENTIFICATION

	June 1992	May 1993	Difference	March 1992	Difference 1992-93
Parti Socialiste	63.1	63.8	+0.7	64.1	-0.3
Génération Ecologie	54.4	54.6	+0.2	na	na
Les Verts	31.6	49.1	+17.5	na	na
UDF	43.1	57.6	+14.5	57.7	-0.1
RPR	38.0	49.3	+11.3	50.8	-1.5
Parti Communiste	20.8	24.4	+3.6	43.7	-19.3
Front National	21.3	23.4	+2.1	25.8	-2.4
Combined ecologists	45.3	53.5	+7.2	57.7	-4.2

Note: figures for March 1992 show percent expressing support for the European Community.

Truly impressive is the correspondence between positive attitudes towards the European Community reported in the Eurobarometer survey conducted over two months prior to the announcement of the referendum and the actual vote of partisan identifiers reported seven months after the ballot in the BVA poll. With the exception of PCF partisans, all differences between the two items across samples are contained within the margins of error. Thus the data contain a paradox. On the one hand, partisan identification is evidently a significant and durable factor in determining voter attitudes towards European integration in general and the Maastricht Treaty in particular, which should reassure those who fear its decline. On the other hand, splits within party elites over the issue are reproduced at the mass level, and this too appears to be an enduring phenomenon.

One final piece of evidence was assembled to examine the possible dislocating effects of a vote against the party position in the Treaty referendum. The post-referendum sample contained both a question about reported partisan identification and a reconstruction of voting preferences in the March 1993 legislative elections. These two items were matched for respondents; those who voted in March 1993 in accordance with their declared partisan situation were placed in one category, while those who opted for a voting choice contrary to their declared partisan affiliation were placed in a second (these were labeled "switchers"). A second variable was created that related the individual vote in the referendum to whether the respondent's party had campaigned for or against the treaty. Those who voted against the party position were labeled as "defiers" (it should be noted that the procedure restricted this part of the analysis to partisans of the PS, GE, PCF, and FN).

These new variables were explored. Out of the 729 respondents who were declared partisans of these parties, 333 (or nearly 46 percent) had behaved in a manner contrary to the official party position during the Maastricht vote. From the for-and-against parties group, 76 were identified who were "switchers"; 43 of these (57 percent) were also "defiers." The cross-tabulation of these two variables yielded a chi-square coefficient of 4.91, significant at the .05 level (.0267). This result indicates a statistically significant positive relationship between defying the party position in the referendum and crossing party lines in the subsequent legislative election. No causality is implied, but it does suggest that the relative strength of partisanship is also enduring for individual voters. It should also be noted that neither defiers nor switchers are less interested in politics than others; in fact 70 percent of defiers and 59 percent of switchers declared that they were either very interested or interested in politics, compared to 54 percent and 55 percent respectively of their more compliant counterparts.

Finally, those who defied the party position on the Maastricht referendum tended to be both younger and less educated than others; neither gender, income, or left-right orientation appeared to correlate with party identifiers who voted against the party position in September 1992. Age and education level together allowed the correct prediction of 74 percent of those who voted with their party and 52 percent who voted against, overall 64 percent of those included in the analysis. This last result is intriguing, for it suggests two quite different possibilities. The first is that, given that partisan identification is acquired over time, it seems that younger voters would be more likely to defy party positions. The second possible interpretation is that younger voters are simply less attached to party positions, entering the political arena in an era of anti-partyism and voter volatility. In the post-referendum sample there was no correlation evident between the lack of party identification and age, meaning that the critical factor is the strength of that identification, for which no stand-alone item was available on the survey.

So, to summarize this section, the following can be stated. First, voter orientations towards Maastricht at the individual level were in part determined by factors related to models of voter behavior that have been developed exogenous to that particular issue. Second, party loyalties were placed under great strain as a result of this referendum; however, these strains are evident in the broader issue area of European integration and transcend the immediate episode of the referendum. Third, these strains have had a subsequent impact upon voter behavior. While it cannot be argued that European integration alone cuts across party lines and produces voter dislocation, it is another policy area where the party elite find themselves at odds with their supporters.

Conclusion

This chapter has demonstrated that the Maastricht referendum result was neither the earthquake nor the abnormal event that many observers initially labeled it to be. While it must be cautioned that an over reliance can sometimes be placed on survey data at the cost of good qualitative and contextual analysis, the patterns in the electorate revealed through the information presented above are quite fascinating. Despite the apparent depth of support for the Maastricht Treaty that was initially thought to be present, the solidification of the no electorate in retrospect looks somewhat less surprising than has sometimes been argued. Perhaps what is more surprising, given the findings in the first part of this chapter, is the disjunction between elite-level support for the treaty and mass-level attitudes. As the second part of the analysis has shown, these patterns in the electorate persist beyond the Maastricht debate and are symptomatic of wider orientations towards European integration.

The constitutional amendments enabling the Maastricht Treaty were established in the National Assembly in early May 1992 by a margin of 398 votes for to 77 against, with 99 abstentions. Clearly this vote distribution was quite at odds with the outcome of the referendum; the only party group to oppose the amendments was the PCF. Studies of party elites and supporters have demonstrated a strong correlation between the political positions of party elites and their supporters, which is not necessarily contradicted by the findings presented above. The strength and persistence of partisanship is one of the interesting discoveries.

But it is noteworthy that the political elite in France, with the exception of the PCF and the FN, displays a strong pro-integration bias. Even within the parties that split over the referendum, the principal leaders all supported the yes position (Giscard d'Estaing, Chirac, Waechter). Those who opposed the treaty, such as Pasqua, Séguin, and de Villiers, were regarded as dissidents by their respective party organizations. While this study has shown that those campaigning against the position of their party's leadership in the name of the party commanded a significant portion of the vote, it may be that the greater effect of European integration on the party system lies in the distancing of the political class from the mass electorate. A no vote was not only a vote against the treaty but it was also a vote against all of the leading presidential contenders *(présidentiables)* within the "parties of government."[30]

The resonance of the Maastricht referendum can be detected in 1994 European elections, where the PS, the UDF, and the RPR garnered an underwhelming 40 percent of the vote, compared to a similar total for the PCF, the FN, and the anti-Maastricht movement of Philippe de Villiers. While the addition of the Mouvement des Radicaux de Gauche (MRG) list headed by Bernard Tapie meant that pro-Europe forces counted for about half the electorate, the presence of anti-Europe ecologists—the anti-European section of the RPR that nonetheless voted with the party—and "other" lists who were in the main anti-Europe, meant that the other half was almost certainly anti-integration.

From a policy perspective, this is troubling. The European Union is increasingly present in the domestic arena, both through direct action and through the filtration of European law. Yet it is not being met with unbridled enthusiasm on the part of its clients. There is a paradox. As French policy elites argue for the migration of power to the European level to solve increasingly complex issues arising from interdependence, they are being challenged by their constituents who have frequently challenged the elites' own use of that power. The party system that emerged around the newly enabled policymaking institutions of the Fifth Republic is coming under stress as those same institutions evolve in the European context. Perhaps the "national revolution" of Lipset and Rokkan is being undone; or perhaps a "supranational revolution" is in the making. Whichever is the case, it surely challenges the capacity of the French system to effectively aggregate interests.

The additional concern since the presidential elections of 1995 is that the institutional hegemony of the Right magnifies the importance of the fracture within that particular portion of the electorate. President Chirac had been noticeably more reticent on the European issue throughout his campaign (which really began many months before the election), as a consequence of the Maastricht morass. Ho ever, the demands of office have impelled him to reiterate, at least on a symbolic level, the depth of French involvement in and commitment to the construction of Europe. While Chirac as president may have outgrown his campaign machine, the RPR in particular is faced with the task of redefining itself and forging an ongoing relationship with the electorate. European integration complicates this task.

To conclude, the findings of this study provide mixed comfort for those concerned about party democracy in France in the 1990s. On the one hand, partisan identification remains important among the electorate, even in cases where dominant issues cut through party lines. On the other hand, the fact that the issue in question, European integration, reveals rather different patterns of support at the elite and the mass levels is of concern. As many have remarked, the Maastricht debate in Europe in general highlighted the technocratic and elite-driven nature of the integration process. The French data may simply reflect the democratic deficit inherent in the structure and operations of the European Community, and as long as the institutions of that body remain seemingly beyond citizen influence, the mass public may have greater difficulty in supporting integrative efforts than their appointed leaders.

Notes to Chapter 12

1. Popularly known as the Maastricht Treaty, named after the Dutch town where the Treaty had been approved at a meeting of the European Council in December 1991.
2. Mitterrand alluded to this on his return from Sarajevo in June when he remarked that the yes vote would reach 60 percent of the electorate *(L'Express,* September 18-24, 1992).
3. A SOFRES poll in May showed a two-to-one majority in favor of the Treaty, although 40% of respondents were uncommitted *(Le Monde,* May 20, 1992).
4. A. Appleton, "Maastricht and the French Party System: Domestic Implications of the Treaty Referendum," *French Politics and Society* 10, no. 4 (fall 1992).
5. *Le Monde,* May 4, 1992.
6. *Le Monde,* May 14, 1992.
7. Ibid.
8. This was done on July 1st, when it was decided to open the official campaign on September 7 and to hold the referendum on September 20.
9. *Le Nouvel Observateur,* July 30-August 5, 1992, p. 29.
10. *Le Nouvel Observateur,* June 11-17, 1992, p.31.
11. Ibid.
12. *Le Monde,* June 23, 1992.

13. *Le Monde*, July 7, 1992.
14. *Le Nouvel Observateur*, July 2-8, 1992, p.34.
15. *Le Nouvel Observateur*, September 10-16, 1992, p. 24.
16. *L'Express*, September 18-24, 1992.
17. A. Appleton.
18. Eurobarometer 37.0 was provided by the Inter-University Consortium for Political and Social Research at the University of Michigan. BVA Period 272 and BVA Period 273 were made available by the Banque de Données Socio-Politiques at the CIDSP in Grenoble. I gratefully acknowledge the assistance provided by the CIDSP and its director, Bernard Bouhet.
19. S. M. Lipset and S. Rokkan, "Cleavage Structures, Party Systems, and Voter Alignments" in S. M. Lipset and S. Rokkan, eds., *Party Systems and Voter Alignments* (New York: The Free Press, 1967).
20. Ibid.
21. See, for example, S. Rokkan, "Norway: Numerical Democracy and Corporate Pluralism" in R. Dahl, ed., *Political Oppositions in Western Democracies* (New Haven: Yale University Press, 1966); D. Butler and D. Stokes, *Political Change in Britain: Forces Shaping Electoral Choice* (New York: St. Martin's Press, 1969); R. Putnam, *Making Democracy Work: Civic Traditions in Modern Italy* (Princeton: Princeton University Press, 1993).
22. E. Allardt, "Past and Emerging Cleavages" in O. Stammer, ed., *Party Systems, Party Organizations, and the Politics of the New Masses* (Berlin: Free University Press, 1968).
23. R. Inglehart, *The Silent Revolution: Changing Values and Political Styles Among Western Publics* (Princeton: Princeton University Press, 1977).
24. See S. Flanagan and R. Dalton, "Parties Under Stress: Realignment and Dealignment in Advanced Industrial Societies" *West European Politics*, 7, no. 4, (winter 1984); S. Flanagan, R. Dalton, and M. Lewis-Beck, eds., *Electoral Change in Advanced Industrial Democracies: Realignment or Dealignment?* (Princeton: Princeton University Press, 1984).
25. S. Flanagan and R. Dalton, p. 19.
26. H. Kitschelt and S. Hellmans, "The Left-Right Semantics and the New Politics Cleavage," *Comparative Political Studies* 23, no. 2, (July 1990).
27. This proposition was investigated and confirmed for the French case by P. Converse and R. Pierce, *Political Representation in France* (Cambridge: Harvard University Press, 1986).

28. R. Pierce, H. Valen, and O. Listhaug, "Referendum Voting Behavior: The Norwegian and British Referenda on Membership in the European Community," *American Journal of Political Science* 27, no. 1, (February 1983).
29. E. Todd, "Le grand retour de la France jacobine," *Le Nouvel Observateur*, September 24-30, 1992.
30. Séguin and Pasqua began to be thought of as *présidentiable* only in the wake of the referendum with the unexpected breakthrough of the no vote.

Chapter 13

National Interest, the Dilemmas of European Integration, and Malaise

David R. Cameron

As the Mitterrand era came to an end and the Chirac era began, France was afflicted with a malaise, a sense of unease, that reflected both a dissatisfaction with the present and a diffuse anxiety about the future. In large part, this sense of malaise resulted from the accumulation of a plethora of social, economic, and political problems—high levels of unemployment despite an economic recovery, increasing evidence of a fracture sociale, urban decay and squalor that was becoming increasingly visible, and innumerable scandals and indictments of political officials and economic leaders—coupled with the apparent inability of the nation's political institutions to rectify those problems. Although the constitution of the Fifth Republic endowed the presidency with considerable powers, Mitterrand, in his last years in office, appeared weakened and unable to resolve those problems not only by old age and ill health but, also, by the demise of French Socialism as a political force and his own diminished popularity. And although the government headed by Edouard Balladur after the 1993 legislative elections commanded a large majority in the National Assembly, it often appeared to act more as a caretaker—prudent, cautious, maintaining the status quo, attempting to please all and offend none in the run-up to the 1995 presidential elections—rather than as the instrument of a newly elected conservative majority. As a result, although powerful in formal institutional terms, both the president and the government appeared curiously passive, incapable of addressing the multitude of social and economic problems facing the country, and unable to chart a course for the future.

After his election as President, Jacques Chirac brought to the Elysée a refreshing sense of vigor, dynamism, and moral authority and there was good reason to imagine that the malaise that had afflicted France in the last years of the Mitterrand presidency would give way to a new sense of governmental capacity and competence, if only because of the new president's energy, vitality, and drive—traits that early on had earned him the nickname le bulldozer. And yet within weeks of his assumption of office, Chirac (and his Prime Minister Alain Juppé) experienced a dramatic decrease in popularity that contributed to an equally dramatic further erosion in the French public's perception of governmental competence. And as the popularity of Chirac, Juppé, and the government in general reached new depths, France experienced a sustained three-week strike throughout the public sector in late November and the first half of December 1995, that gave expression to all of the grievances, dissatisfaction, and sense of malaise that had accumulated in French political life in the late 1980s and 1990s.

In addition to everything else the strikes of November–December 1995 and the deep-seated collective sense of malaise that underlay the strikes may have represented, they were also responses to and expressions of dissatisfaction with France's evolving role in, and relation to, the European Union—dissatisfaction that, paradoxically, grew stronger as the country's commitment to Europe deepened. Indeed, to a very large extent they were the direct result of policy proposals that derived from the European commitments undertaken by Mitterrand and various governments during his two seven-year terms. And even after the strikes had ended the continuing malaise and grievances that generated them, coupled with the unusually low popularity levels of the new president and government, constituted a dilemma of the first magnitude for Chirac and the French government. Their dilemma—how to honor the commitments to Europe while also alleviating the high levels of unemployment and raising their own low levels of popularity—was made more acute by the fact that the president's party, the *Rassemblement pour la République* (RPR), remained deeply divided over Europe and found itself facing a growing anti-Europe opposition on the Right, a public that was increasingly skeptical about the value of participation in the European Union, and the prospect of legislative elections in early 1998.

This chapter examines the European sources and symptoms of the French malaise, as they appeared in the last years of the Mitterrand era, and the dilemmas posed for President Chirac and his governments by France's deepened commitments to Europe. In the first section of the chapter, I consider the several steps by which France's commitment to Europe deepened in the 1980s and early 1990s. Beginning with the creation of the European Monetary System in the late 1970s and culminating with the negotiation and approval of the Treaty on European Union, France committed itself to pursuing, with its partners in the Community, an economic policy that increasingly emphasized deregulation, liberalization, fiscal restraint, price stability, and a strong currency. In addition, the government relinquished some degree of control over its economy, either to the European Commission or, more recently, to the newly independent *Banque de France*. As its commitment to Europe deepened, France's preferences and interests became increasingly intertwined with, and often indistinguishable from, those of its European partners—especially those of Germany, its most important trading partner and closest political ally in the Community. And as that happened, its sense of national interest increasingly came to be defined in terms synonymous with its growing European identity.

In the second section of the chapter, I consider to what extent and in what ways the attitudes of French citizens to Europe have changed in recent years. Data from a series of Eurobarometer surveys suggest that support for the Community increased in France and the other member states throughout the 1980s as France, and the other members, adhered to the nascent European monetary regime and committed themselves to the European initiatives of the 1980s. But the data also suggest a sharp erosion in support for Europe throughout the Community in the post-Maastricht era—one that was especially sharp in France. A number of reasons are adduced for the erosion of support for the Community in France.

In the third section of the chapter, I consider the dilemma that European integration poses for France in general, and President Chirac in particular, in the late 1990s. It is a dilemma created by the deep and formalized commitment to Europe, on one hand, and the erosion in public support for the Union, low levels of popularity of the president and government, and persisting high levels of unemployment, on the other. If France is to qualify for the third and final stage of the Economic and Monetary Union in 1999, for example, the government must pursue a policy of fiscal contraction and austerity, notwithstanding the current low rates of economic growth and high levels of unemployment, and it must do so at a time when the public has become increasingly skeptical about the benefit of EU membership, the president and prime minister have suffered sharp erosions in their popularity, and the governing parties face legislative elections in 1998. The dilemma faced by Chirac and his government involves more than simply choosing between a policy of fiscal contraction that honors France's European commitments to EMU and one of domestic reflation that would allow them to increase the rate of economic growth, reduce unemployment, increase their personal popularity, and improve the electoral fortunes of the governing parties. Rather, the dilemma involves something more complex: whether they can achieve *both* sets of objectives simultaneously—that is, whether they can honor their European commitments *and* attend to the economic problems facing the country as well as their own political concerns—and if so, how. That, I suggest, is the real dilemma of European integration that France and Chirac face in the coming years.

Deepening the Commitments to Europe

After de Gaulle resigned as president in 1969, his successors sought to relaunch the Community, hoping to move it beyond the disputes over British membership and the right of members to exercise a veto in the Council that had dominated the Community—and French policy toward it—in the 1960s. Pompidou reopened the possibility of British membership and, along with his colleagues, endorsed the concept of Economic and Monetary Union and committed France, with its partners, to achieving EMU by 1980. Later, after Britain, Ireland, and Denmark had joined the Community, Pompidou's successor, Giscard d'Estaing, renewed the commitment to EMU and, with his friend and colleague Helmut Schmidt, introduced two institutional innovations—a European Council composed of the national leaders and direct election of the European Parliament—that transformed politics within the Community. And later still, near the end of his term, Giscard, with Schmidt and a few others, created the European Monetary System (EMS) to alleviate the fluctuations and volatility among exchange rates that were wreaking havoc with the Common Agricultural Policy and impeding the development of the Common Market. After defeating Giscard in 1981, François Mitterrand presided, during his two *septennats*, over a further deepening of France's commitment to

Europe—a deepening that led the Community to undertake sweeping new initiatives, first to institute a single internal market and, later, to transform itself into a Union. In this section, we consider the successive steps by which that commitment to Europe deepened, beginning with the creation of the EMS in 1979 and culminating with the Treaty on European Union signed at Maastricht in early 1992.[1]

The European Monetary System

By the end of the 1960s, the European Community had established a Common Agricultural Policy, featuring common prices for agricultural commodities, and a tariff-free Common Market in goods and services. The success of both depended, crucially, on the maintenance of stable exchange rates among the participating states—which largely explains why the Community began to explore, immediately after the establishment of both, the creation of an Economic and Monetary Union.[2] In 1971, the Bretton Woods fixed exchange rate regime—whose premises had already been called into question by the willingness of American governments to tolerate relatively high rates of inflation in the late 1960s—teetered on the brink of collapse after the Nixon administration's decision, in August 1971, to close the Treasury's "gold window" and the subsequent decision, at the International Monetary Fund's (IMF) Smithsonian conference in December 1971, to devalue the dollar and widen the fluctuation range between the dollar and other currencies. In order to dampen the greater fluctuation among currencies that could occur in the new exchange rate regime, in April 1972, the Europeans introduced the "snake," a targeted fluctuation range for their currencies that was one-half the width of the new band.

While the "snake" was designed to dampen the volatility and fluctuation among European Community currencies, it had no mechanism for joint interventions by central banks to defend weak currencies, nor any norms about the appropriate behavior of countries with weak and strong currencies, nor any institutional framework for negotiating realignments when interventions and changes in interest rates failed to maintain the existing rates. As a result, when weak currencies sank to the bottom of their fluctuation bands with other currencies, they simply fell through the floor and out of the "snake." Thus, by 1976, the British pound, the Irish punt, the Italian lira, and the French franc had all dropped out—the franc, in fact, twice, once in January 1974 and again in March 1976. By that time, only the German mark and the currencies of several of Germany's small neighbors (including some that were not members of the EC) remained in the "snake." Clearly, for a group of states committed to common prices for agricultural commodities, and a Common Market in goods and services, the existence of a core of currencies closely linked to the mark and another group that floated was deeply problematic.

The European Monetary System came into being in March 1979, in order to create what Helmut Schmidt, then the German chancellor and one of its principal architects, called a "zone of monetary stability."[3] Conceived in the wake of the demise of the Bretton Woods exchange rate regime, the OPEC price shock of 1973—74, increasing rates of inflation, and increasing exchange rate volatility, the EMS represented an effort to repair the defects of the "snake." While retaining some features of the "snake," such as its parity grid of currencies and the fluctuation range of + 2.25 percent for each currency, it introduced several changes—most notably, an exchange rate mechanism through which the grid could be monitored and changes in exchange rates implemented, a credit facility through which countries could borrow foreign exchange in order to defend their currencies, an expectation that both strong-currency and weak-currency countries would intervene in currency markets or adjust interest rates and macroeconomic policy in order to defend existing rates, and an institutional framework for negotiating realignments when interventions and changes in monetary policy proved incapable of defending those rates.

For countries with strong currencies, the EMS provided obvious advantages. By tying their currencies to weaker ones, it offered the prospect of dampening the rate of appreciation in the value of their currencies and thus dampening currency-based increases in the prices of their goods in export markets. At the same time, the EMS diminished the likelihood that its trading partners would enhance the competitiveness of *their* exports by devaluing their currencies or allowing them to float downward. On the other hand, for countries with weak currencies that had fallen out of the "snake," membership in the EMS meant committing themselves to a strong-currency policy, relative to the policy they had previously pursued, in order to keep their currencies close to the mark. That meant pursuing a monetary policy that targeted the exchange rate rather than domestic growth and that kept interest rates high enough to maintain the currency within its ERM band. It also meant pursuing, on the domestic front, a policy of price stability or, at the least, disinflation sufficient to bring the rate of inflation down to the level that existed in the strong-currency countries, since any difference in inflation would cause the currency of the country with the higher rate to become overvalued vis-à-vis the currency of the country with the lower rate and therefore susceptible to downward pressure within the ERM. Finally, membership in the ERM meant that, compared with the immediate past, the weak-currency countries would forsake the option of altering relative prices and enhancing the competitiveness of their goods in domestic and export markets, and thereby stimulating domestic growth, by allowing their currencies to float downward and depreciate vis-à-vis the strong currencies.

If it is obvious, from a calculation of economic gain, why the strong-currency countries would support EMS and be likely to join (and, as in Germany's case, play a leadership role in its creation), it is not immediately obvious why *weak*-currency countries—most notably, those which had dropped out of the "snake"—would want to join. And, indeed, some of them did not; although participating in the discussions leading to its creation, Britain decided not participate in the ERM, and Italy joined only after obtaining a wider + 6 percent band for itself. But France *did* join—largely, it seems, because of Giscard d'Estaing's close friendship with Helmut Schmidt and his willingness to accommodate Schmidt's preferences, his perception that EMS would solidify and extend the Franco-German partnership in the Community, and his aversion (honed by years of service as finance minister) to inflation and exchange rate instability. In addition, the French commitment undoubtedly reflected Prime Minister Raymond Barre's single-minded pursuit of a strong franc as a means of controlling inflation as well as his continuing commitment, from his days in the European Commission, to reduce, if not eliminate altogether, the margins of fluctuation among currencies.[4] As we have noted elsewhere, the commitment to the EMS proved costly for France (and, ultimately, to Giscard and Barre as well): Nominal and real interest rates rose sharply, the rate of growth dropped and the rate of unemployment increased, the franc became increasingly overvalued, the trade account deteriorated, the country moved into a recession by the second half of 1980, and the electorate decided not to renew Giscard's term in May 1981.[5] Despite the adverse economic effects, however, the commitment to the EMS had been made, and it became the basis for an even deeper commitment to Europe in the 1980s.

Mitterrand's "Grand Tournant"

When François Mitterrand and the Socialist-dominated government came to power in 1981, the country had been in a recession for nearly a year and the rate of unemployment was drifting upward, to more than 7 percent.

Given its partisan identity, it was hardly surprising that, in addition to enacting a number of the social reforms to which the Socialist Party and its candidates had pledged themselves, the government sought to reflate the economy through fiscal and monetary policy. But what *is* surprising is that within a year of coming to power, the government retreated from its initial reflationary path and pursued, instead, a policy of *rigueur* marked by reductions in spending and the budget deficit, and higher interest rates and a contraction of the money supply. As a result, public spending was cut, revenues raised, the budget deficit stabilized (relative to GDP), and "real" interest rates raised.

As we have discussed elsewhere, the Socialist government's peculiar turn from reflation to *rigueur* and, eventually, austerity—peculiar politically because it occurred so early in the Mitterrand presidency, at a time when the government still commanded a secure majority in the *Assemblée*, and because it contributed to the erosion of the government's electoral base and, ultimately, its demise—was, to a large extent, the product of its choices in the domain of exchange rate policy.[6] Indeed, for that reason, the *tournant* occurred in stages that were defined by the three realignments of the franc vis-à-vis the mark and other currencies in the ERM in 1981-83. Thus, it was immediately after the first devaluation, in October 1981, that Jacques Delors, the minister of finance, called for a "pause" in reforms and proposed a combination of spending cuts and freezes, and restrictions on the flow of credit. It was immediately after the second devaluation of the franc, in June 1982—and, in fact, an explicit condition of Germany's agreement to revalue the mark a second time in eight months—that the government cut spending, increased revenues, stabilized the budget deficit, and reduced the money supply. And it was immediately after the third devaluation, in March 1983—again, as an explicit condition of German agreement to revalue the mark once more—that the government instituted another major cut in expenditures, as well as increases in personal and social insurance taxes, that, taken together, introduced a net contractionary effect in fiscal policy for the first time since 1980.[7]

That each devaluation was accompanied by a successively more contractionary fiscal and monetary policy was not coincidental. Because the three realignments were negotiated within the ERM and required the acquiescence of France's partners, including those (most notably, Germany) for whom revaluation of their currency would diminish the competitiveness of their exports not only in France but throughout the Community, they never fully eliminated the overvaluation of the franc vis-à-vis the mark that had occurred since the advent of the ERM in 1979.[8] As a result, fiscal and monetary policy had to be deployed, both to support a franc that remained overvalued and to contract demand that was fueling increases in prices (which in turn decreased the competitiveness of exports) and in the consumption of imports (which, coupled with the decrease in exports, contributed to the continued trade deficit).

The turn to a more contractionary macroeconomic policy in 1982 and 1983 did not, in and of itself, represent a deepening of France's commitment to Europe. Indeed, as some of the statements of France's leaders suggested—most notably, those by François Mitterrand himself in June 1982 and again in March 1983, when advised that France could not withdraw from the ERM—the realignments, and the domestic contraction that accompanied them, provoked anger and bitterness.[9] Nevertheless, in one fundamental sense the turn to a more contractionary macroeconomic policy *did* represent a deepening of the country's commitment to Europe. For when Mitterrand and the Socialist government chose to keep the franc in the ERM, negotiate a modest devaluation, and accept domestic contraction as a necessary accompaniment, rather than withdraw it from the ERM and allow it to float—an action that would have let it depreciate by the full amount of its overvaluation and, in so doing, would have lessened the need for a contractionary macroeconomic policy—they assigned a higher priority to continued membership in the ERM than to maximizing domestic growth, exports, employment, and, ultimately, their own political well-being.

France, Germany, and European Defense

The growing commitment to Europe was not confined to the economic realm. The early years of the Mitterrand presidency also witnessed a significant 'Europeanization' of French foreign and defense policy, through which its objectives began to converge to a greater degree than at any previous time in the Fifth Republic with those of its partners. In the name of national *grandeur* and sovereignty, de Gaulle had sought to avoid subordination within the NATO alliance, notwithstanding the fact that its partners in the Community—most notably, Germany—were deeply committed to it. Indeed, France had dramatized its independence, by creating a nuclear *force de frappe* (strike force) targeted *à tous azimuths* (in all directions), by withdrawing from NATO's Military Committee in 1966, and by ordering the removal of

NATO installations from its territory in 1967. Relations with the alliance improved during the Pompidou and Giscard presidencies, and Giscard was in fact often rumored to prefer a return to the integrated military command. But Gaullism and its legacy of ambivalence remained a strong force in French politics, and despite Giscard's personal relationship with Helmut Schmidt, France remained largely noncommittal. Thus, for example, France was not involved in NATO's 1979 decision to modernize and upgrade its intermediate-range missiles, despite the fact that the impetus for the decision had come as much from Schmidt as from the United States.[10]

When François Mitterrand entered the Elysée in 1981, few observers anticipated that French foreign policy vis-à-vis Europe would change dramatically, and fewer still anticipated that a new policy would be characterized by a more supportive stance toward NATO and cooperation in defense with Germany. For although Mitterrand's long-standing hostility toward de Gaulle could have been expected to lead him to reject the principal tenets of Gaullist foreign policy, he was nevertheless a Socialist who had won election through an alliance with the most orthodox Communist party in western Europe, who had subsequently invited that party to enter the government, and who had been supported by parties that campaigned for peace, progressive disarmament, and the "zero-zero" solution (no SS-20's, and no Pershing II's and cruise missiles in Europe). Moreover, Germany was led by a right-wing Social Democrat who made no secret of his preference for Mitterrand's opponent, and, after 1982, by a Christian Democrat. Despite all that, however—and despite the Gaullist continuities in certain aspects of policy[11]—French policy *did* begin to change after Mitterrand's election.

In July 1981, Mitterrand, accompanied by eight of the new ministers, traveled to Bonn for one of the recurring "friendship summits" envisioned in the Treaty of Cooperation that de Gaulle and Adenauer had signed at the Elysée in 1963. At the summit, Mitterrand signaled his support for Schmidt's position—then under attack in his own SPD—by stating that the Soviet modernization had created "a new superiority" and threatened the balance of power, and the peace, in Europe.[12] In the next summit, in Paris in February 1982, the two leaders agreed in criticizing the Soviet Union both for the Polish government's institution of martial law the previous December and for its invasion of Afghanistan. And they emphasized the necessity of close relations between their two countries, and between Europe and North America.[13] Later that year, after Schmidt had been removed from office by a vote of no confidence, his successor, Helmut Kohl, traveled to Paris for the first of his many summits with Mitterrand. In a meeting that emphasized security policy, the two leaders agreed to activate for the first time in 19 years the portion of the 1963 Treaty that concerned cooperation in defense, and they spoke of the need to develop a "common security policy." France, for its part, committed itself to modernizing its tactical nuclear forces with longer range weapons and to increasing consultation and cooperation with Germany about targeting decisions for those forces—a concern of the Germans since, given the range of the missiles, the targets were most likely to fall within Germany![14] And in January 1983, in an address to the German Bundestag on the twentieth anniversary of the Elysée Treaty, Mitterrand warned of the "excessive armaments of the superpowers" and argued that only a firm commitment by a united alliance to deploy the new missiles would lead to success in the Intermediate Nuclear Forces (INF) talks then underway in Geneva. Coming shortly after the Soviet foreign minister's visit to Germany, during which he had called upon Germany not to deploy the new Pershing missiles, Mitterrand's speech not only appeared to bring France closer to the German (and American) position, and to provide an endorsement of Helmut Kohl in the election campaign then underway, but also to place it in a more openly confrontational stance vis-à-vis the Soviet Union than at any earlier time in the Fifth Republic.[15] Several months later, culminating that progressive gravitation toward the German position, Mitterrand and Kohl agreed, in their two-day summit in May 1983, that NATO should deploy the missiles in December as planned if the Geneva talks did not produce a satisfactory outcome.[16]

The 1984 Council Presidency

On January 1, 1984, France assumed the rotating presidency of the Council of Ministers of the European Community. Taking over after a Greek presidency that was generally seen as a failure, the French presidency confronted a multitude of divisive issues such as rising costs for the Common Agricultural Policy, a British demand for a budget rebate, demands by the European Parliament for "Political Union" and a greater role for itself in decision-making, increasing evidence of barriers to the free flow of goods, services, capital, and people in the Community, and the question of membership for Spain and Portugal. Not all of these problems were resolved in the first half of 1984, but many of them were, and, in addition, the Community embarked on important new initiatives. In retrospect, the French presidency constituted, as some have noted, a turning point for the Community.[17] Just as important, however, it also represented a turning point for France, a moment in which its commitment to Europe deepened as its president, after having recognized in 1983 (with some bitterness) the extent to which macroeconomic policy was constrained by participation in the EMS, committed himself wholeheartedly and unambiguously, for the first time, to the economic project of European integration.

There were signs of Mitterrand's newfound commitment to Europe even before France assumed the presidency in 1984. In his speech to the Bundestag in January 1983, for example, he had called upon the Community to surmount its "family quarrels" and find again its dynamism.[18] And in his December 1983 New Year's Eve television address, he had said that "1984 will be the year of Europe, for better or worse.... First in the world on the commercial level, Europe lacks a political will, the awareness of what it is worth, of what it can be. France, which is European, does not wish to miss this opportunity."[19]

Early in the presidency, Mitterrand met with Kohl at Edenkoben to discuss the various financial issues confronting the Community. At the close of the talks, he spoke of "the political construction of Europe, which can not content itself with living on memories."[20] Several days later, as part of a tour of Community capitals that he made with an entourage of ministers, Mitterrand delivered what was advertised as his "grand discours européen" and set out a broad agenda for the Community—controlling agricultural spending, creating a single internal market, creating a permanent secretariat for the European Council, accepting Spain and Portugal as members, creating a social "space," a cultural "space," even creating a European-manned space station![21] And several months later, before the European Parliament, he returned to many of these themes. "We are," he said, "in a phase where destiny hesitates again. For too long, Europe delays itself in derisory quarrels.... [I]t is necessary to reunite the creative faculties which together built Europe."[22] Saying that all of the issues confronting the Community had been resolved except the matter of the British budget contribution and rebate, he supported again the Iberian enlargement, called for new initiatives in culture, space, transportation, and employment, and called for the development of a common defense. And, addressing himself to the Parliament's project to develop a new treaty instituting a European Union, he stated he was prepared to examine and defend the project—which, among other things, would increase the power of the Parliament and the Commission and reduce the national veto—and called for discussions and then an

Intergovernmental Conference of "interested states" to deal with the matter.[23] Especially noteworthy was Mitterrand's reference to "interested states;" the first explicit suggestion by any European leader that integration might proceed at multiple speeds and have a "variable geometry," it represented a veiled warning to Britain that its obstinacy over the budget issue would not be allowed to delay progress in the Community. And it signaled that France clearly intended to locate itself in the inner core and on the "fast track" of European integration.

The French presidency concluded with the meeting of the European Council in Fontainebleau in June 1984. The meeting was remarkable for the agreement it achieved on three distinct, but linked, issues. First, the lingering dispute over the size of the budget rebate that Britain would receive as partial compensation for its large net contribution was settled.[24] Second, the leaders formally pledged themselves to "the creation of a genuine economic union"; asked the Council of Ministers to examine a series of proposals the Commission had been preparing over the past several years to strengthen the internal market by eliminating all non-tariff barriers and other impediments to the free flow of goods, services, capital, and people; and invited the Commission to report on its progress in regard to the internal market in time for the European Council meeting in Milan one year hence.[25] And third, the leaders created the Ad Hoc Committee on Institutional Affairs to examine the operations of the European institutions and suggest improvements to the Council by March 1985. Germany was induced to provide a disproportionate amount of the increase in the British rebate in exchange for agreement on the internal market and possible political reform. Britain was convinced to accept a modest increase in its rebate and creation of the Ad Hoc Committee in exchange for agreement on the internal market. And for itself, France accepted the creation of a single internal market and the possibility of institutional reform, neither of which had heretofore figured prominently among its objectives in Europe. In concocting this package deal, the French presidency demonstrated not only its cleverness but also a commitment to Europe that set the stage for one of the Community's most important initiatives of the 1980s—the Single European Act (SEA).

The Internal Market and Institutional Reform: The Single European Act

In March 1985, the Commission—by then headed by Jacques Delors, the former French finance minister—issued a White Paper containing some three hundred proposals that, taken together, would eliminate virtually all existing barriers to a single internal market. In the same month, the Ad Hoc Committee on Institutional Affairs issued its report, calling upon the European Council to convene an Intergovernmental Conference (IGC) to draft the amendments to the Treaty of Rome necessary for the creation of a European union and, in particular, proposing an extension of the use of majority voting and an increased role for Parliament in debating and amending Commission proposals.[26] Later that month, the European Council endorsed the White Paper and its recommendation that the proposals be implemented in full by the end of 1992 (hence "EC92") and called upon the Commission to prepare a detailed program for its next meeting, three months hence. It also referred the Ad Hoc Committee's report to that meeting—although without endorsement, because of the disagreements that existed within the Committee.

At its meeting in Milan in June 1985, the European Council endorsed the Commission's proposals for the creation of a single market, as well as Delors' proposal that an IGC be convened to consider both reports.[27] The IGC—essentially a series of meetings of the Council of Ministers—drafted Treaty amendments that represented an amalgamation of the earlier Commission proposals for a single internal market and those of the Ad Hoc Committee. The amendments were incorporated into a Single European Act that the European Council approved in late 1985 and the member states subsequently ratified.[28] In it, the members committed themselves to the creation of "an area without internal frontiers in which the free movement of goods, persons, services and capital is ensured" by the end of 1992. And they stipulated that the nearly three hundred proposals would be implemented through a 'cooperation procedure' that gave Parliament a greater role in amending and approving Commission directives, and, further, that, except for those dealing with taxation, employment, and the movement of persons, all directives would require only a 'qualified' (i.e., weighted) majority.[29]

For France, the SEA represented a further deepening of its commitment to Europe, one that was especially significant because it appeared to contravene, in several respects, traditional beliefs about the proper role of the state and the appropriate allocation of power between the member states and the European institutions. For one thing, in ratifying the SEA and incorporating it into the Community treaties, France committed itself to the creation of a single internal market through the application of the principle of "mutual recognition," by which standards and regulations would be reduced to the "lowest common denominator."[30] In short, it would be a market that was liberalized and deregulated, one in which the member states would inevitably lose control over the flow of goods, services, capital, and people. For a state such as France, that had a strong and long-standing *étatiste* tradition of regulation, this represented a radical departure.[31] Moreover, this liberalized, deregulated market was more likely to work to the advantage of Germany, with its powerful export industry, and Britain, with its well-developed international financial sector, than to that of France. It would, in addition, require the dismantling of many of the traditional statist devices through which France had sought to protect its firms in the domestic market and assist them in export markets. Furthermore, the SEA substantially expanded the role and authority of the supranational institutions of the Community, something that was heretofore anathema in the Fifth Republic. Not only did Parliament obtain more power to amend Commission directives—something that had been the prerogative of the Council—but the Commission itself obtained significant powers to write directives that pertained to all aspects of national economic life. Finally, the SEA introduced a large dose of majority voting in the Council, something that, for the country that had provoked the "empty chair" crisis in the 1960s in order to enshrine its right to exercise the national veto, was, if anything, even *more* of an anathema.[32] For France to commit itself to the SEA, therefore, constituted, implicitly at least, a quite remarkable departure from some traditional notions of its "national interest."

The Resurrection of EMU

Economic and Monetary Union was an old idea in the Community, one that had first appeared in the late 1960s, had been formally endorsed by the leaders of the Six and the Council of Ministers, and had been implemented, only to be derailed by the collapse of the Bretton Woods regime, the OPEC oil price shock, and other related developments in the mid-1970s.[33] The SEA resurrected the idea of EMU and returned it to the agenda of the Community, by proclaiming in its Preamble that one of its objectives was the "progressive realization of economic and monetary union." But, more than anything else, it was the French government, paradoxically, the *cohabitation* government headed by Jacques Chirac and dominated by the neo-Gaullist party that initiated the drive for EMU that culminated, several years later, in the Treaty on European Union signed at Maastricht.[34]

After the Mitterrand *tournant* of 1982-83, realignments in the ERM became increasingly infrequent. The German mark took on the role of "anchor" currency in the ERM, and, as it did, the monetary policy adopted by the German central bank, the Bundesbank, became, in effect, the monetary policy of all the ERM members; as two knowledgeable observers said, "Most of Europe has been turned into a Deutsche Mark zone. The Bundesbank in Frankfurt has become Europe's de facto central bank. Other EMS participants have to ape a German monetary policy in which they have no formal say."[35] Not all governments were prepared to leave the Bundesbank's domination in monetary policy unchallenged, however. Most notably, the French government headed by Chirac was unwilling to do so; in January 1987, with the franc hovering near its floor and believing that to be the result of the mark's *under*valuation rather than the franc's *over*valuation, the French government deliberately let the franc fall through its floor against the mark, in order to force the Bundesbank to intervene in support of the franc and the German government to revalue its currency.[36]

Several months later, prompted by the January crisis, Edouard Balladur, minister of economics, finance, and privatization in the Chirac government, called upon the Community to strengthen the EMS in such a way as to reduce the asymmetry of influence that existed between countries with strong currencies and those with weak ones. Balladur's proposals, made in July and reiterated in August, led to the Basle-Nyborg Agreements of September 1987 between the member states' central bank governors and finance ministers that created a credit facility to support intramarginal interventions in defense of weak currencies. Important as they were, however, the agreements hardly addressed the problem of the imbalance of influence, and benefit, within the EMS, and in December, Balladur called for a larger reform and circulated proposals to that effect to his colleagues in the other member states. Prepared in the wake of renewed attacks on the franc that had forced France to raise its interest rates just as the presidential election campaign was getting underway (one in which Chirac planned to run), Balladur's proposals sought to introduce more symmetry in the EMS, especially in terms of the obligations of participating member-states to defend currencies under attack. He also called for larger credit facilities to support such interventions. And he proposed that, in order to present a common European posture vis-à-vis other currencies, the Community create a common currency that would be managed by a single central bank.

More than the generalities in the SEA's Preamble, it was the Balladur initiative that started the movement toward EMU and began the process that culminated in the year-long Intergovernmental Conference of 1990-91 and, eventually, the Treaty on European Union that was signed in Maastricht in February 1992. Balladur's proposals were soon endorsed by Italy and the German foreign minister, Hans-Dietrich Genscher, and Genscher—in charge of setting the agenda for the European Council meeting that would occur in Hannover in June 1988, at the conclusion of the German presidency—put the matter on the meeting's agenda. The Council referred it to a committee composed largely of the central bank governors and chaired by Delors. The committee's report, issued in April 1989, called for a movement in stages to EMU. At its meeting in Madrid in June 1989, the European Council agreed to start the first of the three stages of EMU in July 1990, and to start after that date the IGC that would negotiate the treaty amendments necessary for the second and third stages. The IGC began in Rome in December 1990 and culminated in the meeting of the European Council at Maastricht in December 1991, at which time the leaders agreed to create, by 1999 at the latest, a single central bank charged with formulating a single monetary policy and managing a single currency formed by the irrevocable locking of exchange rates among the national currencies.

Through all the twists and turns in the negotiations of EMU, France remained, with its allies in Belgium, Italy, and the Commission, in the vanguard of the effort to create a new European Central Bank and a single currency.[37] The French advocacy of EMU, obviously, was not motivated by a desire simply to create new supranational institutions; rather, it was motivated by a desire to lessen the Bundesbank's control over European monetary policy. Nevertheless, France's advocacy of EMU did represent a deepening of its commitment to Europe, for in advocating EMU it was supporting an institutional innovation that, if fully implemented, would constitute the most far-reaching extension of supranational authority in the Community's history. For a state that, more than any other founding member of the Community, had sought to maintain national sovereignty against the incursions of supranational forces, that was a significant extension of its commitment.

German Unification and Political Union

One of the great defining events of the twentieth century, the end of the Cold War, began in 1989. Although begun by policies put into effect by Mikhail Gorbachev and the Soviet leadership, the critical turning point—the point at which controlled reform orchestrated from above by Communist leaders was displaced by spontaneous revolution from below—came in the fall of 1989 in the German Democratic Republic (GDR). On November 9, 1989, following weeks of demonstrations and the flight of tens of thousands of its citizens, the leadership of the GDR opened the Wall in Berlin. Designed to quell the outflow by allowing unrestricted travel from

East to West, the move backfired and precipitated a cascade of events that, within a year, resulted first in German Economic and Monetary Union (GEMU) and then, on October 3, 1990, the unification of the two Germanies.[38]

On November 28, 1989, Helmut Kohl proposed—without prior consultation with his Community colleagues (or the wartime Allies or even his foreign minister)—a "ten-point program" which envisioned the formation of a number of joint Federal Republic-GDR working commissions, followed by "confederative structures" and, eventually, "state unity." At the time, unification seemed some distance in the future—perhaps, Kohl thought, five years, if all went well.[39] Nevertheless, the specter of German unification, with all the memories it conjured up and all the questions it raised about relations among the members of the Community, the stability of the other Communist regimes in the East, and the alliance systems in Europe, created a mood of considerable apprehension among the leaders of the Community.

As the leaders of the Community gathered in Strasbourg, less than two weeks after Kohl's speech, for a meeting of the European Council, it was by no means certain they would endorse the German chancellor's ambitious program. And indeed, by his own admission, the German chancellor ran into an "icy climate" at Strasbourg.[40] A number of leaders—most notably, Margaret Thatcher of Britain and Ruud Lubbers of the Netherlands—expressed their apprehension about the possible ramifications, both in the Community and in the East, of unification, as well as their irritation at Kohl's failure to consult with them before announcing his "ten-point program." Mitterrand, for his part, had made his concerns known well before the meeting; after Kohl's speech, he had arranged to visit the GDR in late December without first advising Kohl of his plans, had declined to join Kohl at the opening of the Brandenburg Gate, and, just before the Strasbourg meeting, had met with Gorbachev in Kiev, where he warned, among other things, that existing frontiers—especially the Oder-Neisse boundary between the GDR and Poland—must be inviolable.[41]

Despite their apprehensions and concerns, however, the leaders of the Community approved, in principle, German unification. In concluding their meeting, they issued a declaration on eastern Europe which stated that they sought "the establishment of a state of peace in Europe in which the German people finds again its unity through free self-determination . . . in a context of dialogue and East-West cooperation . . . [and] situated in the perspective of European integration."[42] In exchange, Kohl agreed to support Mitterrand's proposal to begin the Intergovernmental Conference on EMU in December 1990, rather than at some undefined later date as Germany preferred, so that the second stage of EMU could begin as early as January 1993.[43]

In the campaign for the March 1990 elections for the GDR's *Volkskammer,* the timetable for unification was shortened dramatically, as Kohl called for quick unification under Article 23 of the Basic Law and opened negotiations with the GDR for German Economic and Monetary Union (GEMU). When Kohl's Christian Democratic Union (CDU) won a landslide victory, the pressure for an abbreviated transition to full unification increased still more. Understanding that any acceleration in the pace of unification would require French acquiescence, Kohl met with Mitterrand in April and obtained the French president's acceptance of an accelerated process of unification and the program of GEMU. As in December, French acquiescence was predicated upon a German commitment—in this case, to "accelerate the political construction of Europe." Thus, declaring that "the moment has come to transform the relations among member states into a European union," Kohl and Mitterrand called for the preparation of a second Intergovernmental Conference, this one on "political union" and running concurrently with the IGC on EMU, that would, among other things, "assure the integration and coherence of economic and monetary policy... and define and put into practice a common foreign and security policy."[44] Called together one week later, the European Council endorsed the idea of political union. And as it did, it also endorsed Kohl's accelerated timetable for unification, saying:

> the Community warmly welcomes German unification. It looks forward to the positive and fruitful contribution that all Germans can make, following the forthcoming integration of the territory of the G.D.R. into the Community. We are confident that German unification... will be a positive factor in the development of Europe as a whole and of the Community in particular.... We are pleased that German unification is taking place under a European roof.[45]

The bargain struck between Germany and its Community partners at Strasbourg and Dublin represented, from the Community's perspective, an effort to "bind in" Germany, at a time when events were likely to attract German attention and interests—both economic and geopolitical—away from the Community, to the East. In agreeing to move more rapidly to the second stage of EMU and to institute a Common Foreign and Security Policy, in return for the Community's acquiescence to its accelerated timetable for unification, Germany would, it was hoped, deepen its commitment to the Community. As important as the effort to "bind in" Germany was, however, the Strasbourg and Dublin decisions also signaled a deepening of *France's* commitment to the Community. For not only did France commit itself to an early move to the second stage of EMU and a Common Foreign and Security Policy but it committed itself to the pursuit of those objectives with a unified Germany. In other words, it committed itself to continuing the process of European integration despite the fact that its principal partner would be larger and, in all likelihood, more powerful—both in economic and geopolitical terms—than itself in the future.

Maastricht: The Treaty of European Union

In December 1991, the heads of state and government of the Community, meeting as the European Council, gathered in the Dutch city of Maastricht to settle the last unresolved issues before the two Intergovernmental Conferences and to approve the Treaty on European Union that amalgamated the proposals on EMU and "political union." The most ambitious effort ever undertaken by the Community, the Treaty committed the member states to moving to the second, transitional stage of EMU on January 1, 1994 (assuming, of course, that all 12 member states ratified the Treaty) and to the third and final stage of EMU soon thereafter. In that final stage, the member states that satisfied the so-called "convergence criteria" would transfer the responsibility for monetary policy from their central banks to a new European Central Bank, irrevocably lock the exchange rates among their currencies, and adopt a single currency.[46] In addition, the Treaty committed the member states to pursuing greater cooperation in the domains of foreign and security policy, on one hand, and justice and home affairs, on the other.[47]

By the time the European leaders gathered at Maastricht, the Treaty was virtually complete and in final form, and their approval was assumed to be a formality. However, at least one important change was made by the leaders at Maastricht—one that was initiated by France and that symbolized the depth of its commitment to the Community and to EMU. When the Treaty came out of the IGC, it stipulated (Article 109j.3) that the Council would decide no later than the end of 1996 whether a majority of states satisfied the "convergence criteria" and, if so, when the third and final stage would begin. On the evening before the meeting of the European Council, Mitterrand dined with Giulio Andreotti, the Italian prime minister, and persuaded him to agree to support the insertion of an additional article into the Treaty that would enable the Community to avoid the real possibility that it would remain forever in the transitional second stage, for lack of a majority of states that satisfied the "convergence criteria." With the support of the Italians, the French drafted the additional article (109j.4) and an accompanying protocol (10) stipulating that, in the event a majority of states had not satisfied the criteria by the end of 1996 and a date for the beginning of stage three had not been set by the end of 1997, the third stage would start on January 1, 1999 and would include whichever states qualified as of mid-1998.[48] The French amendment, agreed to by Mitterrand's colleagues, assured that the Community would get to the third and final stage of EMU in a finite and relatively short period of time. As the 1997 deadline increasingly came to be seen as unrealistic and was eventually waived, this "irreversibility clause," with its 1999 deadline, loomed as one of the most consequential clauses in the entire Treaty.[49]

The Rise and Fall of Public Support for Europe

For the better part of a decade, as France renewed its commitment to the European Community and adhered to the emerging norms of the European monetary regime, and as the Community committed itself to creating a single internal market and then to moving toward Economic and Monetary Union, the French and European publics likewise became increasingly committed to Europe. But just as that decade-long process of commitment and institutional innovation was coming to fruition at Maastricht, support for European integration began to erode, both among the publics of the member states of the Community in general and the French public in particular. What is especially noteworthy is the extent to which, as a result of that erosion, the French public had become, by the mid-1990s, one of the *least* supportive in the Union. In this section, we shall describe briefly some aspects of that erosion and suggest some of the reasons for it.

Since 1973, the Eurobarometer surveys conducted by the Community twice a year in each of the member states have asked samples of citizens whether they think membership in the Community is "a good thing" or "a bad thing" for their country and whether they think their country "has benefited" or "has not benefited" from membership.[50] Figure 13.1 presents two summary measures of the extent of support for the Community and Union in Europe, obtained by pooling the responses from the surveys conducted in the member states between 1981 and May 1995. The data in figure 13.1 suggest that the proportion of Europeans who thought membership was a "good thing" and who thought their country had benefited from its membership increased steadily throughout the 1980s until early 1991, but

FIGURE 13.1
SUPPORT FOR THE EUROPEAN COMMUNITY/UNION IN THE MEMBER STATES, 1981–95

(Percent of Pooled National Samples Saying Membership is "Good Thing," "Bad Thing," "Has Benefited" Country, "Has Not Benefited" Country)

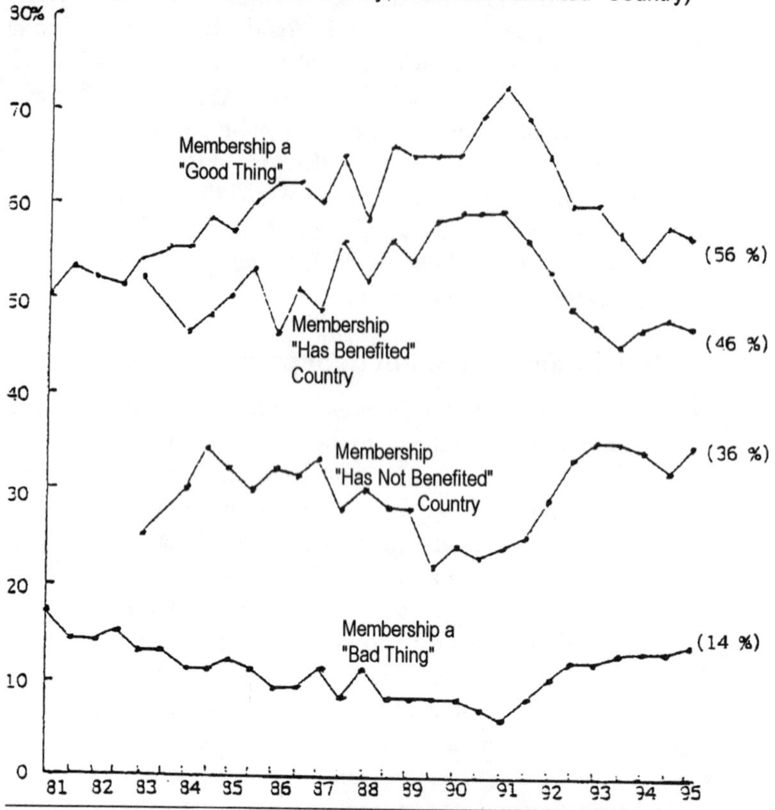

Source: European Commission, *Eurobarometer: Trends, 1974–93* (Brussels: European Commission, May 1994); European Commission, *Eurobarometer: 41, July 1994* (Brussels: European Commission, September 1994); European Commission, *Eurobarometer: 42, December 1994* (Brussels: European Commission, Spring 1995); and European Commission, *Eurobarometer: 43, Autumn 1995* (Brussels, European Commission, 1995).

decreased sharply thereafter. Indeed, support decreased to such an extent that, even after a slight resurgence in late 1994, the proportion of the European public that believed membership was a "good thing" remained below 60 percent, some 15 percentage points below the peak registered in early 1991 and roughly at the level registered in the early 1980s. Likewise, by 1993 and 1994, less than one-half of the European public thought their country

FIGURE 13.2
Support for the European Community/Union in France, 1981–95

(Percent of National Samples Saying Membership in Community/Union is a "Good/Bad Thing," "Has/Has Not Benefited France")

Membership is a "Good Thing" or "Bad Thing"

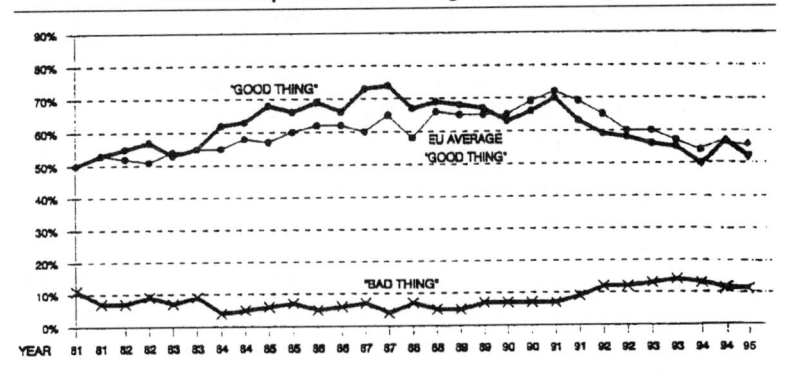

Membership "Has Benefited France" or "Has Not Benefited France"

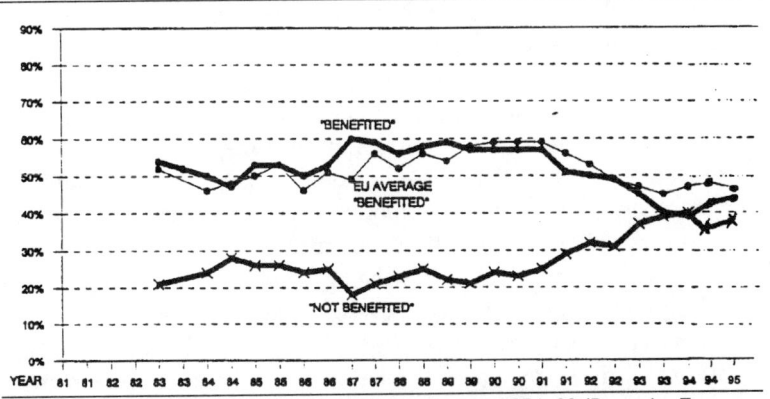

Source: European Commission, *Eurobarometer: Trends, 1974–93* (Brussels: European Commission, 1994), pp. 77-78, 93; European Commission, *Eurobarometer: 41*, July 1994 (Brussels: European Commission, 1994); and European Commission, *Eurobarometer: 43, Autumn 1995* (Brussels: European Commission, 1995).

had benefited from membership, compared to nearly 60 percent between late 1989 and early 1991. Conversely, the proportion saying membership was a "*bad* thing," which had declined steadily in the 1980s from about 15 percent to close to 5 percent by 1991, more than doubled after that date and reached 14 percent in the spring of 1995. And the proportion saying their country had *not* benefited from membership, which had decreased from more than 30 percent to only slightly more than 20 percent in the 1980s, increased sharply in 1992 and 1993 and, after a slight dip in 1994, rose again to 35 percent in the spring of 1995.

Figure 13.2 presents the responses of the samples of French citizens to these Eurobarometer questions. The data in figure 13.2 suggest that throughout the 1980s the French public became increasingly supportive of the Community and that, at least until 1988 or thereabouts, it was more supportive not only in terms of its earlier levels but also relative to the levels registered in the European public as a whole. Thus, whereas only 50 percent of the French public thought membership was a "good thing" when Mitterrand took office, by 1987 roughly 75 percent believed it to be a "good thing." And while the French public in 1981 was no more supportive of the Community than the EC public in general, by 1987 it had become considerably *more* supportive than the EC public, despite the fact that the level of support in the latter had increased. Likewise, throughout the 1980s an increasing portion of the French public believed membership had benefited the country. And the perception that membership was beneficial increased more within the French public in the mid-1980s than it did in the EC as a whole.

The data in figure 13.2 suggest that, after increasing in the early and mid-1980s by an unusually large amount relative to the increase in the EC as a whole, support in France for the Community began to erode. They suggest that erosion began relatively *early*, indeed, as early as late 1989! And they suggest that support for the Community in France eroded *more sharply*—especially after 1991—than in the EC in general. Indeed, the erosion was so substantial that France shifted from being a country in which support was relatively *high*, compared with the level of support in the EC as a whole, to one in which support was relatively *low*, compared with that in the EC. Thus, whereas a relatively *large* portion of the French public in the period between 1984 and 1988 said membership was a "good thing" that had benefited the country, after 1989 a relatively *small* portion said that was the case. Conversely, more French citizens said that membership was a "bad thing" that had *not* benefited the country; thus, after 1989-90 the proportion saying membership was a "bad thing" more than doubled (admittedly from a very low level in the single digits), while the proportion saying the country had *not* benefited from membership drifted upward from about 20 percent to nearly 40 percent by 1993 and 1994. In fact, by 1994, the combined effect of the decrease in the proportion believing France *had* benefited from membership and the increase in the proportion believing it had *not* resulted in roughly as many French citizens believing the country had *not* benefited from membership as believed it *had!*

In order to better comprehend the degree to which support for the Community and Union has eroded in France in recent years, tables 13.1 and 13.2 provide the responses in each of the 12 member states to the two questions pertaining to membership in March 1991—the moment when support for the EC reached its apogee—and May 1995. The data in table 13.1 consist of the responses in each member state to the question whether membership was "a good thing" or "a bad thing" for the country; the data in table 13.2 consist of the responses to the question whether the country has benefited or has not benefited from membership.

The data in table 13.1 suggest a surprisingly *low* level of support in France for the Community and Union both in 1991 and 1995, compared with that registered in other member states, and a relatively *large* erosion in support over that period. In early 1991, for example, 70 percent of the French population thought membership was a "good thing"—a figure that, while substantial, was nevertheless lower than the ones recorded in all the other member states except Denmark and the United Kingdom. By May 1995, that proportion had dropped to 53 percent, a level that was lower than the ones observed in all the other member states (excluding the three—Austria, Finland, and Sweden—which entered the Union on January 1, 1995) except the United Kingdom, the bastion of "Euro-skepticism," and Portugal and Spain, which experienced altogether exceptional deteriorations in support for Europe in the post-Maastricht period. As a result, the difference between the proportions of the French population saying membership was a "good thing" or a "bad thing" dropped from 63 percent in 1991 (the third lowest level after Denmark and the United Kingdom) to 41 percent in 1995 (the lowest outside Denmark, the United Kingdom, Spain, and Portugal and the three new member states). While not the largest decline in support in the Community, that *was* one of the largest and was exceeded only by the precipitous declines in Spain, Portugal, and the United Kingdom.

Table 13.2 presents the responses in 1991 and 1995 in each of the member states to the question whether the country had benefited from membership in the Community/Union. As with the responses to the question whether membership was a "good thing" or a "bad thing," the data in table 13.2 suggest a surprisingly *low* degree of support in France and a

TABLE 13.1
EROSION IN SUPPORT FOR THE EUROPEAN COMMUNITY, 1991–95:
Percent Believing Membership Is a "Good Thing" or a "Bad Thing"

	March 1991 Percent Saying Membership Is a			May 1995 Percent Saying Membership Is a			Change in Percent Saying Membership is "Good Thing" or "Bad Thing," 1991–95		
	"Good Thing"	"Bad Thing"	Net	"Good Thing"	"Bad Thing"	Net	"Good Thing"	"Bad Thing"	Net
Netherlands	89	2	87	79	6	73	-10	+4	-14
Luxembourg	83	4	79	80	5	75	-3	+1	-4
Italy	79	2	77	73	6	67	-6	+4	-10
Portugal	79	3	76	46	14	32	-33	+11	-44
Spain	78	3	75	44	22	22	-34	-19	-53
Ireland	78	5	73	79	5	74	+1	0	+1
Greece	76	6	70	63	9	54	-13	+3	-16
Belgium	75	4	71	67	9	58	-8	+5	-13
Germany	71	6	65	57	11	46	-14	+5	-19
France	70	7	63	53	12	41	-17	+5	-22
Denmark	61	18	43	54	21	33	-7	+3	-10
U.K.	57	13	44	43	24	19	-14	+11	-25
Austria				40	21	19			
Finland				47	18	29			
Sweden				39	33	6			

Source: European Commission, *Eurobarometer: Trends, 1974–93* (Brussels: European Commission, 1994); and European Commission, *Eurobarometer. 43, Autumn, 1995* (European Commission, 1995).

TABLE 13.2
EROSION IN SUPPORT FOR THE EUROPEAN COMMUNITY, 1991–95:
PERCENT BELIEVING COUNTRY HAS BENEFITED/NOT BENEFITED FROM MEMBERSHIP?

	March 1991 Percent Saying Membership			May 1995 Percent Saying Membership			Change in Percent Saying Membership Has/Has Not Benefited Country, 1991–95		
	Has Benefited Country	Has Not Benefited Country	Net	Has Benefited Country	Has Not Benefited Country	Net	Has Benefited	Has Not Benefited	Net
Ireland	83	11	72	87	7	80	+4	−4	+8
Portugal	82	8	74	58	28	30	−24	+20	−44
Netherlands	77	10	67	68	16	52	−9	+6	−15
Greece	76	12	64	72	19	53	−4	+7	−11
Luxembourg	73	12	61	73	16	57	0	+4	−4
Denmark	69	21	48	63	26	37	−6	+5	−11
Belgium	68	13	55	57	22	35	−11	+9	−20
Italy	64	14	50	52	24	28	−12	+10	−22
Spain	58	25	33	28	60	−32	−30	+35	−65
France	57	25	32	44	38	6	−13	+13	−26
Germany	55	29	26	47	34	13	−8	+5	−13
U.K.	47	37	10	38	44	−6	−9	+7	−16
Austria				44	36	8			
Finland				36	41	−5			
Sweden				22	50	−28			

Source: See Table 13.1.

relatively *large* degree of erosion in support after 1991. Thus, in 1991, 57 percent of the French public thought France had benefited from membership in the Community—a figure that, while substantial, was lower than those observed in all of the member states except Germany and the United Kingdom. By early 1995, only 44 percent of the French population thought the country had benefited from membership—a figure that was lower than those observed in *all* of the member states except Spain and the United Kingdom (and the three new member states). And whereas in 1991, a substantially larger portion of the French population thought membership had benefited the country than thought it had not (57 percent to 25 percent), by 1995 nearly as many French citizens thought membership had *not* benefited the country (38 percent) as thought it *had* (44 percent). Only in Spain and the United Kingdom (as well as Finland and Sweden), where public opinion in the aggregate perceived membership to be disadvantageous for the country, was the public more doubtful about the advantages of EU membership. And only in Portugal and Spain had public support for the Community and Union, as measured by the change in the difference in proportions saying membership had or had not benefited the country, deteriorated as much since 1991.

Why Did French Support for Europe Erode?

A careful perusal of the data in figure 13.2 suggests that, until the late 1980s, the French public was disproportionately *more* supportive of Europe than those in other member states, both in thinking that membership was a "good thing" and in believing that membership benefited the country. But beginning roughly in 1989, that support began to erode, to such an extent that by 1990 the French public was *less* supportive than the European public in general. And after early 1991, support in France, as in the rest of the Community, eroded at an accelerating rate.

Why did support for Europe begin to erode in France in the late 1980s, just as the new European initiatives were gathering momentum? And why did it drop even more sharply after 1991? To some extent, of course, the erosion was not unique to France but, rather, common to *all* of the European publics. Some of the erosion that occurred in France, then, may simply have reflected a more widespread European fatigue, skepticism, and anxiety—fatigue in the wake of so much institutional innovation in the past decade, skepticism in the face of the grandiose vision of European Union, and anxiety about Europe's uncertain future after the end of the Cold War. Nevertheless, having said that, the erosion in support for Europe *was* especially acute in France—even more so if we take, as its starting point, the level of support in 1987 or thereabouts.

One possible source of the erosion in French support for the Community is suggested in figure 13.2 by the timing of the crossover of the trendlines in support in France and the EC as a whole. If that crossover identifies the moment in which French support shifted from being *high*, relative to the EC as a whole, to *low*, relative to the EC as a whole, it is surely intriguing and suggestive that it occurred in the fall of 1989—immediately in the wake of the historic events in Germany and Czechoslovakia. While difficult to corroborate with survey data, it is at least plausible that those events—and, in particular, the dramatic move by Germany to pursue some form of unification—may have introduced, in the midst of the collective euphoria that swept Europe, at least some small degree of anxiety in the French public about the future role and influence in the Community of a possibly unified, inevitably eastward-oriented Germany; certainly, such an anxiety weighed heavily on those French and Community leaders who spoke, as the events unfolded, of the need to "bind in" Germany to the Community.

In addition to the possible effect of the developments in Germany and eastern Europe in 1989 and later, the decline in French support for Europe may have resulted from the adverse consequences of an economic policy that, after 1987, was predicated upon the maintenance of parity in the ERM between the franc and the mark. Some of these consequences are suggested in table 13.3. Maintaining a franc fort at a time when the franc remained overvalued vis-à-vis the mark (even after the realignments of 1986-87), when the German rate of inflation was lower than the French rate (as was the case until 1991), and when German interest rates were rising (as occurred throughout the period between 1987 and late 1992), required French interest rates to be raised, despite the decreasing rate of inflation.[51] As a result, both nominal and "real" interest rates rose sharply; by the early 1990s, short-term rates were in the vicinity of 10 percent, meaning that with a current rate of inflation of 2 to 3 percent "real" interest rates were very high, around 7 percent. Those high rates contributed, in turn, to a sharp downturn in the economy. Thus, after having exceeded 4 percent a year in the late 1980s, in the wake of the realignments of 1986-87, the rate of economic growth dropped sharply in 1990 and 1991, and ultimately the economy went into a recession that resulted in a negative growth rate of 1.5 percent in 1993. That, in turn, caused the level of unemployment to rise sharply, so much so that by late 1994 it had risen to nearly 13 percent,

TABLE 13.3
THE COSTS OF THE *FRANC FORT*:
INTEREST RATES, GROWTH, UNEMPLOYMENT, AND TRADE, 1979–95

	Nominal Short-Term Interest Rates	"Real" Short-Term Interest Rates (Nominal Rate minus Rate of Inflation)	Percent Change, "Real" GDP	Percent Labor Force, Unemployed	Balance of Trade with EC (in Billions of dollars)
1979	9.8	-1.0	3.2	5.8	-1.4
1980	12.2	-1.4	1.6	6.2	-5.0
1981	15.3	1.9	1.2	7.4	-5.4
1982	14.6	2.8	2.5	8.1	-10.0
1983	12.5	2.9	0.7	8.3	-8.4
1984	11.7	4.3	1.3	9.7	-7.0
1985	9.9	4.1	1.9	10.2	-7.7
1986	7.7	5.0	2.5	10.4	-7.8
1987	8.3	5.2	2.3	10.5	-9.6
1988	7.9	5.2	4.5	10.0	-7.0
1989	9.4	5.8	4.3	9.4	-8.4
1990	10.3	6.9	2.5	8.9	-7.3
1991	9.6	6.4	0.8	9.4	0.2
1992	10.3	7.9	1.3	10.4	3.2
1993	8.6	6.5	-1.5	11.6	5.7
1994	5.8	4.1	2.9	12.3	5.4
1995(est)	6.6	5.1	2.4	11.8	6.4

Source: Data on interest rates, inflation, growth, and unemployment from OECD, *OECD Economic Outlook 58, December 1995* (Paris: OECD, 1995), pp. 57-61, A4, A19, A24, A39; and earlier volumes. Data on trade from International Monetary Fund, *Direction of Trade Statistics Yearbook, 1995* (Washington, D.C.: IMF, 1995), and earlier volumes. Trade data for 1995 are for first ten months only.

which represented more than 3.2 million workers out of a work force of some 26 million.

The causal connections between exchange rate policy in the ERM, domestic macroeconomic policy, and economic outcomes are, of course, complex and difficult to comprehend, and it is by no means obvious that the French public understood them, nor that its diminished support for Europe reflected that understanding. Nevertheless, it *is* the case that many leading figures—for example, Jean-Pierre Chevènement on the Left and Philippe Séguin and Alain Madelin on the Right, among others—had articulated the linkages and made them known to the public.[52] It is at least a plausible conjecture, therefore, that the erosion of public support for the Community reflected dissatisfaction with the performance of the economy—

TABLE 13.4
The Relation Between Unemployment and Support for the European Union Across the Member States
(Entries are Correlation Coefficients, N = 12)

	Percent of Respondents Saying:				
	Membership Is "Good Thing/Bad Thing"		Country "Has/Has Not Benefitted"		
	Total Saying Membership is "Good" 5/95	Net "Good" – "Bad" 5/95	Change in Net "Good" – "Bad" 3/91–5/95	Total Saying Country Has Benefited 5/95	Net "Has Benefited" – "Has Not Benefited" 5/95	Change in Net "Has Benefited" – "Has not Benefited" 3/91–5/95
Average Percent Unemployed, 1991–94	-.30	-.34	-.31	-.37	-.42	-.39
Percent Unemployed, 1994	-.37	-.39	-.45	-.47	-.52	-.54
First-Order Change, Percent Unemployed, 1991–94	-.52	-.51	-.78	-.65	-.70	-.84

Source: For measures of support for membership, see table 13.1. For the data on levels of unemployment, see *OECD Economic Outlook 58, December 1995* (Paris: OECD, 1995), p. A24. Excludes Austria, Finland, and Sweden, which joined the EU on Jan. 1, 1995.

most notably, the unusually high level of unemployment—and a perception that that performance derived, in part, from the country's rigorous adhesion to the ERM and, more broadly, its membership in the Community.

Support for that conjecture can be found by comparing the variation across the member states of the Community in rates of unemployment, on one hand, and measures of change in support for the Community, on the other. Table 13.4 presents the correlation coefficients across the 12 member states between several measures of unemployment and the measures of support discussed earlier. The data in table 13.4 suggest a consistent inverse relationship between the levels of unemployment and support for the Community. Moreover, they suggest a very strong statistical association between the first-order change in the rate of unemployment between 1991 and 1994 and the change over that same period in the net proportion of the member states' citizens who said that membership was a "good thing" rather than a "bad thing" (r = -.78) and that membership "has benefited" rather than "has not benefited" their country (r= -.84). That is, the deterioration in support for the Community, as measured either by the change between 1991 and 1995 in the difference in each country in the proportion saying membership was a "good thing" rather than a "bad thing," or that it "has benefited" rather than "has not benefited" the country, was greatest in the countries in which the rate of unemployment increased most dramatically after 1991. Put differently, one of the major reasons support for the Community deteriorated as much as it did in France (as well as in Spain, Portugal, and Belgium) after Maastricht may have been the relatively large increase in the level of unemployment.

It is interesting to note, also, that the deterioration in support for the Community after 1991 seems to have been most acute in those countries whose currencies participated in the ERM but were not part of its so-called hard inner core and that remained in the ERM throughout the 1992-93 exchange rate crisis, most notably, Spain and Portugal and, to a lesser degree, Belgium and France. Thus, we find a moderate inverse correlation (r = -.35) between the measures of erosion in net support for the Community between 1991 and 1995 and a simple dummy variable which assigns a value of 1 to all countries that were members of the ERM, but *not* part of its hard inner core, and remained within it throughout the 1992-93 crisis, and 0 to all the rest.[53] To some extent, then, the erosion of support in such countries as Spain, Portugal, Belgium, and France may have resulted from the decision to remain in the ERM when doing so invited continuing speculative attacks on their currencies and led inevitably to further fiscal and monetary contraction and further increases in rates of unemployment that were already relatively high.

There were undoubtedly other, non-economic factors as well that contributed to the erosion of public support in France for Europe in the late 1980s and early 1990s. Of these, perhaps the most important involved the combined effect of rising dissatisfaction with Mitterrand and the Socialist governments during the president's second *septennat*, on one hand—a dissatisfaction that was registered in high disapproval ratings of the president and various prime ministers in public opinion surveys—and, on the other, the growing identification of both Mitterrand and the government with the Community as France's commitment to it deepened in the 1980s. The combined effect was, we suspect, a transference of public dissatisfaction and disapproval from the president and government to the Community with which both were closely associated. That such a transference of dissatisfaction occurred is suggested by, among other things, the fact that it was just as Mitterrand's personal popularity dropped sharply, from relatively high levels, in mid-1991 that the erosion in public support for Europe accelerated.[54]

The corrosive effect on support for the Community of growing disapproval of Mitterrand and the government may have begun in the late 1980s and early 1990s, as the president's term wore on, as scandals began to proliferate, as the governments, lacking a majority in the *Assemblée*, confronted repeated censure motions, and as successive prime ministers—first, Michel Rocard and then, most notably, Edith Cresson—lost what little popularity they once had. But the clearest evidence of a spillover of disapproval from Mitterrand to the Community appeared in 1992, in the evolution of public opinion during the campaign to ratify the Maastricht Treaty.

Table 13.5 provides the results of public opinion surveys over a period of five months in 1992 that asked respondents whether they would vote for or against the Treaty in a referendum. Soon after the Constitutional Council reported in early April 1992 on the changes in the French constitution that would be necessary in order for the Treaty to be ratified, the National Assembly began to consider the constitutional changes.[55] Even after the vocal opposition to the Treaty registered in the Assembly in May—101 deputies voted in favor of Séguin's motion to reject the Treaty outright, and 77 voted against the constitutional amendments that were necessary to allow ratification (with 99 others abstaining)[56]—support for the Treaty remained close to 70 percent. And it remained at that level when, immediately after Denmark's

TABLE 13.5
THE TREATY ON EUROPEAN UNION:
THE RATIFICATION PROCESS IN FRANCE AND PUBLIC SUPPORT, APRIL–SEPTEMBER 1992

DATE	PERCENT YES	
April 9		Constitutional Council reports on constitutional changes required prior to ratification of Treaty.
April 12		Mitterrand television interview, calls for ratification of Treaty. Raises possibility of referendum.
April 22		Government adopts draft law to revise constitution as necessary step for ratification of Treaty.
May 6		Motion in National Assembly to reject entire Treaty defeated, 101 in favor, 396 against. (58 of 126 RPR deputies vote in favor.)
May 13		National Assembly approves constitutional revisions necessary for Treaty, 398 in favor, 77 opposed, 99 abstentions. (5 RPR deputies vote in favor, 31 vote against, 88 abstain.)
May 15	68	(Sofres)
June 2		50.7 percent vote against Maastricht Treaty in Danish referendum.
June 3		Mitterrand announces French referendum to ratify Treaty.
June 4	69	(CSA)
June 8	63	(BVA)
June 11		Motion in Senate to reject entire Treaty defeated, 120 in favor, 196 against. (All 91 RPR senators vote in favor.)
June 17		Senate votes to approve constitutional revisions necessary for Maastricht Treaty, 192 in favor, 117 against.
June 19		Assembly approves Senate's constitutional revisions, 388 to 43.
June 23		Congress approves constitutional changes, 592 to 73.
June 24	56	(CSA)
July 1	61	(Sofres)
August 2	57	(IFOP)
August 5	56	(BVA)

Date	Poll	Firm
August 19	53	(CSA)
August 25	51	(IFOP)
August 25	49	(BVA)
August 25	51	(Sofres)
August 26	48	(IPSOS)
August 28	47	(CSA)
September 2	51	(BVA)
September 2	53	(IPSOS)
September 3		Mitterrand television debate with Séguin, comments by others including Helmut Kohl.
September 4	55	(CSA)
September 6	56	(IPSOS)
September 7	54	(CSA)
September 7	52	(CSA)
September 8	53	(Sofres)
September 8	50.5	(IFOP)
September 9	51	(CSA)
September 10	53	(IPSOS)
September 10	51	(ISL)
September 11	52	(CSA)
September 12	53	(IFOP)
September 12	52	(Sofres)
September 12	50	(BVA)
September 20	51.04	Referendum on Maastricht Treaty.

Source: Poll results (with polling firm in parentheses) reported in *Financial Times*, August 27, 1992, p. 2; August 29-30, 1992, p. 3; September 3, 1992, p. 1; September 7, 1992, p. 1; September 8, 1992, p. 1; September 9, 1992, p. 1; September 10, 1992, p. 4; September 11, 1992, p. 4; September 12-13, 1992, p. 1; and September 14, 1992, p. 2. Events in government and parliament reported in *Le Monde*.

rejection of the Treaty in *its* referendum, Mitterrand called a referendum in France, to be held on September 20. Yet by late August, support for the Treaty had plummeted to less than 50 percent, and it was ultimately approved by the thinnest of margins, a very *petit oui* of 51.04 percent.[57] While many factors contributed to that decline, it appears, in retrospect, that, rather than having increased his own diminished popularity by supporting a popular issue, Mitterrand's strong advocacy of the Treaty very nearly caused its defeat.

The Maastricht referendum campaign did more than just sharpen the critique of Europe and give voice to the public's accumulating dissatisfaction with a president who, by then, had been in office for more than ten years and a Socialist Party that appeared increasingly incapable of governing. It stimulated the further mobilization of opposition to Europe, both by existing parties and by new ones. Thus, as table 13.6 suggests, a variety of movements and parties devoted to rolling back the tide of European integration attracted new supporters in elections after 1992. On the Left, Chevènement's new *L'Autre Politique* (The Other Policy) won 2.5 percent in the 1994 European Parliament elections. And notwithstanding the end of the Cold War and the obsolescence of its *raison d'être*, the Communist Party—whose electorate had been overwhelmingly opposed to the Maastricht Treaty—retained the support of roughly 9 percent of the voters. A movement straddling the Left and Right, *Chasse, Pêche, Nature et Traditions* (Hunting, Fishing, Nature, Traditions), that is dedicated to the suppression of the Community's directive 79-409 pertaining to hunting, won 4 percent. On the Right, Philippe de Villers' *Majorité pour l'Autre Europe* (Majority for the Other Europe) appeared on the scene in 1994 and won 12.3 percent of the vote, and running in a crowded field in the 1995 presidential election, de Villiers won 4.7 percent of the vote. And further to the Right, Jean-Marie Le Pen, the leader of the *Front National* (National Front)— a party whose degree of hostility to Maastricht was rivaled only by the Communists and which, tellingly, had contested the 1994 European election as *Contre l'Europe de Maastricht-Allez la France!* (Against the Europe of Maastricht, Let's Go France!)—won 15 percent in the first round of the 1995 presidential election. Thus, when taken together, the anti-Europe "right of the Right" comprised about 20 percent of the vote, above and beyond the substantial number of "Euro-skeptics" who continued to support the neo-Gaullist RPR, the UDF, and their presidential candidates.

As important as the adverse economic consequences of the *franc fort*, the transference of dissatisfaction with the Mitterrand presidency to the

TABLE 13.6
THE MOBILIZATION OF OPPOSITION TO EUROPE, 1992--95

	Percent of Supporters Voting 'No' in Maastricht Referendum, September 1992	Percent of Vote, National Assembly, March 1993	Percent of Vote, European Parliament, June 1994	Percent ofVote, President, First Ballot, April 1995
LO (Workers' Struggle)/Laguiller '95		1.8	2.3	5.3
PC (Communists)/Hue'95	92	9.2	6.9	8.6
L'Autre politique (Chevènement)			2.5	
PS (Socialists)/Jospin '95	26	17.6	14.5	23.3
"Presidential Majority"		1.8		
MRG/Energie Radical		0.9	12.0	
Génération Ecologie	31	3.6	2.0	
Verts/Union des écol. pour l'Europe (Greens)/Voynet '95		4.0	3.0	3.3
Nouvelle Ecologie		2.5		
L'Europe commence à Sarajévo			1.6	
CPNT (Hunting, Fishing, Nature, Traditions)			4.0	
UDF (Union of French Dem.)	42	19.1		
UPF (Union for France) (RPR+UDF)			25.6	
RPR (Neo-Gaullists)/ Chirac & Balladur '95	67	20.4		39.4*
Diverse Right		4.7		
Majorité pour l'autre Europe/de Villiers '95)			12.3	4.7
FN (National Front/Contre l'Europe de Maastricht - Allez la France!)/Le Pen '95	95	12.4	10.5	15.0

* In the 1995 election, Chirac won 20.8 percent of the vote and Balladur 18.6 percent.
Source: 1992 vote based on exit polls conducted by SOFRES for TF1 - RTL - *Le Figaro*, reported in *Le Monde*, September 25, 1992, p. 7. Election results reported in *Le Monde*, March 23, 1993, p. 1; June 15, 1994, p. 12; April 25, 1995, p. 1.

European Community, and the mobilization of opposition during and after the Maastricht referendum were, the erosion of support for Europe did not derive *exclusively* from factors involving only French domestic politics. To some considerable extent, it reflected, also, the fact that Europe *itself* was in crisis after Maastricht. Indeed, it experienced severe and protracted crises in the two domains that figured most prominently in the Treaty on European Union—exchange rate policy and EMU, on one hand, and "political union," featuring, among other things a "Common Foreign and Security Policy," on the other. Both crises surely caused support for Europe to erode in France and, indeed, throughout the Community.

In the domain of EMU, after more than five and a half years during which no realignment had occurred, the ERM exploded in the late summer of 1992 in a series of speculative attacks and devaluations that lasted nearly a year, until eventually the fluctuation bands were widened from ± 2.25 percent to ± 15 percent in early August 1993.[58] In all, seven devaluations occurred—three involving the Spanish peseta, two the Portuguese escudo, and one apiece the Italian lira and Irish punt. In addition, two currencies—the lira and the British pound—were withdrawn from the ERM, the first time in its 13-year history that that had happened. France avoided the humiliation of a forced devaluation or departure of the franc. Nevertheless, the crisis *did* challenge the fundamental assumptions that had guided French economic policy for the better part of the past decade; for despite the fact that the rate of inflation in France was half the German rate, and despite the French government's willingness to pay whatever price was required (in terms of high interest rates, low rates of growth, and high levels of unemployment) to make its commitment to the *franc fort* and parity with the mark credible, the franc came under attack on several occasions. As if that were not enough, it was only through massive German assistance in several coordinated interventions in the markets—first in late September 1992, again in December 1992, and finally in July 1993—that France managed to avoid devaluation. Moreover, when, despite the expenditure of enormous sums, the third Franco-German defense failed to stem the attacks on the franc in the last days of July 1993, the much-vaunted cooperation between France and Germany broke down; Germany refused to lower its interest rates and commit itself to unlimited intervention in support of the franc, and France, for its part, refused to raise *its* rates or devalue, and refused, as well, a widened band for the franc or a suspension of the ERM. Only the last-ditch agreement to widen the ERM's fluctuation bands to ± 15 percent—an action that transformed it into a fundamentally different system—allowed France to maintain the fiction of the *franc fort* and parity with the mark.[59]

In the domain of foreign policy, as well, the Community experienced a crisis after Maastricht—one that not only called into question its capacity to pursue a "Common Foreign and Security Policy" but also its ability to prevent war from occurring again in Europe. The crisis involved, of course, the breakup of the former Yugoslavia. Just as the year-long crisis in the ERM may have caused support for the Community to erode as countries saw their currencies come under attack and were forced to raise interest rates or suffer a humiliating devaluation (or both), so, too, the crisis in the Balkans—especially, of course, the war, "ethnic cleansing," shelling of cities, and human suffering in Bosnia—may have caused support to erode. Support for the Community may have been especially vulnerable to the effects of the wars in the Balkans, of course, because the Community's recognition decisions in 1991-92 had played an important role in bringing about the Bosnian tragedy and then, once war had broken out, it had been unwilling to support and defend the new Bosnian state and had been unable to end the war.[60] Any erosion of support for the Community that derived from its policy toward Bosnia may have been especially marked in France because of the prominent role of French troops in the United Nations' peacekeeping force, the fact that a large number of them were located in Sarajevo (the capital city and focal point of worldwide media attention), and the disproportionate number of casualties suffered by French troops.

The Dilemma of European Integration in the Chirac Era

In their first months in office after the May 1995 presidential election, Jacques Chirac and the new government headed by Alain Juppé confronted a dilemma posed by the juxtaposition of the country's deepened commitment to Europe, on one hand, and the domestic economic situation, on the other. On the one hand, the commitment to Europe, deepened over the course of Mitterrand's two *septennats* and formalized in the Single European Act and the Treaty on European Union, carried with it certain obligations. Most notably, it committed France to continue the deregulation and liberalization of the economy begun by the SEA and "EC92" and, in particular, to impose the fiscal restraint necessary to satisfy the "convergence criterion" pertaining to the budget deficit stipulated as a condition for moving to the third and final stage of EMU.[61] On the other hand, the president and the government inherited from their predecessors an economy marked by low rates of economic growth, high levels of unemployment, high interest rates, and a relatively large budget deficit. Imposing fiscal restraint in order to reduce the budget deficit might well bring down interest rates, and eventually, contribute to an improvement in the rate of growth and diminution in the level of unemployment. For the short term, however, reduction of the deficit—obtained either through reducing public spending or increasing tax receipts and revenues, or both— would have a contractionary effect on the economy that, if anything, would further increase the already-high level of unemployment.

The dilemma was accentuated for the new president and government by the fact that they traced their ideological and political roots to Gaullism and shared de Gaulle's deep skepticism of supranational Europe. It was also accentuated by the political context within which they operated—in particular, by the fact that the growing public opposition to Europe evident in the September 1992 referendum and in subsequent elections (and in the periodic Eurobarometer surveys) was disproportionately concentrated on *their* side of the political spectrum and existed not only "to the right of the Right" in the burgeoning xenophobic *Front National* and the smaller anti-Europe movements, but even within the governing RPR *itself*, by the fact that Chirac had committed himself in the presidential election campaign, above all else, to reducing the high level of unemployment, and by the fact that the government would face elections for the *Assemblée* in less than three years.

The first manifestation of this dilemma appeared very soon after the Juppé government took office, as it sought, in its supplemental budget, to assure that France would satisfy the "convergence criteria" of EMU in time to move, with Germany and other countries, to the third and final stage in 1999 while also addressing the problem of high unemployment. As noted earlier, the "convergence criteria" stipulate, among other things, that the public deficit be less than 3 percent of GDP at the time—presumably in the first half of 1998—the member states of the EU consider which of them (if any) will move to the third stage. In 1994, the deficit had been 6 percent of GDP. After taking office, the new government discovered that, if left unchecked, the 1995 deficit would amount to some 370 billion francs and that, with the additional 60 billion franc deficit in the social security funds, the total public deficit in 1995 would be some 430 billion francs, equivalent to 5.7 percent of GDP.[62] Meanwhile, the government confronted an unemployment rate of 12.2 percent, representing 3.26 million persons, of whom 1.2 million, nearly 40 percent, had been out of work for more than a year.[63] Although the overall rate had come down slightly from its 1994 peak of 12.7 percent, it was estimated that even if the economy continued to grow at its current rate of almost 3 percent a year during the remainder of 1995 and 1996, the unemployment rate would remain well above 11 percent.[64]

How could the government cut the deficit by nearly 50 percent in three years, in order to qualify for the third stage of EMU, and simultaneously reduce the high level of unemployment by a significant amount before the legislative elections scheduled for 1998? How, in particular, could it reduce the deficit by that magnitude when the new president had made the battle against unemployment his foremost priority, when the new prime minister had committed his government, in his declaration to the *Assemblée*, to a *mobilisation générale contre le chômage de masse qui gangrène le corps social* (a general mobilization against the mass unemployment that eats away at the body of society) and had said that *tout le programme de travail que je vous présente aujourd'hui... tient en un seul mot: l'emploi* (the entire program I present today is captured in one word: employment), and when such a prominent advocate of an employment-oriented policy as Séguin sat outside the government and such an opponent of Europe as Le Pen prepared for the next election?[65] Would it not make more sense, politically, to do immediately what the financial markets suspected the government would do sooner or later in any event—concentrate on the employment issue, relax the ambition to reduce the budget deficit to 3 percent in three years, and pursue a higher growth rate by lowering interest rates, even if that meant not satisfying the EMU "convergence criteria" and causing the franc to drop in value?

It is, of course, too soon to know the answers to these questions. However, it *does* appear that, notwithstanding Chirac's considerable ambivalence about Europe, Maastricht, and EMU in the past,[66] he and the government will attempt to honor France's commitments to Europe. The first evidence of this came at Chirac's meeting in Strasbourg with Helmut Kohl the day after his investiture, when he said, "We desire that the commitments undertaken in the Maastricht Treaty be adhered to. They will be. There can't be any question that France would have an economic and monetary policy which did not respect its commitments."[67] Subsequent declarations made it apparent that France would incur the costs necessary to qualify for EMU; thus, after his summit meeting with Kohl in Bonn in October 1995, Chirac reiterated France's intention to fulfill the "convergence criteria" and enter the third stage of EMU with Germany, and immediately thereafter, in a televised address to the country, stated that a reduction of the budget and social security deficits was an imperative that could not be questioned.[68] And still later, as it became increasingly apparent in the spring of 1996 that the 3 percent deficit target for 1997 might be missed, Chirac called for "draconian" cuts in spending—despite the fact that the rate of unemployment had edged steadily upward to 11.9 percent by March 1996 in the wake of a substantial drop in the rate of economic growth in late 1995 and the first half of 1996.[69]

Despite the rhetorical commitment to Europe in general, and EMU in particular, it is not obvious that Chirac and the government can in fact reduce the deficit by an amount sufficient enough to allow France to qualify for EMU in 1999 and also reduce the level of unemployment by a significant amount. Indeed, the record of their first year in office suggests just how difficult it will be to achieve *either* objective—much less *both* objectives simultaneously. The supplemental budget presented by Juppé in June 1995 reduced the projected 1995 deficit by some 50 billion francs to 322 billion francs, by raising revenues some 30 billion francs in the remainder of 1995 (and some 70 billion francs on a full-year basis) and reducing spending by some 19 billion francs.[70] Combined with the anticipated deficit in the social security funds of 60 billion francs, the deficit reduction would have yielded a total public deficit of some 382 billion francs, equivalent to roughly 5.1 percent of GDP. The supplemental budget envisioned further reductions in the deficit in later years sufficient enough to reduce it to an amount equivalent to 4 percent of GDP in 1996 and 3 percent of GDP in 1997, thereby enabling France to qualify for stage three of EMU. It envisioned that the reductions would be achieved entirely through spending cuts, as Chirac's presidential campaign had promised, and by the elimination by 1998 of the deficit in social security funds, through "reforms" in pensions and health insurance.

That a reduction of the deficit (by one percentage point of GDP a year for three successive years) would be exceptionally difficult if not impossible for the government to enact, even with its very large majority in the Assemblée and Senate, became increasingly apparent in the protracted and difficult negotiations in the fall of 1995 over the *projet de loi de finances* (draft budget) for 1996 and the unfolding debate over "reform" of social security. With the rate of growth in the economy decreasing and fiscal receipts for 1995 failing to meet projections,[71] the *projet* proposed a further reduction in the deficit in 1996. But the reduction was relatively modest— some 33 billion francs to 289.7 billion francs (later reduced another 2.8 billion francs by the Assemblée). Even this modest reduction could be attained only by instituting a freeze on the salaries of public employees—an act that, when announced by Juppé in early September, incurred the wrath of the unions and caused them to organize a large strike of public sector workers in October. And the modest scale of the reduction meant that, in order to meet the target deficit of 4 percent of GDP in 1996, the government would have to reduce the deficit in social security funds—in excess of 60 billion francs by late 1995—by more than 30 billion francs. Given the large portion of that deficit, some 35 billion francs, that derived from health insurance, given that health expenses were increasing in 1995 at a rate of 7 percent a year, and given the outcry that greeted the first modest efforts to limit health expenses (raising the charge for hospitalization from 55 to 70 francs a day), it appeared unlikely the government could achieve a reduction of that magnitude in the social security deficit without substantially broadening the revenue base of those funds.[72]

The difficulty that Chirac and the government faced in achieving the EMU-dictated reduction in the budget deficit could be seen in the budget results for 1995. The government actually came very close to its targeted deficit of 322 billion francs, missing it by only 1 billion francs. But because the social security deficit rose to 80 billion francs (20 billion more than anticipated) the combined deficit was some 402 billion francs, 20 billion more than the original target. The higher deficit, combined with the smaller GDP because of the slowdown in the economy in the last quarter of 1995, meant the government missed its target for the 1995 deficit of 5.1 percent of GDP by several tenths of a percentage point.[73]

For 1996, the government aimed for a budget deficit of 287 billion francs, which, with a targeted deficit of 17 billion francs in social security funds, would result in a total deficit of some 304 billion francs, equivalent to about 4 percent of GDP. Yet by mid-1996, the Social Accounts Commission estimated that, largely because of reduced revenues from payroll charges, the social security deficit for the year would be 49 billion francs. This, coupled with the low rate of growth in the first half of the year, led to estimates of the aggregate deficit in 1996 in the range of 4.2 to 4.7 percent of GDP, rather than 4.0 percent.[74] As the government prepared the budget for 1997— the results of which would be critical in determining whether France met the deficit "convergence criterion" for EMU—it proposed a further reduction of 40 billion francs in the deficit to 248 billion francs, and the elimination of the entire social security deficit. By its estimation, those cuts would enable France to meet the criterion. But whether the government would in fact be able to *achieve* those cuts remained doubtful; indeed, during the first half of 1996, the European Commission, the IMF, and the OECD, all estimated that France would miss the 3 percent target with a 1997 deficit somewhere between 3.6 and 4.2 percent of GDP.[75]

Turning from deficit reduction to the attack on unemployment, because of the magnitude of the deficit, the supplemental budget of June 1995 provided considerably less for the fight against unemployment than might have been anticipated from Chirac's presidential campaign rhetoric. Thus, while it raised 30 billion francs in additional revenues in the remainder of 1995 and 70 billion on an annual basis, new spending on such employment-related measures as the *Contrat Initiative-Emploi* (Employment Initiative Contract, CIE), the *Complément d'aide à l'emploi* (employment assistance complement, CAE), and reductions in employers' social security charges was limited to less than 12 billion francs for the remainder of 1995 and some 40 billion francs on a full-year basis.[76] The *projet de loi de finances* for 1996 added little, either in terms of programs or funding, to the attack on unemployment. Thus, it remained an open question whether, in the absence of a significant reduction in interest rates and a substantial increase in the rate of economic growth over the long term, the government would be able to effect anything more than, at best, a modest reduction in unemployment.[77] And indeed, the net effect of government policy vis-à-vis employment over the first year of the Chirac presidency was, at best, meager. In the second half of 1995 only 25,000 new jobs were created (compared to 125,000 in the first half of 1995) and INSEE estimated that there would be a net *decrease* in jobs in the first six months of 1996. As a result, the rate of unemployment, which was 11.6 percent at the time of the presidential election and had dropped to 11.4 percent in August 1995, increased steadily upward to 11.9 percent by March 1996 and above 12 percent by the summer.[78]

The problem of reducing both the large budget deficit and the high level of unemployment was only the first and most immediate manifestation of a dilemma that is likely to confront Chirac and the Juppé government throughout their terms in office, as they attempt to honor France's deep, and formal, commitments to Europe while also retaining their popularity and electoral support with a public that is increasingly disillusioned with the vision of European union. While it is likely to be most visible, and most acutely felt, in the economic realm —largely because EMU figures so prominently in the near future of the Union and because Chirac and the Juppé government assigned such importance to the reduction of unemployment—it is also likely to appear in *many* domains of policy throughout the Chirac presidency. Indeed, the dilemma of choosing between European commitments and domestic political and economic imperatives is likely to extend beyond the realm of national policy to relations with the other member states of the European Union. For ultimately, it reflects not simply a disjuncture between the inherited commitments of the government to its

European partners and the attitudes of the French public but something more fundamental—a collective uncertainty, in the wake of the sustained deepening of the commitment to Europe in the 1980s and early 1990s, about whether a distinctive "national interest" still exists, apart from the new-found European identity, and, if so, whether that interest is best served by further European integration. For a president and government that draw their support and inspiration from a movement whose founder was guided by *une certaine idée de la France* (and who also had a certain, and quite different, idea of Europe), and that surely retain as an article of faith their movement's belief in an overarching national interest, that is the true dilemma of European integration. How that dilemma is resolved will, in all likelihood, determine the course of events in France, and the Union, in the next several years.

Conclusion

As the Mitterrand era ended and the Chirac era began, France was afflicted with a malaise that reflected both a dissatisfaction with the present and a diffuse anxiety about the future. To a large extent, that malaise was the product of domestic factors—above all, the accumulation of social and economic problems that the nation's political institutions appeared unable to alleviate, notwithstanding their formal powers. However, it also derived, to some extent, from international sources—most notably, the growing dissatisfaction with a European Community and Union to which the country had become ever more deeply committed over the course of Mitterrand's two *septennats*.

This chapter has examined the European sources and symptoms of the French malaise in the last years of the Mitterrand era and as the Chirac presidency began. It began by tracing the series of decisions by which France deepened its commitment to Europe, beginning with the creation of the European Monetary System in the late 1970s and culminating with the agreement to create an Economic and Monetary Union (and a political union as well) in the early 1990s. That deepening of commitment to Europe brought with it a commitment to economic policies that emphasized deregulation, liberalization, fiscal restraint, and a strong currency, and as France committed itself to Europe, and those new policies, its preferences and interests became increasingly intertwined with those of its partners—indeed, to such an extent that the prevailing sense of national interest became conflated with, and subsumed within, its European identity.

Data from a series of Eurobarometer surveys suggested that for a time during the 1980s the deepening commitment to Europe was accompanied by increasing support for the Community from the French public. But beginning in late 1989, and accelerating just as the deepening of the commitment to Europe reached an apogee at Maastricht, public support in France (and the other member states of the Community) eroded dramatically. By the end of the Mitterrand presidency, the level of support in France was among the lowest observed in any member of the Union, for reasons having to do with anxieties about the newly unified Germany, the adverse economic consequences of the *franc fort* policy, the apparent tendency of citizens to transfer their disapproval of Mitterrand and the Socialist governments to the Community with which the latter were closely identified, the mobilization of opposition to Europe during and after the 1992 referendum on the Union Treaty, and the post-Maastricht crises in the Community involving the ERM and the wars in the Balkans.

The juxtaposition of a deepened, and formalized, commitment to Europe and a public that is increasingly skeptical about, and hostile to, the Union creates a dilemma for Jacques Chirac and the government headed by Alain Juppé, and the chapter concluded with a discussion of some facets of that dilemma. The dilemma—whether to honor the various commitments to Europe agreed by their predecessors, when doing so may hinder their ability to address the multitude of social and economic problems for which they will undoubtedly be held accountable—is accentuated by the fact that they represent a Gaullist tradition that is deeply suspicious of supranational Europe and govern with a party that is deeply divided over Europe, that confronts a hostile anti-Europe opposition "to the right of the Right," and that faces the prospect of legislative elections in less than two years. Given that context, it is not surprising that Chirac spoke, almost wistfully, at his investiture of his hope that the French would become *plus patriotes et en même temps plus européens* ("more patriotic and at the same time more European")[79] for only when that happens will Europe represent a venue for French leadership in pursuit of the national interest rather than a source of commitments that are costly both in economic and political terms.

In closing, it is appropriate to return to the issue with which I began—the malaise that afflicts the collective political psyche of the country. After the 1995 presidential election, it appeared that the malaise that afflicted the French political consciousness in the 1980s and 1990s might be supplanted by a new vigor and dynamism as Jacques Chirac brought the force of his personality to the issues of the day. Perhaps that malaise will turn out to have been only the natural collective psychological response in the last days of a presidency that had lasted too long; perhaps Chirac's reinvigoration of the presidency, and his forceful assertion of the national interest in the international arena, will in time alleviate those feelings of dissatisfaction and anxiety and allow the French to regain the confidence they seemed to lack in the face of domestic problems and international uncertainties.

It is, of course, much too soon to say whether that will happen. However, there is some reason to believe it *will* in fact happen, if only because of the force of personality and energy of the president. It is hard to imagine, for example, that Chirac could tolerate the degree of institutional passivity and inertia in the face of social and economic problems that existed in the last years of the Mitterrand presidency. On the other hand, it is by no means certain that it will happen in the immediate future, and indeed, evidence from public-opinion surveys accumulated in the first weeks and months of the Chirac presidency suggested that, far from diminishing, the French malaise was *deepening* at an accelerating rate. Within weeks, it appeared that the new president's honeymoon with the French public would be remarkably short-lived and that the French public was no less discontented with its governors in the Chirac era than it had been in the last years of the Mitterrand era. Thus, as table 13.7 indicates, in the first several months of Chirac's term, his popularity and that of Juppé and his government, plummeted dramatically. Reflecting the cumulative effect of a series of discrete events—Chirac's decision in June 1995 to resume nuclear testing, the abrupt dismissal in late August of Alain Madelin as minister of economy and finance, Juppé's peremptory decision in early September to freeze public sector salaries, the possibility that came to light in October that the prime minister had violated the law in renting an apartment from the city of Paris while he was an assistant mayor—superimposed upon the continuing economic problems of high interest rates, low growth, and high unemployment, and the growing realization that, because of the EMU constraint on the budget, "reform" was increasingly becoming synonymous with deficit reduction, the public dissatisfaction with Chirac and Juppé, and with the way France is governed in general, was unprecedented in its magnitude.[80] Thus, paradoxically, regardless of how much Chirac's victory may have brought a new dynamism to the Elysée and the French government, the French malaise not only continues but has deepened to such an extent as to dramatically erode support for the president,

TABLE 13.7
THE SHORT HONEYMOON OF JACQUES CHIRAC:
THE FRENCH PUBLIC'S VIEWS OF CHIRAC AND THE JUPPÉ GOVERNMENT, MAY–DECEMBER 1995

"What opinion do you have of Jacques Chirac as president of the Republic?"

	Good	Bad	Net
May	62	22	+40
June	55	27	+28
July	51	33	+18
September	44	47	-3
October	36	56	-20
November	32	61	-29
December	37	59	-22

"What opinion do you have of Alain Juppé as Prime Minister?"

	Good	Bad	Net
May	59	18	+41
June	52	25	+27
July	50	31	+19
September	43	44	-1
October	29	62	-33
November	29	63	-34
December	31	65	-34

"Are you satisfied or dissatisfied with the way in which France is governed?"

	Satisfied	Dissatisfied	Net
May	36	44	-8
June	38	46	-8
July	38	48	-10
September	32	61	-29
October	22	73	-51
November	22	72	-50
December	26	71	-45

Source: BVA surveys, reported in *Paris Match*, July 6, 1995, p. 54; August 3, 1995, p. 80; September 28, 1995, p. 96; October 26, 1995, p. 92, and December 28, 1995, p. 58.

the prime minister, and the institutions of the Fifth Republic. This was true before the strikes of November–December 1995 and only became more obvious in the wake of those events. Whether Chirac can reverse that deterioration in popularity and the sense of malaise that accompanies it will largely determine the success or failure of his presidency. And whether he can do this will ultimately depend on his ability to deploy the force of his personality and the powers of his office to create policies that address and alleviate the social and economic problems of contemporary France—above all, the problem of recurring low growth and high unemployment—while at the same time maintaining and honoring France's accumulated commitments to the European Union. More than anything else, this is, and will remain, Chirac's foremost challenge.

Notes to Chapter 13

1. The heads of state and government, meeting as the European Council, had agreed to the Treaty at their meeting in Maastricht in December 1991. But the Treaty was formally signed by the foreign and finance ministers of the member states in Maastricht in February 1992.

2. See, among many, D.C. Kruse, *Monetary Integration in Western Europe: EMU, EMS and Beyond* (London: Butterworth, 1980).

3. See the declaration read by Schmidt at the conclusion of the European Council meeting in Bremen in July 1978, reported in European Commission, "The European Monetary System," *European Economy* 3 (July 1978): 67. For the definitive account of the creation of the EMS, see Peter Ludlow, *The Making of the European Monetary System: A Case Study of the Politics of the European Community* (London: Butterworth, 1982).

4. Giscard served as secretary of state in the Ministry of Economy and Finance in 1959-62 and as minister in 1962-66 and 1969-74. Schmidt served as minister of finance in 1972-74. Giscard became president and Schmidt chancellor in May 1974. Barre served as vice president of the Commission in charge of monetary affairs in the late 1960s and early 1970s and, in that capacity, played a major role in the development of proposals to eliminate the margins of fluctuation between currencies and to create, by stages, an Economic and Monetary Union. He became prime minister in August 1976, after Jacques Chirac resigned.

5. See David R. Cameron, "From Barre to Balladur: Economic Policy in the Era of the EMS," in Gregory Flynn, ed., *Remaking the Hexagon: The New France in the New Europe* (Boulder, Col.: Westview, 1995), chapter 7, especially pp. 124-26.

6. See David R. Cameron, "Exchange Rate Politics in France, 1981-1983: The Regime-Defining Choices of the Mitterrand Presidency," in Anthony Daley, ed., *The Mitterrand Era* (New York and London: New York University and Macmillan, 1995), chapter 3.

7. For a discussion of the negotiations surrounding the three realignments, including the commitments about macroeconomic policy made by France to Germany and its other partners, as well as the details of the subsequent policy, see Cameron, "Exchange Rate Politics."

8. Based on the accumulated difference in inflation rates between France and Germany since March 1979, by October 1981 the franc was overvalued vis-à-vis the mark by roughly 20 percent. The devaluation that month of the franc by 3 percent and revaluation of the mark by 5.5 percent thus eliminated less than one-half of the overvaluation. That, coupled with the continued difference of roughly seven percentage points between the German and French rates of inflation, made a second realignment, and then a third, inevitable. See Cameron "From Barre to Balladur," 127, table 7-4.

9. See, for example, Mitterrand's comment in 1983 quoted in Serge July, *Les Années Mitterrand: Histoire baroque d'une normalisation inachevée* (Paris: Grasset, 1986), p. 96.

10. In December 1979, NATO agreed to deploy 108 intermediate-range Pershing II ballistic missiles in Germany, in place of 108 short-range Pershing IA's, and 464 ground-launched cruise missiles—also intermediate-range (1500 miles)—in Germany, Belgium, the Netherlands, Britain, and Italy, beginning in December 1983 unless United States-USSR negotiations on intermediate-range nuclear forces had produced an agreement by that time. The immediate impetus was the USSR's deployment of the several hundred new SS-20 missiles, which had a considerably longer range (3000 miles) than the SS-4's and SS-5's they were designed to replace, were mobile, and had three independently targeted warheads. By 1979, some 260 SS-20's had been deployed, thereby doubling the number of warheads targeted on western Europe. The first European leader to call for a western response was Helmut Schmidt, in a speech at the International Institute for Strategic Studies in London, in October 1977. For discussions of the NATO decision, see Linda P. Brady and Joyce P. Kaufman, eds., *NATO in the 1980s: Challenges and Responses* (New York: Praeger, 1985).

11. See Stanley Hoffmann, "Mitterrand's Foreign Policy, or Gaullism by any other Name," in George Ross, Stanley Hoffmann, and Sylvia Malzacher, eds., *The Mitterrand Experiment* (New York: Oxford, 1987).

12. See *Facts on File*, 41 (July 17, 1981): 502; and *Le Monde*, July 14, 1981, pp. 1, 4.

13. *Facts on File*, 42 (February 26, 1982): 131-35; and *Le Monde*, February 27, 1992, p. 1.

14. *Facts on File*, 42 (October 29, 1982): 808; and *Le Monde*, October 22, 1982, pp. 1, 4.

15. See, *Facts on File*, 43 (January 21, 1983): 25; and *Le Monde*, January 21, 1983, pp. 1, 3.

16. After several rounds of the United States-USSR negotiations at Geneva had produced no settlement, the German Bundestag voted, on November 23, 1983, to deploy the first battery of Pershing IIs. The next day the Soviet

Union walked out of the talks. Eventually, in 1987, the United States and the USSR agreed to eliminate the Intermediate Nuclear Forces.

17. See Andrew Moravcsik, "Negotiating the Single European Act," in Robert O. Keohane and Stanley Hoffmann, eds., *The New European Community* (Boulder, Col.: Westview, 1991).

18. *Le Monde*, January 21, 1983, pp. 1, 3.

19. *Le Monde*, January 3, 1984, p. 6.

20. *Le Monde*, February 4, 1984, p. 18.

21. *Le Monde*, February 9, 1984, pp. 1, 7.

22. *Le Monde*, May 25, 1984, pp. 1, 4; and *Le Monde*, May 26, pp. 1, 3.

23. The draft treaty, approved by the Parliament in February 1984, was frequently referred to as the Spinelli project, after its principal sponsor, Altiero Spinelli, an Italian Communist MEP who was the rapporteur of the parliamentary commission that drafted it.

24. For a discussion of the budget rebate issue, see David R. Cameron, "The 1992 Initiative: Causes and Consequences," in Alberta M. Sbragia, ed., *Euro-politics: Institutions and Policymaking in the "New" European Community* (Washington, D.C.: Brookings, 1992), chapter 2, especially pp. 59-62.

25. Ibid., 33-34.

26. For extensive discussions of these two reports, see, among many, Cameron, "The 1992 Initiative;" and Moravcsik, "Negotiating the Single European Act."

27. Although amendments to the Treaties of the Community/Union require the approval of all member states, the convening of an IGC requires approval by only a majority. At Milan, Britain, Greece, and Denmark opposed convening such a conference, but all three agreed to participate.

28. The SEA was agreed by the European Council at its meeting in December 1985, was formally signed by the foreign ministers in February 1986, and, after some delay in ratification, went into effect on July 1, 1987.

29. See Article 13 of the SEA. To be approved by a 'qualified' majority, directives must receive the support of a weighted 'super-majority' (i.e., about 70 percent) of the Council, where the member states are assigned weights roughly proportional to their relative populations.

30. The principle of mutual recognition emerged from the European Court of Justice in 1979 in the *Cassis de Dijon* case. See Martin Shapiro, "The European Court of Justice," in Alberta M. Sbragia, ed., *Euro-politics: Institutions and Policymaking in the "New" European Community* (Washington: Brookings, 1992), pp. 128-34.

31. For a classic statement of that tradition, see Andrew Shonfield, *Modern Capitalism* (New York: Oxford, 1969).

32. In mid-1965, France withdrew from the Council of Ministers in a dispute over the right of members to exercise a veto. The "empty chair" crisis was resolved in early 1966 by the "Luxembourg Compromise," by which the member states agreed to protect the "vital" interests of a member against an adverse majority vote in the Council by continuing to negotiate. France (but not the other member states) understood the Compromise to mean that if no agreement resulted, the directive under consideration was rejected.

33. See Kruse, *Monetary Integration*.

34. For a detailed discussion of this later EMU initiative, see David R. Cameron, "Transnational Relations and the Development of European Economic and Monetary Union," in Thomas Risse-Kappen, ed., *Bringing Transnational Relations Back In: Non-State Actors, Domestic Structures, and International Institutions* (Cambridge: Cambridge, 1995), chapter 2.

35. See Nicholas Colchester and David Buchan, *Europower: The Essential Guide to Europe's Economic Transformation* (New York: Random House, 1990), pp. 160-61.

36. Ultimately, the German government *did* revalue the mark, by 3 percent. (The Dutch guilder was revalued by the same amount, and the Belgian-Luxembourg franc by 2 percent).

37. For an account of these negotiations, see Cameron, "Transnational Relations."

38. On German unification, see, among many, Timothy Garton Ash, *In Europe's Name: Germany and the Divided Continent* (New York: Doubleday, 1993); Peter H. Merkl, *German Unification in the European Context* (University Park, Penn.: Pennsylvania State University Press, 1993); Elizabeth Pond, *Beyond the Wall: Germany's Road to Unification* (Washington, D.C.: Brookings, 1993); and Philip Zelikow and Condoleezza Rice, *Germany Unified and Europe Transformed: A Study in Statecraft* (Cambridge: Harvard, 1995).

39. On the "ten-point program" and Kohl's views, see Garton Ash, *In Europe's Name*, 343-56 and 384-98; Pond, *Beyond the Wall*, 137-38; and Zelikow and Rice, *Germany Transformed*, 118-25.

40. Pond, *Beyond the Wall*, 156.

41. See *Le Monde*, December 8, 1989, pp. 1, 2.

42. *Le Monde*, December 12, 1989, p. 5.

43. The Delors Committee issued its report on EMU in April 1989. The European Council agreed at Madrid in June that the first stage would begin on July 1, 1990 and that an IGC to draft the Treaty amendments necessary for stages two and three would be convened sometime after the first stage had begun. The leaders anticipated the IGC would last one year and the ratification of

the amendments by the member states would take the better part of another year. At Strasbourg, the leaders (without a vote, although Mrs. Thatcher was opposed) agreed to start the IGC in December 1990. See *Le Monde*, December 8, 1989, pp. 1, 2.

44. See *Le Monde*, April 20, 1990, pp. 1, 4.

45. Quoted in "German unity welcomed," *Financial Times*, April 30, 1990, p. 2.

46. The "convergence criteria" stipulate the conditions that must be satisfied by states in order to move to the third and final stage of EMU. They include the rate of inflation, the size of the government's budget deficit and the public debt, the degree of stability of exchange rates, and long-term interest rates. They are described in Article 109j.1 and Protocol 6 of the Treaty.

47. For a useful discussion of the Treaty, see, among many, Andrew Duff, John Pinder, and Roy Pryce, eds., *Maastricht and Beyond: Building the European Union* (New York: Routledge, 1994).

48. On the discussion and negotiation of article 109j.4 and protocol 10, see *Financial Times*, December 11, 1991, p. 2; and December 12, 1991, p. 2.

49. At their meeting in June 1995, the finance ministers agreed unanimously, over the strenuous objections of the Commission, that the 1997 deadline was unrealistic. At their meeting in Cannes one week later, the European Council retained 1997 as a possible date for the move to stage three of EMU, although there was an informal consensus in support of the finance ministers' position. See *Le Monde*, June 21, 1995, p. 1; and *Le Monde*, June 28, 1995, p. 4.

50. The full wording of the questions is as follows: "Generally speaking, do you think that (respondent's country's) membership in the Common Market is a good thing, a bad thing, or neither?" and "Taking everything into consideration, would you say that (respondent's country) has on balance benefited or not from being a member of the EC?" The former has been asked since 1973, the latter since 1983. The responses are reported in European Commission, *Eurobarometer: Trends, 1974-93* (Brussels: European Commission, May 1994); *Eurobarometer: 41, July 1994* (Brussels: European Commission, September 1994); *Eurobarometer: 42, December 1994* (Brussels: European Commission, spring 1995); and *Eurobarometer: 43, Autumn 1995* (Brussels: European Commission, 1995).

51. By the end of 1987—the year in which French and German exchange rates were last realigned—the franc was overvalued vis-à-vis the mark by roughly 12 percent. The difference between the French and German inflation rates, while diminishing each year after 1987, nevertheless totaled roughly 6 percent by the end of 1990, suggesting the franc was, by then, overvalued by about 18 percent relative to the mark. (After 1990, that overvaluation was reduced by a few percentage points as the German rate of inflation exceeded the French rate.) The German discount rate was increased on nine consecutive occasions between mid-1988 and mid-1992, from 2.5 percent to 8.75 percent. On the

overvaluation of the franc, see Cameron, "From Barre to Balladur," 127, table 7.4, n. 40, p. 155. On German interest rates, see *Financial Times*, July 17, 1992, p. 1.

52. Chevènement had been one of the leading advocates of an exit from the ERM when he served in the Mauroy governments in 1981-83. Séguin and Madelin had voiced their opposition to participation in the ERM in the 1992 debate over the Maastricht Treaty and at various moments during the subsequent ERM crisis. Séguin was selected by Mitterrand to represent the opposition to the Treaty in a three-hour nationally-televised debate on September 3, 1992.

53. We have arbitrarily identified Germany, the Netherlands, and Luxembourg as belonging to the hard inner core of the ERM. Italy and the United Kingdom, both of which dropped out of the ERM in September 1992, and Greece, which never joined, are also assigned a value of 0. All others are assigned a value of 1.0.

54. Surveys conducted by BVA in 1991 found that the proportion of the French public having a good opinion of Mitterrand as president actually *rose*, to more than 60 percent, in February and March (in part, no doubt, a result of the Gulf War). But by December, that figure had dropped to 35 percent. Conversely, the proportion having a bad opinion of him as president was less than 30 percent in March but rose to more than 50 percent in December. The trend lines crossed in September. See *Paris Match*, January 1, 1992, p.7.

55. Once the constitutional changes required by Maastricht (pertaining to the creation of a single currency and the extension of the suffrage in local elections to citizens of other member states) had passed both the National Assembly and the Senate, Mitterrand had the option of either calling a referendum or convening a "Congress" composed of the Assembly and Senate that would have to approve the revisions by a 60 percent majority. In the end, he did both.

56. Séguin's motion to reject the Treaty was defeated by a vote of 396 to 101. Among the 101 supporting the motion were 58 of the RPR's 126 deputies, a few non-RPR center-right deputies, all 26 Communist deputies, and Chevènement and a handful of Socialists. The constitutional amendments were approved by a vote of 398 to 77, with 99 abstentions. Of the RPR deputies, five voted in favor, 31 against, and 88 (including Chirac) abstained.

57. The margin of approval of the Treaty was even thinner in metropolitan France—50.82 percent. It won approval in only 9 of the 22 regions and 42 of the 96 *départements*.

58. For a detailed discussion of the crisis, see David R. Cameron, "British Exit, German Voice, French Loyalty: Defection, Domination, and Cooperation in the 1992-93 ERM Crisis" (paper presented at the Annual Meeting of the American Political Science Association, Washington, D.C., September 1993).

59. For an account of the dramatic events and negotiations of July and early August 1993, see Cameron, "British Exit, German Voice, French Loyalty."

60. Glenny argues "the death sentence for Bosnia-Hercegovina was passed in the middle of December 1991 when Germany announced that it would recognize Slovenia and Croatia unconditionally on 15 January 1992." See Misha Glenny, *The Fall of Yugoslavia: The Third Balkan War* (New York: Penguin, 1994), p. 165.

In a "very conflictual" ten-hour meeting only one week after the European Council meeting in Maastricht in December 1991, the foreign ministers considered whether and when to recognize Slovenia and Croatia, both of which had declared their independence in June, 1991. Under great pressure from Germany, which had argued for recognition since the summer (and whose chancellor had already promised their leaders recognition by Christmas), the ministers agreed to heed the advice of the five-man commission of constitutional court members headed by Robert Badinter of France and created by the EC's Peace Conference at The Hague as to which former republics should be granted recognition, and to do so on January 15, 1992. But the day after the ministers' meeting, Kohl announced at the CDU Congress in Dresden that Germany would recognize Slovenia and Croatia on January 15. In January, after the Badinter Commission had advised that Slovenia and Macedonia (which had also applied for recognition) satisfied its criteria but that Croatia did not, because of insufficient guarantees of minority rights, the ministers, under pressure from Germany, agreed to recognize Slovenia and *Croatia*. In recognizing the latter, they failed to require, as a condition of recognition, institutional means by which the Serb minority could share power in the new state and simultaneously retain its ties to Serbia. The ministers also stipulated that Bosnia-Hercegovina, the fourth applicant for recognition, need only conduct a referendum to establish a mandate for independence—despite the fact that, as the Croatian referendum of 1991 had demonstrated, a majority could be obtained without the support of the Bosnian Serbs. The referendum was conducted, in late February 1992, the Bosnian Serbs boycotted it and an overwhelming majority voted in favor of independence, independence was duly declared, and recognition extended in early April 1992. Immediately thereafter, the war began. On the ministers' decisions, see *Le Monde,* December 17, 1991, p. 4; December 18, 1991, pp. 1, 3; and January 16, 1992, pp. 1, 4.

61. The criterion stipulates that the combined deficit of all levels of government must be less than 3 percent of GDP unless it has 'declined substantially' and 'comes close to' 3 percent or is judged to be 'exceptional'. The decision on entering stage three of EMU on January 1, 1999 will be made on the basis of the budget performance in 1997.

62. As it prepared the supplemental budget, the Juppé government found that the Balladur government had included 47 billion francs in proceeds from privatization to reach its projected deficit for 1995 of 275 billion francs. In

addition, revenues were running some 11 billion below projection and expenditures some 38 billion above projection. The "real" deficit, therefore, was likely to be 371 billion francs. See *Le Monde*, June 2, 1995, p. 8; June 18-19, 1995, p. 5; June 23, 1995, pp. 1, 7; June 24, 1995, pp. 1, 6-7; and *Financial Times*, June 23, 1995, pp. 1, 3, and 12.

63. *Financial Times*, June 2, 1995, p. 3. As of August 1995, the government used a new method for calculating the rate of unemployment in accord with a ruling by the *Conseil d'Etat* pertaining to the application of a 1991 law. The new method excluded from the definition of unemployed those seeking employment who worked more than 78 hours a month and reduced the aggregate number of unemployed by roughly 300,000. Using the new measure, the rate of unemployment in May 1995 was 11.6 percent. See *Le Monde*, September 2, 1995, pp. 1, 22; and *Financial Times*, November 1, 1995, p. 16.

64. See the estimates for growth and unemployment in 1995 and 1996 reported in *Le Monde*, May 19, 1995, p. 4. As will be noted, the growth forecasts for the remainder of 1995 and 1996 proved to be far too optimistic.

65. See Chirac's investiture address on May 17, 1995, reported in *Le Monde*, May 18, 1995, p.1, and Juppé's declaration before the *Assemblée* on May 23, 1995, reported in *Le Monde*, May 25, 1995, p. 66. Séguin decided to retain the presidency of the *Assemblée* rather than take a position in the Juppé government.

66. Chirac abstained in the May 1992 vote in the *Assemblée* on the constitutional amendments pertaining to the Maastricht Treaty but supported the Treaty in the September referendum. In November 1994, at the start of his presidential campaign, he called for another referendum on EMU prior to France's moving to the third stage but was soon persuaded to withdraw the proposal. In May 1995, during the campaign, Chirac again called for a referendum—this time on the institutional reforms and other changes that might be negotiated in the Maastricht-mandated Intergovernmental Conference scheduled for 1996.

67. *Le Monde*, May 20, 1995, pp. 1, 2.

68. *Le Monde*, October 27, 1995, p. 2.

69. The unemployment rate (calculated according to the new formula) had dropped from 11.6 at the time of the presidential election to 11.4 percent in August 1995. In September 1995, the government had forecast that the economy would grow by 2.8 percent in 1996; by the spring of 1996, it was forecasting a growth rate of 1.3 percent for the year. See *Financial Times*, March 26, 1996, p. 3; and May 1, 1996, p. 2. By mid-1996, the European Commission, the OECD, and the IMF all were forecasting that France would miss its 1997 deficit target of 3 percent of GDP. See *The Economist*, April 20, 1996, p. 43; and *Financial Times*, June 3, 1996, p. 2.

70. Most of the additional revenues came from an increase of two percentage points in the Value Added Tax (TVA), from 18.6 to 20.6 percent, that went into effect on August 1, 1995. The taxes on wealth and on corporate profits were also increased by 10 percent.
71. By mid-October, 1995, INSEE was estimating that the rate of economic growth in 1996 was likely to be in the range of 2.5 percent, rather than the 2.8 percent assumed in the draft budget. And largely because of the declining rate of growth, by the fall of 1995 the fiscal receipts appeared to be some 30 billion francs below the figure estimated in the 1995 budget and some 20 billion francs below the figure estimated only a few months earlier in the supplementary budget. See *Le Monde*, September 13, 1995, p. 7, and October 15-16, 1995, p. 5.
72. That such an overhaul would be undertaken, however, was suggested in September 1995 by Jean Arthuis, the minister of economics, finance, and the plan. He suggested that the fiscal reform advocated by Chirac in the presidential election might involve shifting some 400 billion francs over five years from social contributions to other taxes and that, as part of that reform, the revenue basis of social security might be enlarged. In June 1996, Juppé announced the government would propose a five-year program of tax reform in the fall that would eliminate loopholes and many deductions in the income tax and broaden its base (roughly one-half of all households currently paid no income tax), lower tax rates for all, and shift taxes for health from wage earners and companies to a new universal health charge to be paid by all. Although not acknowledged, the net effect, of course, would be a substantial increase in aggregate tax revenues. See *Le Monde*, September 28, 1995, pp. 1, 8; October 3, 1995, p. 7; October 11, 1995, p. 1; and *Financial Times*, June 4, 1996, pp. 17-18.
73. See *Financial Times*, March 1, 1996, p. 1.
74. Ibid. On the estimated 1996 social security deficit, see *Financial Times*, June 10, 1996, p. 2; and June 11, 1996, p. 3. In early 1996, the European Commission estimated the deficit for the year would be 4.2 percent of GDP; in May 1996, the OECD estimated it would be 4.7 percent. See *Financial Times*, May 16, 1996, p. 2; and June 3, 1996, p. 2.
75. During the first quarter of 1996, the European Commission and the IMF predicted a 1997 deficit of 3.6 percent. In May, the OECD predicted a deficit of 4.2 percent, which it subsequently reduced slightly after the French government argued that an estimate of 3.8 percent was more appropriate. See *The Economist*, April 20, 1996, p. 43; and *Financial Times*, June 3, 1996, p. 2. The uncertainty about the size of the deficit derived, of course, not only from uncertainty about the proposals for spending cuts that would be put forward in the 1997 budget in September 1996 but also about the effects of the five-year reform of taxes that would be announced at that time, as well as the rate

of growth in the economy in 1997 (which the government generously estimated at 2.8 percent).

76. The CIE involved a subsidy to employers of 2,000 francs per month for two years, and an exoneration from all charges for social security on the portion of salary below the monthly minimum wage (SMIC) of 6,250 francs for each new hire of a person who had been unemployed more than one year. If the person is over 50, the exoneration from social charges remains until retirement. The cost of the CIE was estimated at 3.2 billion francs for the remainder of 1995. The CAE involved a subsidy of 2,000 francs per month for nine months to employers for each hire of a person under 25. It was estimated to cost 2.4 billion francs for the remainder of 1995. Finally, all firms received an exoneration of employers' social charges on employees at or near the minimum wage equal to a maximum of 10 percent of the charges paid on those receiving the SMIC and diminishing to 0 for employees earning 20 percent or more above the SMIC. The cost of this was estimated to be 5.4 billion for the remainder of 1995. See *Le Monde,* June 24, 1995, p. 6.

77. That the employment-generating measures would have, at best, only a modest impact was the conclusion of a detailed analysis conducted by the *Observatoire français des conjonctures économiques* (OFCE). The OFCE estimated that all of the measures taken together would be likely to generate 175,000 new jobs by the end of 1996, while the increase in the TVA that accompanied the measures would reduce the rate of economic growth by about 0.6 percent and result in a loss of 30,000 jobs. Taken together, the job measures and tax increases, when coupled with the natural increase in the labor force, would leave roughly three million persons unemployed. On the OFCE analysis, see *Le Monde,* July 13, 1995, p. 6. See, also, the interview with Jean-Paul Fitoussi, the president of OFCE, in *Le Monde,* October 10-15, 1995, p. 10.

78. See *The Economist,* April 6, 1996, p. 52.

79. From Chirac's investiture address. See *Le Monde,* May 18, 1995, p. 1.

80. See Jean-Luc Parodi, quoted in *Le Monde,* July 25, 1995, p. 6.

Chapter 14

A Testing Time for the Pursuit of Grandeur

Jolyon Howorth

"Hourra pour la France!" exclaimed Charles de Gaulle in February 1960 upon hearing the news of the first French nuclear test. Possession of the nuclear weapon conferred on France a peculiar status and rank that successive presidents of the Republic have successfully exploited in three major ways. First, entry to an exclusive club, coinciding with permanent membership in the United Nations Security Council, guaranteed, throughout the duration of the Cold War, that France would stride the diplomatic stage if not like a colossus, then at least like a serious player. Second, the French bomb ensured military and therefore diplomatic "superiority" over Germany, thus helping to cement what would otherwise have been a very unbalanced Franco-German partnership in the new Europe. The fact that the French bomb was able to be presented as rigorously bleu-blanc-rouge also conferred a type of one-upmanship over Britain, which remained highly dependent on the United States.[1] Third, under the situation of nuclear stalemate that occurred after the Cuban missile crisis, the French bomb contributed to the complexity of the nuclear equation and thereby played a non-negligible role in deterrence. As long as the world was structured by the balance of terror underwritten by the superpowers, the bomb appeared to serve a useful purpose. Furthermore, the discourse that accompanied it, by stressing deterrence and peace (as opposed to the prospect of limited warfare as in NATO's flexible response doctrine), helped ensure the creation of a stable political consensus around French nuclear policy that was never quite matched in other NATO countries.[2]

It is now commonplace to read that, with the end of the Cold War, the disintegration of the Soviet Union, the advent of massive reductions in superpower nuclear arsenals and the reemergence of limited, regional security threats (whose management requires neither nuclear arsenals nor a nuclear doctrine), France has emerged from the events of the past five years as a massive loser on the international stage.[3] There is little doubt that the "nuclear ace" of the Cold War years has been substantially devalued, and along with it the diplomatic "rank" to which all French presidents have attached such importance. It has become increasingly difficult for France, given the emergence of something journalists and politicians have dubbed the "international community," to ignore the considerable impetus that has been assumed by arms control agreements, and particularly by the Nuclear Non-Proliferation Treaty (NPT). Resources have also become a massive headache, not only because of domestic pressures for delivery of a "peace dividend," but also, far more significantly, because the new world disorder of regional instability and limited military intervention requires considerable outlay on conventional weaponry, which France badly neglected during the Cold War years. Its limited participation in the Gulf War and its military frustrations in Bosnia[4] have demonstrated to the world just how small a colossus France really is. The development of new generations of sophisticated conventional weapons carries a price tag that increases exponentially. This introduces yet another dimension to the apparent reduction in France's global influence since 1989: the obvious need to Europeanize its military and security arrangements.[5] Europeanization means, among other things, securing German political and financial support for projects that often meet with German ambivalence.

Jacques Chirac's announcement, on June 13, 1995, that France intended to conduct a new (and final) series of nuclear tests in the South Pacific between September 1995 and May 1996 raised a much bigger international outcry than any other event in France's nuclear history. There are several reasons for this. First, the tests' proximity to the fiftieth anniversary commemorations of the bombing of Hiroshima unleashed a worldwide flood of emotion and passion. Second, France's decision reversed a universally applauded moratorium on tests (imposed by François Mitterrand in April 1992), a moratorium also respected by the other nuclear powers except China.

To that extent, the resumption of testing was perceived by world opinion as a significant step backwards. Third, it allowed a coalition of Pacific lobbies, from the semi-official Japanese "never-again culture," Polynesian independence movements, and environmental groups such as Greenpeace, to the Australian and New Zealand governments, to vent their moral outrage (via the televised media) to the entire world. Fourth, it touched a raw European nerve, revealing once again the depth of the anti-nuclear culture, particularly in the Nordic countries. Above all, perhaps, it refocused the world's attention on the political dimension of a question that had been filed away in the euphoria of the Cold War's demise: what is the purpose of nuclear weapons in the year 2000? These questions emerged against the backdrop of an important domestic debate that has intensified within the French defense establishment over the last five years.

What Chirac actually proposed on June 13 was, on the surface, quite straightforward; France needed to conduct a series of seven or at most eight further tests in order to guarantee the *sûreté, sécurité et fiabilité* ("safety and reliability") of its existing nuclear arsenal and to allow it to master the techniques of laboratory simulation. The test program would last from September 1995 to May 1996 and would allow France to formally ratify the NPT. In a further statement to the French senate on July 12, 1995 Chirac gave technical details of the proposed tests. One test was required to complete a series of 22 previous tests perfecting the TN-75 warhead for the new M-45 submarine-launched missile. Two tests were required to verify the stability of the trigger devices for French nuclear warheads. A further four tests, with the possibility of a fifth, would be required to perfect the calibration of the instruments involved in mastering the technique of nuclear test simulation in a laboratory in a program called PALEN (Préparation à la Limitation des Essais Nucléaires).[6] It is interesting to note that these technical details did not coincide with the aims and objectives expressed by leading experts prior to Chirac's senate statement.[7] Finally, Chirac suggested that the silo-based missile site on the Plateau d'Albion would eventually be closed down, leaving France with an airborne and a seaborne deterrent but no land-based system. It is in the context of the internal French debate on nuclear weapons that Chirac's decision must be scrutinised if it is to be properly understood, not merely via widely proliferated televised images of French marines storming the anti-nuclear Greenpeace ships Rainbow Warrior and Vega.

François Mitterrand, during his 14 years at the Elysée, authorized 86 nuclear tests in the South Pacific, three times more than de Gaulle, and approximately half of all of France's nuclear tests.[8] In the eyes of commentators and caricaturists alike, Mitterrand acquired a reputation as a devout apostle of nuclear deterrence. Yet, on May 5, 1994, he bared his soul to the media and explained in great detail the rationale behind his decision, two years previously, to impose a moratorium on testing. In so doing, he hinted at the alternative agendas lurking behind the French debate. He even attempted to preempt what he feared would be a future president's (Chirac?) desire to resume testing, by arguing that it would be morally and politically impossible for any successor to reverse his moratorium.[9] Mitterrand's reasons for imposing the moratorium are logically consistent with the nuclear stance that he adopted throughout his presidency. They also reflect the arguments of the mainstream nuclear doctrine in France, which includes traditional Gaullists, reluctant centrists, and converted Socialists. These strategists view nuclear weapons as weapons of deterrence, not weapons of war. They are, therefore, not only legitimate but vitally important. As such, they need to be up-to-date technically and credible. This required tests. Sufficient quantities of nuclear weapons (but no more) are considered essential to ensure their credibility. By 1992, Mitterrand and mainstream politicians believed that those objectives had been met through the test program that he had overseen and that, therefore, there was no further need for tests. Moreover, the French recognized that the world had changed fundamentally since 1989 and that other nuclear powers had frozen their programs, there was no justification for further research into and development of atomic weapons systems. Non-proliferation had become the great political cause of the "international community," and it was incumbent on the existing nuclear powers to show a lead in self-restraint. Mitterrand's own message was clear enough.

But there was another aim behind Mitterrand's speech; namely to head off what he referred to as drift *(dérive)* in French nuclear thinking. He felt he could detect drift in the minds of "des hommes éminents" who nevertheless had "une conception différente" from his own. The first example of drift was sympathy for the notion of ballistic missile defense, as exemplified by the Strategic Defence Initiative (SDI) or the more restricted Global Protection against Limited Strikes (GPALS) programs dear to various United States administrations. For the "nuclear purist" Mitterrand, any attempt to protect the country from nuclear attack was to undermine the very essence of nuclear deterrence, based on the balance of terror. Ballistic missile defense programs were, in his view, profoundly destabilizing. A second example of drift was support for mobile missile systems instead of the fixed silos of the Plateau d'Albion. The latter represented, in mainstream thinking, an unequivocal target, an attack against which would constitute a definitive act of aggression. Mobile missiles, however, ran the risk of being perceived by an adversary as legitimate roving targets whose "surgical" removal might be interpreted as falling short of an act of war. A third example of drift, according to Mitterrand, was the view that France's short-range, prestrategic nuclear systems were to be used as potential tactical weapons in the style of NATO's "flexible response," rather than as the "ultimate warning shot." The final, and most dangerous example of drift, he argued, was the recent penchant "in statements by leading politicians" in favor of the development of a new generation of miniaturized, low-yield nuclear weapons for use against countries with the capacity to threaten France.[10] It is not insignificant that all of these elements of "drift" were, in the early 1990s, clearly detectable in sections of the political Right close to Jacques Chirac.

David Yost has defined this new camp within the French defense establishment as being characterized by a "more operational" approach to nuclear weapons as opposed to the traditional mainstream "less operational" approach.[11] Yost prefers this distinction to one which posits a stark dichotomy between "nuclear war-fighting" and "deterrence," his argument being that all factions in France are concerned with preventing war. The difference between the two positions is nevertheless considerable, and it is worth noting the impressive degree of support for the "more operational" lobby that became apparent in the early 1990s. In November 1990, François de Rose, long-term opponent of the Gaullist approach to nuclear weapons, first inverted the mainstream doctrine of the deterrence "of the strong by the weak" (dissuasion du faible au fort) by calling for the deterrence "of the weak by the strong" (la dissuasion du fort au faible).[12] The idea that French nuclear weapons might need to be redeployed against third world countries with a capacity to exercise state terrorism in one form or another gained respectability after the Gulf War, when a variety of commentators argued openly in favor of the development of a new generation of nuclear weapons with a "surgical strike" capacity.[13] Prior to 1993, these ideas were limited to a tiny fringe of iconoclastic individuals. However, with the advent of the right-wing government in 1993, the mainstream approach to deterrence was increasingly questioned by a wide swath of defense experts from across the political spectrum, many of whom suggested adopting *dissuasion du fort au faible* or, more dramatically, *dissuasion du fort au fou* ("deterrence of the mad by the strong"), as a serious option.[14]

Perhaps the most significant development in French nuclear strategy was the publication in October 1993 of a report by the parliamentary defense commission that recommended that France shift to a "nuclear use strategy."[15] About this time official statements, including those by the defense minister and the prime minister, and finally by Mitterrand himself in a major press conference in May 1994, began to reassert "Gaullist orthodoxy" by explicitly ruling out any prospect of France's shifting to a nuclear use doctrine. It is within this context that Chirac's decision to resume testing must be examined. His decision was taken on the advice of a commission of experts established in July 1993 by Mitterrand (in consultation with Balladur). The commission was composed of Hubert Curien, former Minister for Research (who has close ties to the nuclear industry); Jean Teillac, High Commissioner for Atomic Energy; Henri Conze, General Delegate for Armaments; General Philippe Vougny, presidential *Chargé de Mission* for Space and Strategic Doctrine; Roger Baleras, Director of Military Applications at the Atomic Energy Commission (CEA); and Robert Dautray, Scientific Director at the CEA. It was presided over by Admiral Jacques Lanxade, Chief of the General Staff. The commission was to analyze the need for further French nuclear tests. The exercise was not dissimilar to asking a synod of bishops to pronounce a statement on the existence of God. The commission originally reported to Mitterrand in September 1993, advocating a series of twenty further tests, but the outgoing president, Mitterrand, overruled the recommendation and upheld the moratorium.[16] Chirac decided to cross the Rubicon. Why?

Among the obvious reasons is the fact that Chirac projected an image as a decisive "hard-liner," determined to make a clear break with Mitterrand's allegedly soft approach to security issues. He was also keen to assume a "Gaullist" posture.[17] Chirac had implied during his presidential campaign that he would not maintain the moratorium on testing. His entourage includes many who have argued most energetically not only in favor of resuming nuclear tests, but also in favor of the "more operational" approach to nuclear doctrine. Pierre Lellouche, Chirac's strategic advisor; Jacques Baumel, now the dean of defense "experts" within the RPR; Admiral Jean Bétermier, Baumel's main adviser; Vincent Lanata, former Air Force chief of staff; and Henri Conze and Roger Baleras, two key members of the Lanxade commission, have all recently advocated a "more operational" stance.[18] The timing of the announcement was fairly self-defining. Since Chirac has insisted that France will ratify the NPT in 1996, then a last-minute series of eight tests had to be conducted as soon as possible. To have made the announcement during or even after the Hiroshima commemorations would have been virtually unthinkable, even for a "Gaullist."

However—and this is where the issue becomes more complex—the Chirac government has strenuously and repeatedly denied that the projected tests have anything to do with the development of new generations of usable low- or variable-yield nuclear warheads. Moreover, the most vocal elements of the "more operational" lobby have kept a very low profile throughout the recent controversy. There has been no overt advocacy of a test program with objectives other than those officially stated by the government. Yet the importance of the government's stated objective in pursuing the tests is disproportionate to the high political price it has paid for them. Three controversial issues require discussion: first, the nature and purpose of the tests themselves; second, their effect on the environment; and third, their political repercussions.

As to the nature and purpose of the tests, two distinct but interconnected issues emerge. The first is whether tests were necessary in order to obtain the results the government states as its objective. Many eminent scientists, including leading researchers in the CEA, argued that they were not.[19] Unidentified sources suggested that even the Lanxade Report concluded that the one programmed test for the TN-75 warhead was not necessary.[20] Furthermore, many argued that if France still needed tests to verify the reliability of its nuclear weapons, then the test program in the past had been a failure. As for the simulation program, Mitterrand himself, in his May 4, 1994 press conference, specifically stated that *il faut que le programme de simulation se fasse sans essais nouveaux* ("the simulation program should be conducted without new tests"), arguing that French scientists possessed the technical know-how (not to mention the resources) to achieve this. Moreover, despite frequent reports that France had remained ignorant of the results of American simulation experiments, it was revealed in September 1995 that France and the United States are in fact collaborating closely on the nuclear simulation program.[21] The positions adopted by advocates or opponents of the tests are political rather than technical. Michel Tatu, one of the most respected experts in the field, adopted an impartial position: *le dossier tel qu'il est présenté par Paris ne permet guère au `non-spécialiste non-prévenu' de se prononcer sur le bien-fondé des essais nucléaires de Mururoa* ("The case presented by Paris scarcely permits the unfamiliar non-specialist to make a judgment on the appropriateness of the nuclear tests in Mururoa.")[22] Those in the know were not talking, and those doing the talking did not really know.

However, there is little doubt that matters were not as straightforward as the government suggested. A report by three eminent American nuclear scientists[23] who conducted a detailed inquiry in France in November 1994 quoted members of the Lanxade commission as admitting that laboratory simulation exercises could in no way replace actual nuclear tests. They also argued that a recent parliamentary report on simulation was full of substantial errors about the technical processes involved and about its political and military function.[24] The American report was highly skeptical about the official reasons given for the tests and concluded that, since there was no reason to conduct tests for the stated purposes, the real reasons had to do with the development of new warheads. This is the second issue connected with the tests themselves.

The most credible alternative explanation for the tests appeared to be that which was advanced by *Le Monde*'s Jacques Isnard the day Chirac announced the end of the moratorium: the development of the long-range stand-off missile, Air-Sol Longue Portée (ASLP). This missile would have a range of over a thousand kilometers and a precision error (CEP) of only a few meters. If equipped with an extremely low-yield warhead (of the order of 0.1 kiloton, for example), the weapon could have a devastating "surgical strike" capacity. This is precisely the type of "usable" weapon that those who urged the resumption of tests advocated.[25]

Numerous reports suggested that France and the United States were hoping to exclude tests on weapons with extremely low yields from the Comprehensive Test Ban Treaty (CTBT), but in mid-August 1995 both Paris and Washington confirmed that they would insist that the CTBT ban all tests whatever the yield (the "zero option").[26] However, reports also indicated that the United States recently conducted tests on these very low-yield weapons and that these tests cannot be detected by other countries. Those in France who suggested that the real purpose of the current tests may well be the development of the ASLP were by no means marginal "crazies." They include notable figures from the mainstream such as Pascal Boniface and leading defense journalists such as Jean Guisnel.[27]

The lengths to which the government was forced to go in denying such hypotheses suggest that there was at least some connection between smoke and fire. However, the fact is that there may be no more than a dozen or so individuals in France who know the whole truth about the tests. The rest is surmise.

As far as the environmental impact is concerned, the debate is somewhat more clear-cut. The government stressed repeatedly that France invited three independent scientific teams to test the environment of Mururoa and that the results proved there is less radioactivity around the atoll than there is in the center of Auckland or at the Châtelet metro station.[28] The presence of Cesium 137 around the atoll has been attributed to earlier atmospheric tests. However, although all three teams were satisfied that there was no immediate danger of an environmental catastrophe, they reserved judgment as to the long-term effects of the testing. Masses of vitrified radioactive waste have been frozen into the atoll's basalt by each successive test. The impact on this waste of ocean water seepage, the seismic effects of subsequent tests, and future geological (especially volcanic) activity is uncertain.[29] The French government drew maximum political and scientific mileage out of various official reports published in New Zealand and Australia in mid-August 1995 testifying that levels of radioactivity in the vicinity of the nuclear atolls were insignificant and that there was no immediate health threat, but scientists have formulated alternative views that are much bleaker.[30] While it seems fairly certain that there is no immediate environmental danger, the environmental jury is still out on the long-term effects. Given that nuclear waste remains radioactive for hundreds of thousands of years, that jury is likely to remain out indefinitely.

The French government has always insisted that Polynesia is the least populated spot on the planet. Fewer than 5,000 people live within a one-thousand-mile radius of Mururoa. But that argument, however factual, hardly stands up against the far more political and diplomatic charges leveled by Canberra, Auckland, and Tokyo concerning the atavistically "colonial" exercise of power by a European country in what the Pacific-rim countries consider to be their own back yard. Australians and New Zealanders remain unimpressed by the French claim that Polynesia is as much a part of "France" as is the Auvergne. This leads to the third main issue emerging from the current controversy: the political and diplomatic fallout. Did the tests, whether necessary or not, exact a price that France did not expect to pay and that it can ill afford?

There can be no doubt that the incoming Chirac government seriously underestimated the level and intensity of the opposition that would be aroused by the ending of the moratorium. Three distinct issues arise in this connection: the impact of the tests on the NPT and the CTBT; their impact on France's image in the world; and their impact on France's place in Europe. These three issues stand in an ascending order of difficulty for France. Arguments by opposition politicians such as Laurent Fabius, Pierre Mauroy, and Lionel Jospin that resumption of testing would jeopardize the ratification in 1996 of the NPT and compromise the signing of a CTBT appear to have been misguided. These arguments were informed by one of the motives the outgoing Socialist government used to justify the moratorium: namely, that an end to French tests would encourage non-nuclear states to agree to an indefinite extension of the NPT, thereby perpetuating France's membership in the exclusive nuclear club (and, simultaneously, securing Germany's permanent exclusion). Yet despite the resumption of tests the 178 state signatories to the NPT accepted its unlimited extension on May 12, 1995. Furthermore, there have been no signs that non-nuclear states are considering changing their position on a 1996 ratification of the NPT as a result of the French tests, although opponents of the test program constantly name this threat as the main reason for halting the tests. In fact, the French government's high-profile assurances about its intention to ratify the NPT and its determination to conclude a CTNT that prohibits all tests have, if anything, created positive spinoff from the test program for the international community. Russia was quick to follow the French and American lead in advocating a "zero option" for the CTBT. The outrage expressed by governments around the world was moral and diplomatic. Their criticisms did not go so far as to question the juridical bases of the major arms control agreements; France, it would appear, has successfully ridden out this particular storm.

The same cannot be said about France's image in the world. The virulence and universality of the opprobrium that accompanied the resumption of the tests was unprecedented. The celebrated headline (in French) in the Sydney Morning Herald, "Pourquoi les Français sont des connards" ("Why the French are idiots"), sets the tone. To counter this perception, the French government took the extraordinary step of dispatching special emissaries (35 deputies or senators, all long-term specialists in defense policy) to countries around the world and charged them with explaining the policy behind the resumption of testing.[31] A similarly drastic step was deemed necessary during the Gulf crisis when Mitterrand dispatched emissaries to the capitals of the Muslim world to explain his volte-face towards Iraq; France has still not recovered its lost prestige in the Arab world. Moreover, government ministers worked overtime composing text after text aimed exclusively at damage control.[32] That damage has been varied. Despite unofficial boycotts of French goods in many countries around the world, French trade was not seriously effected. Governments, for the most part, refrained from encouraging commercial sanctions.[33] The Pacific region continues to function as a marketplace. But the political and cultural fall-out has been devastating. France was just beginning, in large part as a result of the moratorium, to win back some measure of acceptance in the Pacific region. But the recent outbreak of Francophobia, more extreme than ever before, cannot help but seriously impair France's future efforts to reestablish its position in the region. The protests against the resumption of testing were inextricably bound up with the resurgence of independence movements in both Polynesia and New Caledonia, and the cause of "decolonization" was taken up with a vengeance in Tokyo and Santiago just as it was in Canberra and Wellington. The fact that the protests, this time, spread to Latin America was a serious blow for France. As *Le Monde* editorialized the day after the first of the new tests, the Chirac government, by acting as an "orgueilleux cavalier seul" ("proud loner") was guilty of seriously mismanaging *le crédit international de la nation* ("the nation's international credit").[34]

The explanation for the extent of the protest movement lies primarily in the fact that the post–Cold War world has deligitimized nuclear weapons. For a "second-tier" country like France to break ranks with a moratorium respected by the superpowers was perceived as an act of supreme arrogance that nothing (least of all the questionable results of the tests) could justify. The fundamental difference between de Gaulle's "Hourra pour la France!" and Chirac's "irrevocable" decision to resume testing is that the former comment, set in the Cold War context and uttered by a widely respected figure such as the general, commanded the (no doubt grudging) respect of many actors around the world. The latter decision, however, came in a very different era and was made by a very different man. It provoked disbelief, anger, and extreme resentment. The Chirac government failed to realize that the possession of nuclear weapons no longer conferred either grandeur or (still less) respect. *Le Monde*'s editorial again hit precisely the right note:

Here is a country which has neither the planes nor the helicopters necessary for rapid intervention in a military theater which concerns it the most—Europe—and which is starting to modernize a nuclear weapon, the deterrent capacities of which are less and less evident.[35]

Once the tests were completed and France finally plugged the boreholes on Mururoa and Fangataufa, Hermés scarves and Moët et Chandon helped restore something of France's image. But it was not easy, and those commentators in Paris who argued that, whatever the real reason behind the tests, the political price in terms of international prestige would ultimately prove to be too high may yet have the last word.

France's most difficult task, however, lies in Europe. The lifting of the moratorium opened a Pandora's box of enormous complexity. In their efforts to justify the resumption of tests, French officials emphasized the notion that France was not doing this for itself, but for the whole of Europe.[36] France's suggestion that its nuclear weapons might become "European weapons" was by no means new and goes back to the very start of its nuclear history.[37] By the summer of 1995, this suggestion had become an issue which was as significant as it was sensitive. Ever since January 1992, when Mitterrand delicately intimated the notion of a "European nuclear deterrence," there has been an increasing number of winks and nods in the same direction.[38] The 1994 Livre Blanc states boldly that "the problematic of a European nuclear doctrine is destined to become one of the major questions in the construction of a common European defense. With nuclear weapons, European defense autonomy is possible. Without them, it is not."[39] Such a doctrine is conceptually linked in the French mind to the development of a European identity. The current dispute over nuclear tests has done nothing to help the development of that identity. Au contraire.

Prior to the resumption of tests, some progress did seem to be discernible. French nuclear doctrine was evolving in interesting directions. Perhaps most intriguing was the development of the notion of dissuasion *par constat*, which is usually translated (erroneously in the eyes of its authors) as "existential deterrence." This notion was developed in the 1980s by a number of "intellectual generals" such as Claude Leborgne, Charles-Georges, and Fricaud-Chagnaud.[40] The concept offered an approach to nuclear weapons and nuclear doctrine attractive not only to the non-nuclear members of the European Union, but also to Britain. "Existential deterrence" is predicated on the growing interdependence at every level between the nuclear and non-nuclear states of the European Union. It stresses the logical impossibility of identifying and specifying the "vital national interests" of any given state (including France). It assumes not only the continued existence of nuclear weapons (and nuclear powers) in the European theater, but also the existence of serious conventional forces to deter surprise attacks or nuclear blackmail. The notion is developed at some length in Fricaud-Chagnaud's recent book on French defense policy, whose provocative title—*Mourir pour le Roi de Prusse?*—symbolically posits the starkness of the security option now facing France.[41] Advocates of "existential deterrence" argue that it avoids the pitfalls of most other approaches to a common European nuclear deterrence, such as extended deterrence, concerted deterrence, or shared deterrence.[42]

There had been progress, too, on the Franco-British front. The Franco-British Joint Commission on Nuclear Policy and Doctrine was formally established as a permanent group in July 1993. Their discussions have focused on two issues: detailed mutual exploration of each side's nuclear doctrine, which revealed (apparently surprisingly) that the doctrines are quite similar and largely compatible; and the NPT, CTBT, and shifts in the nuclear doctrine of the other nuclear powers. Above all, the commission developed an excellent working relationship in which both sides realized that agreement on nuclear doctrine was within reach. The commission still faced the enormous problem of persuading the other European partners to adopt a Common Foreign and Security Policy (CFSP) that contained a nuclear dimension, but discreet discussions with Germany conducted simultaneously were revealing growing support within the CDU and CSU for the notion of a European deterrent. This "softly, softly" approach, with an open-ended time scale, seemed to be gaining acceptance as the EU moved into the Intergovernmental Conference in the spring of 1996.[43]

The controversy over the French tests seriously compromised the CFSP process in several ways. First, by making the announcement on tests with no prior consultations, Chirac revived the more atavistic aspects of nation-state independence associated with de Gaulle and reawakened long dormant strains of virulent Francophobia across the continent. Second, the tests split the European governments into three groups. While no government actually applauded France's move, the British maintained an embarrassing neutrality, respectful of France's "sovereignty." At the opposite end of the scale, the Danish, Swedish, Finnish, and Dutch governments engaged in varying degrees of overt denunciation. The Danish prime minister personally joined a bicycle protest rally from Copenhagen to Paris. In Oslo, police watched sympathetically as demonstrators dynamited a Citroën 2CV in front of the French embassy. A third group of governments, including those of Germany, Spain, Italy, and Greece, expressed various forms of "regret" about the decision, while recognizing France's right to do as it pleases. The polarization of governmental positions around the nuclear issue does not bode well for the progress of talks in the forthcoming Intergovernmental Conference on CFSP. Popular opinion has been dramatically radicalized in every country and has once again projected the nuclear issue to the forefront of the European debate, a development all governments would have preferred to avoid.

The resurgence of popular protest against nuclear weapons was the biggest obstacle to the almost daily French pleas to its 15 European partners to embrace the tests on behalf of the entire European Union. Even in France, the decision to resume testing proved highly unpopular, with polls recording a 60 percent disapproval rate. But the much more serious problem in the medium term has been the political polarization that has occurred as a result of Chirac's decision. The only party leader to applaud Chirac's decision was the new Spanish conservative prime minister José Maria Aznar, but growing numbers of CDU deputies in Germany were forced to approve the notion of a European deterrent, a move that has intensified SPD opposition. In Britain, too, the issue became one that Labour and Conservatives were likely to contest in the upcoming elections. The more "party politicized" the debate becomes, the less likely it is that Europe's 15 leaders will actually agree on a framework for discussions about a nuclear doctrine. Prior to the summer of 1995, the problem of the "Euro-deterrent" was primarily institutional. It has now become intensely political and thereby much less manageable.

If Chirac, echoing de Gaulle, had exclaimed, when the final test was concluded in May 1996, "Hourra pour l'Europe!," the reactions would likely have ranged from anger to embarrassment, from irritation to hilarity. The prospects of even a ripple of applause were negligible. Paradoxically, it may well prove that the tests, and particularly the arrogant style of their presentation, will doom moves towards a European deterrent. Given that the creation of such a deterrent, based solidly on the French bomb, had become a major plank in French security policy, the resumption of tests may well prove to have been a counter-productive miscalculation.

Notes to Chapter 14

1. France's political independence from Washington was absolute in theory (whatever that actually means in practice) but was developed with American tech-

nical assistance. See Richard Ullman, "The Covert French Connection," *Foreign Policy* 75 (summer 1989).
2. See Philip H. Gordon, *A Certain Idea of France: French Security Policy and the Gaullist Legacy* (Princeton: Princeton University Press, 1994); on the consensus, see Jolyon Howorth, *France: The Politics of Peace* (London: Merlin, 1984).
3. Recent contributions to this discussion are to be found in David S. Yost, "Nuclear Debates in France," *Survival* 36, no. 4 (winter 1994-95); Edward A. Kolodziej, "French Nuclear Policy: Adapting the Gaullist Legacy to the Post–Cold War World," in Michael Mazurr and Alexander Lennon, eds., *Toward a Nuclear Peace: the Future of Nuclear Weapons* (Boston, St. Martin's Press, 1994); David G. Haglund, "France's Nuclear Posture: Adjusting to the Post–Cold War Era," in *Contemporary Security Policy* 16, no. 2 (August 1995); BASIC, "French Nuclear Policy Since the Fall of the Wall," British-American Security Information Council, 1993, *Défense Nationale*, special issue, (February 1993).
4. See David S. Yost, *France and the Persian Gulf War: Political-Military Lessons Learned* (Monterey, Calif.: Naval Postgraduate Institute, 1992); and Howorth, "French Policy in the Conflict" in Alex Danchev, ed., *International Perspectives on the Gulf War* (London: Macmillan, 1994); and "The Debate in France over Military Intervention in Europe," *Political Quarterly* 5 (1994).
5. See in particular, *Livre Blanc sur la Défense 1994*, (Paris: UGE 18 October 1994), especially chapter 3.
6. Although Chirac's senate intervention was never formally published, its main points were summarized in Chirac's press conference on July 14, 1995. Ambassade de France, London, *Statements*. This was the first time a French president had ever given details of a forthcoming test program.
7. The dean of French defense journalists, *Le Monde*'s Jacques Isnard, originally reported that the tests were to develop the new generation of M-5 warheads as well as to perfect the long-range stand-off missile (ASLP) to be carried by Rafale (*Le Monde*, June 15, 1995, p. 12). Neither of these programs was officially recognized in Chirac's July statement.
8. In an extraordinary move in early August, France published complete details of all its nuclear tests since 1960. *Le Monde*, August 2, 1995.
9. Summarizing the attitude of his political opponents who, he claimed, were already planning to reverse his decision once he left office, Mitterrand exclaimed:

> "Eh bien, je vous dis, Mesdames et Messieurs: après moi, on ne le fera pas! On ne le fera pas parce que la France ne voudra pas offenser le monde entier en relançant le surarmement nucléaire, en blessant l'ensemble des pays qui n'en sont pas détenteurs, en bafouant les pays du Tiers-Monde et l'ensemble des pays pauvres. . . . [J]e fais confiance à mon successeur et à mes successeurs. Ils ne pourront pas faire autrement.

Bien entendu, ils auraient tort de faire autrement, mais comme ils ne le pourront pas, je n'approfondirai pas la discussion."
Propos sur la *Défense* 42 (May 1994): 32.

10. Mitterrand, Ibid.

11. Yost, "Nuclear Debates in France," *Survival* 36, no. 4, (winter 1994-95). A much longer version of that paper appears as "Nuclear Weapons Issues in France," in John C. Hopkins and Weixing Hu, eds., *Strategic Views from the Second Tier: the Nuclear Weapons Policies of France, Britain and China* (New Brunswick, N.J.: Transaction Press, 1995), pp. 19-104. I am grateful to David Yost for sending me copies of his important work.

12. *Le Monde,* November 9, 1990.

13. Ewen Faudon [pseud.], "La Guerre avec l'Irak et la programmation militaire française," *Libération,* February 27, 1991; Jean-Louis Gergorin, "Deterrence in the Post–Cold War Era," *Adelphi Paper* no. 226, (London: IISS, 1992), p. 12.

14. Howorth, "The Debate in France," 108, n. 6.

15. Assemblée Nationale, *Avis présenté au nom de la commission de défense nationale: Tome IV, Dissuasion Nucléaire,* no. 583, October 7, 1993. The report was written by Jacques Baumel.

16. The Lanxade Report has never been made public (in either version) and is classified *secret défense*. However, some details have been leaked by those in the know, primarily those opposed to its recommendations. See, for example, Pascal Boniface, "En soufflant sur le feu nucléaire, Chirac joue à l'apprenti sorcier," *Le Nouveau Quotidien,* June 15, 1995.

17. See Thierry Bréhier, "L'Image d'un 'chef,'" *Le Monde,* June 15, 1995.

18. Henri Conze and Jean Picq, "L'Avenir de la Dissuasion nucléaire," *Défense Nationale,* (February 1993); Roger Baleras cited in *Le Monde,* May 4, 1993, p. 14. For Lellouche and Baumel references, see article cited in footnote 14 above.

19. See "Des scientifiques désapprouvent," *Libération,* June 16, 1995, p. 3; "La reprise des essais nucléaires dans le Pacifique réveille des craintes parmi les scientifiques," *Le Monde,* June 21, 1995, p. 30.

20. Boniface.

21. "Les chercheurs français et américains vont coopérer dans le domaine de la simulation des essais nucléaires," *Le Monde,* September 1, 1995, p. 4.

22. Michel Tatu, "L'Avenir de la Bombe," *Le Monde,* August 12, 1995, p. 1.

23. Richard Garwin, a senior researcher at Los Alamos from 1950 to 1993 and vice-president of the Federation of American Scientists; Ray Kidder, a senior engineer at the Lawrence Livermore Laboratories for 35 years and adviser to

the United States Congress on nuclear issues; and Christopher Payne, a senior researcher at the Natural Resources Defense Council. See the details in their 50 page report. Discussions in Paris regarding the necessity of nuclear tests for maintaining a reliable French nuclear force under a comprehensive test ban appear in *Libération,* July 14, 1995, p. 2.

24. Assemblée Nationale. Rapport au nom de la commission de défense: les simulations nucléaires, no. 847 (December 15, 1993), by René Galy-Dejean.

25. The best overview of this thesis is Jean Guisnel, "Les militaires français rêvent d'une mini-bombe atomique, *Libération,* July 14, 1995, p. 4.

26. "Paris s'engage à soutenir l'interdiction en 1996 de tout essai nucléaire," *Le Monde,* August 11, 1995; "M. Clinton se prononce pour l'abandon total de tout essai nucléaire," *Le Monde,* August 13-14, 1995. On the complexities of this issue, see Michel Tatu, "Essais nucléaires: le casse-tête de l'option zéro," *Le Monde,* August 16, 1995.

27. Boniface has argued this in a variety of articles: *Libération,* June 9, 1995; *Le Nouveau Quotidien,* June 15, 1995; *Le Monde,* June 16, 1995; *International Herald Tribune,* July 13, 1995.

28. Teams led by Haroun Tazieff (1982), Hugh Atkinson (1984), and Jacques-Yves Cousteau (1987) gave a cautious but relatively clean bill of health to the atolls. See "Trois missions n'ont pas permis de faire toute la lumière sur les conséquences des expériences," *Le Monde,* June 21, 1995, p. 30.

29. The leading French volcanologist Pierre Vincent is especially convinced of the latter danger. See his "Mururoa: un `stockage' de déchets radioactifs à haut risque," *Le Monde,* July 12, 1995, p. 11.

30. Florence de Chagny, "Des scientifiques australiens et néo-zélandais minimisent l'impact des essais nucléaires français sur l'environnement," *Le Monde,* August 17, 1995. For the "pessimistic" reports, see Bengt Danielsson, "Poisoned Pacific: The Legacy of French Nuclear Testing," *Bulletin of the Atomic Scientists* (March 1990): 22-31; and Tilman Ruff, "Bomb Tests Attack the Food Chain," ibid., pp. 32-34; Greenpeace, *Testimonies: Witnesses of French Nuclear Testing in the South Pacific,* 1990; Natural Resources Defense Council, *French Nuclear Testing, Nuclear Weapons Data Center Working Paper* 1989: 1, (Washington, D.C., 1989).

31. "M. Millon envoie des `missi dominici' à l'étranger," *Le Monde,* September 6, 1995.

32. Charles Millon, "Refonder le consensus sur la défense," *Le Monde,* June 30, 1995; Millon, "L'idéologie de la paix contre la cause de la paix," *Le Monde,* August 5, 1995; Alain Juppé, "La Dissuasion c'est la paix," *Figaro,* August 26, 1995; "Chirac Répond," *Le Point,* September 2, 1995.

33. At the end of July, a number of military contracts were lost in both New Zealand and Australia but in early August, 97 percent of shareholders in Australia's second largest life insurance company, National Mutual Life, voted in favor of being taken over by the French group AXA. The biggest losses were sustained by small traders suffering from unofficial boycotts of French goods.

34. "La Boîte de Pandore," *Le Monde*, September 8, 1995, p. 13.

35. "Deux images de la France," *Le Monde*, July 16-17, 1995, p. 10.

36. This became the centerpiece of Prime Minister Juppé's traditional opening speech to the annual session of the Institut des Hautes Études de Défense Nationale on September 7, 1995 (reported in *Le Monde*, September 8, 1995, p. 2).

37. See Howorth, "France and European Security: Rereading the Gaullist 'Consensus,'" in Brian Jenkins and Tony Chafer, eds., *France and the New World Order* (London, Macmillan, 1995), pp. 17-38. The most recent (and in many ways best) addition to a growing literature on the subject is Bruno Tertrais, "Quelle dimension européenne pour la dissuasion nucléaire?" *Relations internationales et stratégiques* 17 (summer 1995).

38. François Mitterrand in *Le Monde*, January 12-13, 1992, p. 1; Jacques Delors in *Le Monde*, January 7, 1992, p. 3; Jacques Lanxade in *Le Monde*, October 23-24, 1994, p. 9; Alain Juppé, "La France et la Sécurité européenne," *Défense Nationale*, (April 1995), p. 6; François Fillon, "Dissuasion nucléaire et élargissement," in *Ministère de la Défense, Un Nouveau Débat Stratégique* (Paris: Sirpa, 1993), p. 63; François Léotard, "L'effort de défense: une volonté politique," in *Défense Nationale*, (October 1993), p. 14.

39. *Livre Blanc*, 98.

40. Claude Le Borgne, *La Guerre est morte mais on ne le sait pas encore*, (Paris, Grasset, 1987); Charles-Georges Fricaud-Chagnaud, "L'Europe de la dissuasion et des solidarités actives," *Stratégique* 29 (1986): 7-20.

41. Charles-Georges Fricaud-Chagnaud and J. J. Patry, *Mourir pour le roi de Prusse?* (Paris: Publisud, 1994).

42. See Daniel Vernet, "Nucléaire: la difficile dissuasion concertée," *Le Monde*, July 20, 1995.

43. See *Le Monde*, February 29, 1996.

About the Contributors

John T. S. Keeler is professor of political science and director of the Center for West European Studies at the University of Washington. He is the author of *Réformer: Les Conditions du Changement Politique* (Presses Universitaires de France, 1994) and *The Politics of Neocorporatism in France: Farmers, the State and Agricultural Policy-making in the Fifth Republic* (Oxford University Press, 1987) as well as numerous articles in journals such as *Comparative Politics, Comparative Political Studies, West European Politics* and *French Politics and Society*. He also edited a special issue of *Comparative Political Studies* (1993) on "The Politics of Reform in Comparative Perspective" and is a contributing editor for *Pouvoirs*. He has been a research associate or visiting professor at the Institut d'Etudes Politiques de Paris, the Centre de Sociologie des Organisations, the London School of Economics and Political Science and the University of Tübingen. Under the auspices of a Parliamentary Development Project funded by the U.S. Agency for International Development, he recently served as a consultant to the Supreme Rada of Ukraine on constitutional development in France.

Martin A. Schain is professor of politics and chair of the Center for European Studies, New York University. He is the co-editor and author of *The Politics of Immigration in Western Europe* (Cass, 1994); *The State, Socialism and Public Policy in France* (Methuen, 1985); *French Politics and Public Policy* (St. Martin's, 1980); the co-author of *Politics in France* (HarperCollins, 1992); and the author of *French Communism and Local Power* (St. Martin's, 1985).

John S. Ambler is professor of political science at Rice University. He is author of *The French Army in Politics* and *The Government and Politics of France* and editor and co-author of *The French Socialist Experiment* and *The French Welfare State*. His recent research has focused on the politics of education in industrialized democracies. He is writing a book on the politics of education in France.

Andrew M. Appleton is associate director of the Division of Governmental Studies and Services at Washington State University. He teaches courses and has published in the area of political parties and electoral behavior. He is co-editor (with Daniel S. Ward) of *State Party Organizations* (Congressional Quarterly, 1996).

Frank R. Baumgartner is associate professor of political science at Texas A&M University. He is the author of *Conflict and Rhetoric in French Policymaking* (University of Pittsburgh Press, 1989), the co-author of *Agendas and Instability in American Politics* (University of Chicago Press, 1993), and the author or co-author of numerous articles and book chapters on policymaking, interest groups, and agenda-setting in French and American politics. He serves as program organizer for the Conference Group on French Politics and Society of the American Political Science Association.

David R. Cameron is a professor of political science and chair of the Council on West European Studies at Yale University. He is the author of many papers and articles on French Politics, most recently "Exchange Rate Politics in France, 1981-1983: The Regime-Defining Choices of the Mitterrand Presidency," in Anthony Daley, ed., *The Mitterrand Era;* and "From Barre to Balladur: Economic Policy in the Era of the EMS," in Gregory Flynn, ed., *Remaking the Hexagon: The New France in the New Europe.* He has also written on developments in the European Community and Union, most recently, "The 1992 Initiatives: Causes and Consequences," in Alberta M. Sbragia, ed., *Euro-Politics: Institutions and Policymaking in the `New' European Community;* and "Transnational Relations and the Development of European Economic and Monetary Union," in Thomas Risse-Kappen, ed., *Bringing Transnational Relations Back In: Non-State Actors, Domestic Structures, and International Institutions.* He currently serves on the Executive Committee of the European Community Studies Association.

Jolyon Howorth is professor of French civilization at the University of Bath. He also holds a Jean Monnet Chair in European Political Union. He is the co-editor of *Europeans on Europe: Transnational Visions of a New Continent* (London: Macmillan, 1992), *Defense and Dissent in Contemporary France,* (New York: St. Martin's, 1984, *National Defence and European Security Integration* (forthcoming Routledge), and the author of *Edouard Vaillant: la création de l'unité socialiste en France, la politique de l'action totale* (Paris: Syros, 1982), and *France and European Security* (forthcoming, Oxford University Press).

Mark Kesselman is professor of government at Columbia University. He has edited *The French Labor Movement: Economic Crisis and Political Change* (Allen & Unwin, 1984) and *Comparative Politics at the Crossroads* (D.C. Heath, 1996); and contributed to Philip G. Cerny and Martin A. Schain, eds., *The State, Socialism, and Public Policy in France* (Methuen, 1984); Yves Mény, ed., *Idéologies, Partis Politiques, et Groupes Sociaux, Pour Georges Lavau* (Presses de la Foundation Nationale des Sciences Politiques, 1989); Paul Godt, ed., *Policymaking in France: From de Gaulle to Mitterrand* (Pinter Publishers, 1989); and Anthony Daley, ed., *The Mitterrand Era: Policy Alternatives and Political Mobilization in France* (New York University Press, 1995).

Amy G. Mazur is assistant professor of political science at Washington State University. She is co-director of the cross-national "Research Network on Gender, Politics, and the State" and directs the research for this project in France. She is author of *Gender Bias and the State: Symbolic Reform at Work in Fifth Republic France* (University of Pittsburgh Press, 1996); and co-editor (with Dorothy McBride Stetson) of *Comparative State Feminism*. Other recent publications include, "The Interplay: The Formation of Sexual Harassment Legislation in France" in R. Amy Elman, ed., *European Integration: The New Feminist Challenge* and "Gender and Party Politics in France" (with Andrew Appleton) in J. Lovenduski and P. Norris, eds., *Gender and Party Politics*.

Vivien A. Schmidt is director of the European Studies Program, director of the Center for Democracy and Development in the McCormack Institute of Public Affairs, and professor of public policy and management at the University of Massachusetts at Boston. She has published extensively on comparative public policy and political economy, including *From State to Market? The Transformation of French Business and Government* (Cambridge University Press, 1996), and *Democratizing France: The Political and Administrative History of Decentralization* (Cambridge University Press, 1990), for which she received a special award in France. Her current work focuses on the challenges to the nation-state from the rise of regional and international trade organizations.

Alec Stone is an associate professor in the School of Social Sciences at the University of California, Irvine. His current research interests are European integration, international institutions, and theories of dispute resolution. He is the author of *Governing with Judges* (Oxford, forthcoming), *The Birth of Judicial Politics in France* (New York: Oxford, 1992), and co-editor of The "New Constitutional Politics of Europe," a special issue of *Comparative Political Studies*, 26, no. 4, January, 1994.

Marie-France Toinet died in August, 1995. She was *directeur de recherche* at the Fondation nationale des sciences politiques, Centre d'études et de recherches internationales–CERI. She is the author of *Le système politique des Etats-Unis* (Paris: PUF, 1987), the co-editor of *L'état des Etats-Unis* (Paris: Editions la Découverte, 1990), the editor of *L'Etat en Amerique* (Paris: Presses de la FNSP, 1989) and the co-author of *Les chemins de l'abstention: une comparaison franco-américaine* (Paris: Editions la Découverte, 1993).

David Wilsford is president and professor at the Institute for American Universities in Aix-en-Provence, France. He is the author of *Doctors and the State* (Duke University Press, 1991) and is currently completing a book comparing health care politics in the advanced industrial democracies, *The Political Economy of Health Care*. He served as a German Marshall Fund Research Fellow, Europe, has been a Resident Research Fellow at the Max-Planck-Institut in Cologne, and was editor of *Political Leaders of Contemporary Europe* (Greenwood Press, 1995).

Index

Ambler, John, 15
André, Michèle, 265-6
Appleton, Andrew, 17
Auroux Laws, 146-8, 156
AVFT (Association Européene Contre les Violences Faites au Femmes au Travail), 261, 265-6, 268-9, 272-3

Badinter, Robert, 12, 62, 72
Balladur, Edouard, 2, 3, 5, 40-1, 43, 67-8, 71, 76, 78-9, 113, 116, 126, 128, 130, 135, 169, 187-8, 221, 254, 272, 281, 284, 294, 306, 325, 340
Barre, Raymond, 4-5, 36, 110-1, 284, 331
Baumgartner, Frank, 13, 16, 171
Bayrou, François, 200, 211, 218-19
Benelux countries, 10, 11, 341, 356
Bérégovoy, Pierre, 5, 37, 116-18, 127, 129, 246, 264, 307
Berlusconi, Silvio, 16, 294
Britain, 15, 39, 60, 86, 201, 222, 232, 234, 239, 241, 253, 258-9, 285, 291, 303, 312, 314, 316, 328-9, 331, 349-52, 362, 395-6
business, 9, 13, 105-36, 145-6, 148, 157, 258, 262, 270, 273

Cameron, David, 17, 46
Canada, 258-9, 265, 282
Carignon, Alain, 135
Catholic Church, 213-5, 283, 314
CFDT (Confédération Française Démocratique du Travail), 151, 172, 216, 262, 265, 273
CGT (Confédération Générale du Travail), 89, 146, 151-3, 172, 211, 262, 265
Chaban-Delmas, Jacques, 34
Chevènement, Jean-Pierre, 124, 201, 215, 218, 222, 308, 354, 360
Chirac, Jacques, 1-5, 6-18, 23-5, 35-6, 38-46, 67, 69-70, 74, 76, 78-9, 108, 113, 127, 130, 136, 145, 150-1, 158, 169, 182-3, 188-9, 218, 254, 264, 273, 281, 284, 294, 302, 304-7, 310, 319-20, 325-8, 339, 364-373, 384-90, 392-3, 396
see also Gaullists; RPR
Choisir, 260

CNPF (Conseil National du Patronat Français), 121, 157
Codacionni, Colette, 273
cohabitation, see presidential power
Cohen, Elie, 123, 133
Common Foreign and Security Policy, 18, 361-2, 395-6
Communist Party (PCF), 33, 45, 89, 95, 146, 156, 172, 174-5, 177-8, 180, 209, 211, 218, 248, 270-1, 290-1, 292, 295, 302, 309, 319-20, 360
Constitutional Council, 12-13, 31, 35-7, 46, 53-80, 173, 215, 221-2, 357
constitutional weapons, 26-7, 37-8
corruption, 5, 95, 134-6, 279, 371
Council of State (Conseil d'Etat), 30, 31, 62, 74, 173
Cresson, Edith, 37, 116-17, 127-9, 132, 184-7, 265, 357
Crozier, Michel, 91, 93, 199, 223
CSMF (Confédération des Syndicats Médicaux Français), 240, 245-6, 254
cycle of electoral rejection, 5, 24

Debré, Jean-Louis, 189
Debré, Michel, 26, 30-1, 34, 214, 283, 306
decentralization, 216-7
defense policy, 333-5, 383-96
Defferre Law, 216
Delors, Jacques, 133, 314, 332, 337-8, 341
deregulation, 13, 106, 113, 115, 126
Denmark, 303, 315, 328, 349-51, 357, 395
Devaquet, Alain, 200, 206, 216, 220-22
Dubois, Jean, 143
Duhamel, Olivier, 31
Duverger, Maurice, 33

Ecologists, 177, 308
education policy, 13, 15, 199-224
elections
 1958, 27
 1965, 33, 291
 1969, 289, 295
 1973, 287
 1974, 33
 1978, 290, 292

INDEX 405

1981, 3, 33-4, 145, 209, 287, 288
1984, 176, 179
1986, 177, 177-9, 191, 264, 290, 292
1988, 39, 55, 74, 176-7, 182, 287-8
1989, 287
1993, 1, 5, 40, 177-8, 180, 182, 185, 190, 272, 282, 287-90, 292, 303, 305, 317, 325, 361
1994, 292, 360-61
1995, 1, 5, 7, 9, 23, 40-41, 134, 169, 176, 178, 182, 188-9, 191-2, 292, 305, 326, 361
Emmanuelli, Henri, 135
European Community (EC), see European Union.
European Monetary System, 327-31, 369
European Monetary Union (EMU), 67, 303, 327-9, 339-41, 343-5, 361-9, 371
European Union (EU)9-11, 14, 16-18, 67, 76, 85, 107, 109, 112, 116-21, 131-4, 153, 180, 258, 261, 265, 267, 271, 280, 283, 291, 301-21, 325-73, 394-6
see also Maastricht Treaty; Single European Act

Fabius, Laurent, 5, 34, 62, 112-13, 124, 135, 183, 392
Favoreu, Louis, 80
Feigenbaum, Harvey, 88
FEN (Federation of National Education), 208-211, 217
FMF (Federation of French Physicians), 240, 254.
foulard affair, 183, 186, 219, 286
FSU (Federation of Unified Unions), 211

Gandois, Jean, 157
de Gaulle, Charles, 2, 5, 24-36, 39, 42-3, 46, 56, 110, 216, 223, 246, 328, 333-4, 364, 383, 386, 393, 395-6
Gaullists, 24, 27, 29, 32-3, 35-7, 56, 60, 95, 191, 238, 279, 291, 304, 306, 309, 386-8
see also RPR
gender politics, 16, 155, 257-74
Germany, 10-11, 15, 55-6, 59, 79, 114, 118, 232, 234, 239, 241, 246, 253, 282, 285, 302-3, 327, 329-37, 339-44, 352-3, 362, 370, 383-4, 392, 396
Guigou, Elisabeth, 307
Giscard d'Estaing, Valéry, 4, 24, 35-7, 65, 184, 216, 223, 260, 279, 281, 295, 304, 307-8, 310, 328, 331, 334
see also UDF
Groux, Guy, 151, 158
Guichard, Olivier, 200

Habérer, Jean-Yves, 135
Hall, Peter, 89
Hayward, Jack, 120

health care policy, 9, 15, 146, 231-55, 367
Hersant, Robert, 69-71, 75
Hollifield, James, 92
Howell, Chris, 148
Howorth, Jolyon, 18

immigration policy, 8-10, 13, 14, 16, 72, 76-7, 92, 169-93, 302
Italy, 16, 56, 59, 79, 95, 239, 274, 282, 312, 329, 341, 344, 363, 396

Japan, 15, 156-7, 234, 239, 241, 253, 282, 385, 391, 393
Jones, Bryan, 93
Jospin, Lionel, 2, 45, 188-9, 218, 220, 284, 392
judicialization (of policymaking), 12, 58, 60-1
Juppé, Alain, 1, 2, 11, 41-2, 44, 79, 108, 136, 189, 254-5, 302, 326, 363-4, 366, 368, 370-2

Keeler, John, 12, 77, 80, 94
de Kervasdoué, Jean, 248, 250
Kesselman, Mark, 14, 42
Kohl, Helmut, 302-3, 335-6, 342-3, 365
Kolodziej, Edward, 90

labor movement, 14, 91-2, 143-160, 239-40
see also CFDT; CGT; FEN; FSU; SNES; SNI
Labbé, Dominique, 154
Lang, Jack, 215, 281, 309
Lavau, Georges, 283
LDF (Ligue du Droit des Femmes), 260-1, 268
Léotard, François, 307-8
Le Pen, Jean-Marie, 7, 9-10, 14, 169, 176-7, 188-9, 219, 281, 284-5, 294, 360, 365
see also National Front
Long, Marceau, 186
Longuet, Gérard, 135
Luchaire, François, 55

Maastricht Treaty, 2, 10-11, 13, 17, 43, 67, 115, 118, 131, 134, 283, 301-21, 327, 339-41, 344-5, 349, 356-61, 363, 365, 370
Madelin, Alain, 2, 42, 136, 354, 371
malaise in France, 3, 15, 16, 77, 80, 136, 169, 282, 294, 325, 370
Maschino, Maurice, 202, 211
Mauroy, Pierre, 5, 34, 62, 110, 112, 200, 221, 392
Mazur, Amy, 16
Méhaignerie, Pierre, 43, 187
MG France (Médecins Généralistes de France), 240, 254
Millon, Charles, 281

Minc, Alain, 286
Mitterrand, François, 1, 3-5, 9-10, 12, 13, 15,
    17-8, 23-5, 29, 31, 33-5, 37-43, 62, 65,
    105-6, 108, 115, 118, 128, 131, 133-4,
    176, 214-5, 220-21, 254, 265, 272, 301-5,
    308, 310-11, 325-7, 331-7, 339, 343, 357,
    360, 363, 369-71, 384, 386-9
see also Socialist Party
MLF (Mouvement de Libération des
    Femmes), 260
Monnerville, Gaston, 31
Monory, René, 201, 218
Mouriaux, René, 158

National Assembly, 27, 31-2, 34-7, 40, 43-5,
    55-6, 59-60, 63, 66, 79, 170, 185, 190,
    267, 282, 305, 319, 357, 366
National Front, 9, 14, 169-71, 174-85, 187-
    93, 219, 284, 290, 302, 304, 309, 319-20,
    360, 364
NATO, 333-5, 384, 387
Neiertz, Véronique, 264-9
nuclear weapons tests, 18, 24, 43, 383-96

parliament, 26-30, 32, 37, 43-4, 53, 62-3, 65,
    68, 73-5, 77, 123, 126, 170, 172, 242,
    257, 259, 268, 270, 280
see also National Assembly; Senate
Pasqua, Charles, 11, 13, 45, 71-2, 75-6, 187,
    190, 219, 281, 306-8, 319
Perot, Ross, 16, 294
Peyrefitte, Alain, 2
political parties, see Communist Party;
    Ecologists; National Front; RPR;
    Socialist Party; UDF
Pompidou, Georges, 30, 33-5, 42, 45, 223,
    287, 334
Portugal, 10-11, 55, 335, 349-52, 356, 362
presidential power, 12, 23-46, 53, 56
    hyperpresidential model, 25-35, 41, 45-6
    premier-presidential model (cohabita-
        tion), 25, 37-41, 46
    tempered presidential model, 25, 35-7, 46
prime minister, 12, 23, 25-7, 31, 36, 56, 258
privatization, 4, 9, 13, 114-5, 118, 126-30

Ralite, Jack, 248
Ranger, Jean, 291
Raoult, Eric, 189
Rémond, René, 202, 283
Robert, Jaques, 55
Rocard, Michel, 5, 37, 62, 74, 77, 116-7,
    127-9, 183-4, 186, 265, 357
Roudy, Yvette, 260-1, 264-5, 267
Roussin, MIchel, 135
RPR (Rassemblement Pour la République),
    1, 5, 11, 16, 24, 40-3, 45, 177, 182, 184,
    190, 219, 304-7, 309, 316-7, 320, 326,
    360, 364

Sarkozy, Nicholas, 307
Savary, Alain, 200, 215, 218, 221-3
Schain, Martin, 12, 14, 91-2, 94
Schengen Accords, 10, 76, 189, 302
Schmidt, Vivien, 13
Séguin, Philippe, 11, 43-4, 246, 284, 306-8,
    319, 354, 365
Senate, 31, 45, 55-6, 59-60, 62, 66, 79, 366
sexual harassment policy, 16, 257-274
Shonfield, Andrew, 120
Single European Act, 13, 115, 131, 337-9, 363
SNES (National Union of Secondary
    Education), 209-11, 218
SNI (National Union of Elementary
    Teachers), 209-11
Socialist Party (PS), 3-5, 16-7, 33, 37, 40,
    45, 65, 68-9, 74, 76, 89-90, 95, 106, 111,
    123, 128, 135, 145, 156, 169, 172, 174-5,
    182-4, 203, 206, 209, 218, 220, 238, 248,
    260, 267, 290-2, 294-5, 303-5, 308-9,
    317, 320, 332
Spain, 10-11, 17, 55, 79, 274, 335, 349-52,
    356, 362, 396
Stevens, Anne, 88
Stone, Alec, 12, 46
strike wave of November-December 1995,
    9, 11, 13-14, 18, 42, 136, 144, 150, 158-
    60, 189, 207, 254, 326, 372
Suleiman, Ezra, 88

Tapie, Bernard, 135, 281, 284, 320
Toinet, Marie-France, 16
Toubon, Jacques, 60
Tiersky, Ronald, 5
Touchard, Jean, 283
trade unions, see labor movement

UDF (Union pour la Démocratie
    Francaise), 5, 11, 16, 24, 40, 42-3, 177,
    184, 190, 192, 303-8, 316-7, 320, 360
unemployment, 3-9, 16, 119, 153-4, 156,
    180, 353-6, 365, 368, 371
United Kingdom, see Britain
United States, 3, 15, 16, 55, 60, 68, 86, 93,
    95, 119-20, 147, 157, 201, 203, 212, 220,
    233-5, 238-9, 241, 246, 253, 258-60, 265,
    268-9, 272, 282, 285-8, 290, 294, 296,
    329, 334, 383, 389-90, 392

Vedel, Georges, 44, 55, 283
Veil, Simone, 187, 272
de Villiers, Philippe, 281, 308-9, 319-20, 360

Wilsford, David, 15
women, see gender politics

Yamgnane, Kofi, 187